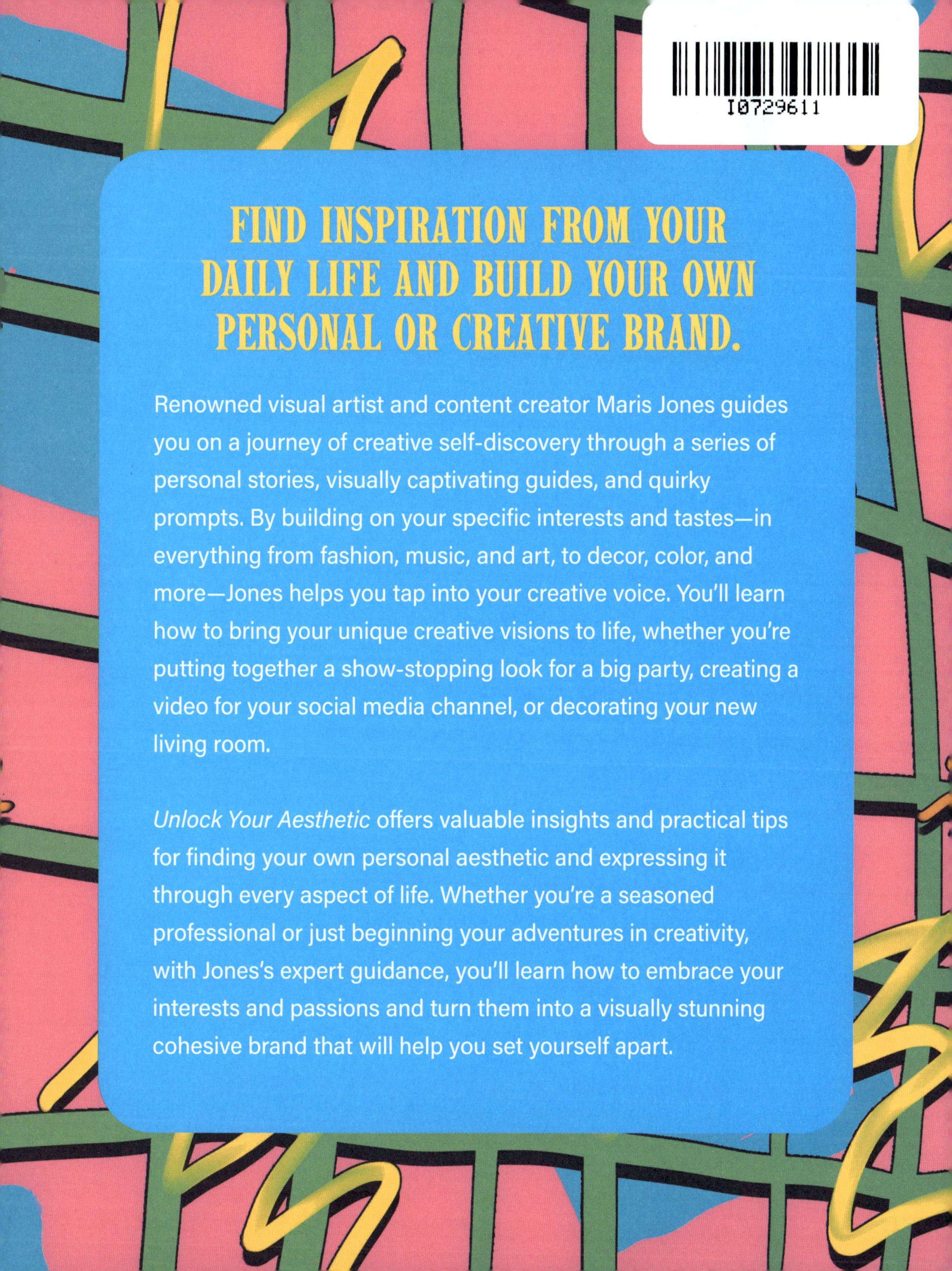

FIND INSPIRATION FROM YOUR DAILY LIFE AND BUILD YOUR OWN PERSONAL OR CREATIVE BRAND.

Renowned visual artist and content creator Maris Jones guides you on a journey of creative self-discovery through a series of personal stories, visually captivating guides, and quirky prompts. By building on your specific interests and tastes—in everything from fashion, music, and art, to decor, color, and more—Jones helps you tap into your creative voice. You'll learn how to bring your unique creative visions to life, whether you're putting together a show-stopping look for a big party, creating a video for your social media channel, or decorating your new living room.

Unlock Your Aesthetic offers valuable insights and practical tips for finding your own personal aesthetic and expressing it through every aspect of life. Whether you're a seasoned professional or just beginning your adventures in creativity, with Jones's expert guidance, you'll learn how to embrace your interests and passions and turn them into a visually stunning cohesive brand that will help you set yourself apart.

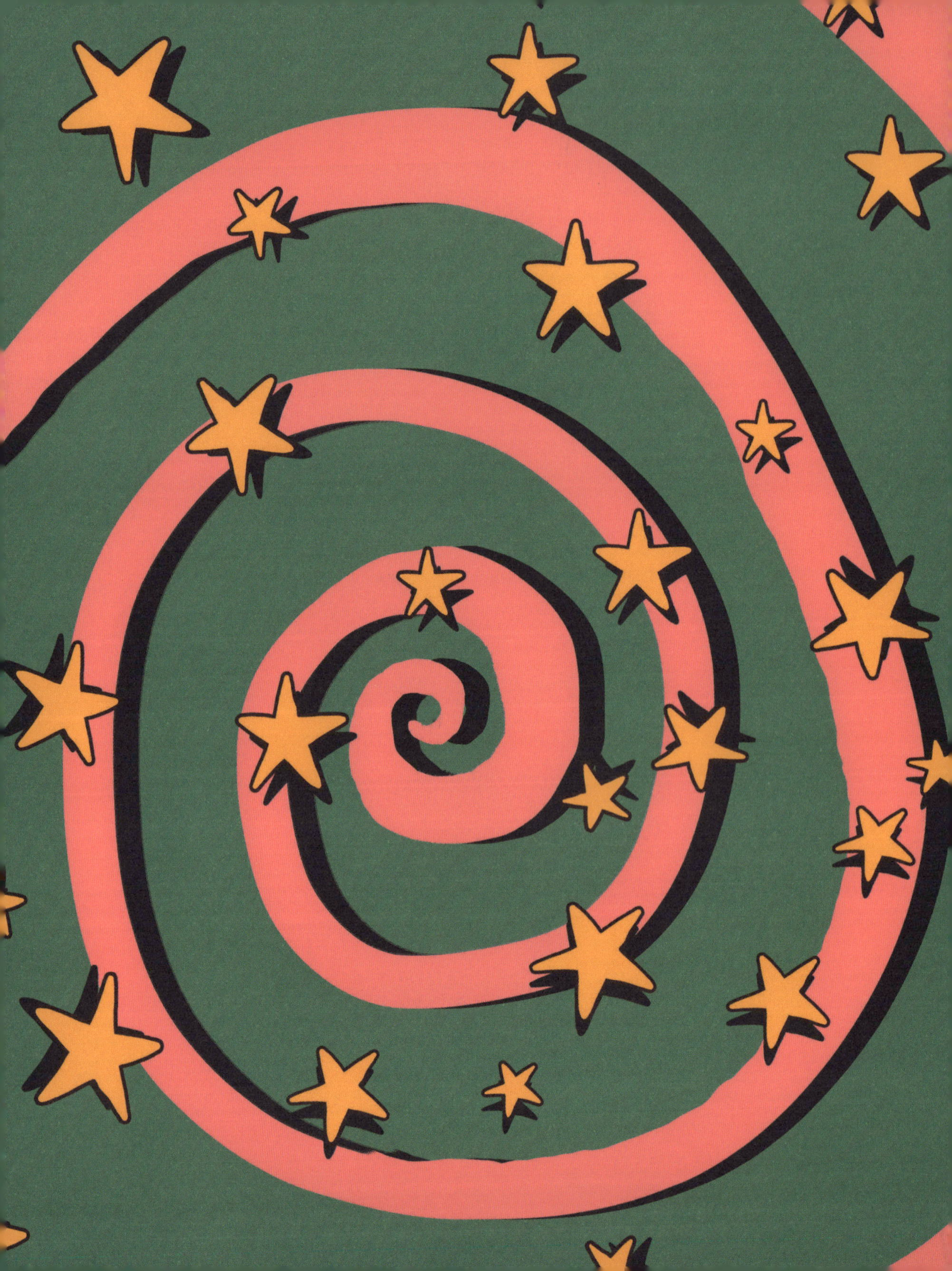

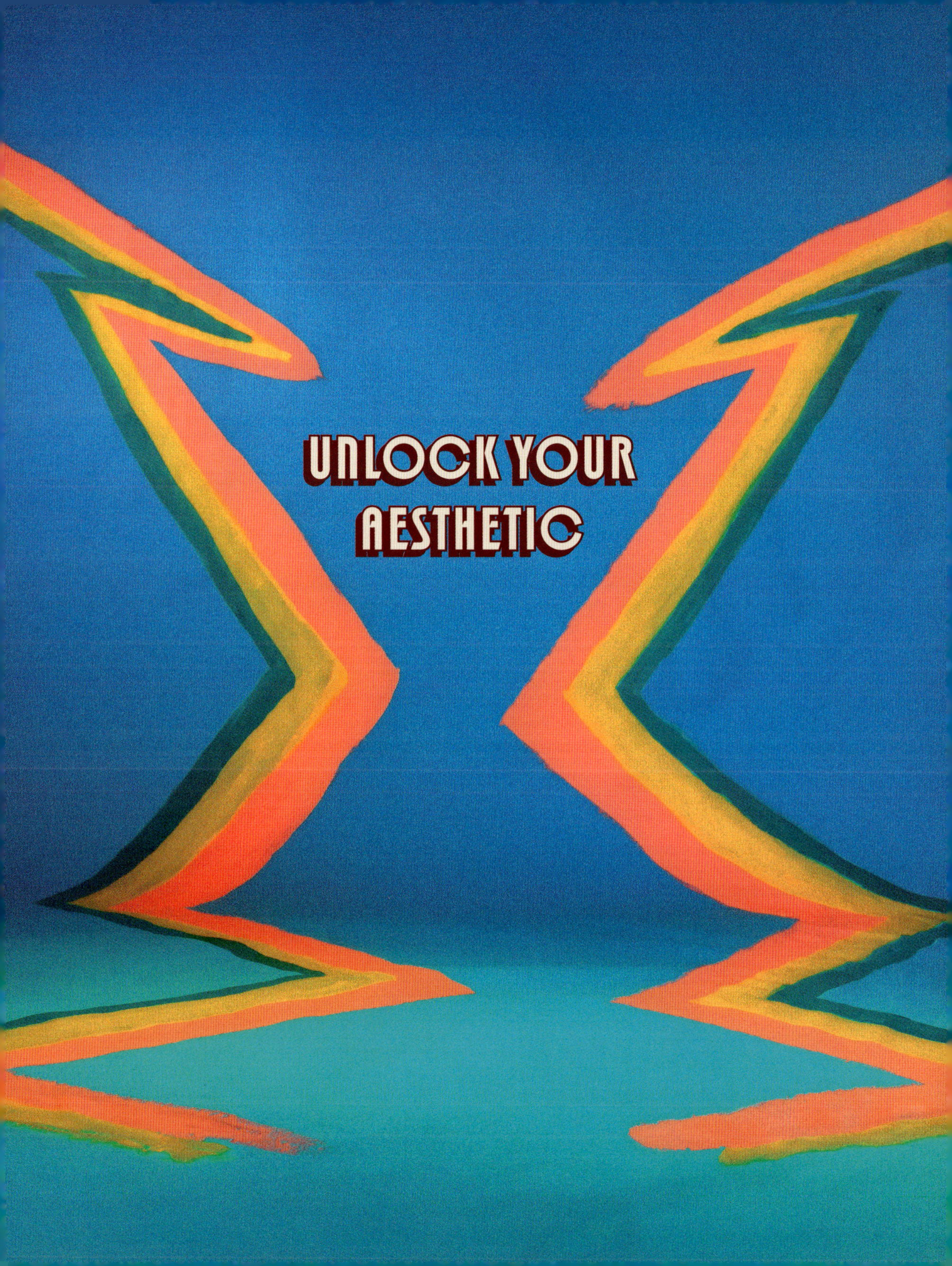

UNLOCK YOUR
AESTHETIC

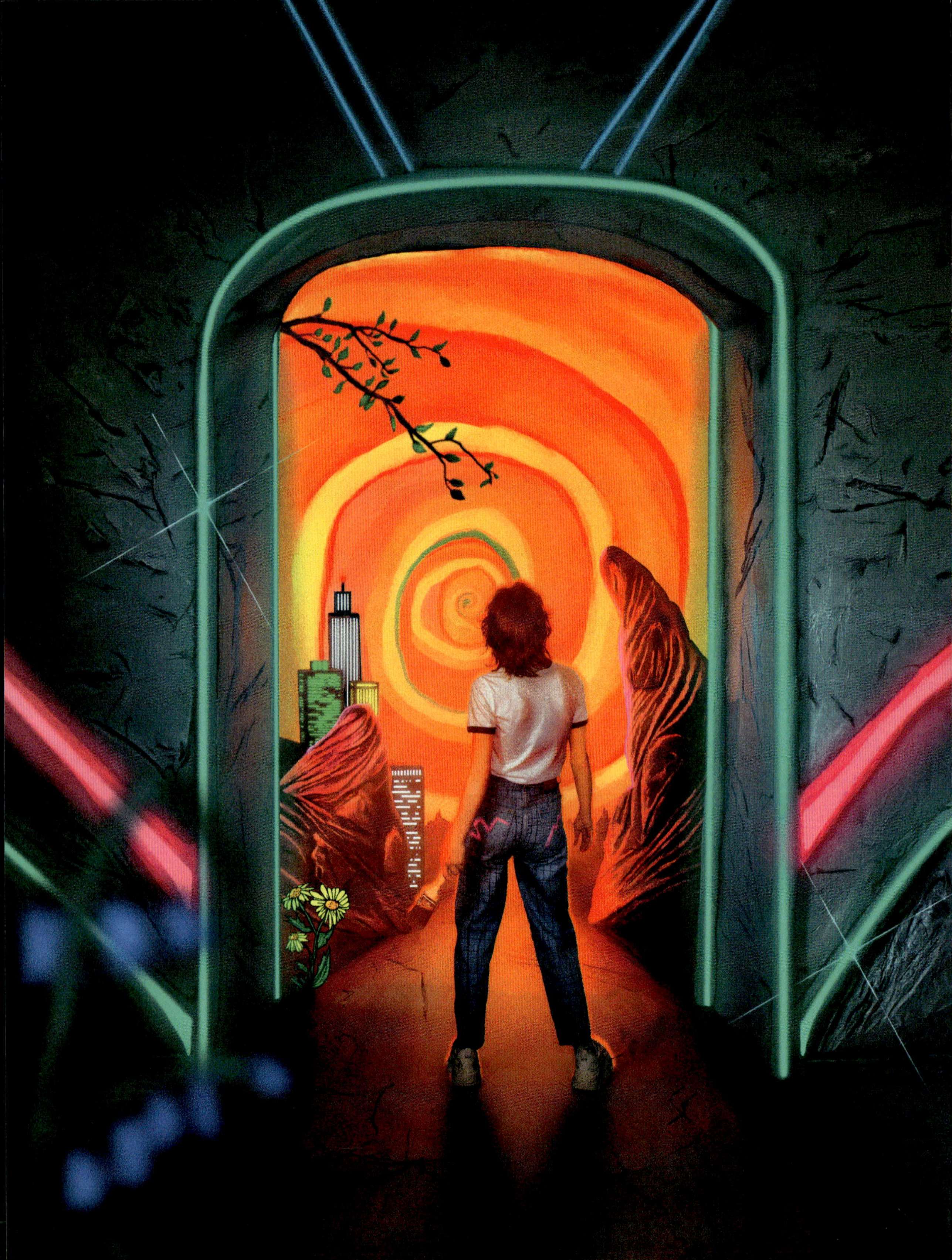

UNLOCK YOUR AESTHETIC

MARIS JONES

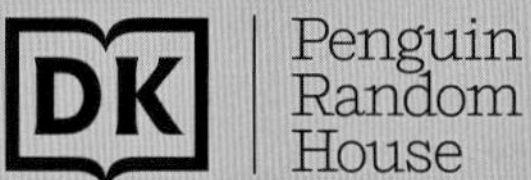

Publisher Mike Sanders
Executive Editor Alexander Rigby
Editorial Director Ann Barton
Art & Design Director William Thomas
Designer Ryan Scheife
Photographer Maris Jones
Copy Editor Tamanna Bhasin
Proofreaders Monica Stone, Tiffany Taing
Indexer Celia McCoy

First American Edition, 2024
Published in the United States by DK Publishing
1745 Broadway, 20th Floor, New York, NY 10019

The authorized representative in the EEA is Dorling Kindersley
Verlag GmbH. Arnulfstr. 124, 80636 Munich, Germany

Library of Congress Catalog Number: 2024934355
ISBN: 978-0-7440-9300-1

DK books are available at special discounts when purchased
in bulk for sales promotions, premiums, fund-raising, or educational use. For details, contact
SpecialSales@dk.com

Printed and bound in China

www.dk.com

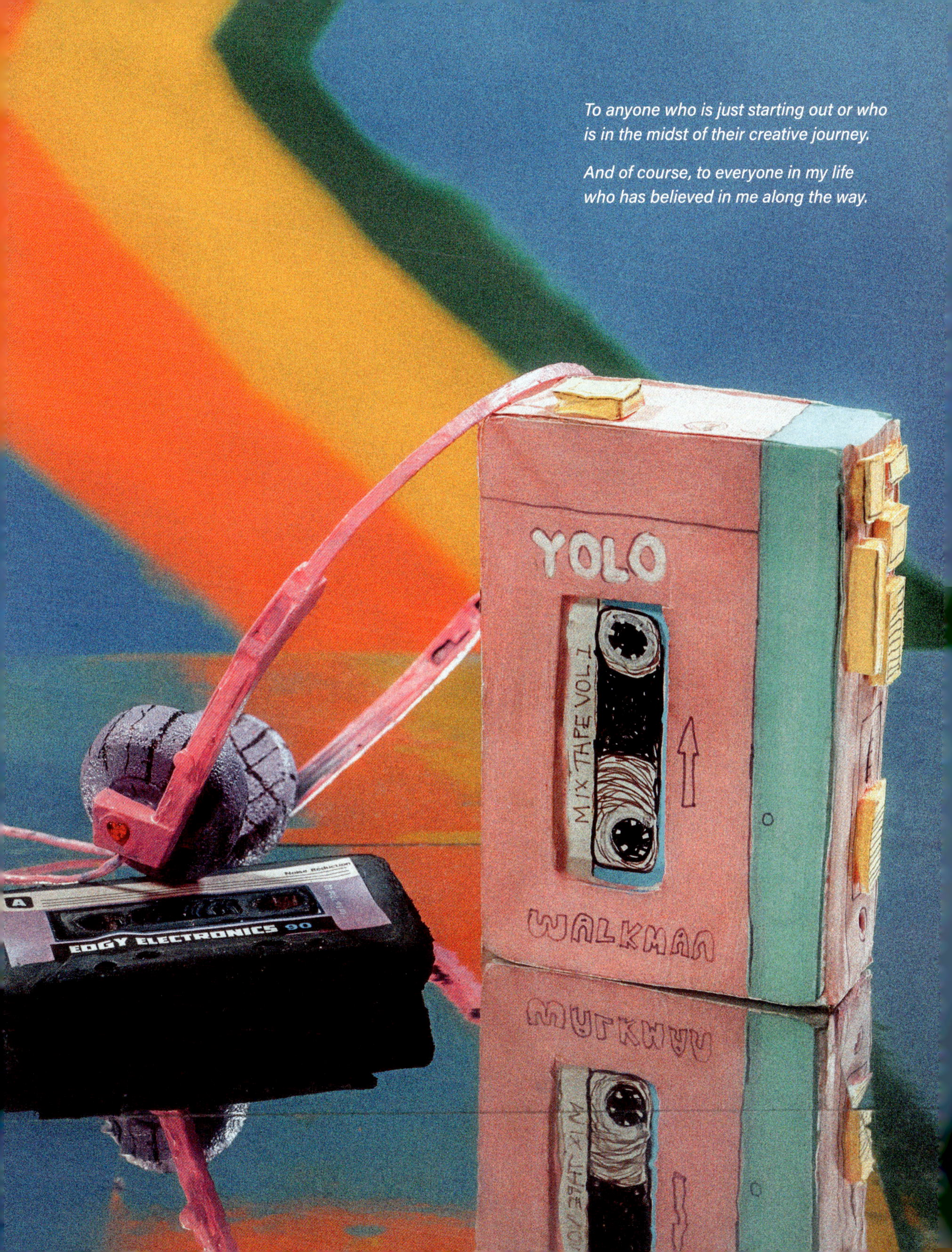

To anyone who is just starting out or who
is in the midst of their creative journey.

And of course, to everyone in my life
who has believed in me along the way.

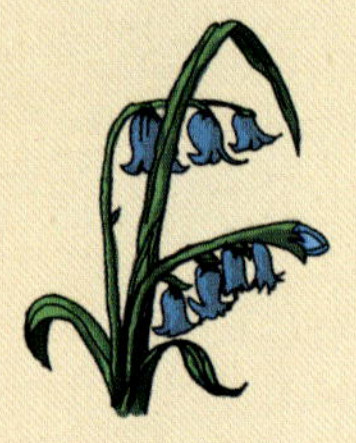 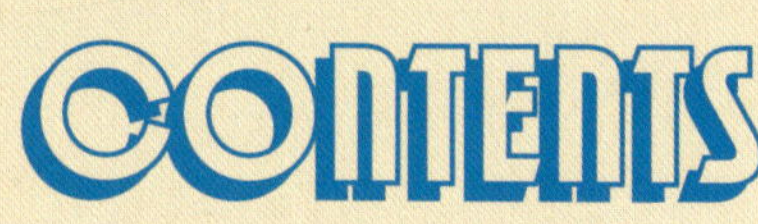 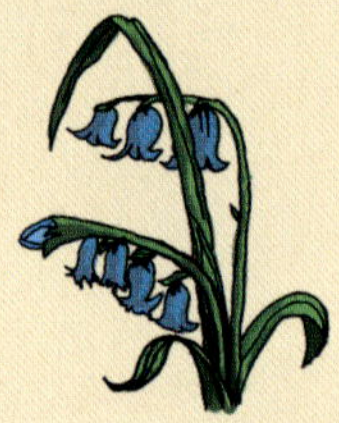

CONTENTS

PART I: GETTING STARTED

Chapter One: Foundations

Chapter Two: What Is an Aesthetic?

Chapter Three: Keywords & Brainstorming

PART II: BUILDING BLOCKS

Chapter Four: Finding Your Medium

Chapter Five: A World of Color

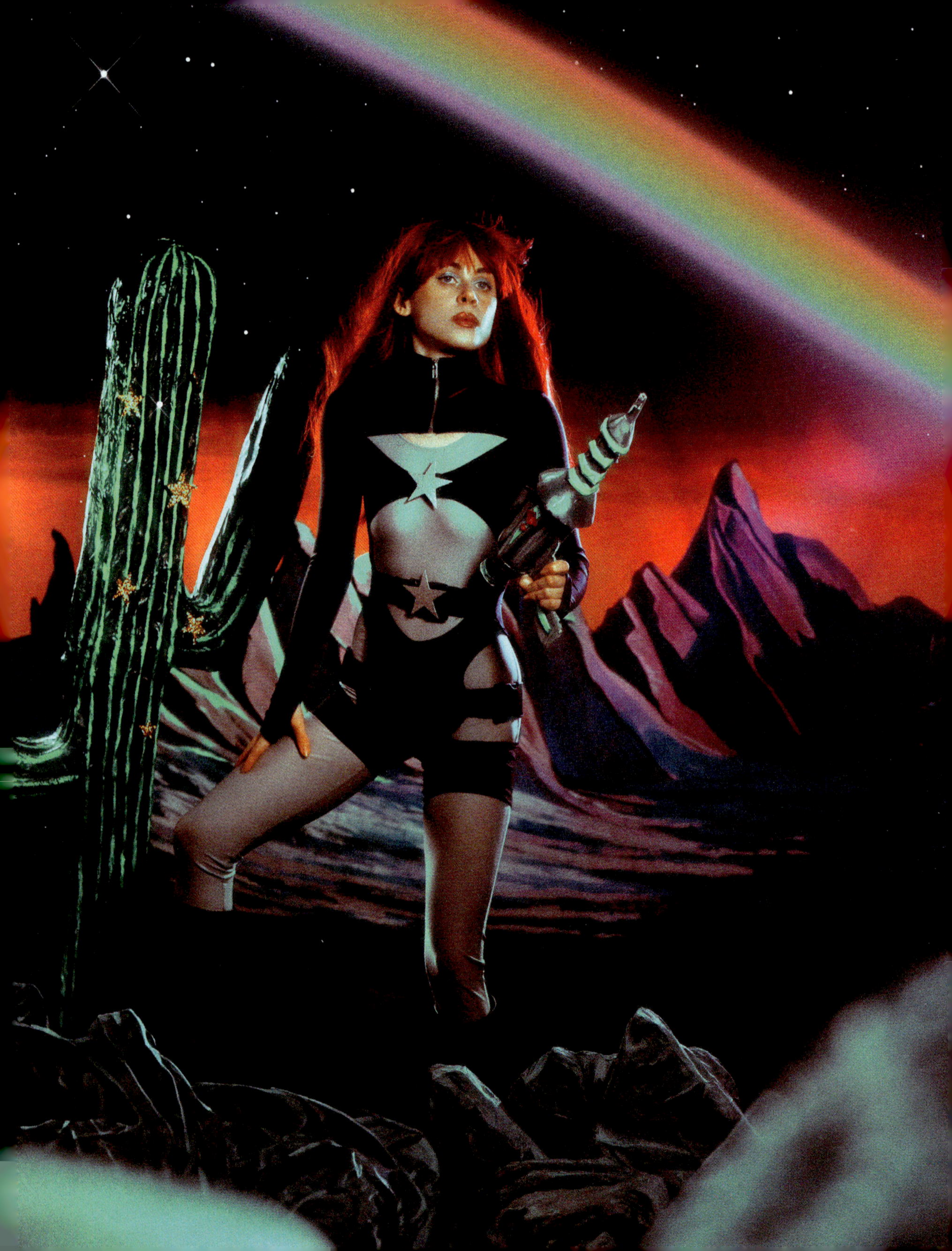

INTRODUCTION

Let me guess, you're feeling frustrated in your quest to find your own personal aesthetic, the visual artistic voice that can help define who you are and what you're aiming to create. It can be disheartening if you're struggling with how to best tap into those very special essences that are needed to expand your imagination. Maybe you've tried reconnecting with your inner child, hoping to unlock a wellspring of creativity, but it's been a challenge. Perhaps you've even tried journaling, an activity that often promises self-discovery, but you've still found yourself drawing blanks. Well fear not, I'm here to help guide you on a journey to unlock your own very special aesthetic once and for all!

Why should I be the person to guide you on your aesthetic journey? Well for starters, I am obsessed with creating. It's pretty much the only thing I enjoy besides eating tomatoes and mozzarella. I've managed to turn my fascination with nostalgia and my passion for design and storytelling into a full-time career.

It all started by trying different things that popped into my head, having fun, and not taking anything too seriously. In 2015, I won Vine of the Year at the Shorty Awards. At age 22, I directed my first nationally syndicated campaign. I've been featured in publications like *Rolling Stone*, *Vogue*, *NYLON*, and *VICE* and have worked on many projects with my childhood music heroes. I owe it all to letting go, trusting my instincts, and staying consistent.

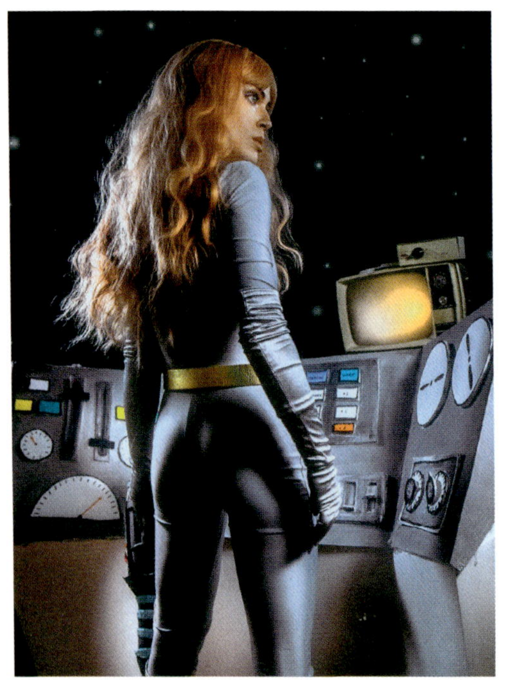
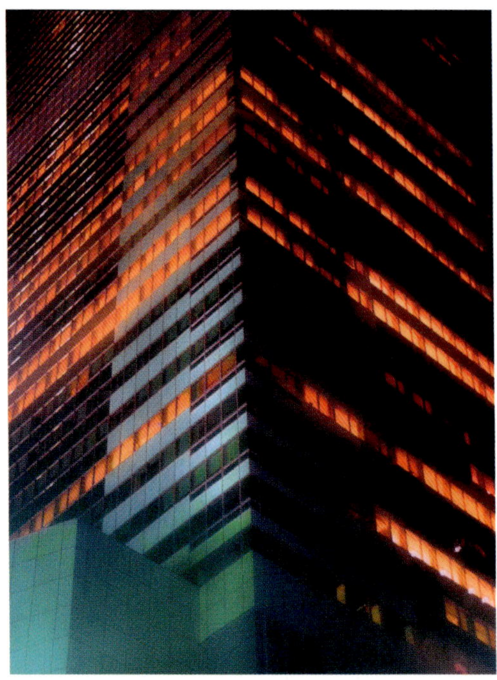
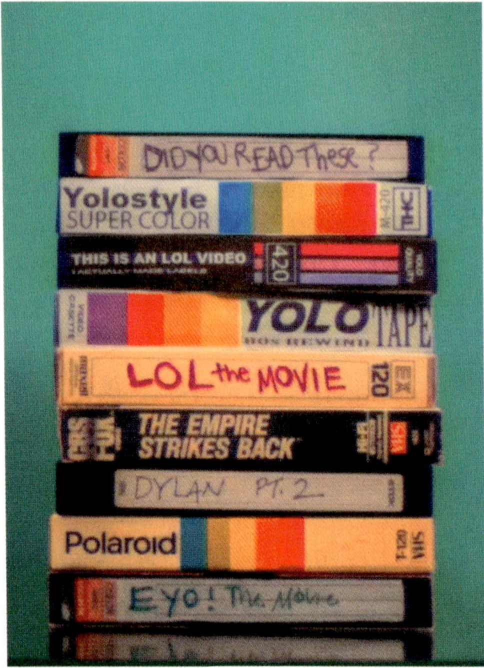

DID YOU READ THESE?
Yolostyle SUPER COLOR
THIS IS AN LOL VIDEO
I ACTUALLY MADE LABELS
YOLO TAPE
BE KIND REWIND
LOL the MOVIE
THE EMPIRE STRIKES BACK
DYLAN PT. 2
Polaroid
EYO! The Movie

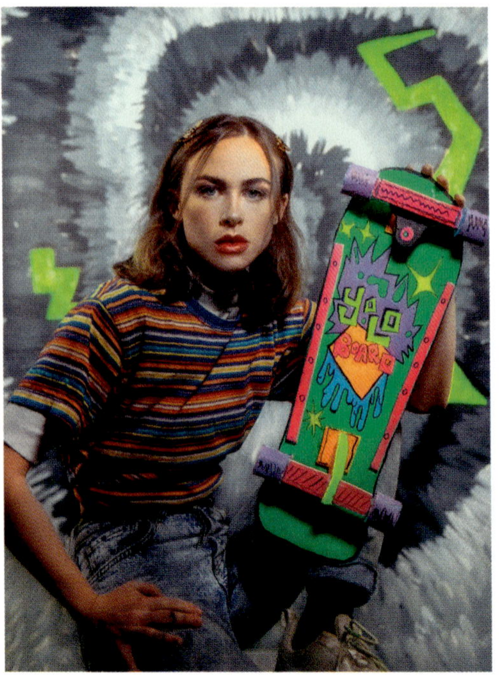

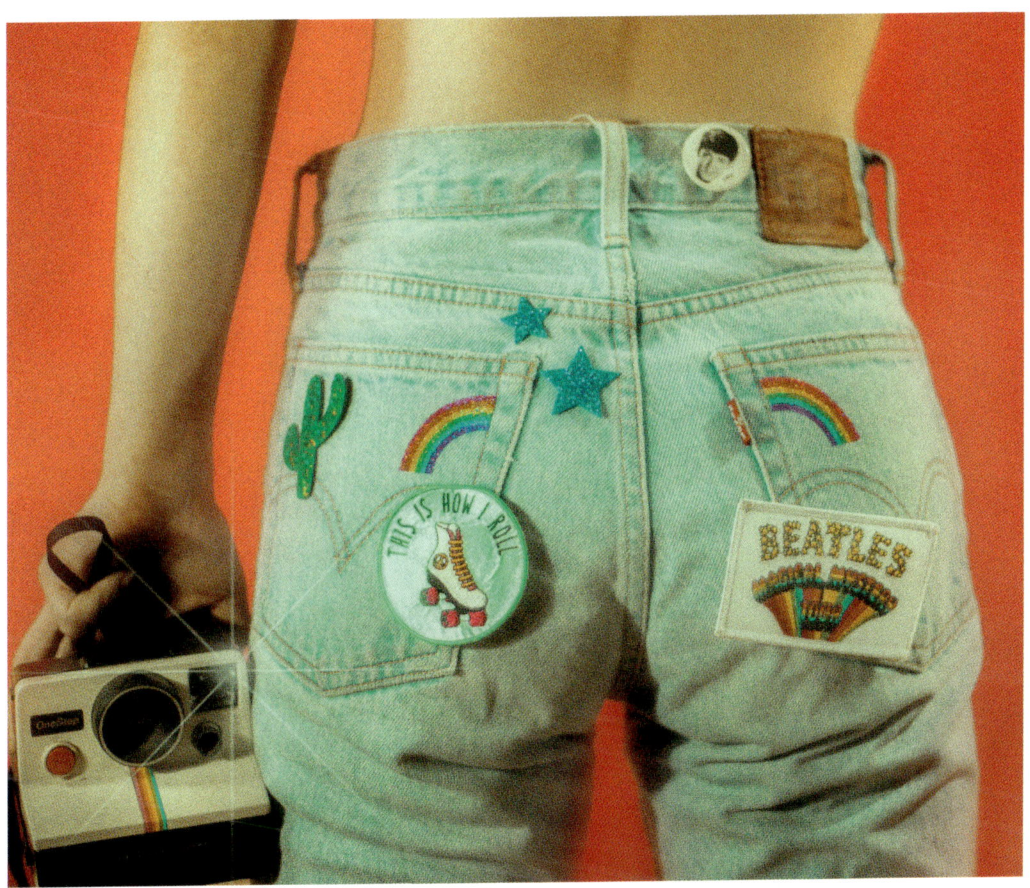

I've always tried my best to embrace every element that has captivated me by incorporating them into my work to create something familiar yet distinctly my own. Instead of fixating on the origins of each reference, I focus on personal resonance, which has allowed me to forge an entirely new aesthetic of my own.

It may seem daunting and complex, but breaking down your life experiences and the elements that have influenced you over time can help paint a clearer picture of your own aesthetic. It's not an overnight transformation, but with consistent effort you can find yourself on a path toward a truly artistic personal aesthetic. My hope is that this book will help you understand that pursuing creativity and finding your artistic voice are attainable goals, no matter what stage of life you're at.

This book is not solely about becoming an artist; it's about discovering who you are. Step by step, we're going to allow your unique aesthetic to emerge naturally.

So let's embark on a journey. Together.

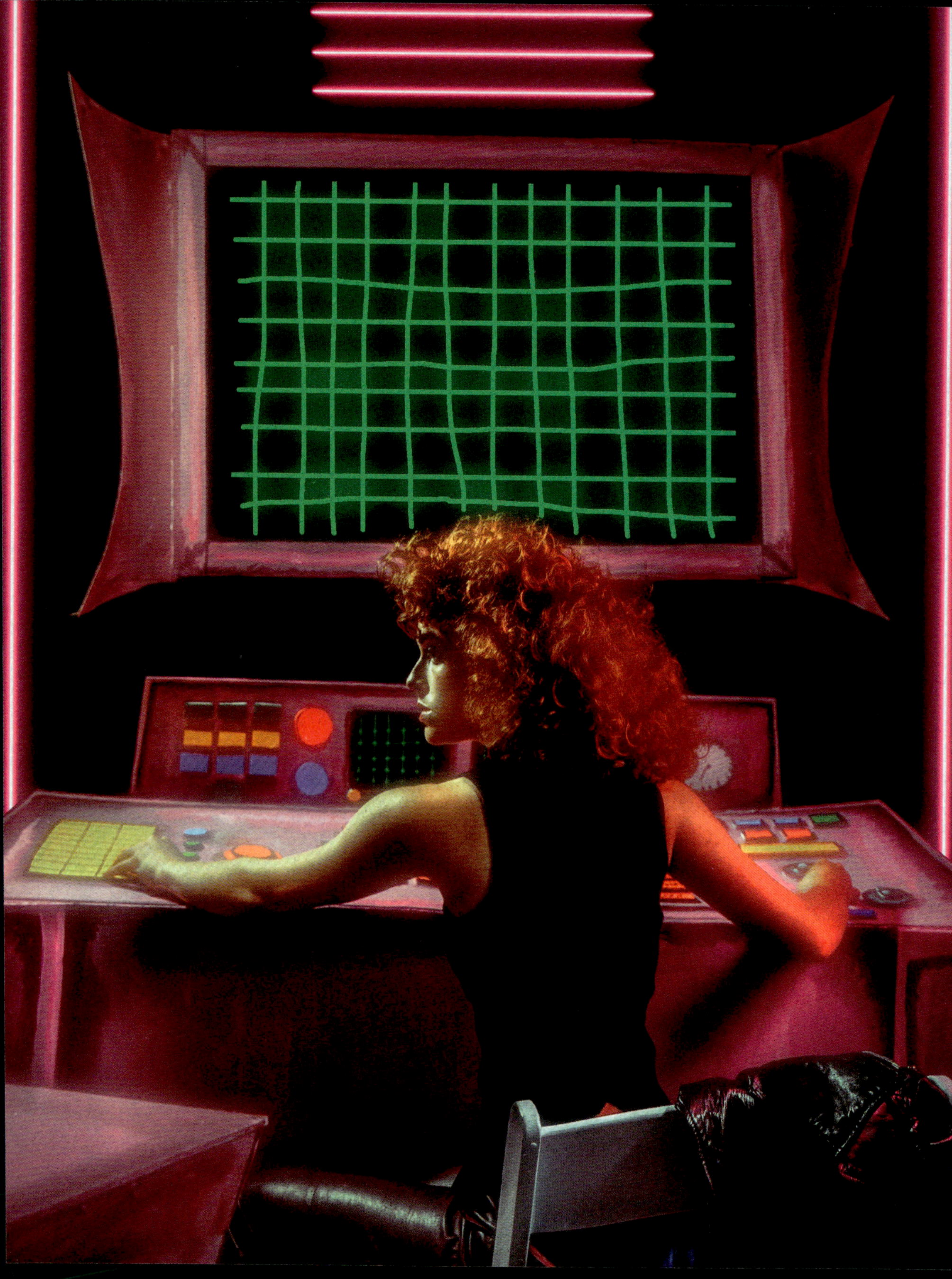

PART I

GETTING STARTED

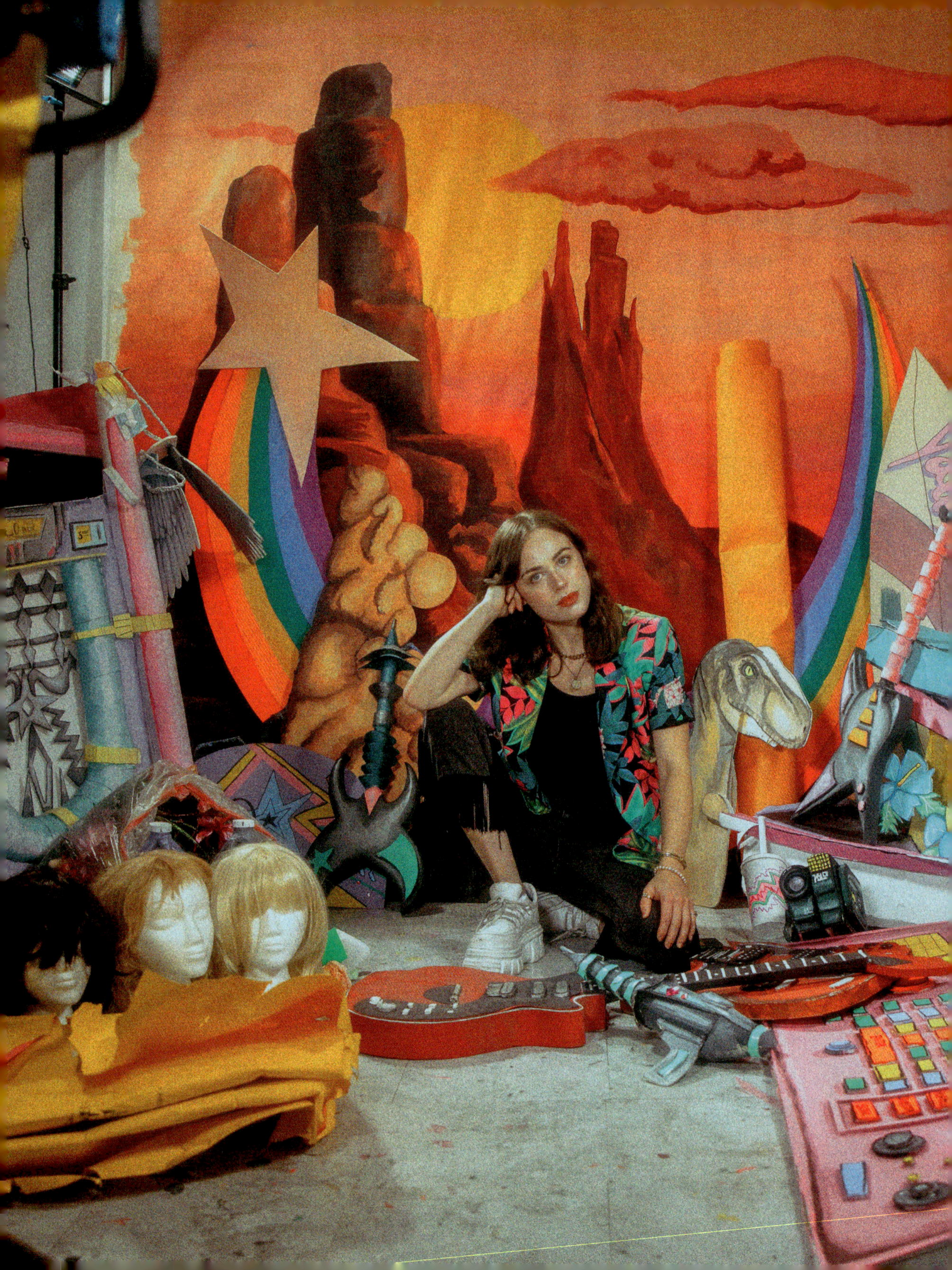

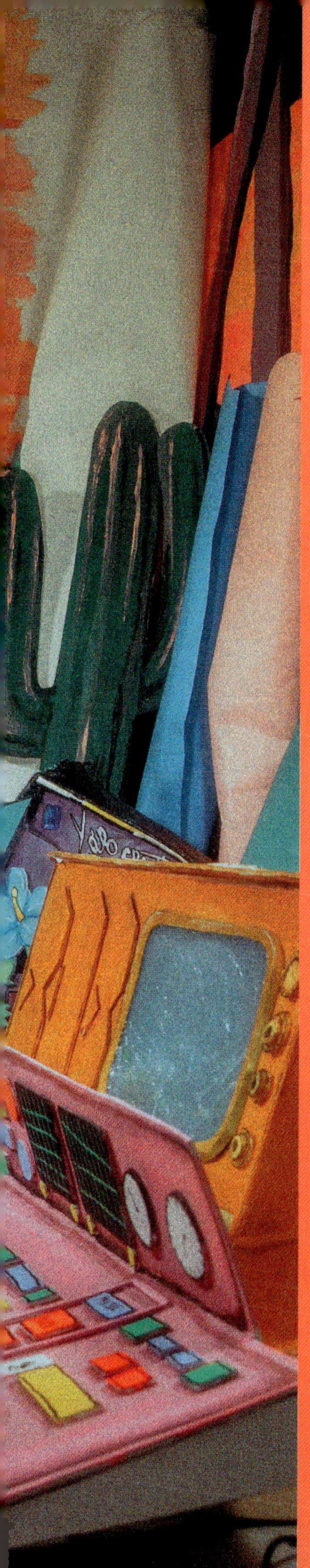

CHAPTER ONE

FOUNDATIONS

FINDING YOUR AESTHETIC

People often ask me, "How did you find your aesthetic?" In a world where we're encouraged to create our own personal brand and showcase it as often as possible on social media, it's no wonder that the term *aesthetic* has become a hot topic. A memorable aesthetic lingers in our minds, leaving a lasting impression. Whether in movies, fashion choices, home design, or art, a memorable aesthetic excites the brain.

Finding your own aesthetic is a complex process. Aesthetics are a culmination of tiny microinfluences that merge and blend together to shape something entirely new. It would be nearly impossible to just come up with a truly unique style right away without taking inspiration from other creative voices.

At first, deciphering your personal aesthetic may seem confusing and exhausting. But trust me, you already possess (most of) the answers. So let's home in on your unique visual identity and dive into the world of creative expression.

YOUTHFUL BEGINNINGS

I never set out to be an artist. In fact, I actively avoided anything art related for most of my life. Coming from a household with two artistic parents, I found the art world to be boring, stuffy, and pretentious. Listening to adults discuss themes, line quality, and the symbolism behind certain pieces felt like a whole lot of bullshit. I associated creativity with the complexities of adulthood, and so I did my best to avoid any form of artistic expression.

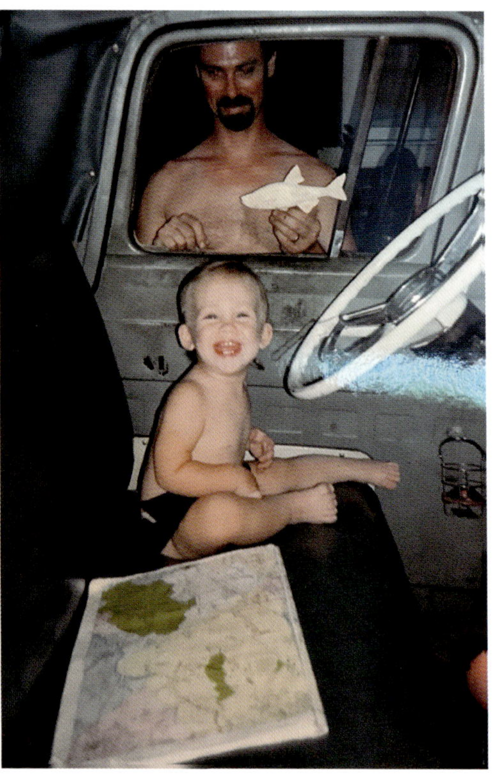

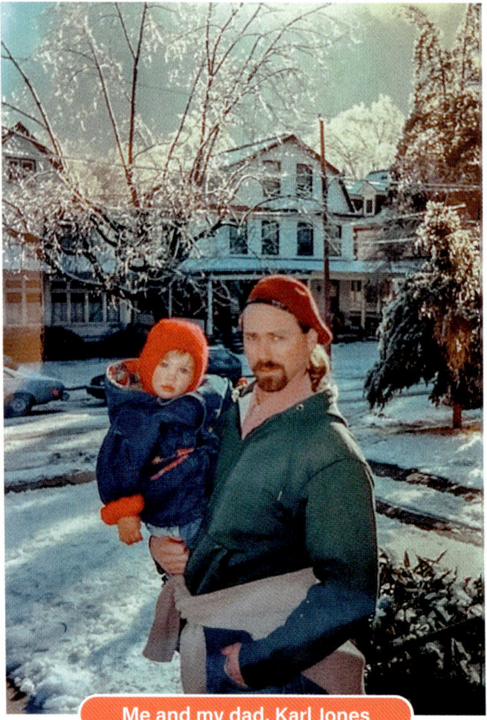

Me and my dad, Karl Jones

Lines and shapes, balls of yarn, naked bodies, geometric patterns that go nicely together, muted colors—I thought this was what art was all about, inaccessible, something above the average person's understanding. Being dragged along with my parents to their friends' art exhibitions was pure agony. Everyone around me seemed to be tearing a page out of the same handbook as to what they believed art should look like. Their work seemed to show someone searching *for* meaning rather than someone making something meaningful *to* them.

I'm not saying that art must be exclusively happy; it absolutely can delve into themes of anxiety, depression, and loss. I just mean that fully unlocking your pathway to productive creative expression and achieving what you set out to produce should make you happy—or at the very least, bring you a certain sense of satisfaction.

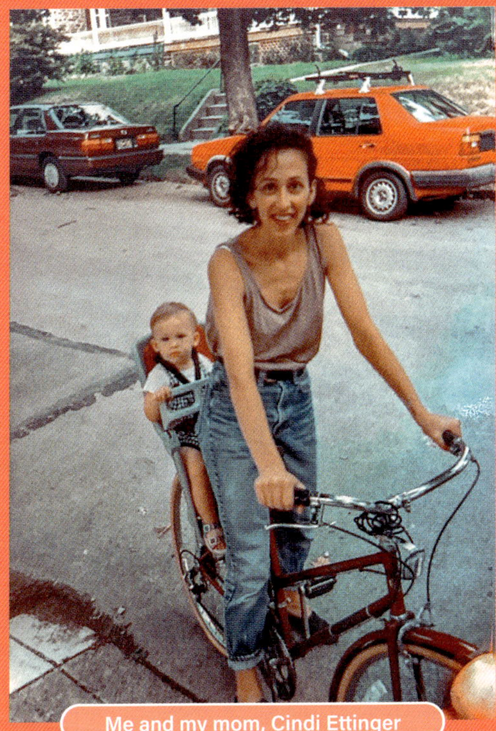

Me and my mom, Cindi Ettinger

While I now understand it all differently, I still believe that, too often, art and creativity are approached in a rigid and obscure manner. In reality, truly meaningful art stems from letting go and having fun. If more people realized that creating art simply means making what they enjoy, we would see a surge of individuals dabbling in the arts.

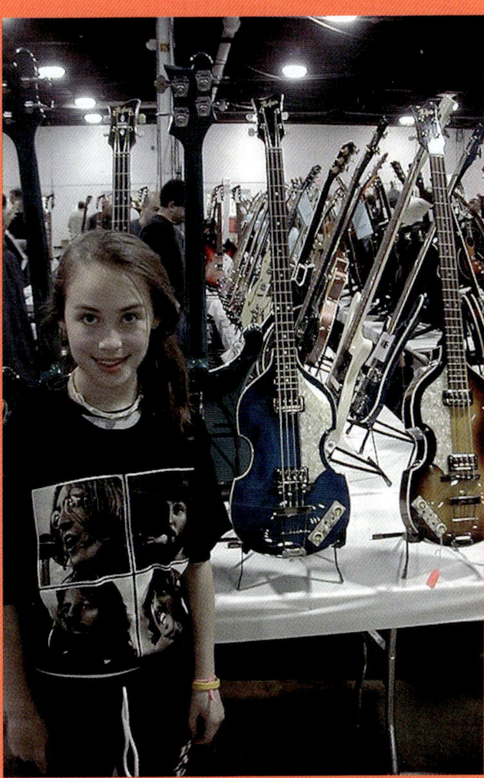

PINPOINTING CHILDHOOD OBSESSIONS

I was born with cerebral palsy, a neurological movement disorder that makes it challenging for me to perform simple tasks that others find effortless. So while I was busy being anti-art as a kid, I was also spending an insane amount of time playing with toys alone. Being alone meant I could control the environment at my own pace, without worrying about other kids.

I spent countless hours daydreaming and doing all sorts of creative stuff. I'd take my toys and stage elaborate plays. By the age of six, my love affair with stop-motion animation began—I animated my toys, bringing them to life in the magical worlds I created. I'd set up little scenes and film videos with the family cameras.

Now, you might wonder what in the world sparked all this creative madness? Well, let me tell you about *Clash of the Titans* (1981). This movie blew my little child brain. It seamlessly blended these incredible stop-motion effects with live-action sequences, and it transported me to a world that felt mystical and real. I vividly remember watching the movie for the first time. Barely five years old, I turned to my father, wide-eyed, and asked, "How did they get that animal to fly like that?"

My dad, being the movie buff he is, was thrilled that I was interested. He told me, "That's the work of Ray Harryhausen, the stop-motion master. Basically, you take an object, snap photos of it in tiny increments, and then put all the photos together to make it look like it's moving on its own."

And just like that, I was hooked! From that day on, I was determined to create whole worlds and scenarios that I couldn't achieve in real life. Damn it, stop-motion was just too cool not to explore.

It's mind-blowing to look at my own work now and see fragments of this early passion woven into my creative pieces. Childhood obsessions hold immense power; they provide a glimpse into who we are and what drives our creativity. They function as one of many building blocks that work together to build our creative makeup as an artist. And guess what? By actively looking back at your own life, you too can start uncovering the elements that have made you who you are.

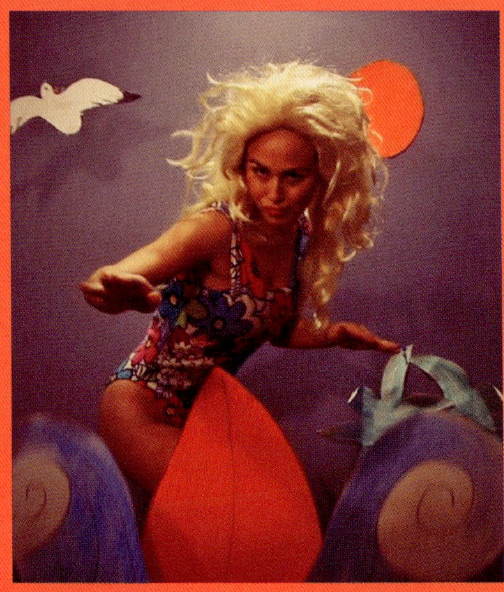

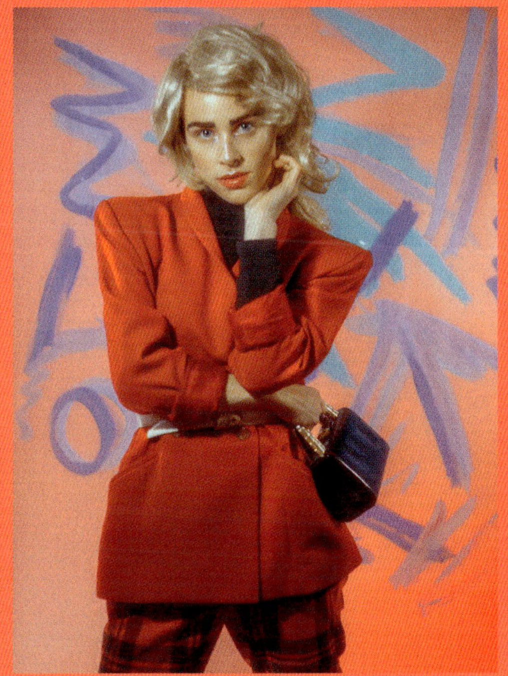
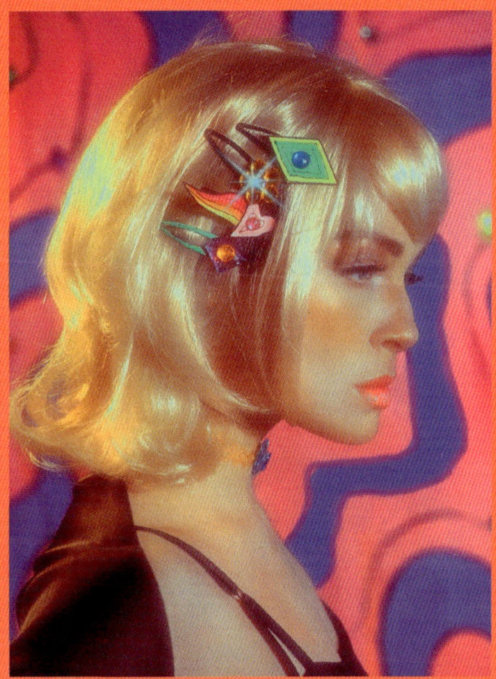
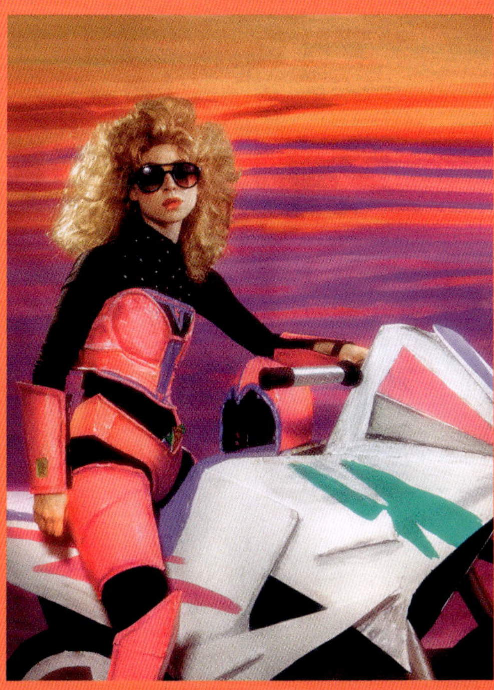
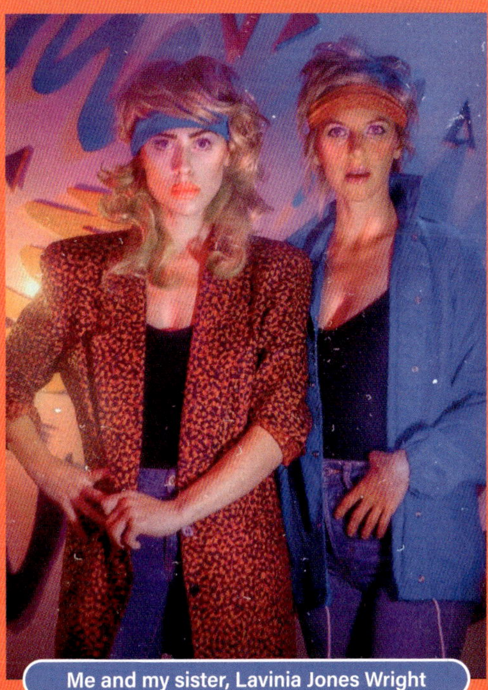

Me and my sister, Lavinia Jones Wright

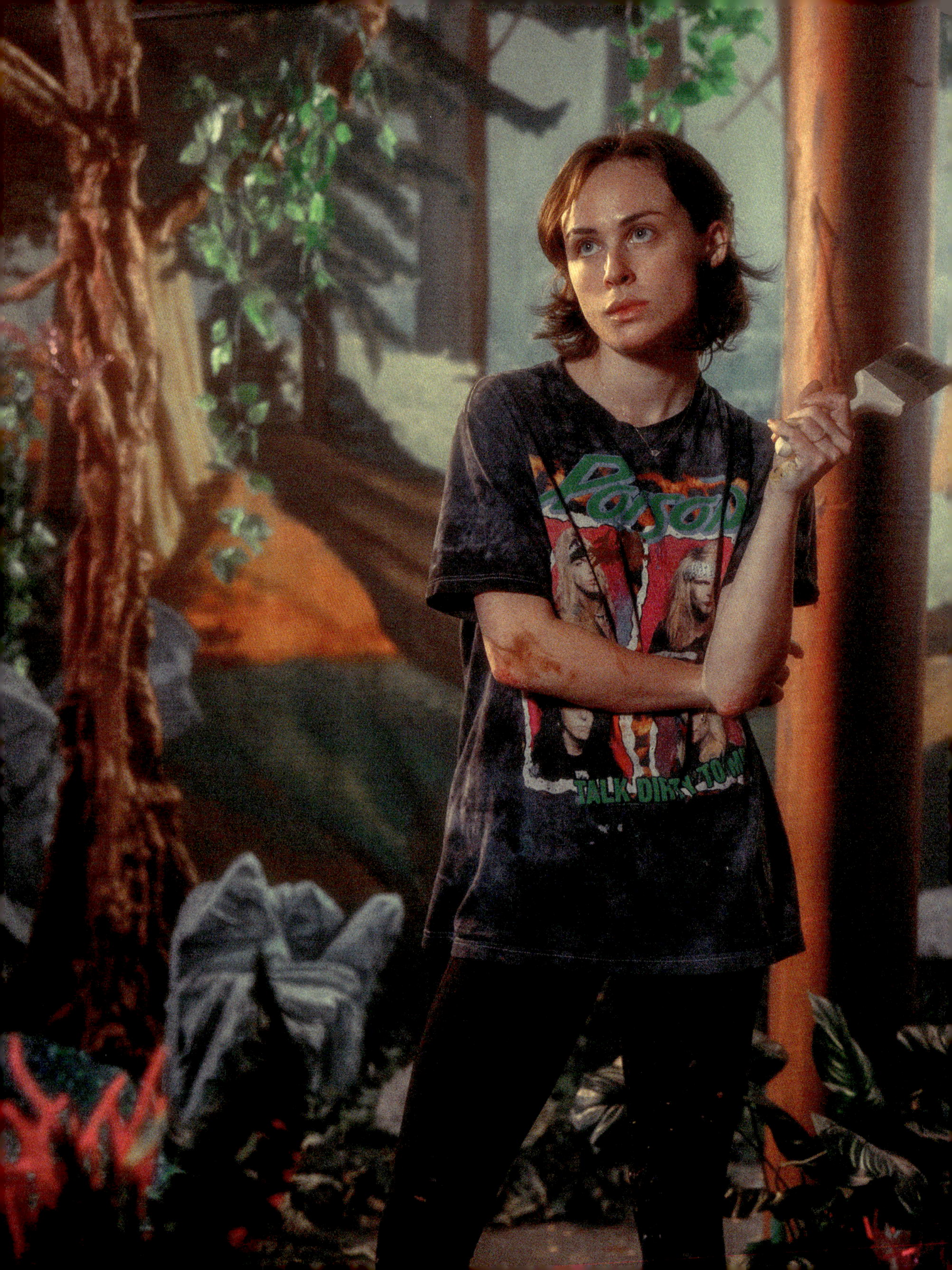

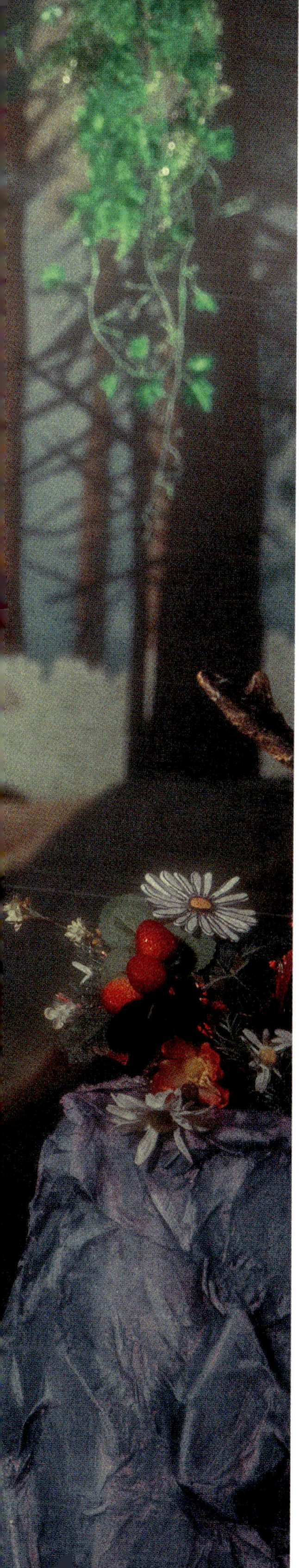

THE ENVIRONMENT AROUND YOU

Because of my dad's passion for nostalgic items, it often felt like our house was a time capsule from 1975. He collected so many things over the years. Everything from plates, cups, clothes, chairs, and even our lawnmower came from previous decades. They formed the baseline for what I found appealing.

By the age of seven, a record player appeared amid my toys, providing the perfect soundtrack to my imaginative adventures. I would spend hours listening to the Partridge Family and discovering obscure B-list garage-rock bands from the 1960s. You know, I genuinely thought it was the music of the 2000s. It was only as I got older that I realized our home was filled with dusty old relics.

As I grew out of my teenage era, I began to appreciate all the vintage stuff my dad brought into our home. These shared experiences with my parents, the love for antiques and the melodies of bygone eras, shaped my creative identity in profound ways. Now, vintage has become an integral part of my artistic style.

Usually, some part of your environment growing up will hold significance to you. It can be an incredibly powerful and rewarding experience to unlock these childhood memories and apply them to your artistic life. Take note of your own environmental impacts now and ask yourself:

1. What is the baseline of my reality?

2. What feels the most natural to me?

3. What kind of music, clothes, decor, and time periods feel the most representative of me?

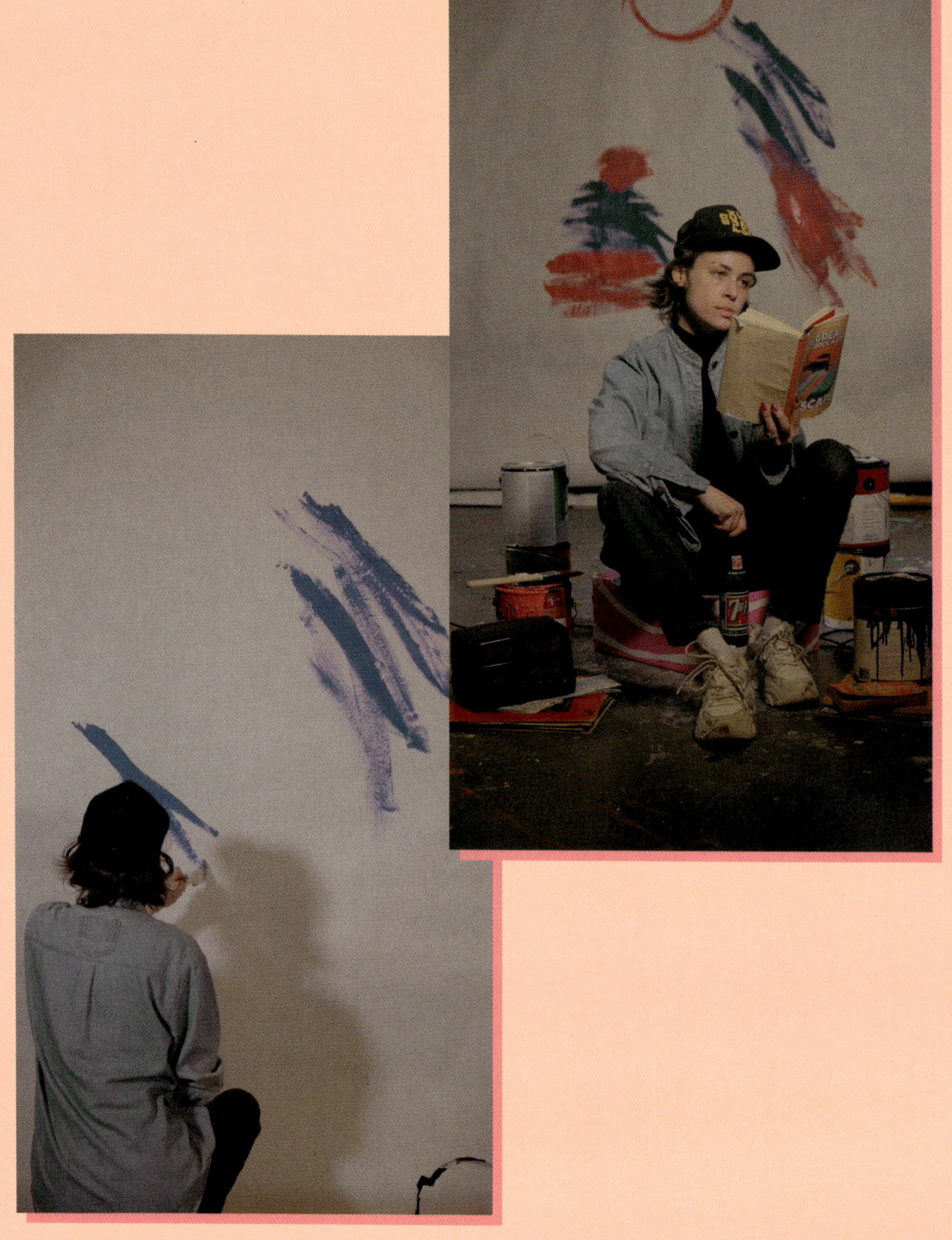

Getting Started

ABILITIES AS ARTISTIC TOOLS

From the age of two until around fourteen, I was convinced by my mother to make holiday cards. She, being a printmaker herself, would bring home these special copper plates for me to etch into. Then she'd take the drawing I etched and print it on a massive printing press.

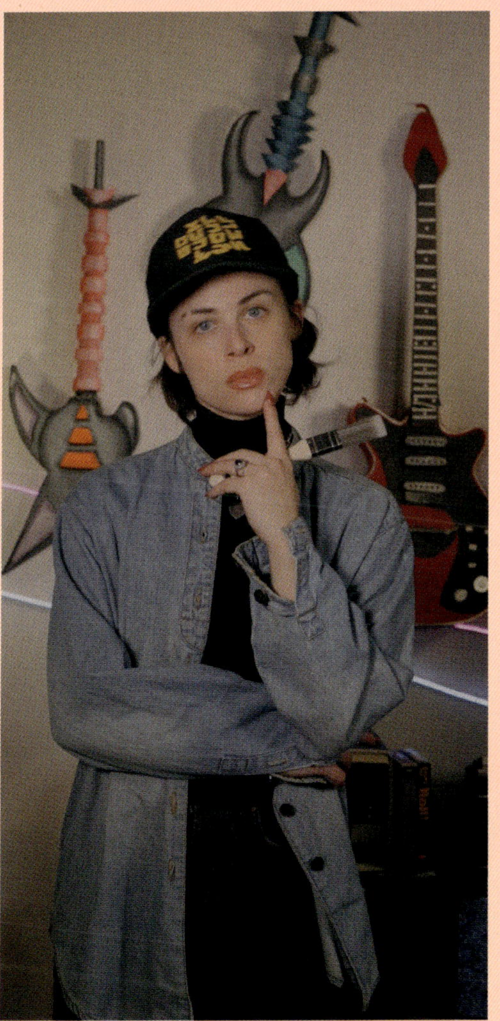

Although I can now appreciate that I had this experience, as a child, I despised making these cards. I was constantly told I had a knack for drawing, even before I understood more than, like, 20 words of English. It became the one thing everyone associated with me. My parents would praise my ability to draw well, telling me how much people loved receiving our cards. But deep down, it was torture for me.

Since I have physical disabilities, holding a paintbrush or a pencil often strains my hand because of the way my muscles work. When I hold anything that has a handle, my muscles tense up and become exhausted. As a young kid, I couldn't fully understand why drawing was so hard for me.

I still don't have a burning passion for drawing. But here's the interesting twist: I don't see drawing as *just* drawing anymore. When I am inspired to draw something, I don't have to try very hard to make it work. It's one of those things that comes naturally to me. I use drawing as a tool to help me achieve the desired artistic outcomes that truly excite me. It's a means to an end—a building block that leads to creating something that is uniquely mine.

So as you can see, leaning on your natural abilities can be super helpful when trying to think of what tools you should work with when you start creating.

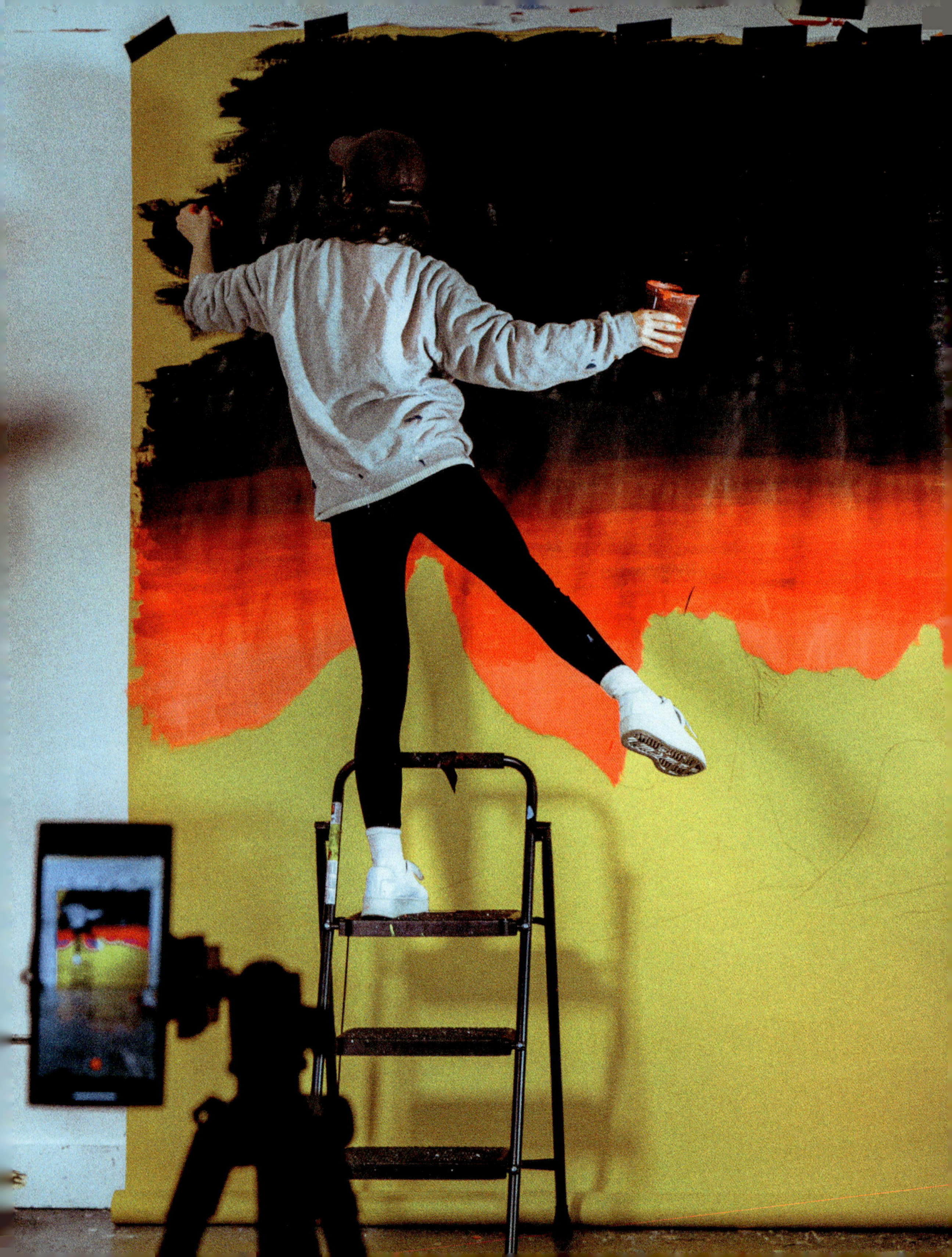

EMBRACE YOUR QUIRKS

School was 100 percent not my thing. I was placed in remedial classes due to my learning disabilities and all sorts of undiagnosed neurodiversity. I knew that the traditional school system wasn't designed for someone like me. But my parents' breaking point was when I failed art in elementary school. They couldn't wrap their heads around it. I mean, me failing math and language classes made sense to them, but art?! That hit home, hard.

My mother decided to call up my art teacher, demanding an explanation. The teacher explained that the grading system was based on fine motor skills, like cutting along the lines, tracing objects, coloring within the borders, and other practical tasks. The teacher, although apologetic upon learning about my cerebral palsy, inadvertently made me realize something important—I'm a bit sloppy. In fact, *sloppy* has been a label I've carried throughout my life. But instead of trying to fit the mold of perfection, I've embraced those crooked lines and unintentional quirks. They've became an integral part of my artistic style.

When it comes to expressing yourself, making sure you can cut along the lines or trace a circle perfectly aren't needed to create from within. Rather than trying to mimic something a certain way, it's better to let your hand create naturally. It's a sure way to create something unique to you. Nobody can make a line quite like you, and nobody will measure a shape quite like you either. You're adding something special to the end result—something that truly reflects who you are as a creative.

Over time and with practice, you'll naturally get better, but the essence of how you first approach something will likely remain. It's a fun and liberating way to bring forth your true creative self. I can't be anyone but me, and neither can you. You can only be you, and that, I think, is super cool.

BREAKING AWAY FROM LIMITING MINDSETS

As I entered my angsty teenage years, new challenges arose. I was still terrible at school, but I was also drifting away from the artistic ambition my parents once saw in me. While most rebellious teenagers wanted to express their artistic side, my teenage rebellion took a different form. I saw my rebellion in conformity. I wanted to experience and participate in all standard teenager activities. I embraced the popular fashion trends of the late 2000s, played around with my hair and makeup, and enjoyed attending sports games and pep rallies. This change confused my parents, who couldn't grasp my new desire to partake in "normal activities" and ignore my creative ones. While my parents lay awake at night, worried that I would become some corporate executive, I was fully aware that I was going to do something bold and creative with my career path.

You don't have to conform to the stereotypical artist lifestyle to be an artist. Creativity is innate, and it comes from within. It's about expressing yourself authentically, no matter how you choose to live your life. When my mom threatened to send me to art school, she thought she was doing something revolutionary by countering my mainstream interests. But little did she know, her efforts only fueled my fire to prove I could be creative on my own terms. I don't have to look or act like an artist to be an artist. And neither do you.

Let go of any doubts or limitations that hold you back. Embrace your true self and believe that you can be both creative and unique in your own remarkable way. As you embark on your own journey of self-discovery and aesthetic exploration, take your time. There's no need to rush or put pressure on yourself. Understand that this process is a gradual one that requires introspection, honesty, and a willingness to delve into the depths of your experiences and influences. Celebrate your unique journey and find joy in the creative expressions that resonate within your soul. Trust in your power to create something truly remarkable, regardless of societal expectations or preconceived notions.

Remember, this is your journey. It is an opportunity to embrace your true self and unlock your creative potential.

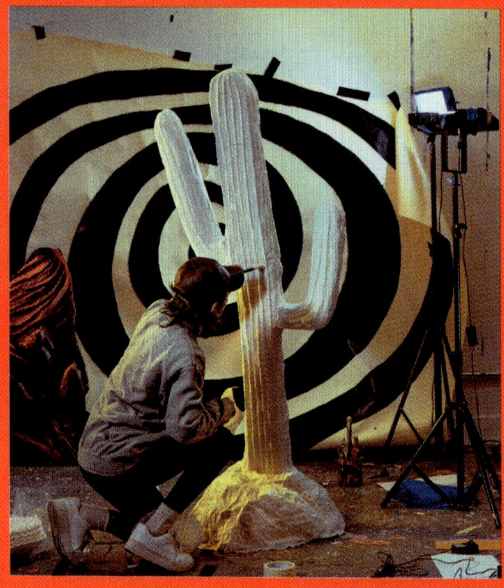

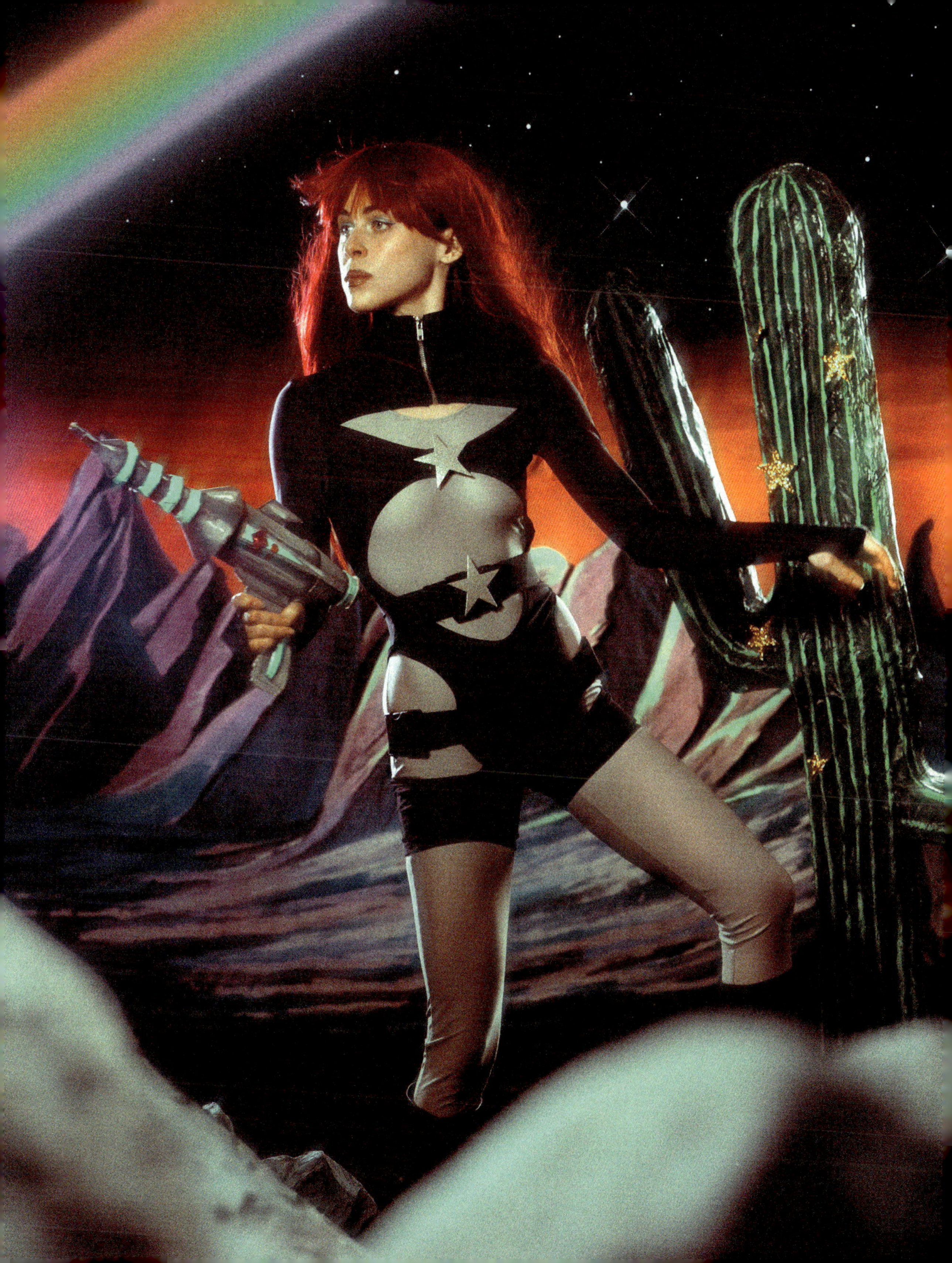

CREATE YOUR AESTHETIC LIST

All these experiences and moments I've shared with you thus far form pieces of the foundation of who I am as a person and as a creative. They shape my art and my life, forming an aesthetic that is uniquely true to myself. When it comes to finding your own aesthetic, remember: don't try to be something you're not. Instead, embrace the elements that speak to you and make you who you are.

Elements that strongly stuck out to me as a child have influenced who I am, serving as building blocks that help inform my creative visions. So let me introduce a helpful exercise that will allow you to reverse engineer who you are visually.

Try and pinpoint the elements you've been drawn to throughout your life and create a master list. All these little pieces can help you find a visual voice of your own, and the master list you create can be applied toward your aesthetic.

As an example, here's my list of artistic influences:

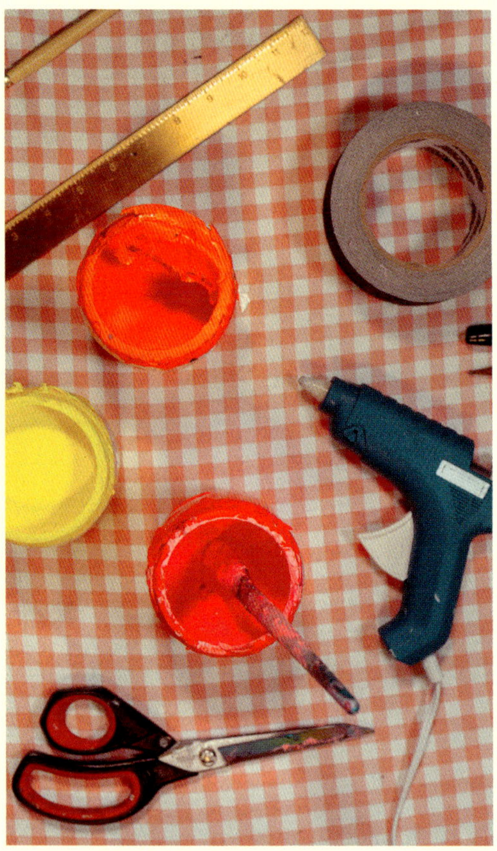

1. Animated Disney movies: I've always been captivated by the illustrations, colors, style, and stories. I love the magical combination of music and imagery.

2. Big puffy sleeves/princess dresses: The silhouette and the exaggerated sleeves of princess dresses fascinate me. This connects to my love of '80s fashion and the Renaissance era.

3. David Bowie: The legendary musician and his unique style blends music, fashion, and art.

4. *The Wizard of Oz*: With its whimsical storytelling and vibrant visuals, this timeless movie holds a special place in my heart.

5. Classic rock and soul music: The energetic and soulful sounds of classic rock and soul influenced my artistic sensibilities.

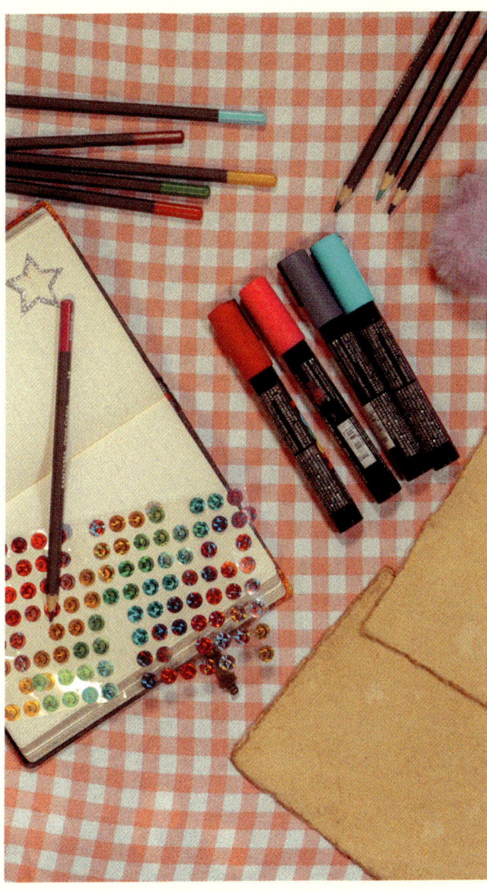

9. Films by Ray Harryhausen: The masterful stop-motion animation work of Ray Harryhausen fueled my passion for the craft.

10. *Muppet Treasure Island*/Jim Henson's creations: The imaginative world of the Muppets and the genius of Jim Henson's puppetry inspired my love for visual artistry.

11. *Cats*: This iconic musical influenced my appreciation for theatrical performances and choreography.

12. *The Chronicles of Narnia*: The enchanting world of Narnia, with its fantastical creatures and epic adventures, resonated with my imagination.

13. Making products and starting a business: The drive to create and turn ideas into tangible products has always been a part of my creative journey.

14. King Henry VIII/the Renaissance: The rich history and decadent style of the Renaissance era, including King Henry VIII, influenced my artistic sensibilities.

15. Colonial Williamsburg: Exploring the historical site of Colonial Williamsburg sparked my interest in the progression of time and the evolution of design.

16. The Beatles: The iconic music and cultural impact of the Beatles shaped my appreciation for music and creativity.

17. Big '80s hair: The bold and voluminous hairstyles of the '80s influenced my love for self-expression through personal style.

6. Old Hollywood musicals: The glamour, music, and dance included in classic Hollywood musicals left a lasting impression on me.

7. Rainbow Brite: This colorful and magical character from my childhood contributed to my love of bright and vibrant colors.

8. *The Nutcracker* with Macaulay Culkin: This enchanting ballet production sparked my fascination with storytelling through dance.

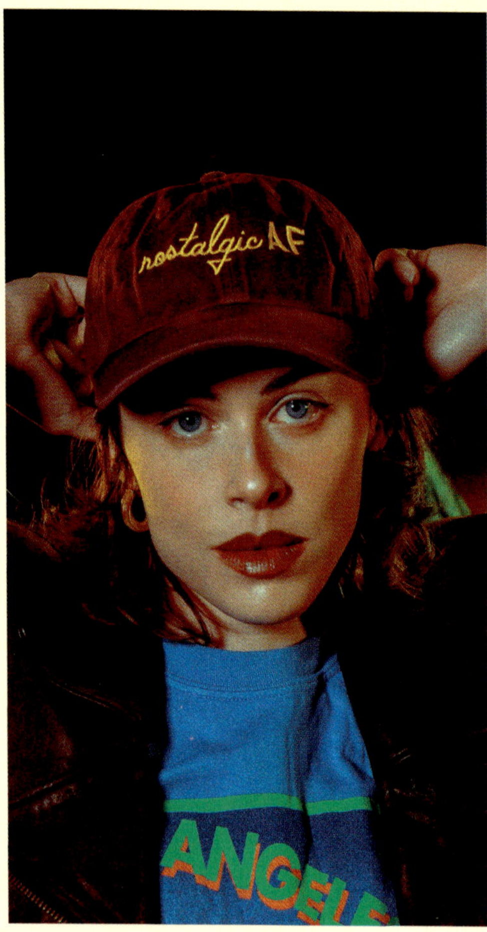

21. Fog: The ethereal quality of fog influenced my aesthetic preferences and sense of atmosphere.

22. *Young Frankenstein*: This classic comedy film shaped my appreciation for humor and creativity in visual storytelling.

23. *Cinema Paradiso*: This heartfelt movie about the love of cinema resonated with my passion for storytelling through film.

24. The Jonas Brothers: My unabashed love for the Jonas Brothers and their music reflects my diverse musical interests and the power of nostalgia.

25. *This Is Spinal Tap*: This mockumentary film influenced my appreciation for satire and humor in creative works.

26. *Do the Right Thing*: Spike Lee's powerful film made me reflect on social issues and the importance of artistic expression in addressing them.

27. '70s rock: The raw energy and rebellious spirit of '70s rock shaped my musical preferences and artistic sensibilities.

28. Disco: The infectious beats and vibrant energy of disco music influenced my love for rhythm and movement.

29. *Koyaanisqatsi*: This experimental film challenged my perception of time, nature, and the human experience.

30. Electronic music: The futuristic sounds and innovative production techniques of electronic music sparked my interest in sound design and composition.

18. Making videos/showing and telling stories: The art of storytelling through video production has become an integral part of my creative expression.

19. Sunsets: The beauty and tranquility of sunsets has always fascinated me and inspired a sense of wonder.

20. Cities at night: The vibrant and mesmerizing cityscapes illuminate at night with new colors and shadows. A whole new city can emerge after sunset.

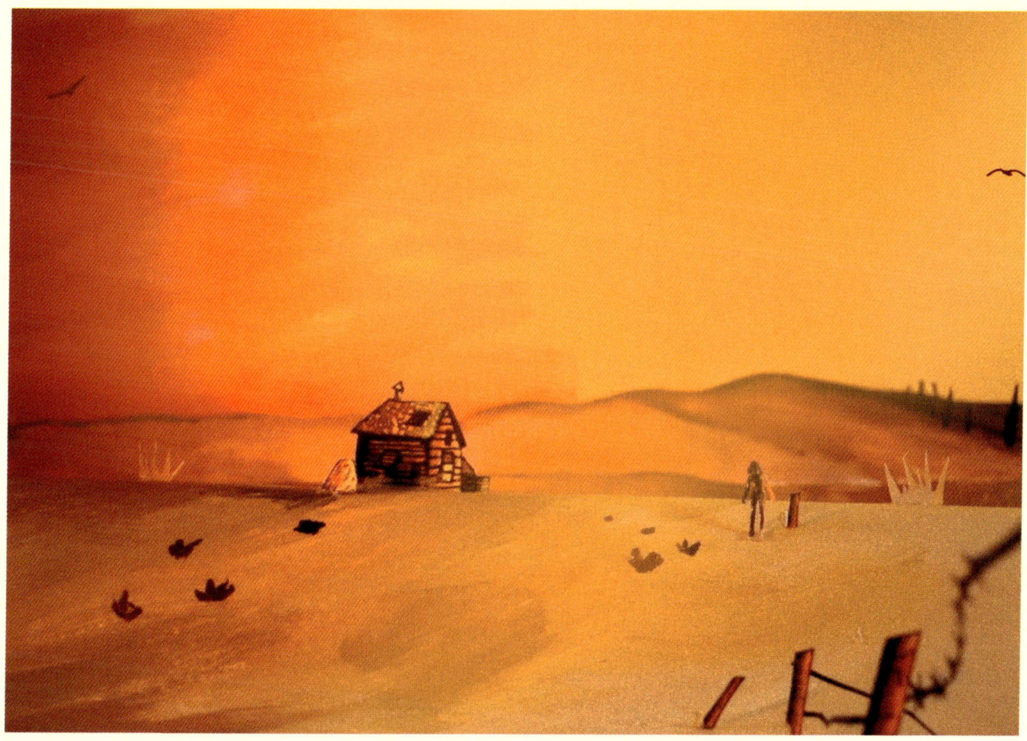

31. '90s hip-hop: The lyrical storytelling and cultural significance of '90s hip-hop have influenced my appreciation for the genre and its artistic expression.

32. *The Rocky Horror Picture Show*: This cult classic film influenced my love for camp, theatricality, and embracing the unconventional.

33. '80s music: The vibrant and diverse sounds of the '80s left a lasting impact on my musical taste and artistic style.

34. Technology: Computer programs give me the ability to mold and manipulate my practical effects, taking my videos a step further and easily enriching them.

35. Statistics: The analytical side of my brain has a fascination with statistics, finding patterns and insights in data.

36. '80s and '90s films: Specifically, the use of soundstage sets that are mostly realistic but still hint at creative artistry really resonated with me.

37. Puzzles or problem-solving games: Engaging in puzzles and problem-solving activities has honed my critical thinking skills and love for challenges.

38. Interior design: Exploring different interior design styles from Art Deco, Regency, midcentury modern, to '80s postmodern influenced my visual composition preferences.

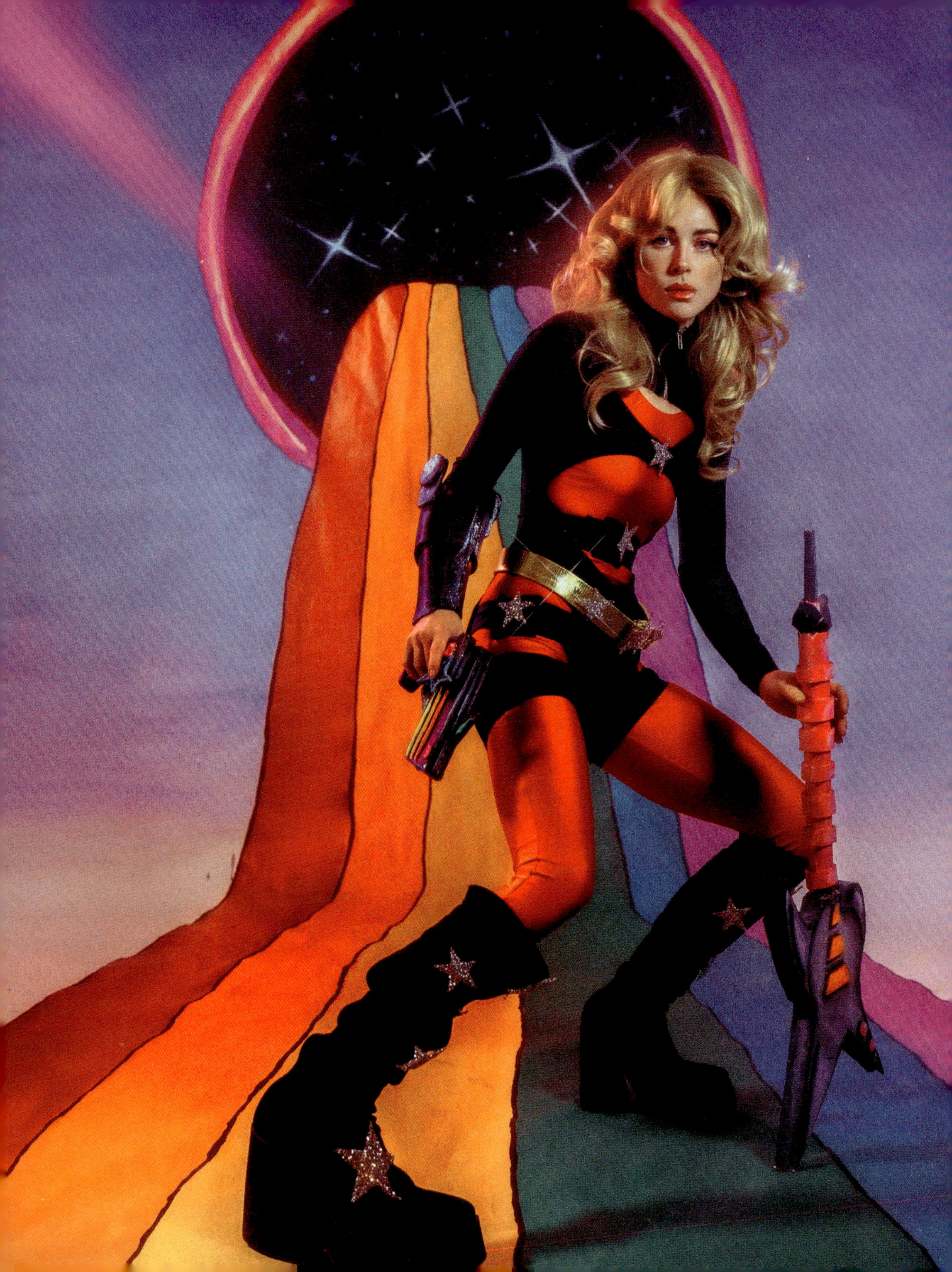

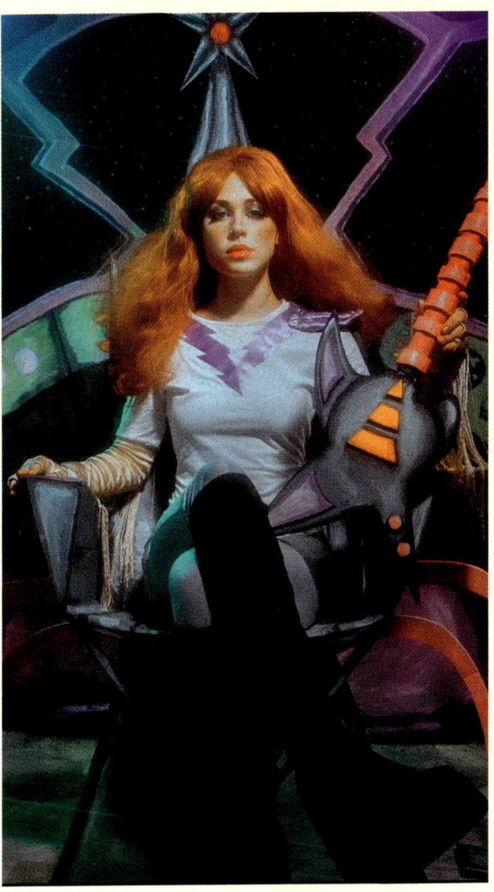

feel warm, powerful, and a bit reflective. My heart can't handle it.

42. Mountainous landscapes: There is nothing more breathtaking. I love how the light plays with mountains and how weather can swirl around them, augmenting their shape and demeanor.

43. Giraffes: No one told them to be so interesting looking. And yet, they are.

44. Video games: I love open-world games, the ones where you can explore and create new things around you. It's like watching a movie where I can control the story.

45. Entertaining/hosting parties: I always enjoyed watching my parents and their friends gather, laugh, consume, and talk. I like to watch people having fun.

46. Swelling music that creates a powerful blast: When music builds up and blasts a thick chord, it feels like a powerful magical spell casting out something unwanted.

47. Underdogs and unexpected heroes: Since I grew up with disabilities, I always felt like people were annoyed by my slow movements and quirky habits. I love a good underdog hero who exceeds expectations.

By going through each item on the list you've written down, you can explore how these attractions and experiences can be applied in various areas of your life—whether it's in art, fashion, interior design, music, filmmaking, or any other creative pursuit. Let's uncover the essence of your aesthetic together.

39. Getting dressed up: I love to morph into different personas. Each one is a piece of me, but none is the same. Dressing up provides me the ability to reinvent myself in new ways.

40. Miniature sets: Using these are an adorable way to build worlds that have never existed. They're an accessible means to create vast landscapes you couldn't otherwise create.

41. Pink: Specifically, orangey-pinks, the color of my favorite type of sunset. It makes me

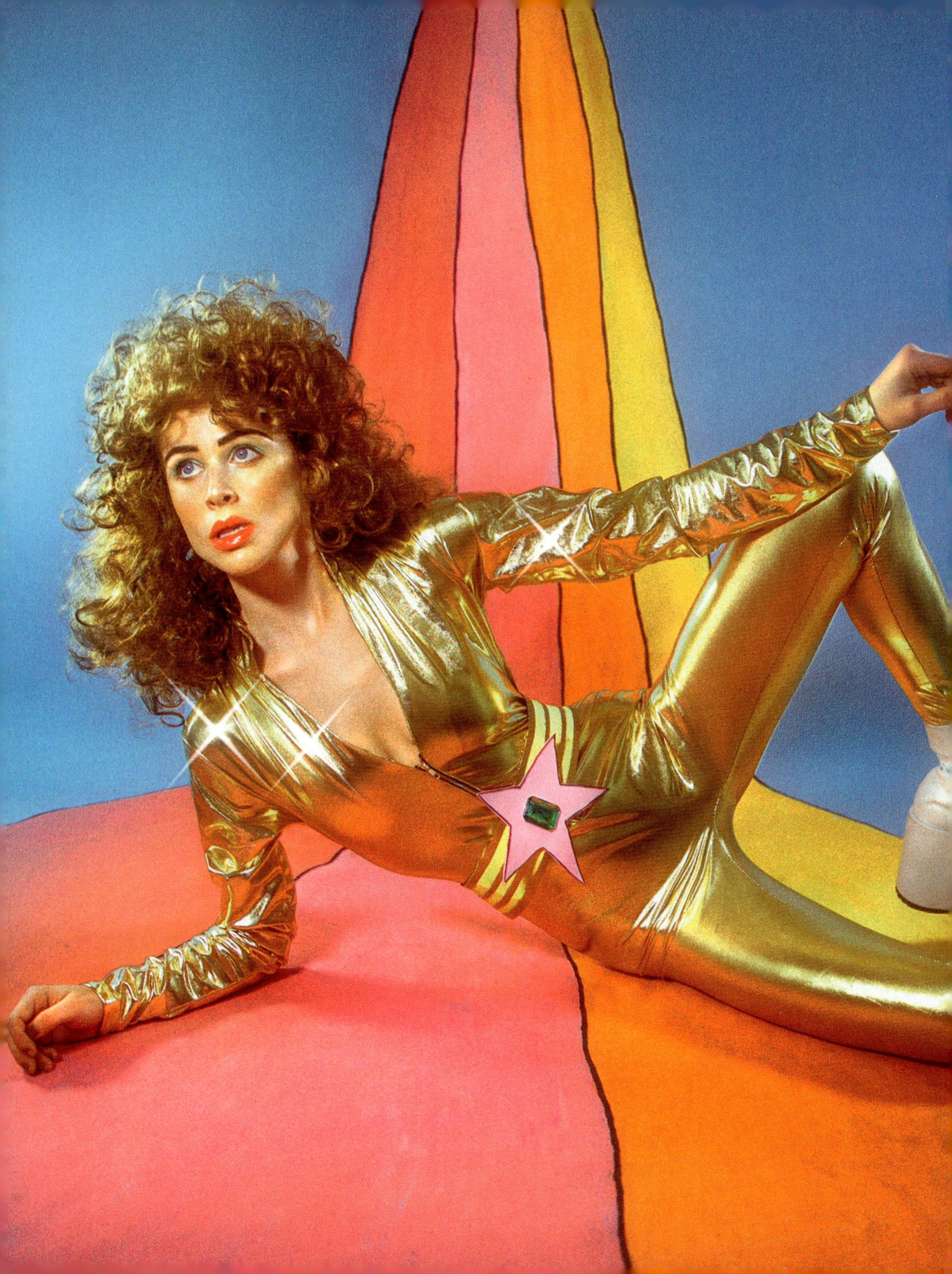

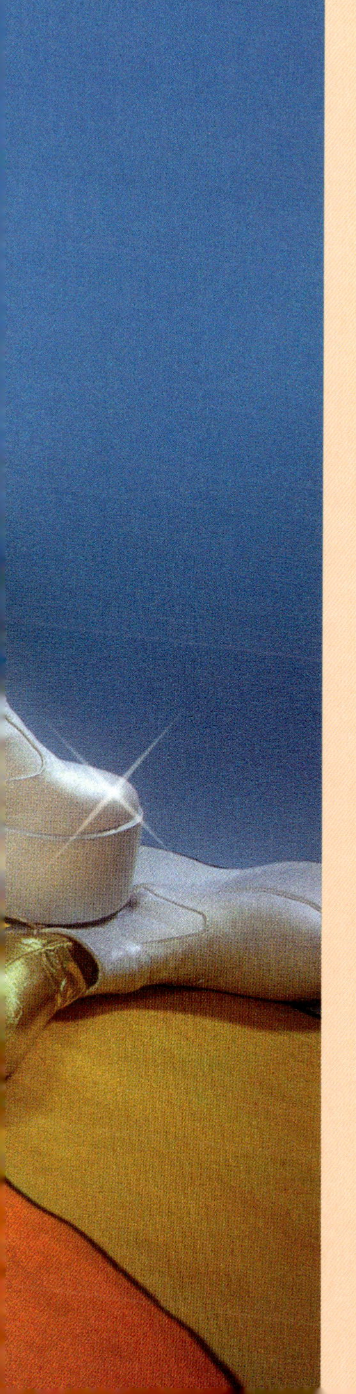

CHAPTER TWO

WHAT IS AN AESTHETIC?

MORE THAN A BUZZ WORD

An aesthetic is the essence that emerges from anything you encounter or observe. It's a fusion of elements that combine to elicit a specific feeling within you, affecting your senses. Aesthetics are not limited to visual experiences; they can also be derived from sounds, thoughts, or ideas.

Aesthetics can be applied to a wide range of areas including art, music, fashion, writing, and more. Ultimately, an aesthetic is a reflection of who you truly are as an individual.

Each of us sees the world through our own unique lens that cannot be duplicated by anyone else. While you may admire and appreciate the aesthetic of a filmmaker, attempting to replicate it wouldn't truly represent your personal aesthetic. You can incorporate elements from various aesthetics into your own unique mix, but your experiences and perspectives make your aesthetic one of a kind. Identifying your aesthetic allows you to create a road map to your individuality and a means to authentically express yourself.

In my eyes, aesthetics are like snowflakes, seemingly similar from a distance but intricate and distinct upon closer inspection. No two are alike, yet they all make sense in their own way!

DISCOVER YOUR AESTHETIC

It's time to delve deeper into the concept of aesthetics. Now that you understand the basic essence of what an aesthetic is, you can begin to recognize patterns and themes in what you are naturally drawn to. By avoiding the creation of a predetermined aesthetic, you can embrace the organic evolution of your own creative voice.

Aesthetics weren't a focal point in my family. Our home was an amalgamation of random artifacts, sentimental items, and objects that my parents found intriguing. There was no intentional cohesion, and I longed for the perfectly arranged furniture and matching colors of my friends' suburban homes.

In retrospect, I realize that my parents unintentionally developed their own aesthetic by amassing things they liked, unified by their understanding of color and shape principles. What they unknowingly instilled in me was an appreciation for aesthetics created without fixating on specific styles, focusing instead on what visually appealed to me.

I want to emphasize that the best way to discover your own aesthetic is to avoid fixating on a specific outcome. When I first started creating, I never concerned myself with how I wanted things to look; I simply created what I could. Over time, I honed and perfected my craft, leading to the development of my unique aesthetic—a culmination of many facets that reflect my essence.

It's so important to trust your instincts when crafting your own unique aesthetic. Your master list from Chapter One will help you discover patterns that provide valuable insight into how your brain perceives the world and what resonates with you. The key lies in observing these patterns and diving deeper into their essence.

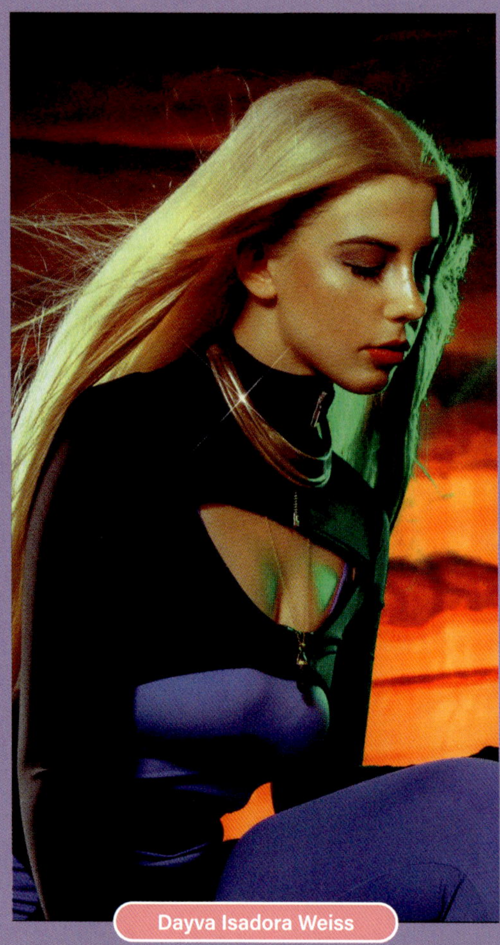

Dayva Isadora Weiss

Getting Started

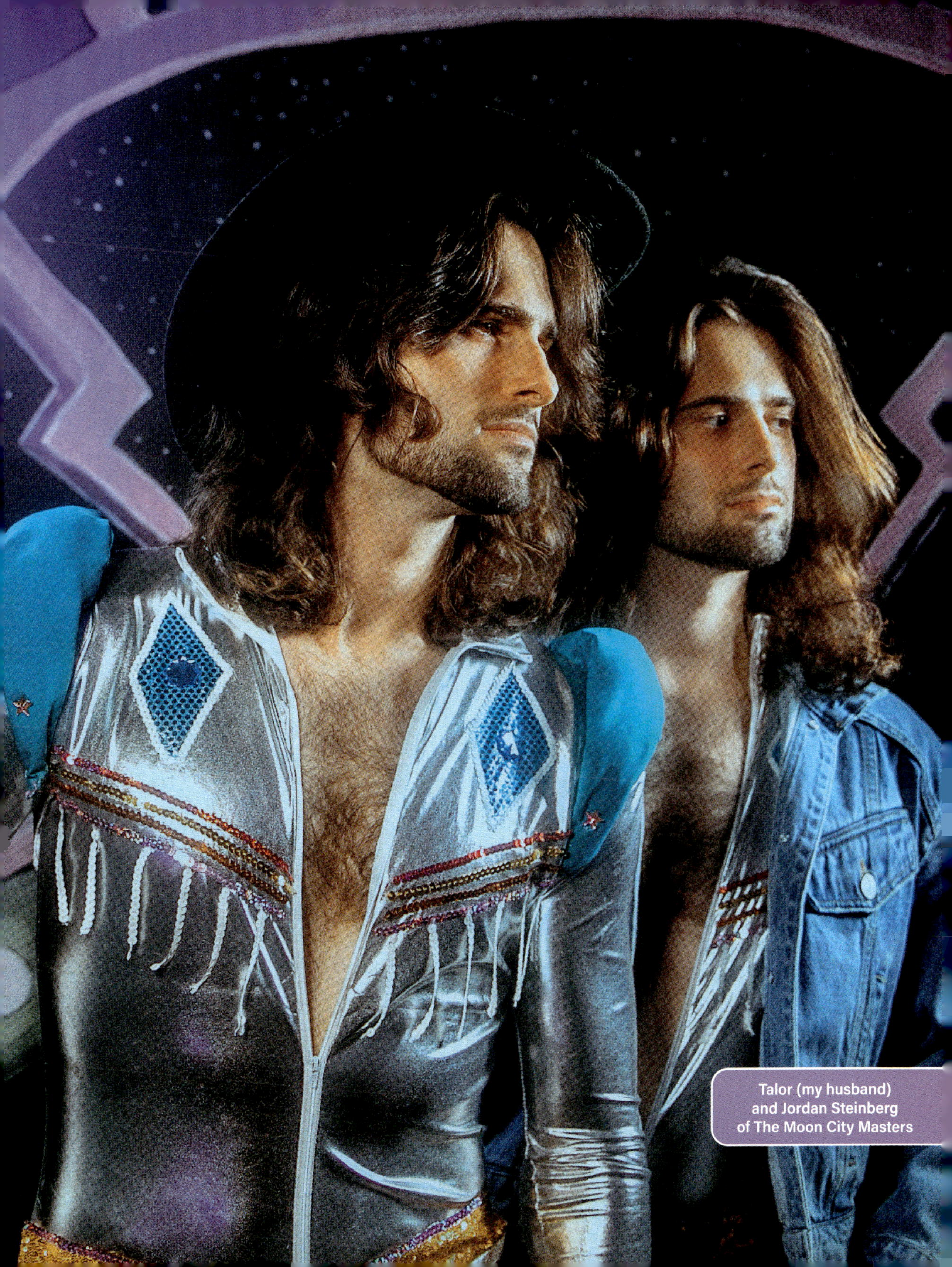

Talor (my husband) and Jordan Steinberg of The Moon City Masters

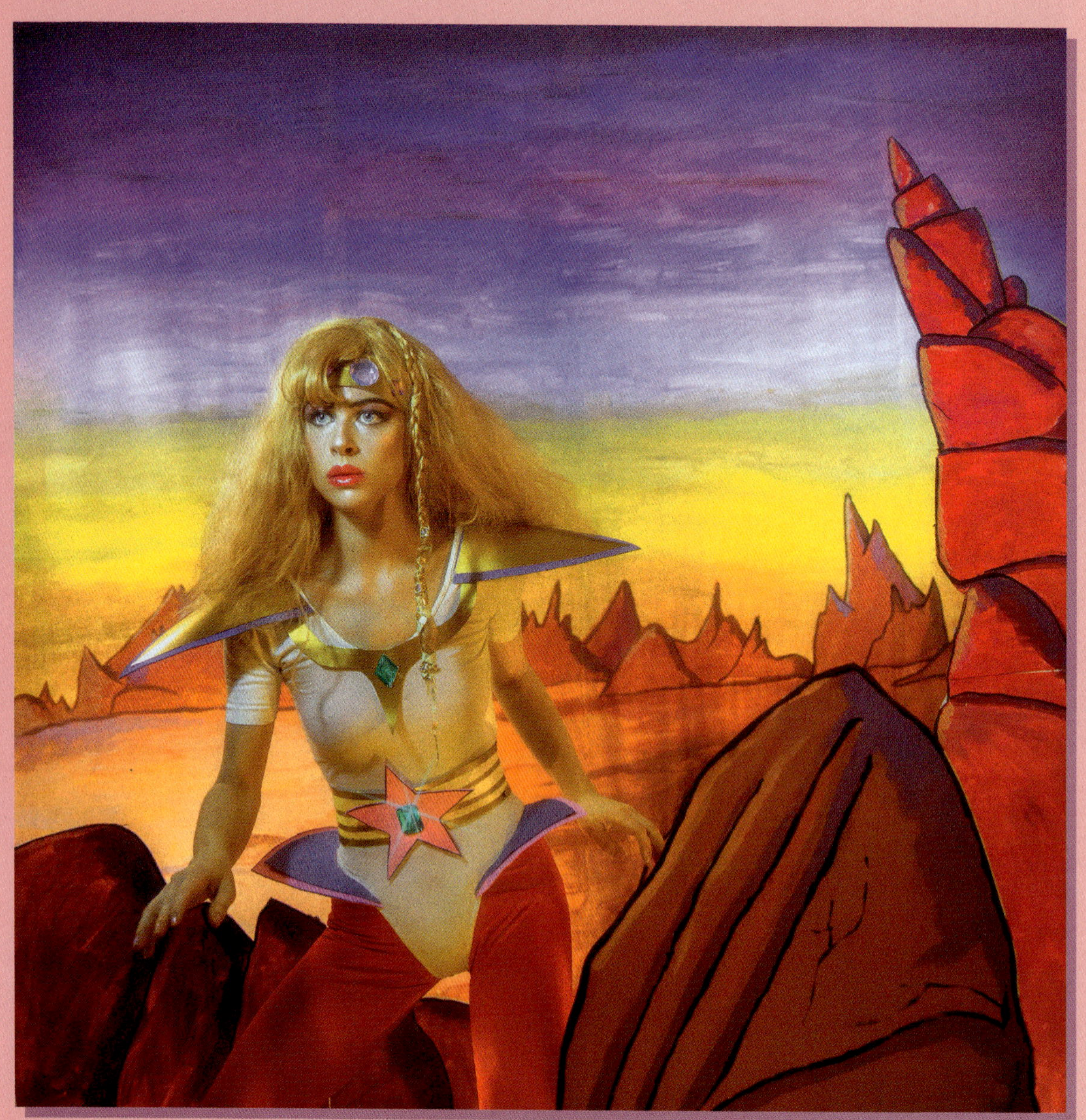

Getting Started

IDENTIFYING PATTERNS

I often liken aesthetics to a mathematical equation—by combining elements I love, I can create something new. Trusting your intuition and attuning yourself to the moments when something feels right is essential. Listen to the voice in your head that says, "Oh yes, this feels right to me," when you look at something. Usually, that first mind spark is an element of who you are. Trust it.

Take time to go down the master list you made earlier and think hard as to why you're drawn to those specific elements. From there, you can highlight the patterns that begin to emerge.

Considering the list I made, here are some examples of patterns I've found:

Over-the-top theatrical outfits: David Bowie, princess sleeves, musicals, '80s style, '70s glam, disco, Rainbow Brite, *The Nutcracker*, *Cats*, and Henry VIII.

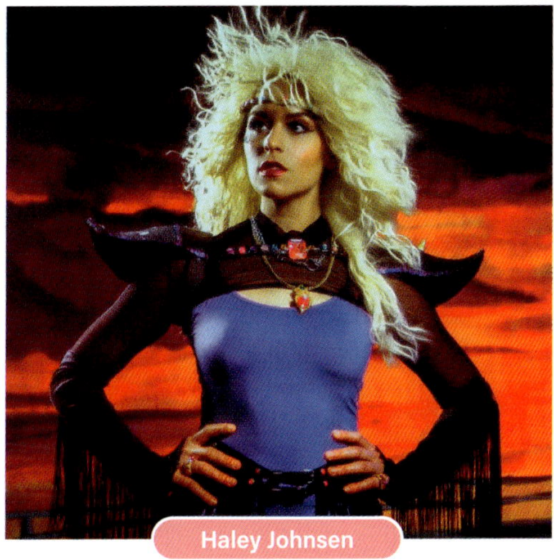

Music and movement relationship: old Disney cartoons, musicals, and rock music when it used to be more theatrical.

Objects coming to life: cartoons, stop-motion, the Muppets, the magic of camera trickery and how we can add magic into the world, and handmade objects used in film sets.

Technology and the idea of growth and progression: coming up with unique technology-based ideas to captivate, and manipulating physical mediums I create with computer programs.

The vibrant natural world and the colors that exist within it: sunsets, cities at night, fog, *Koyaanisqatsi*, mountainous landscapes, the natural world's ever-changing vibrant colors, and shifting light.

Identifying these patterns from my list helps me understand how all these items connect and overlap. This list gives insight into who I am and what I'm into creatively. I love whimsical over-the-top ways to express emotion, I have an interest in tech and manipulation, and I love vibrant colors. How does your list compare? What patterns do you see among the objects and elements you've identified?

As you move forward in your journey of self-discovery, remember to embrace the organic evolution of your aesthetic. Trust in yourself and the process—allowing your aesthetic to emerge naturally from your experiences, influences, and the elements that resonate within your soul.

AESTHETICS ACROSS DISCIPLINES

How can you apply what you've learned about aesthetics so far across different disciplines?

A good place to start is by thinking about the different areas where you would like to home in on your aesthetic.

Aesthetics for art: Art itself is usually a reflection of some sort of element or idea in life. Reflection is key. Reflect on what you have been drawn to and love; reflect on what has made you feel a certain way; reflect on the colors your eyes always snap to; reflect on your core beliefs; reflect on your hopes and desires.

After you spend time reflecting, explore and find inspiration. As an artist, I like to think of aesthetics as the devices used to evoke a certain emotion. We all have ideas and memories attached to certain vibes. Think about the tone you're trying to create with your work. What does that style look like?

Creating a mood board is always helpful when you are trying to achieve a specific style or tone. But then, after you create the mood board and have all your references in your head, *never look at it again*. Instead, let your brain continue to imagine what your work will look like.

Aesthetics for interior design: When I feel lost while designing a space, I tend to scroll through furniture websites. Forget about the price of an item; just pay attention when your brain pinpoints a specific item. What is it that caught your eye? Make a note and keep going.

Once you start to see a pattern emerge, consider the colors and style of the furniture. If you're unsure what the style of a specific piece is, you can always figure it out by searching descriptive terms. After you have identified the styles you like, it will become easier to find more items that fit the same vibe. And remember, the items you're using to decorate your space don't have to all be the same style—they just need to have elements that complement one another!

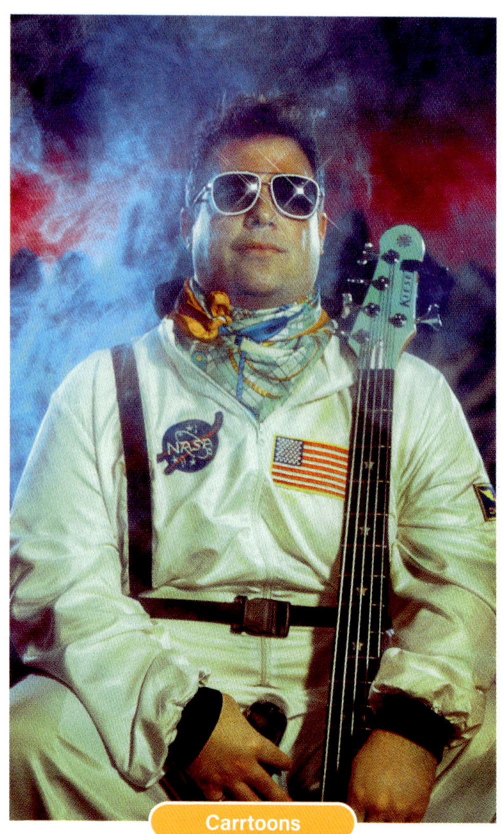

Carrtoons

CINDI ETTINGER
Printmaker

I have always had a desire for adventure and am visually attracted to the interplay of design, pattern, text, and color. I love that these elements can each have their own historical or nostalgic associations and can be used as metaphors. I enjoy looking at old album covers, advertising, graphic design, and book jackets for inspiration. Although my work has changed quite a bit over the years, there is still a thread that is visible across my work, even if it isn't always obvious.

I started painting when I was a teenager and switched to printmaking in college. I found printmaking offered me technical access to the things that influence me visually. There are so many ways to use the print medium. During my time at college, I focused on traditional techniques but always tried to push the limits and use printmaking in experimental ways. I like problem-solving and thinking outside of the box. In the early 2000s, I acquired a letterpress. This press was used in the commercial printing of newspapers and books until the advent of computers and digital processes. As I started using it regularly, I realized how excited I get from using text and graphic elements in my work.

Our home is somewhat eclectic as well. I like contrast; we live with a mix of family heirlooms and contemporary art and accessories. The furniture is basic but the rugs, dishes, pillows, and art are colorful and patterned. I dress that way too: classic clothes with colorful scarves,

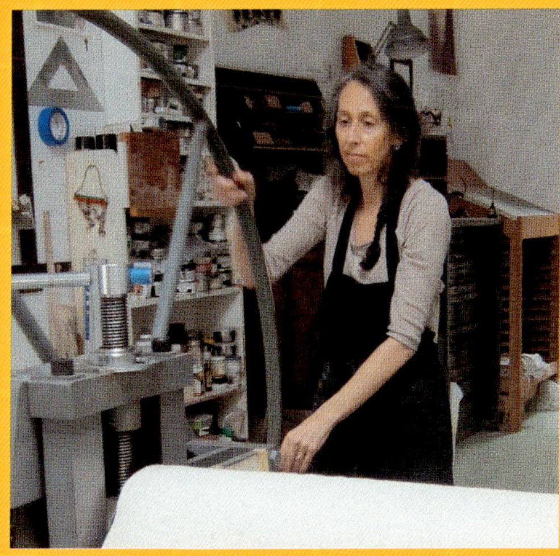

jewelry, etc. You can also see this trend in my artwork.

My creative process is intuitive. When I start working, I rarely know where a piece will end up. Each thing I do brings me to the next phase. When I feel blocked, I review old work and see what I can do differently or what I should stick with. This usually sparks something.

Unconsciously, my work is affected by where I've been, what I've read, or how I feel. My studio is filled with old maps, books, prints, and paper. I use all these elements in my work and combine the old with the new. By using written words and language as a visual element, I am able to bring meaning into my work, while still always adapting my process over time.

CHOOSE YOUR OWN AESTHETIC ADVENTURE

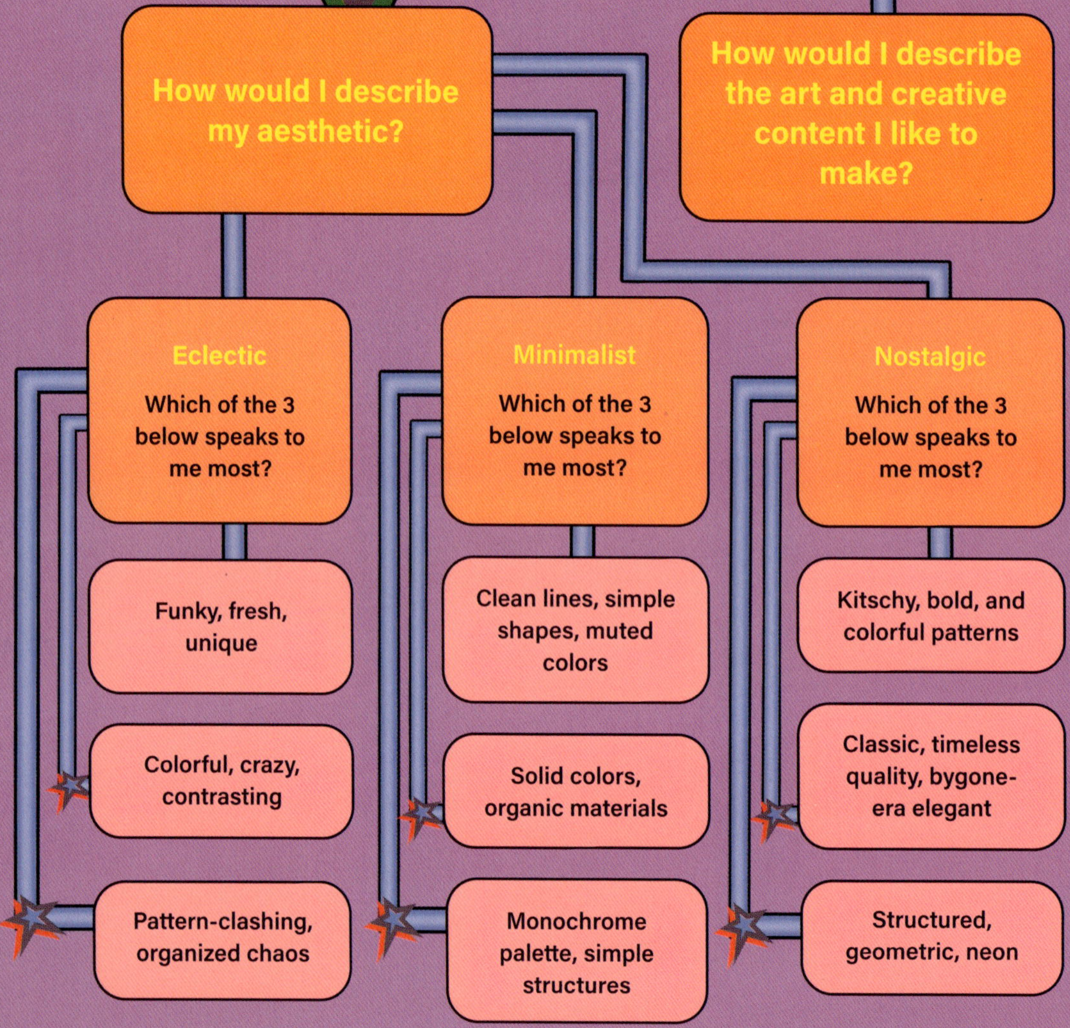

How would I describe my aesthetic?

How would I describe the art and creative content I like to make?

Eclectic
Which of the 3 below speaks to me most?

Funky, fresh, unique

Colorful, crazy, contrasting

Pattern-clashing, organized chaos

Minimalist
Which of the 3 below speaks to me most?

Clean lines, simple shapes, muted colors

Solid colors, organic materials

Monochrome palette, simple structures

Nostalgic
Which of the 3 below speaks to me most?

Kitschy, bold, and colorful patterns

Classic, timeless quality, bygone-era elegant

Structured, geometric, neon

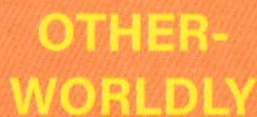

OTHER-WORLDLY

Which of the next 2 options speak to me most?

Surreal

Magical

Magical realism: fantastical, magic moments grounded in reality

Dark magic: hazy, eerie, gothic vibes

Dreamlike: soft, hazy, ethereal

Psychedelic: vivid, bright, bold patterns and colors

TEXTURED

Which of the next 2 options speak to me most?

Layering

Sensory

Interactive: touching, hearing, tasting

Immersive: installations, large-scale, viewed from different angles

Maximalism: mixed media, collaging, many mish-mashed elements

Organic: fabrics, woods, stones, furs

NARRATIVE

Which of the next 2 options speak to me most?

Visual storytelling

Shaping the story

Digital media and video games: stories to interact with

Writing: composing a story with words

Film and television: moving visuals with picture and sound

Comics or photojournalism: sequenced images strung together

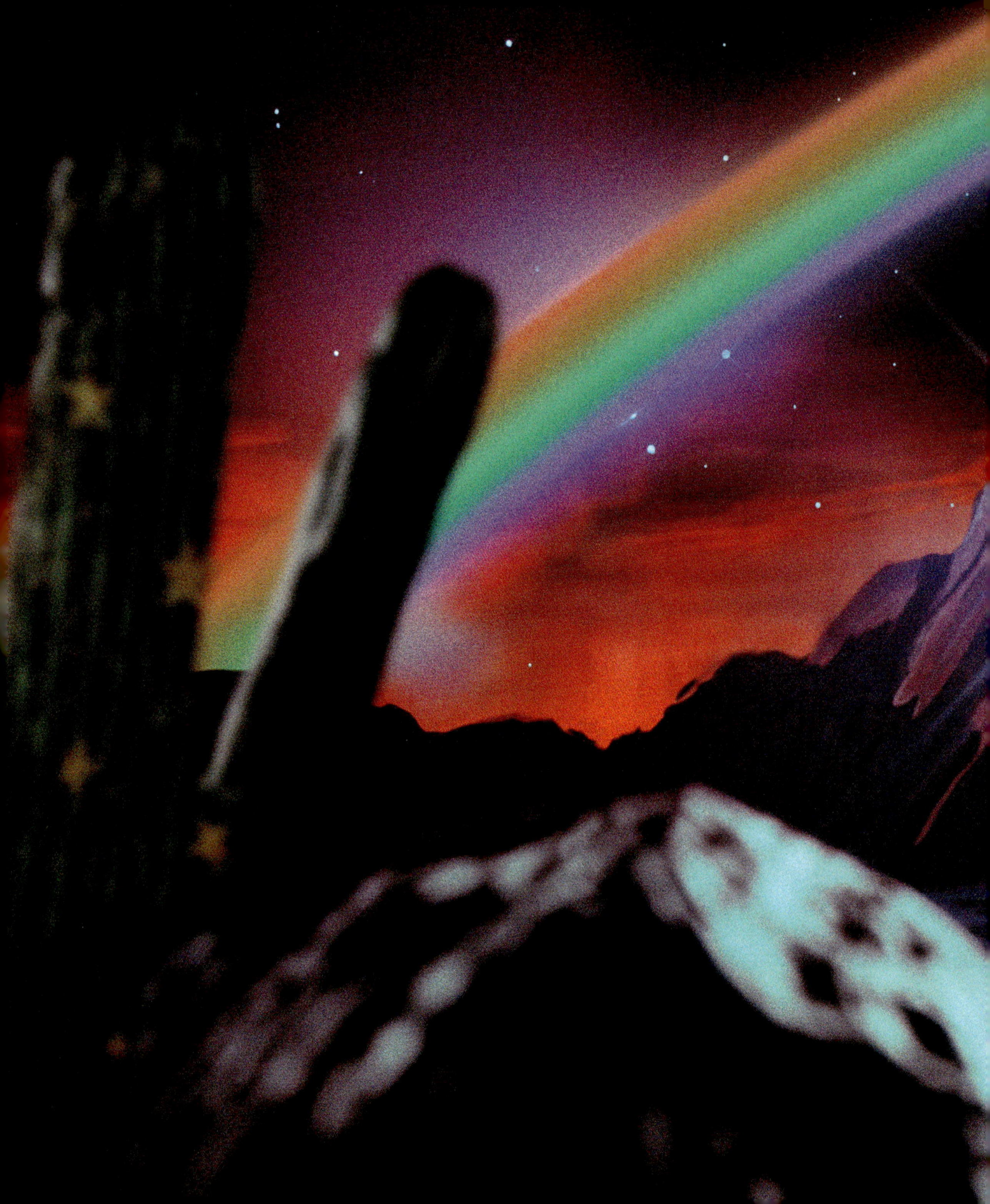

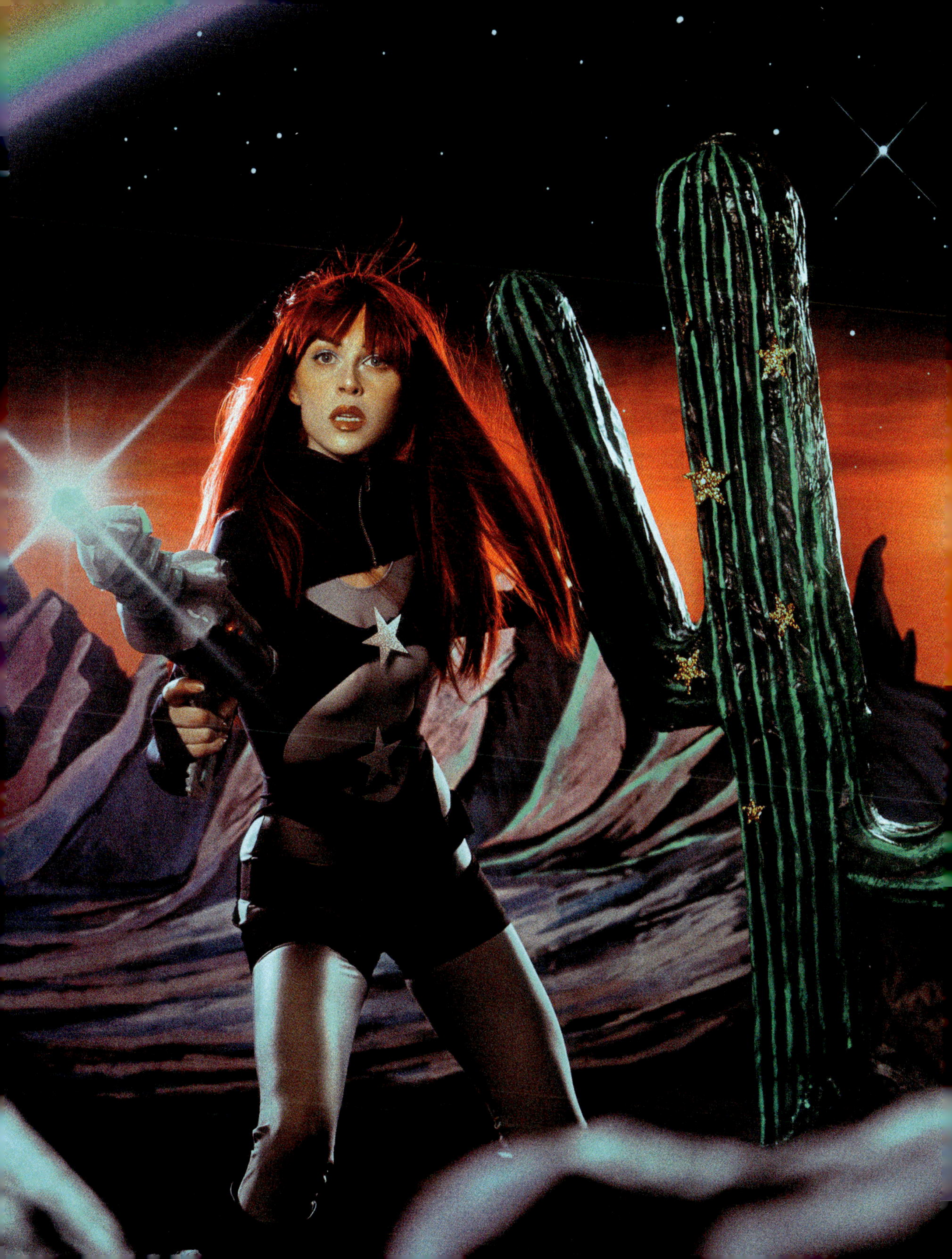

AESTHETIC EXPLORATION EXERCISES

> Try creating things based on the aesthetics you enjoy. Search around and do a bit of research. Then never look at the references again. Instead, try to create something based off what you think the aesthetic is in your head. What do you end up with?

> It's a good idea to work with things you already own! This is a fun way to see if you can use your imagination and creativity to produce something with what you have on hand.

> Try finding objects around your space that you think can go together, and create a little still life with them. Why is it working? Why don't you think it is working?

> Create a collage from magazines. Make one collage using only one magazine. Then make another collage pulling from multiple magazines. Which one do you like better? How do they differ?

> Open up your closet or drawer of clothes. What kind of clothes do you have the most of? Are there any patterns or colors you see repeated often among the items in your wardrobe?

> Look at your recently played song history. What genre of music do you see showing up the most often? Across the different genres you regularly listen to, are there any similarities in the musical composition or mood of the songs? What about the lyrics?

> Film a scene. Set up your camera or phone in a room you like and point it in the direction of where you'd like your scene. Try rearranging items in the scene based on what you see through the lens or in the phone's frame. Don't just use your naked eye on the real space itself. Once you finish moving things around, think about what you came up with. Do you think the result is different because you only looked from the camera's perspective? How is it different?

> Draw something you love. Take a good look at a reference image, then put the image away and don't look at it again. Draw it using two different mediums (like one with a thick marker and another with a pencil). Which of the two do you prefer? View the reference image again. Which medium is the closest representation of what you wanted your drawing to look like?

> Look up from this book and allow your eyes to wander until they come to rest on an object that catches and holds your interest. What do you like about this object? What do you dislike? Where is it from? Does it have a story to tell?

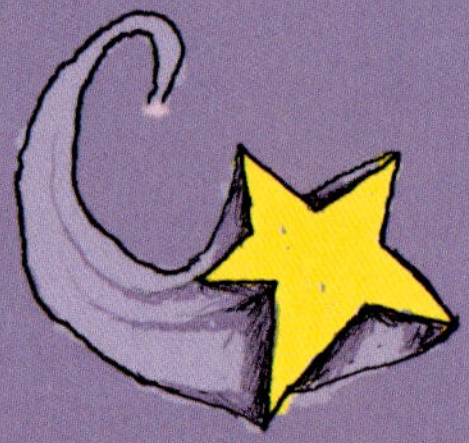

Getting Started

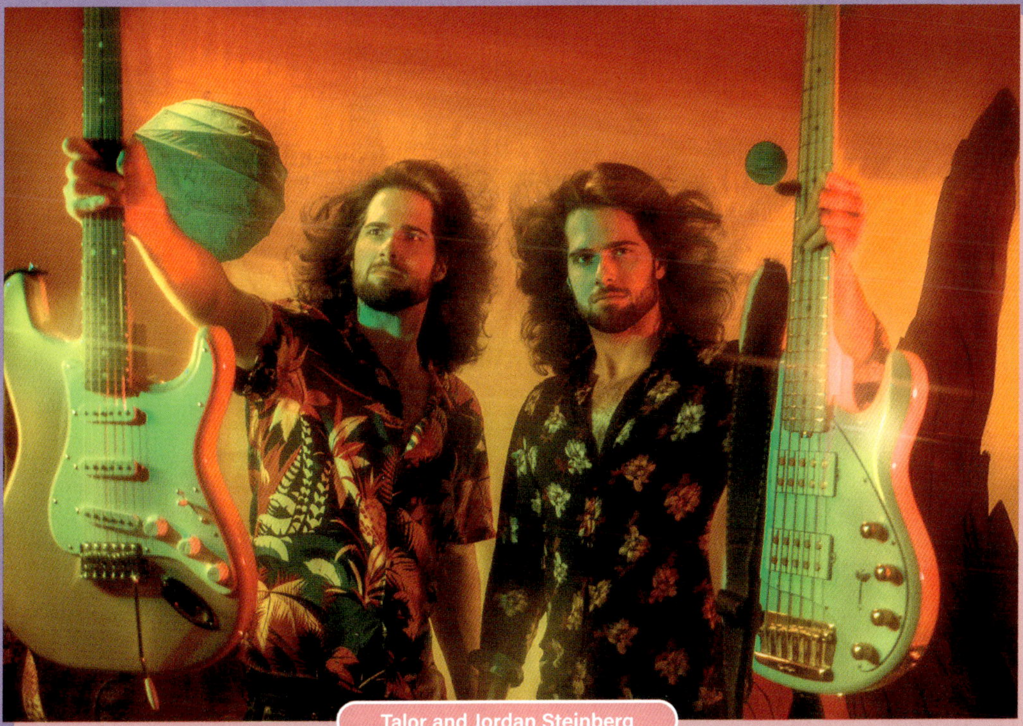

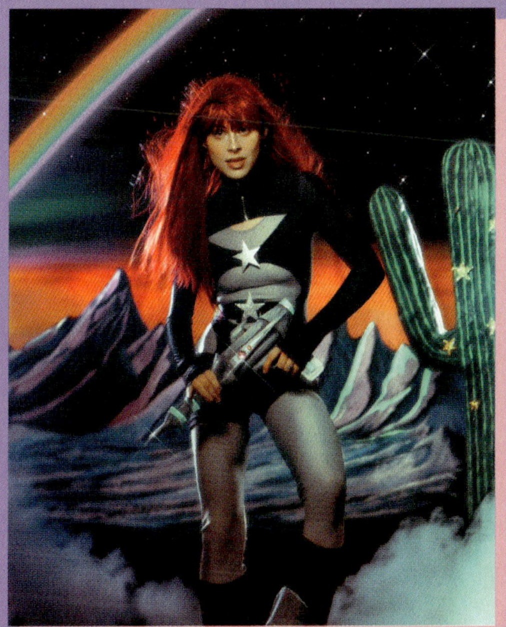

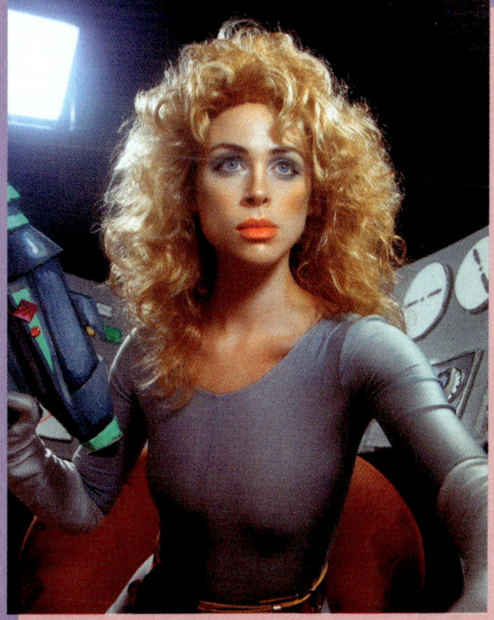

Talor and Jordan Steinberg

QUESTIONS TO CONSIDER

> What types of aesthetics are you drawn to?

> Why are you drawn to them?

> Can you identify some words that describe what you like visually?

> Are there two or three different aesthetics you like a lot? How are they similar? How are they different?

> What emotions do you feel when you think about an aesthetic you'd like to have?

> What colors are you drawn to? Why are you drawn to them?

> What materials and textures come to mind when you think of your aesthetic?

> How do you want your aesthetic to make others feel? How can you get these emotions across through your work or other creative endeavors?

> What are the patterns and themes you've noticed that keep reappearing in your lists?

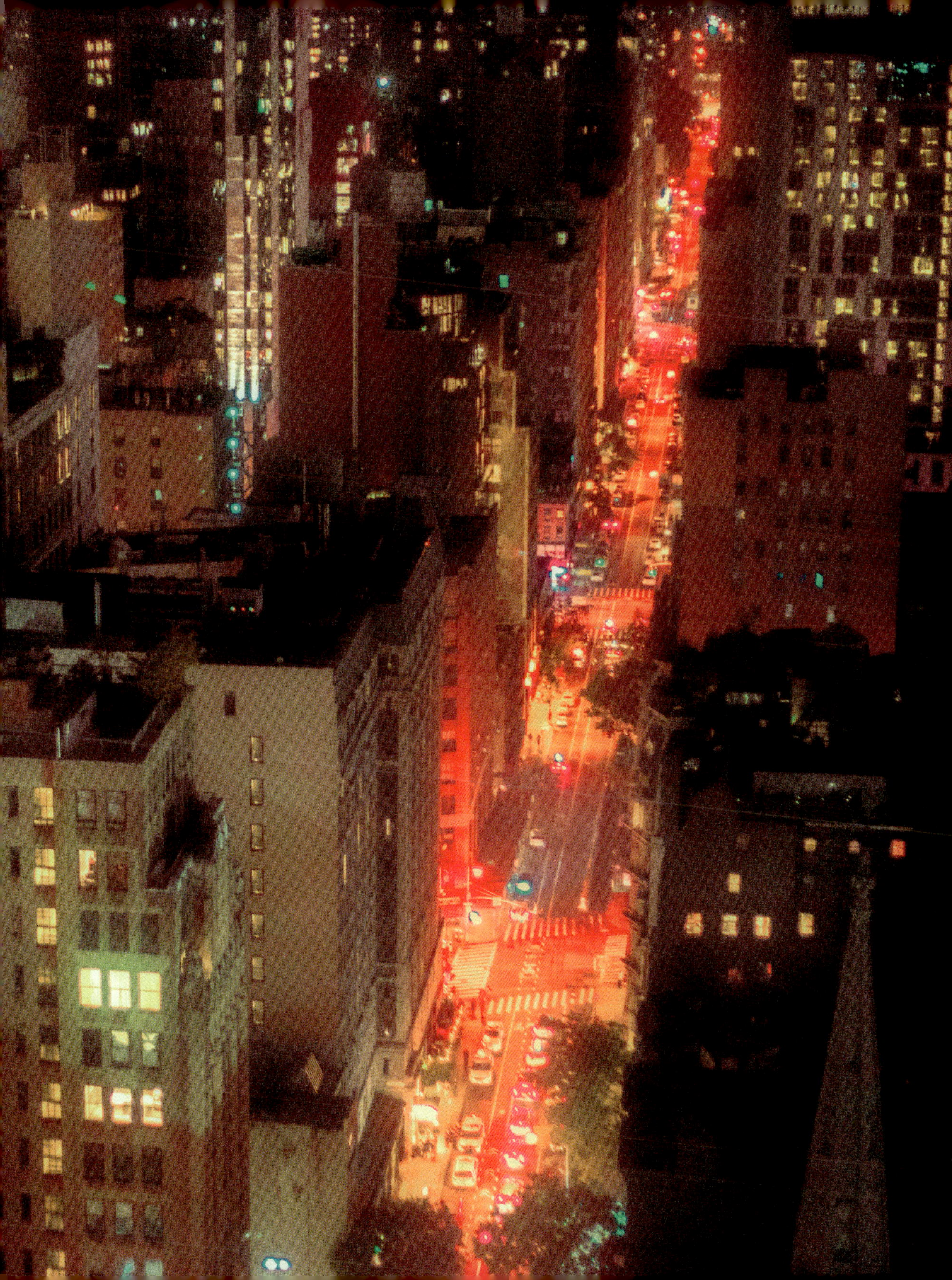

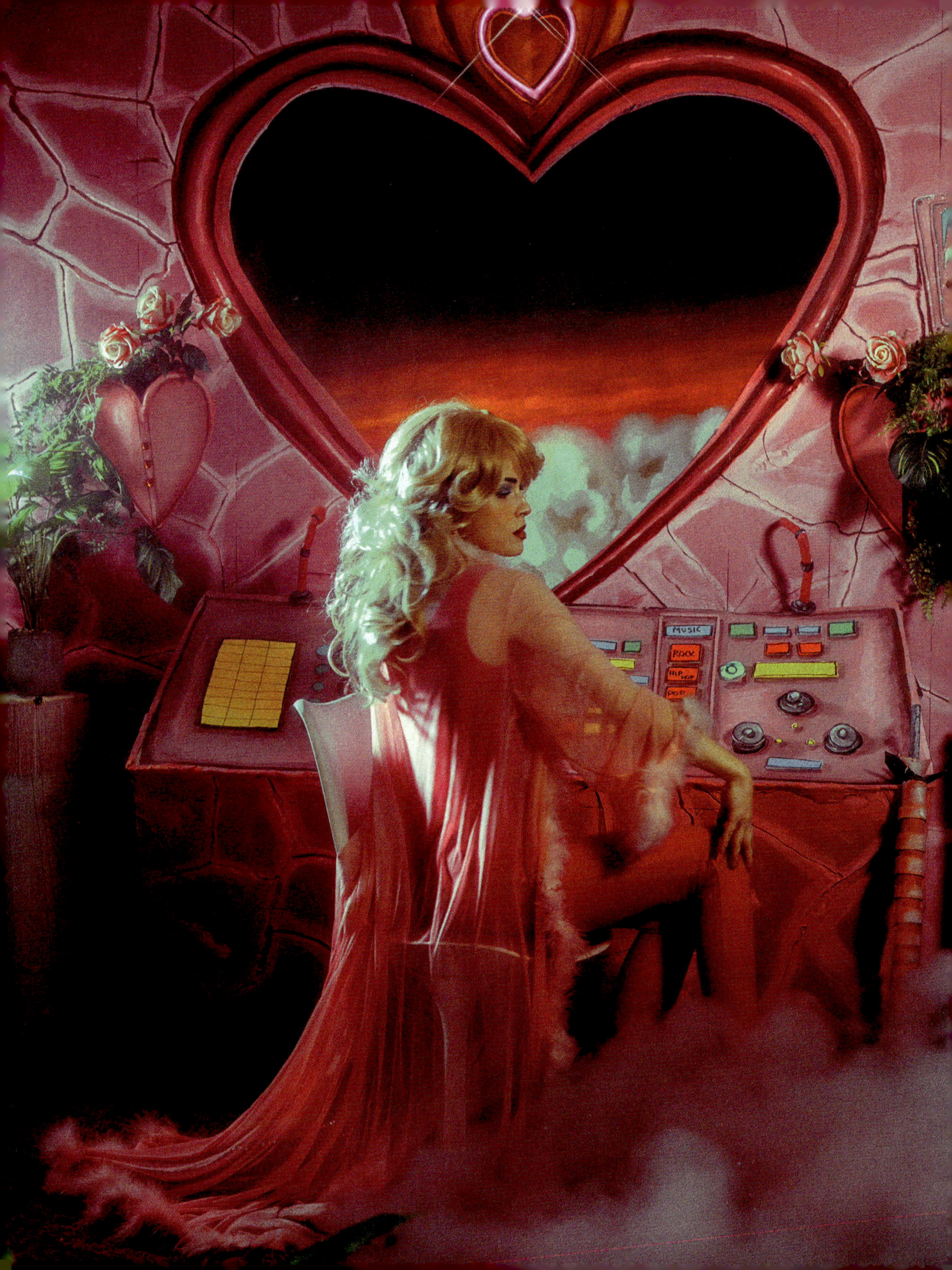
MUSIC
ROCK
HIP HOP
POP

CHAPTER THREE

KEYWORDS & BRAINSTORMING

UNLEASHING THE CREATIVE FLOW

As children, we're often obsessed with something in particular, whether it's a TV show, a fictional character, or a specific song. When I was a kid, with my natural inclination toward creativity, I channeled my childhood preoccupations into various artistic expressions—writing stories, making videos, staging plays, and doodling sketches—all based on whatever obsession I had at the time. I embraced these obsessions wholeheartedly because they ignited my passion and constantly occupied my thoughts. They were fresh, new, and exciting, and more importantly, they inspired me to create.

As adults, our obsessions become more fleeting, like bold moments of intrigue that come and go. By the time we're grown, we've gained more knowledge and experiences, which may temper the pure magic of our reactions. However, that bold intrigue can still fuel our creative endeavors, and it's crucial to seize those moments immediately whenever they arise.

But how do we harness these creative moments? We can begin by breaking them down and uncovering what we want to achieve through the power of keywords and brainstorming. Keywords are the identifiable elements of a thing that break it down into more specific pieces and help define what it is. For example, if you're obsessed with cats, some of your keywords could be **playful**, **fluffy**, **agile**, **feline**, and **pet**. Brainstorming is the process of coming up with these ideas; so in essence, we just brainstormed these keywords after identifying the obsession of cats. Brainstorming can always go in several different ways, which is part of the reason why it's such a creative practice.

Take a closer look at your list of cherished elements that you wrote in Chapter One. Pay attention to the items that call out to you the most, and identify which ones alight a spark of energy within you. Trust your instincts and focus on what excites you rather than worrying about what you think *should* excite you.

TERMINOLOGY TO UNDERSTAND

Semiotics is the language of signs and symbols that we unconsciously use to communicate. Think about emojis and road signs—they convey meaning without words. By understanding how combinations of signs and symbols evoke emotions, we can incorporate them into our creative expressions.

Symbology is a part of semiotics, a special language made up of pictures, shapes, and colors that we use as a society. Basic shapes and symbols have attached meaning that help us further a story along. Using symbols can be an easy way to evoke or convey what you're trying to get across without having to say anything. Symbolism can take something complicated and boil it down to more straightforward components.

Themes play a crucial role in any creative endeavor. They are the big ideas or messages we want to convey to our audience. Let your current emotional state guide your choice of themes since they're an authentic way to infuse truth into your creations.

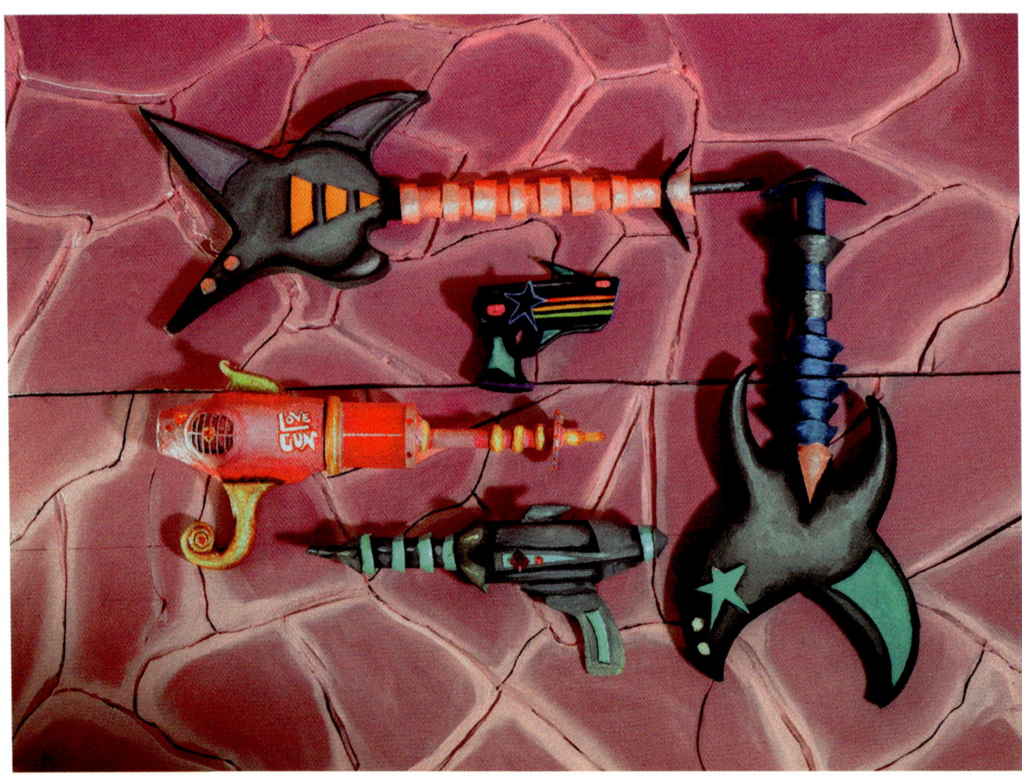

Getting Started

Allegory is a powerful tool that allows us to tell stories with hidden or alternative meanings. By creating a story or visual that can be interpreted as revealing a hidden meaning, we can explore intense topics within the framework of simpler narratives.

Reappropriation involves reshaping the narrative and changing the meaning attached to something else, giving it a new light and fresh perspective. It empowers us to transform negative situations into sources of strength and empowerment.

Motifs are recurring patterns or sequences that serve as clues and visual anchors within a story or creative piece. They can help indicate something or simply create a visually captivating pattern.

Narrative is the main storytelling vessel—it is the way the story is told and the framework of the creative piece that shares information and experiences in an interesting and deliberate manner.

While understanding these terms and concepts is helpful, it's equally important not to overthink the creative process. I've always been against trying too hard to be "deep." Depth emerges naturally when we create from a place of genuine excitement. The themes and concepts we seek will then fall into place effortlessly.

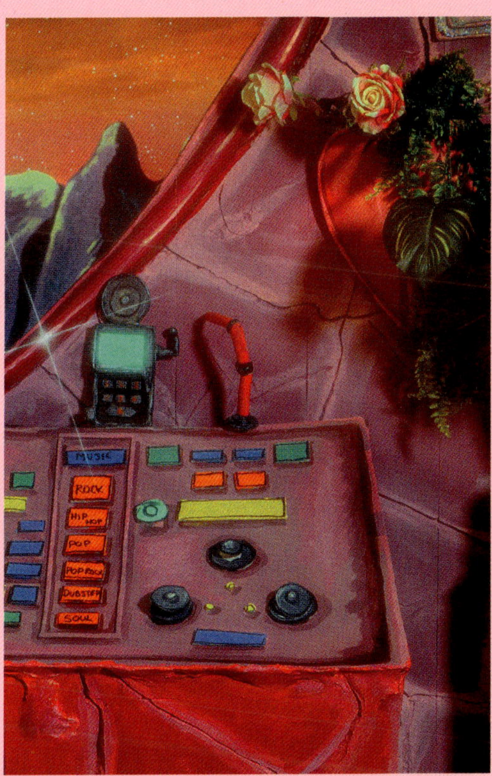

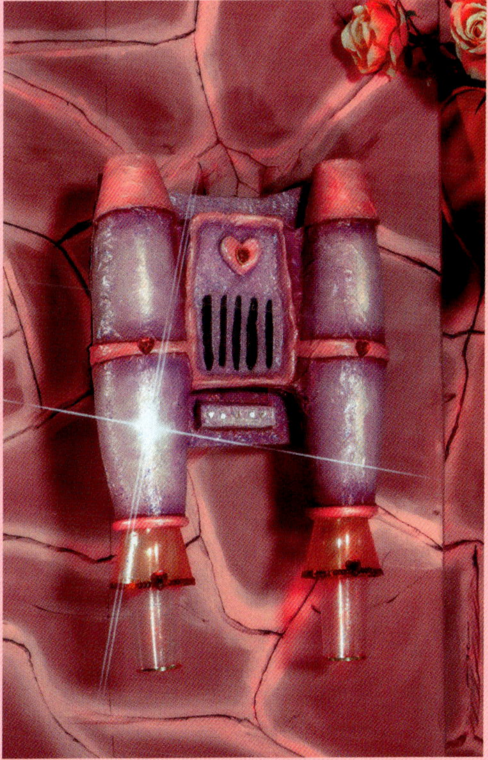

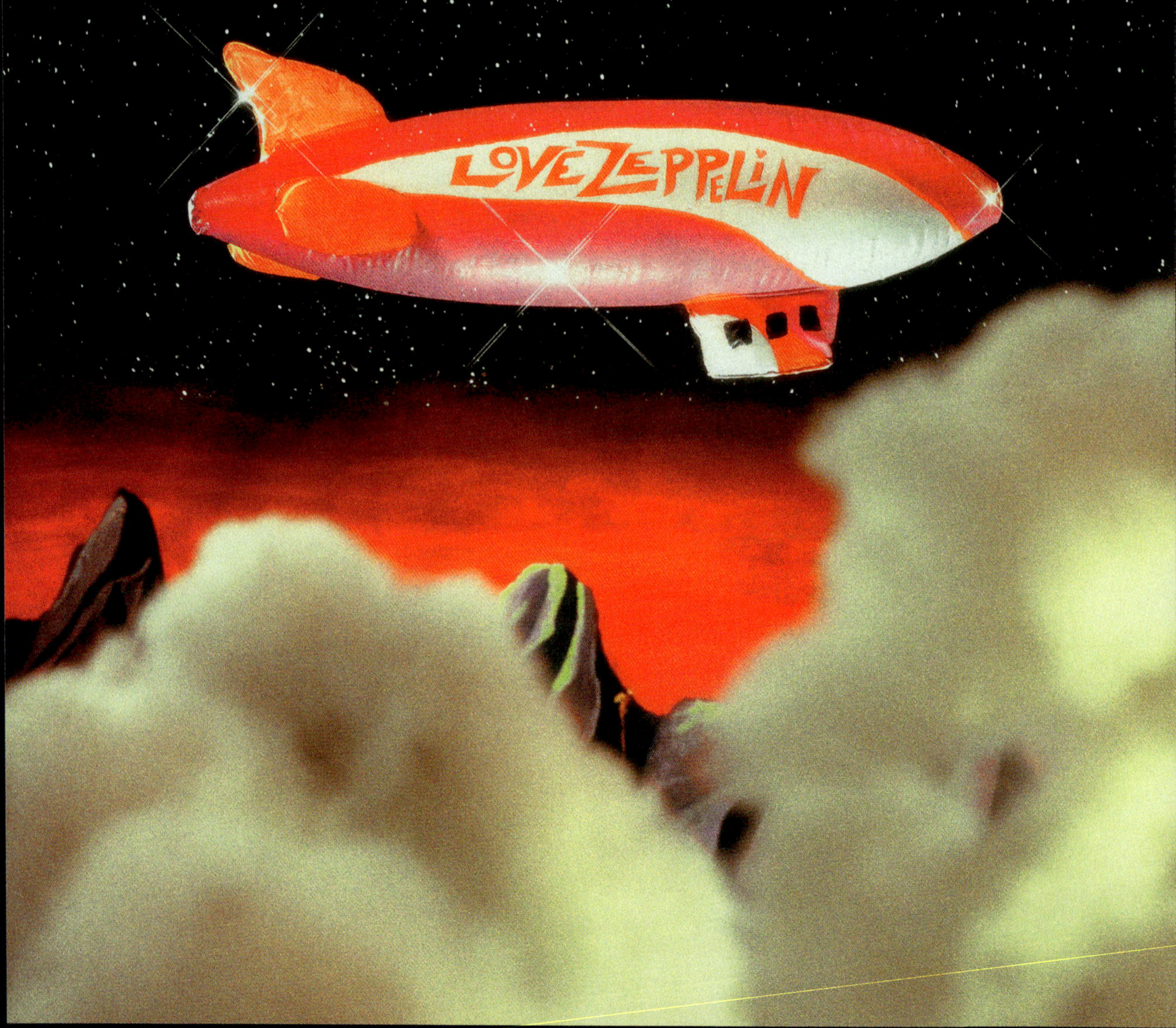

LoveZeppelin

USING KEYWORDS & BRAINSTORMING FOR IDEATION

One of the great things about keywords and brainstorming is that they can both be used interchangeably to lead to the other. You can brainstorm a list of keywords to better develop your concept, or you can use your list of keywords to brainstorm a new idea!

Let me share an example of how I used my own list of keywords to brainstorm a video idea:

I decided I'd love to make something that implements the keywords **disco**, **Studio 54**, and **'70s roller skating**. I started with the idea of what roller skating means to me and thought about what I could create around that keyword.

Roller skating has to do with movement, and as a rule, motion on roller skates typically moves forward. *Forward motion*—what does that symbolize in society? Going places, looking ahead, and rolling with the changes. It's about working hard and resilience. *(Oh would you look at that . . . Do I see a theme appearing?)*

Well, I see that **rainbows** are on my list, so maybe I can incorporate some kind of rainbow road to roll along on. This reminds me of **Nintendo 64**, and that works well since video games are also on my list.

Why would I be rolling on a rainbow to move forward with my life? Maybe it's because I am making a change. Maybe I am doing some spring cleaning—getting rid of the clutter and starting fresh—when I discover an old pair of **dusty** roller skates. The dusty element lets the viewer know it's been a while since I've used the skates. I can also use music and facial expressions to indicate that I'm remembering using them in the past. Nostalgia!

What if I decide to put them on while I am cleaning and transform myself into some **'70s glam/'80s hair** superhero on disco skates?

What if a rainbow road blasts through my window (which could symbolize a portal into another situation)? I would probably decide to take a leap of faith and roll out through the window.

When I think of **disco**, I think of pops of color with lots of black and shimmering sparkles. How about I roll into the stars and reach to catch them? Then I can roll off into the distance, getting lost in the dazzling universe, forever going forward! BAM!

IT'S TIME TO DIVE IN

Your list of cherished elements serves as a road map for your creative projects. It's exciting to discover that you already hold the answers within you. To apply these elements and embark on the brainstorming process, follow these steps:

1. Review your list, and identify the elements that captivate you. Trust your instincts, and search for that spark of energy inside you. Remember, this is about what you genuinely care about, not about what you think you should care about.

2. Consider your emotional state and the general themes that resonate with you. Can you combine your selected elements with these themes?

3. Dive into the symbolic meaning of your chosen elements. How can you use semiotics and symbology to convey your desired message or emotion?

4. Aim to write a concise paragraph with a beginning, middle, and end. Think of it as a puzzle waiting to be solved. Don't worry about practicality at this stage; simply let your imagination run free. You can figure out the execution details later.

5. Let the paragraph you wrote sit for a day. Take a break, listen to music, or go for a walk. Sometimes, giving your ideas space to breathe can lead to valuable insights.

In following these steps, you'll find yourself on a creative brainstorming journey that's fueled by your unique vision and passions. Tackling this at the start of your process before you get too far into creating a new work will allow you to clearly establish the goals you have for your piece, thereby making it a stronger project in the long run.

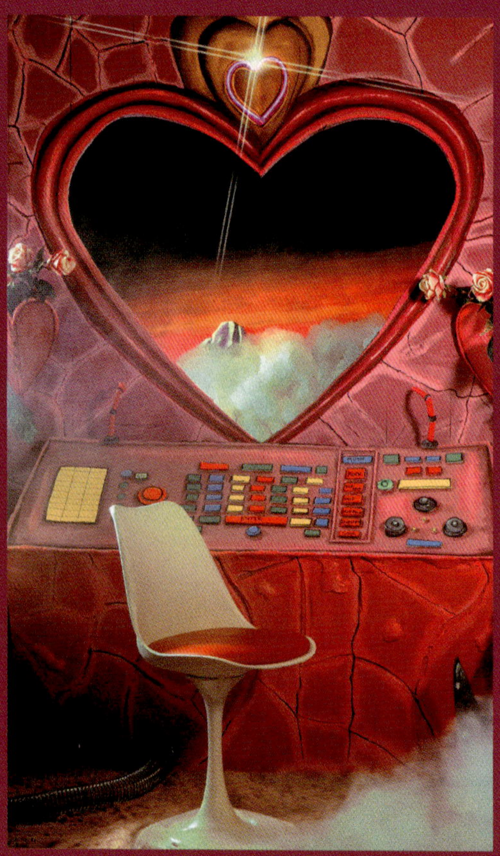

Getting Started

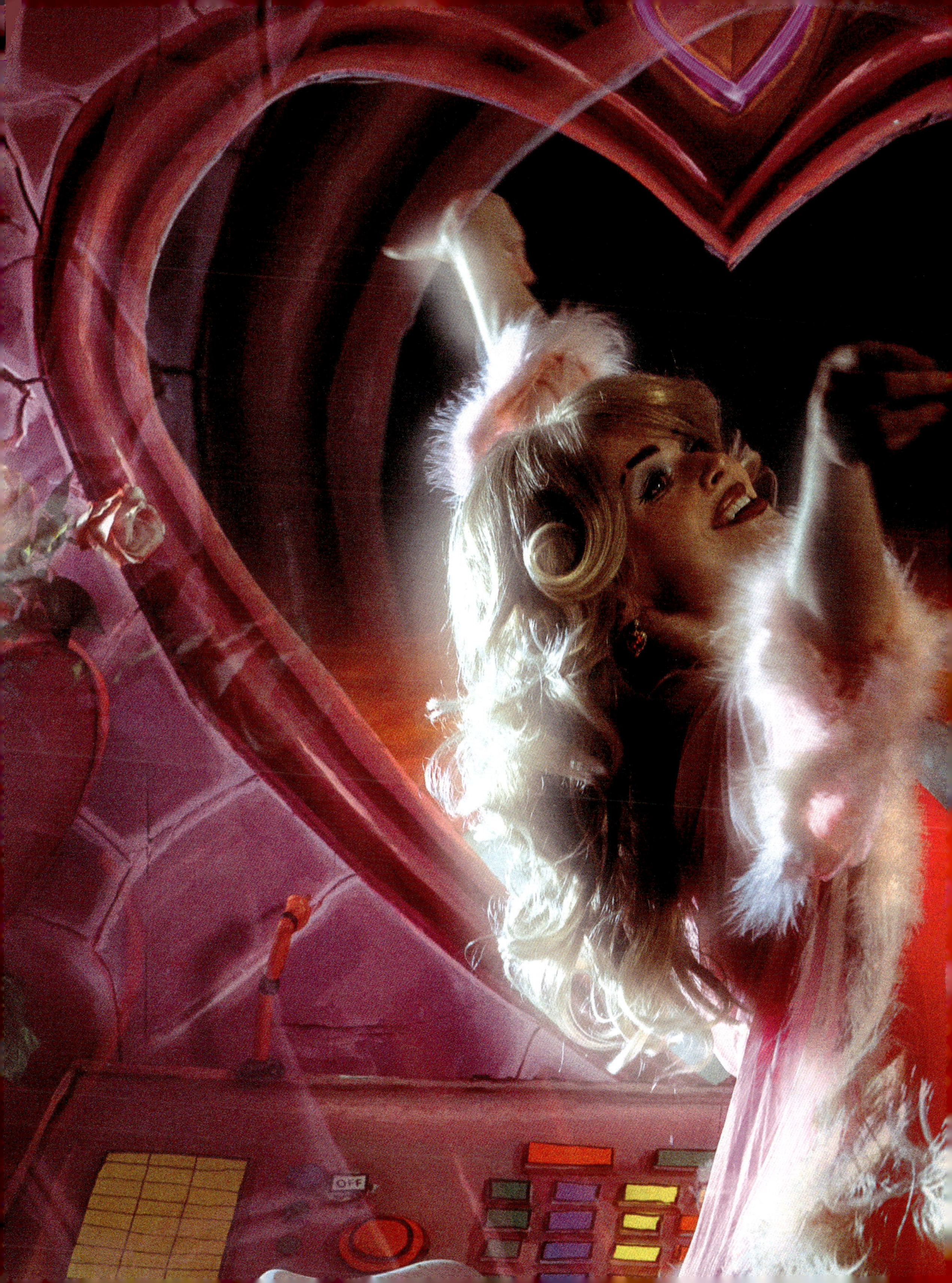

IDEATION ACROSS DISCIPLINES

Let's explore how these concepts can be applied across different disciplines. Each discipline presents its own unique opportunities for creative expression.

Ideation for visual art: Developing an idea starts with a deep dive into your chosen elements. What do they represent to you? How can you incorporate them into your art? Allow your emotions and themes to guide your creative process, and don't be afraid to experiment with them.

Ideation for interior design: Start by identifying what you don't like about your space. What do you want it to feel like? Use your list as a reference and gather some inspiration. Sketch out a rough layout to visualize how different elements could fit together. Consider the emotions you want to convey and select decor elements accordingly. Lastly, set a budget to help prioritize and make informed choices.

Ideation for content creation: Whether informing, teaching, or entertaining, creators can begin by identifying their areas of interest and the type of content they want to create. Find a keyword you love and explore what you want to convey with it. Are you looking to create a fictional narrative, an informative piece, or are you simply showcasing something you love?

ZACHARIAH PORTER
Comedian & Influencer

For me, brainstorming always starts in unexpected places, like grocery stores, fitting rooms, and even theme parks. My notes app is filled with snippets from restaurant chatter and coffee shop queues, drawing inspiration from daily life. My love of creating characters has always been fueled by my obsession with television and movies, as well as from the wisdom of women who raised me. My inspiration runs the gamut from classics, like Carmela Soprano, to personal icons, like my favorite Old Navy manager, who inspired many of my stories.

I love a narrative rooted in universal experiences. Having my jokes resonate with my audience is always top of mind. Remember that you can easily elevate a joke with a good costume; never underestimate the power of a good wig and a sequined blouse. A costume can transform a story from ordinary to extraordinary. For me, brainstorming is just one big game of connecting the dots. Pulling from past experiences and constantly being open to the different possibilities of what your next day could inspire is key! No matter how silly they sometimes appear, every story I create is rooted in authenticity, drawn from real-life encounters, and grounded in relatable storytelling.

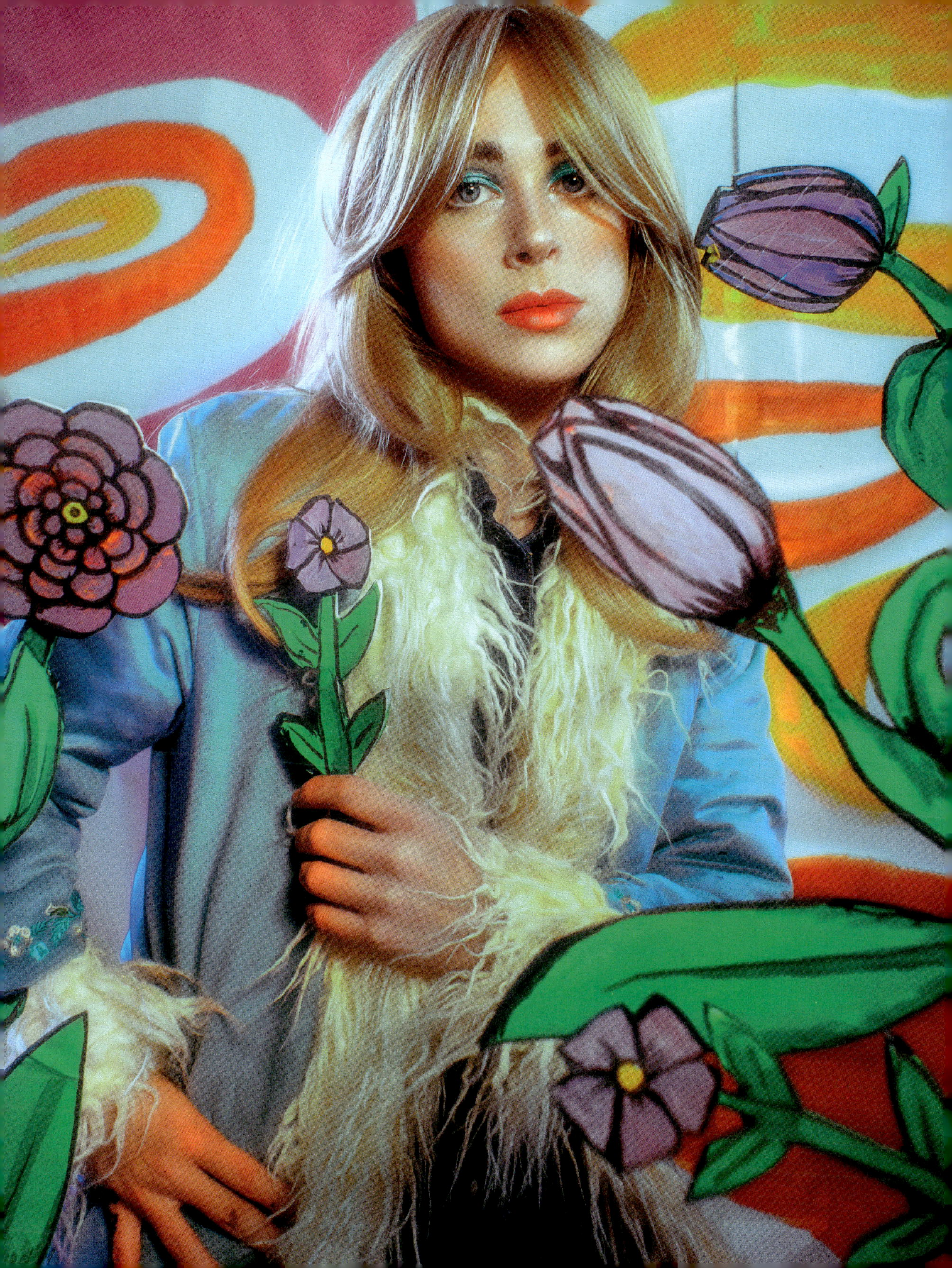

BASIC SYMBOLS
& WHAT THEY MEAN

IF YOU SEE A	THAT MIGHT MEAN
HEART 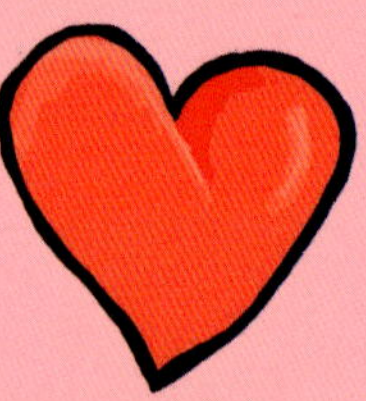	love, warmth
FIRE 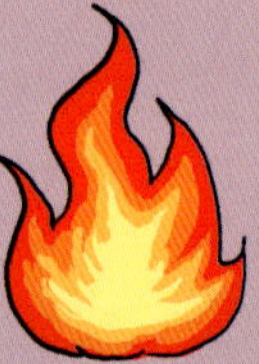	anger, rage, badass
RAIN CLOUD 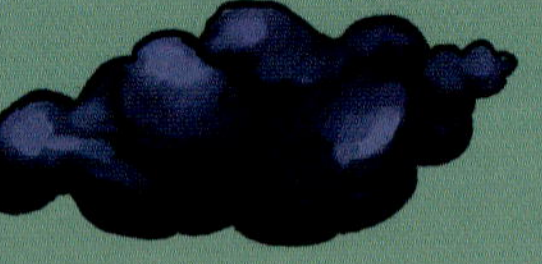	sadness, turmoil, drudgery
STARS 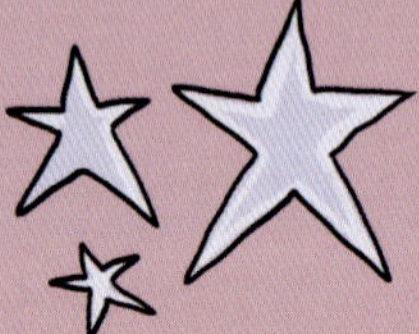	magical moment, out of this world, ethereal
BEAM OF LIGHT	hopeful, answers, clarity

IF YOU SEE A	THAT MIGHT MEAN
RAINBOW	new beginning, fulfillment
LIGHT BULB 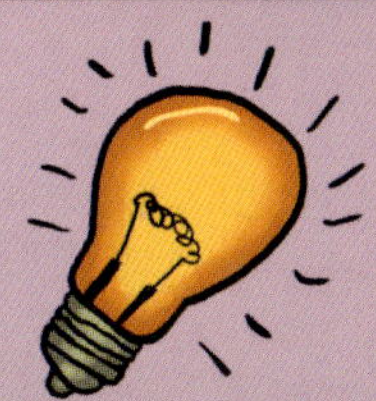	bright idea, intellect
SKULL AND CROSSBONES 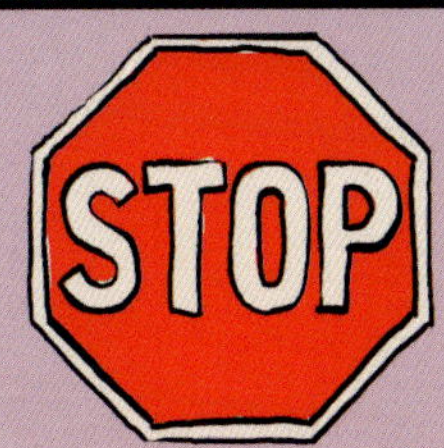	toxic, poison, danger
STOP SIGN 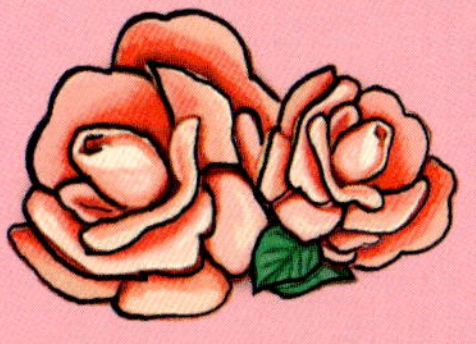	stop, slow down
ROSES	romantic, dreamy, sweet

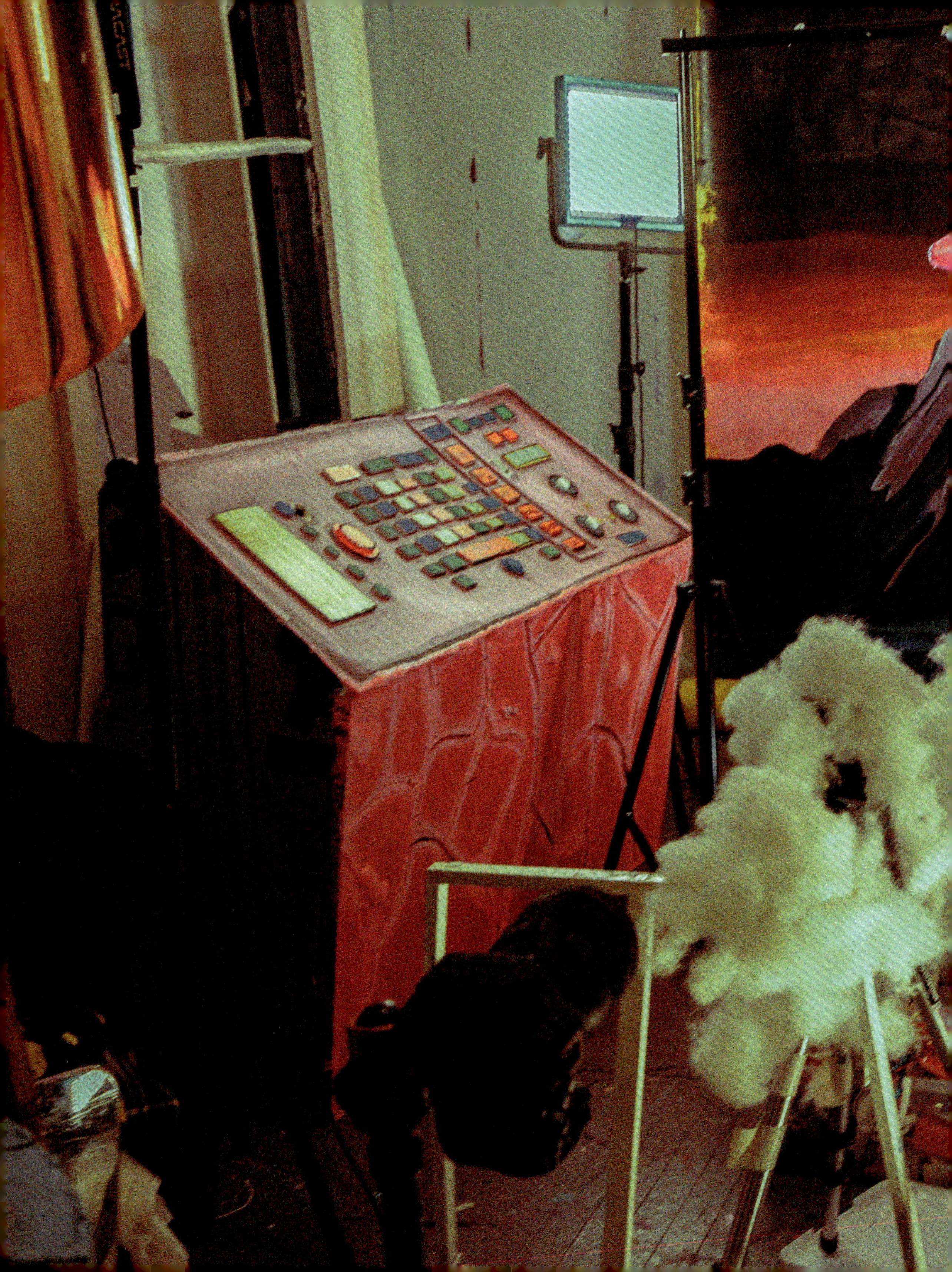

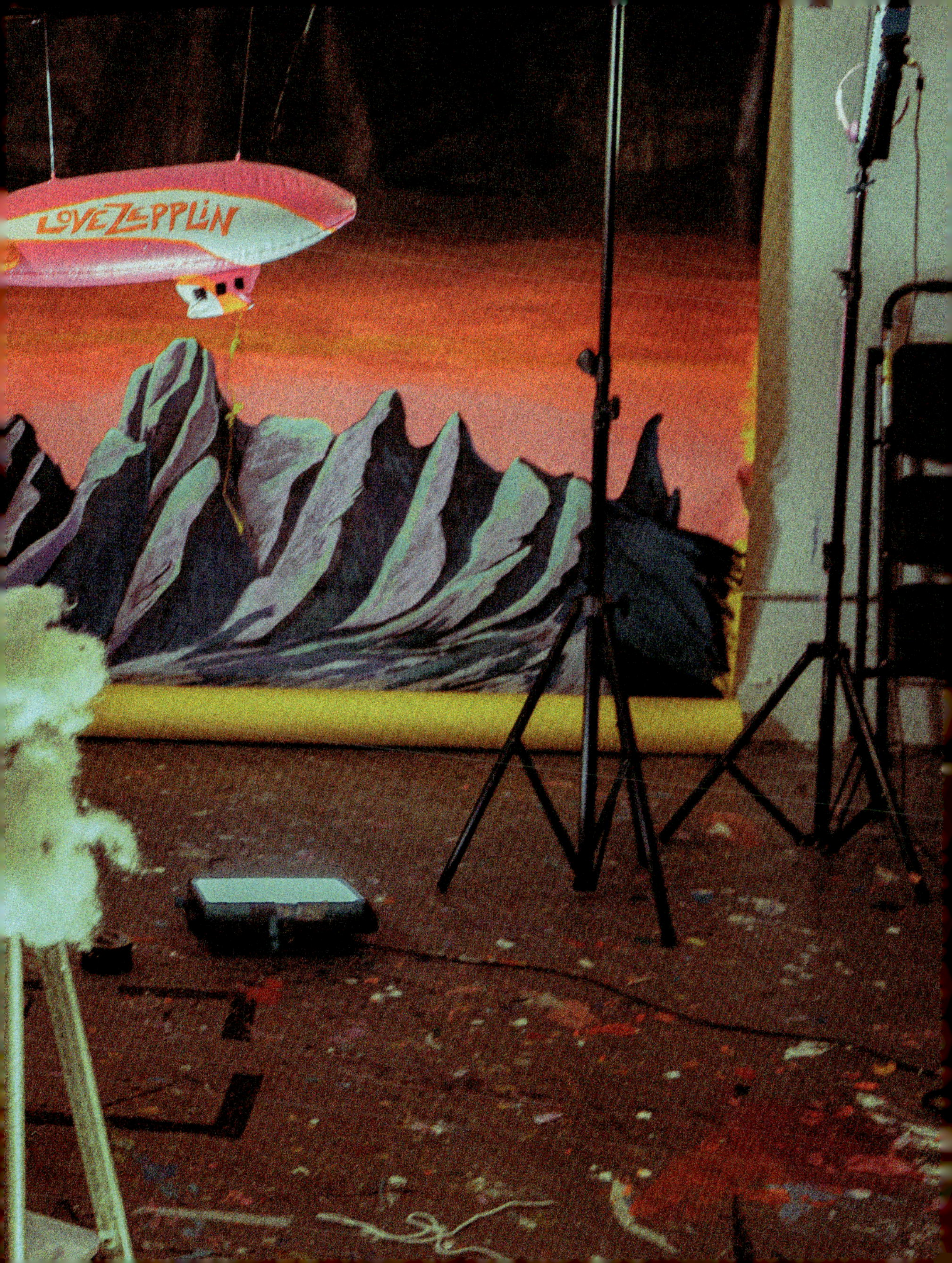

LOVE ZEPPLIN

IDEATION EXERCISES

> Think about something you were obsessed with as a child. Now, write a list of at least ten keywords that can be attached to this obsession, identifying as many different elements of it as you can.

> What keywords would you use to describe yourself and what you're drawn to? Make a list of keywords that identify who you are, what you're doing today, when you feel your best, where you're currently at (both physically and emotionally), why you bought this book, and how you feel right now doing this exercise.

> Use a dictionary or online resource to randomly pick a list of five to ten words. Can you assign these random keywords to a project idea? How challenging is it to

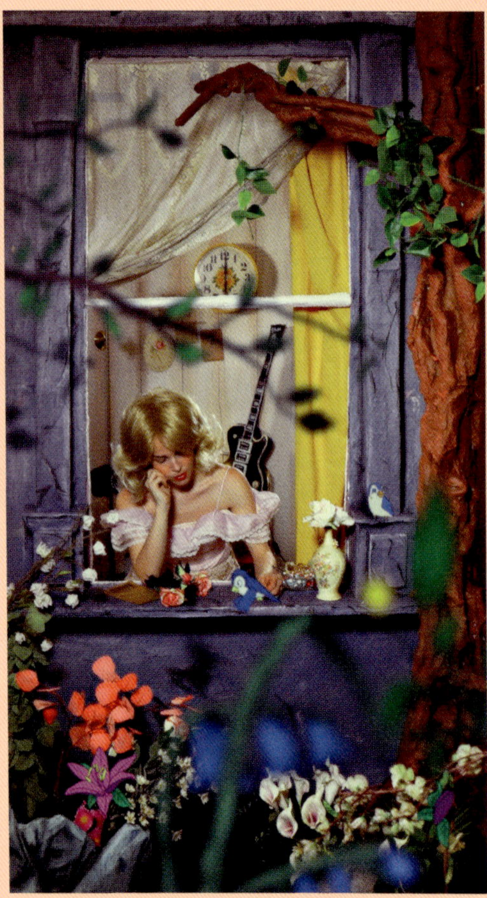

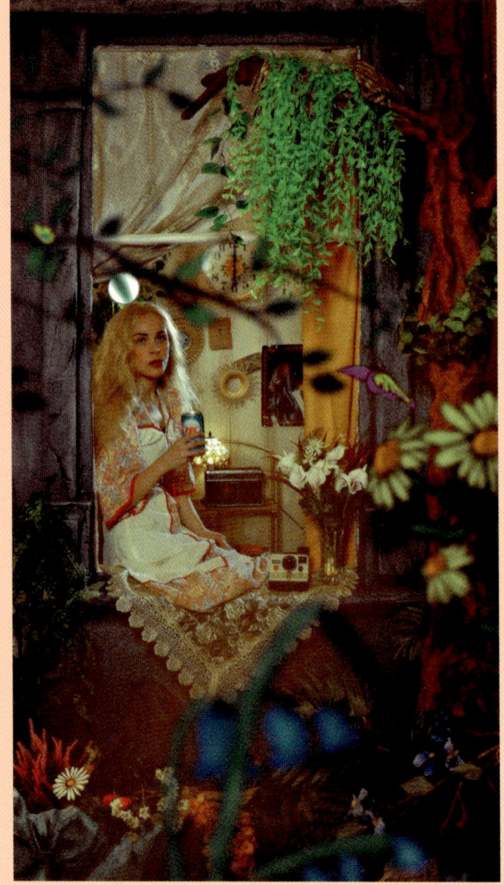

come up with something that incorporates all the random words?

> Write down at least nine different adjectives on separate pieces of paper. Throw them into a hat and select three groups of three, at random. Brainstorm three different project ideas based on the adjective trios you come up with. If you're satisfied with what you come up with, you can even try doing this again to see what other kinds of combinations are possible.

> Identify a few of your favorite creations. If you haven't made anything recently that you're proud of, feel free to identify pieces made by other creatives that have caught your eye. Pull inspiration from these pieces to brainstorm a new idea. Try pulling as many different elements as possible from the various pieces to make your own special kind of mash-up, and then get to work building something all your own!

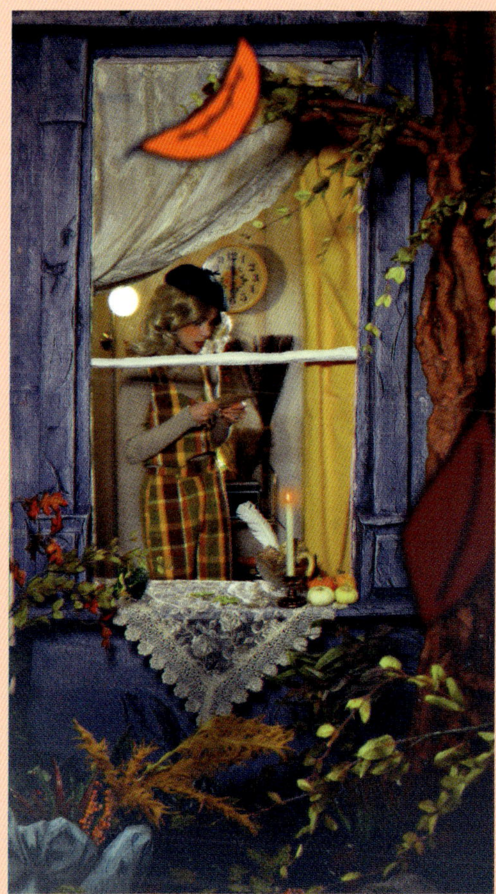

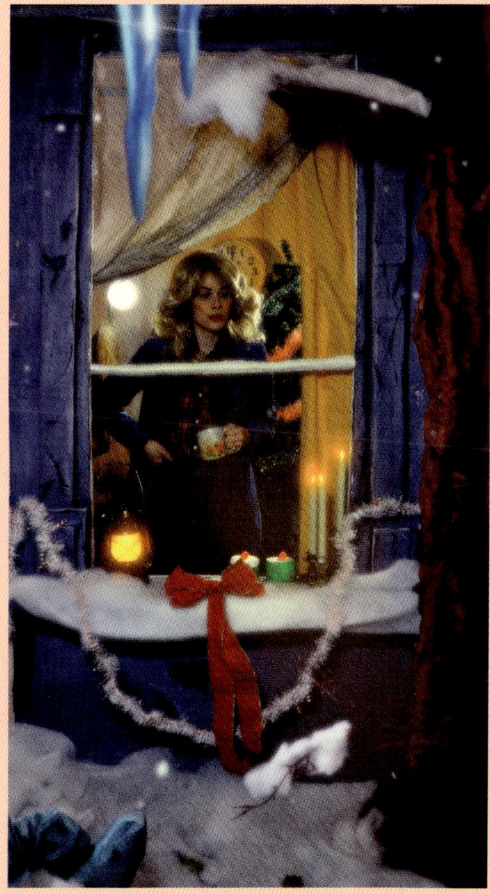

QUESTIONS TO CONSIDER

> Are there any elements on your list that you find yourself particularly interested in right now? What are they, and why do you think they have your attention?

> What's something you were obsessed with as a kid that you have no interest in anymore? Why do you think you liked it so much when you were young? Why aren't you drawn to it any longer?

> What are some of your creative-focused goals? Can you come up with any keywords that could help you identify what creative success looks like to you?

> Do you want to create something that feels bright or something that feels dark? Is your piece meant to be humorous, self-aware, campy, dramatic, or fun? Is there any way it can be all these things at once?

> Do you have any morals you feel strongly about? How will these come into play in your art? Could any of your beliefs be limiting when it comes to your creative expression? What are the ideals you have to hold onto, and what can you let go of?

> Do you want to make something a certain way because you feel it resonates with you or because it's trendy now? What's something you really love that's not trendy? Could you try to create a piece that has the possibility of leading to a new trend?

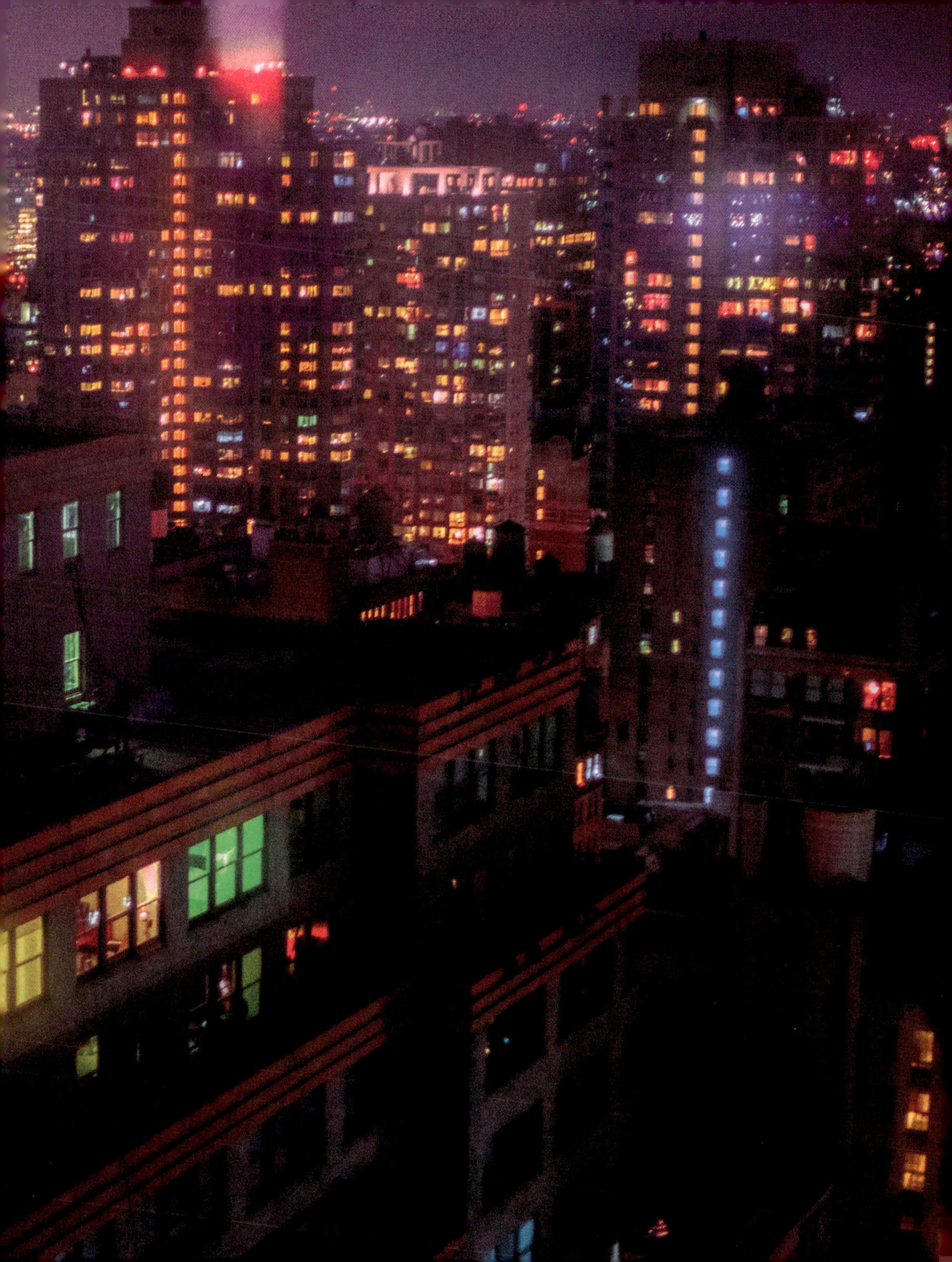

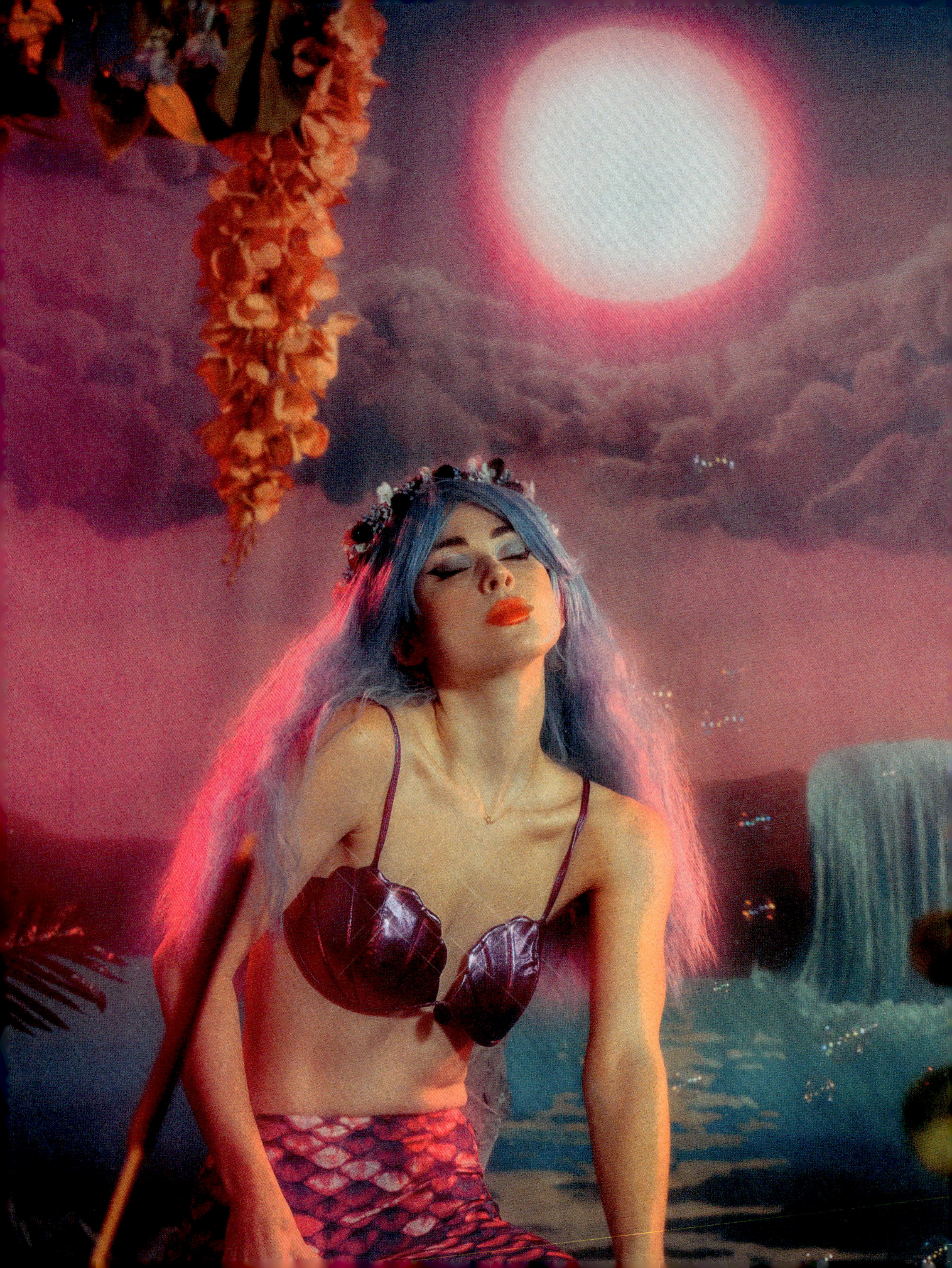

PART II

BUILDING BLOCKS

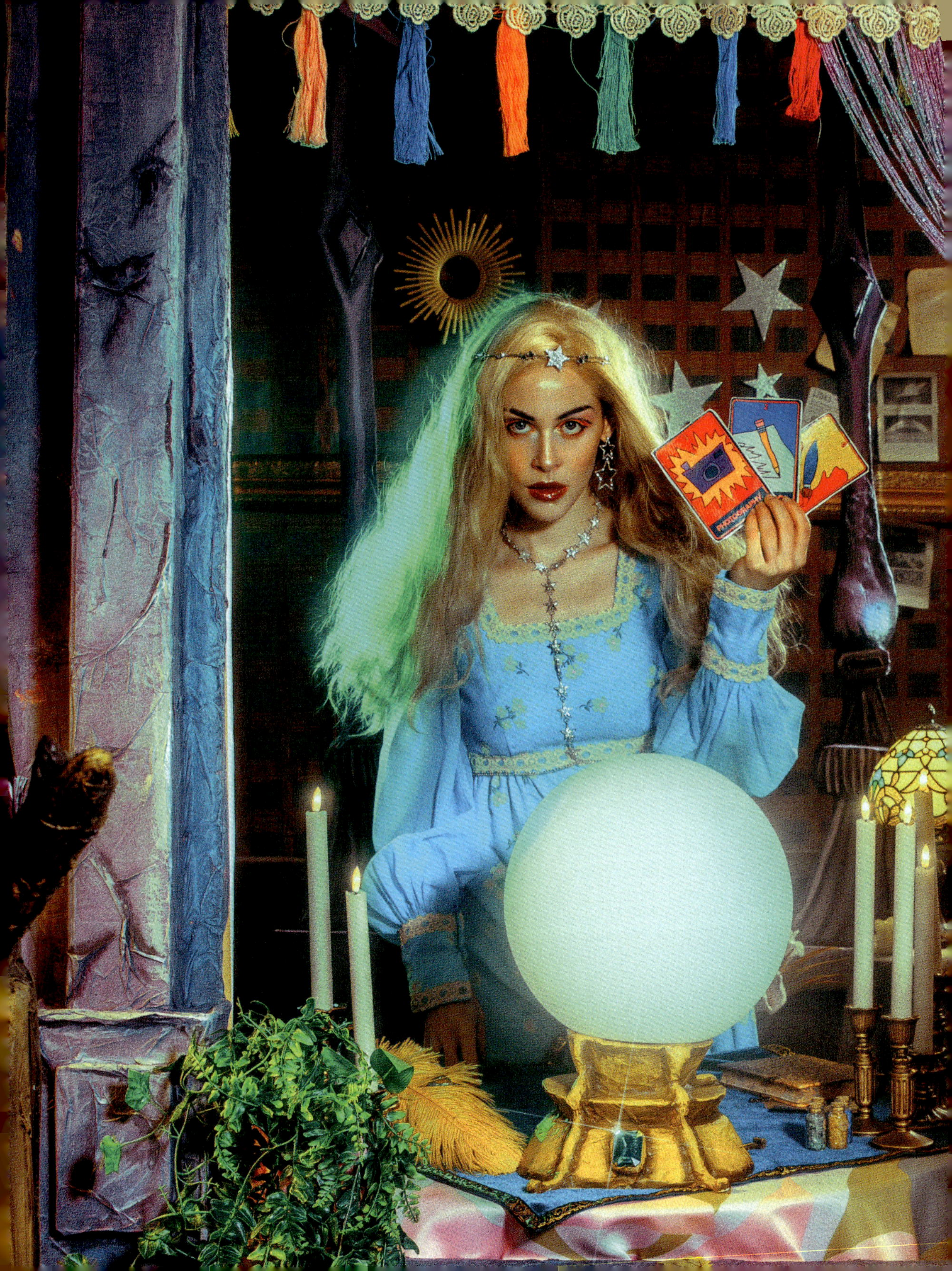

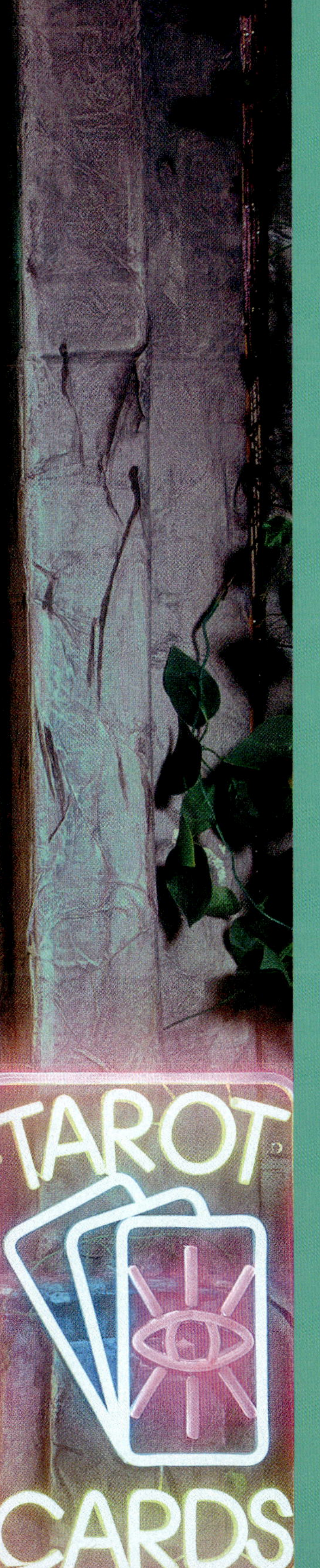

CHAPTER FOUR

FINDING YOUR MEDIUM

USE WHAT YOU'VE GOT

I love creating new pieces with items I already have in my possession. It feels like a puzzle that I have to fit together. Not only am I creating something I love, I'm also playing a fun brain game. Rummaging through your space for objects you own might also help you create new ideas that you never thought you'd come up with.

It didn't take me long to figure out I really enjoy working with just paper, paint, and my crotchety digital Canon EOS 5D Mark IV camera. I am comfortable using them, and I can express myself with them in a way that keeps me satisfied. These three materials always let me start with a blank canvas, allowing my creative progression to unfold naturally. They give me the freedom to create.

When considering mediums, people often start thinking about what type of piece they want to make, rather than what kind of piece they want to visually inject into the world. From the beginning of my creative journey, the one thing I was always sure of was that I wanted to capture whatever I created with my camera. I love the concept of rendering my daydreams life-size and physical through the camera lens. Think about how you envision your artwork holistically and then try breaking that vision down to its most basic parts. This will help you find your medium.

EXPLORE YOUR PLAYGROUND

The summer I was eighteen, I was preparing to move out of my parents' home for the first time. I was transitioning beyond my teenage vibes toward adulthood, yet these changes all felt so ambiguous. Some of my friends were getting jobs as production assistants on film sets, but I felt hesitant to start out my career in a similar way. I knew I wanted to be an editor (or so I thought), but I really didn't know much beyond that. Then I had an exciting thought: What if I stopped worrying about the future and just focused on posting to social media for the rest of the summer, sharing the fun little videos I made with my friends? This became my creative outlet.

My parents had all these old miscellaneous items lying around that worked perfectly as props, so I started making time-progression videos with them. We had a variety of old cameras from different historical decades. As someone who was always fascinated by the concept of time and technological developments, it gave me the idea to create a video about the evolution of this tech. I filmed a little vignette for each decade with the matching camera, piecing together a visual timeline. These videos weren't slick, and I wasn't using anything that was truly period appropriate because I had never created something like this before, but I loved the idea. So I dug deeper.

I also spent a lot of time making little drawings and animating them using a free cell phone–animation application. I used what I had: paper, pens, and an above-average number of vintage props. I was having a lot of fun, but everything I made was pretty simple. I knew I had a ways to go to reach the kind of finished product I envisioned in my mind, but I loved that the concepts I imagined were now being put out into the world. And that alone was a step in the right direction.

At the end of the summer, I packed up and left for New York City with some friends. Four of us lived together in a Brooklyn apartment with very little natural light. When I wasn't continuously searching for jobs, I was coming up with video concepts. One day, I really wished I had a barbell for a workout video I had planned, but I was broke and didn't own one. So I took the paper supplies I used for my stop-motion videos and drew

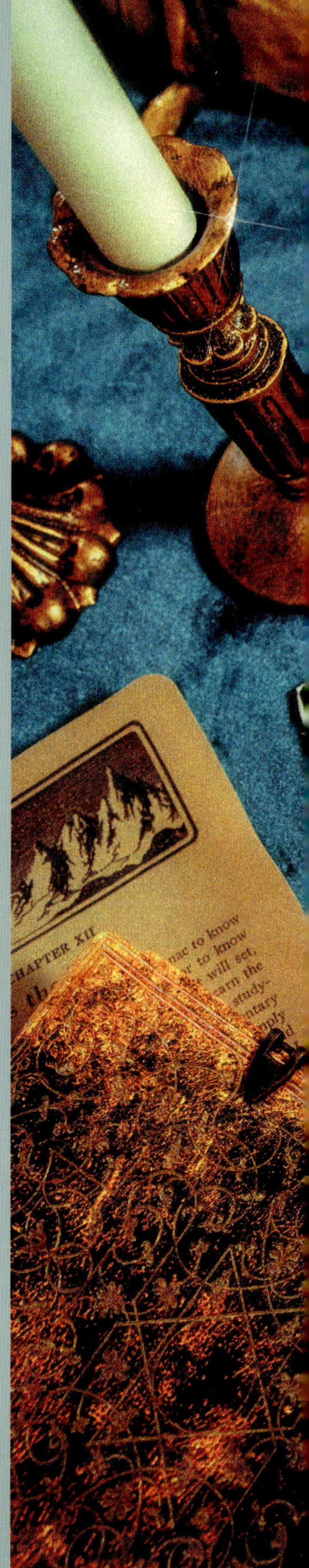

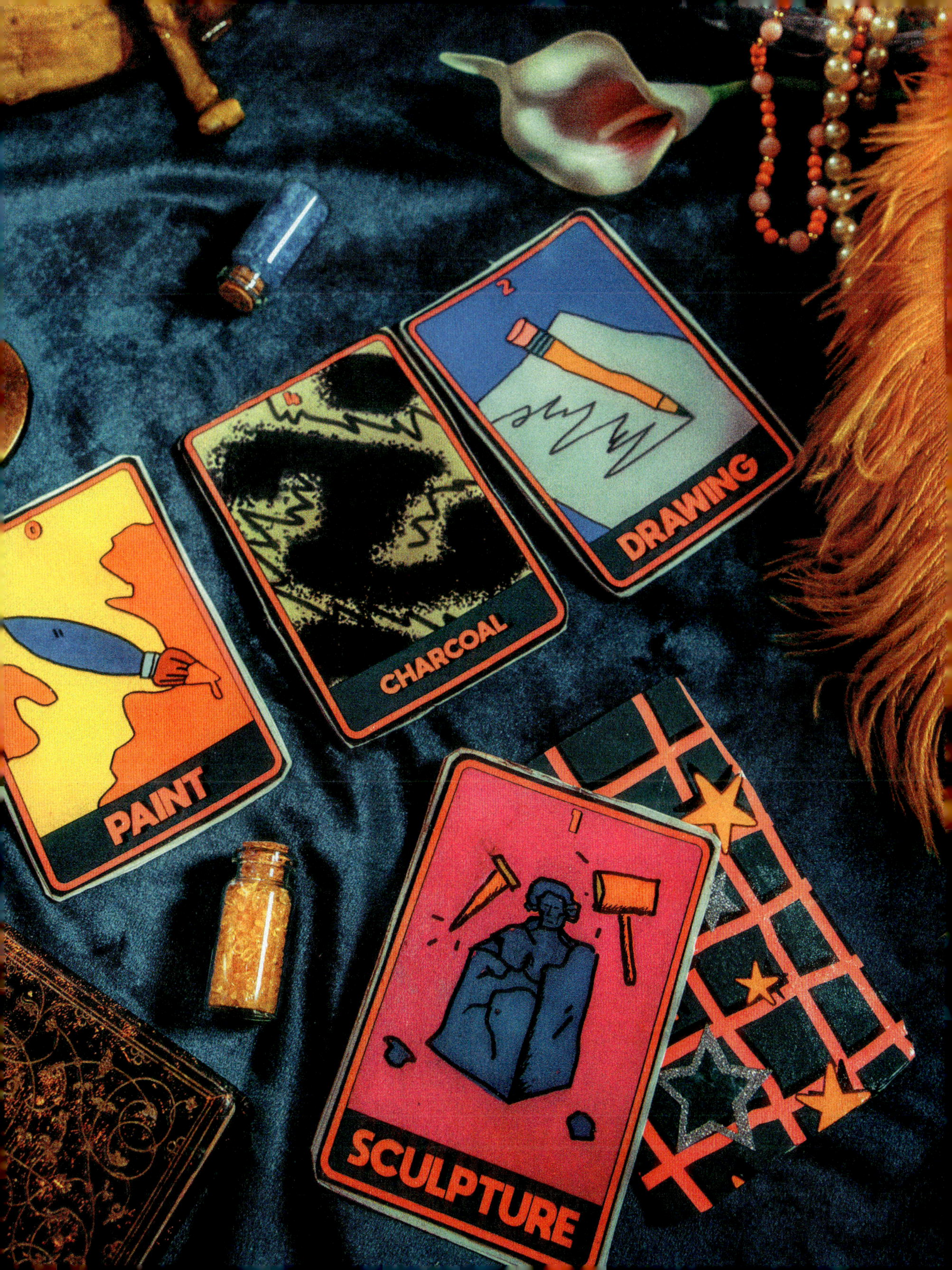

DRAWING
CHARCOAL
PAINT
SCULPTURE

new life-size props on poster board from the dollar store. I began by painting a very simple barbell. I'm pretty sure I used a watercolor set that my roommate already owned.

Happy with how the paper props looked in the video, I decided that using these kinds of props made a lot of sense for my personal aesthetic. (Look back to my aesthetic list, where I mention my love for old Hollywood films—which often utilize flat, 2D props and painted elements.)

Once I made the paper barbell, there was no turning back. I spent the next year drawing prop after prop to create more comedic videos. I used a lamp in our kitchen as my key light and borrowed anything else I needed from my roommates whenever possible. Over the course of that year, I got better at drawing, I became a more skilled painter, and I started to learn how to piece things together in an artistic way.

When thinking about what kind of artistic medium you should start with, I encourage you to begin by looking around your space. What do you already own that you could use to create something new? What kind of medium do you like to use when you're in a making mood? Or perhaps you should even consider what materials you're most skilled at using.

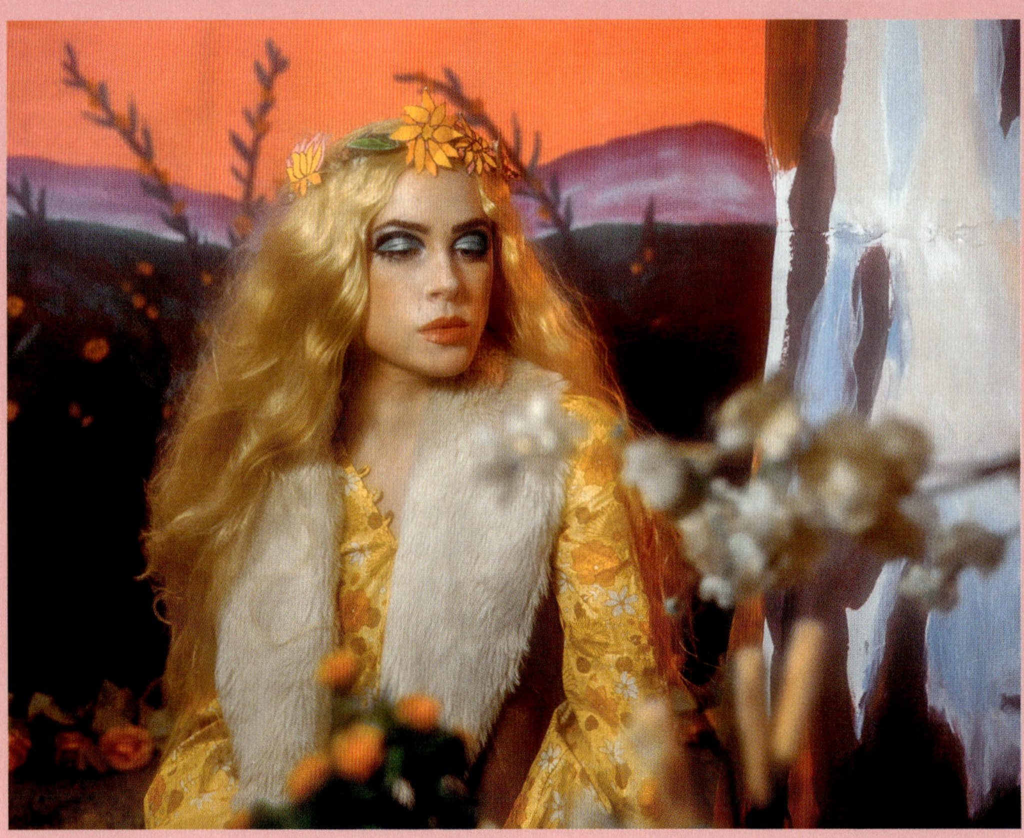

 Building Blocks

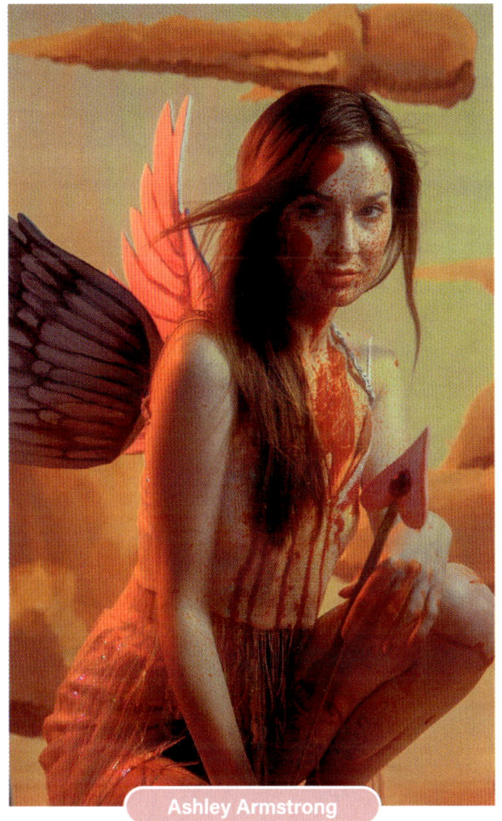

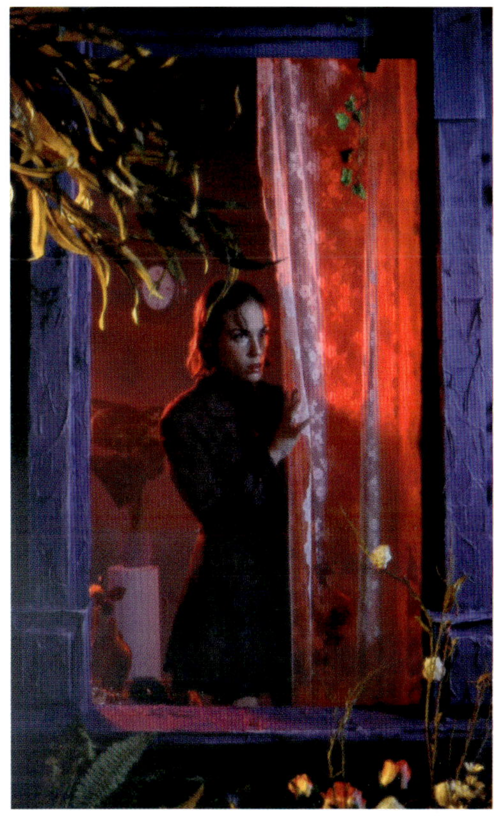

What's something intriguing that you'd like to try out? When thinking about these questions, don't worry about being good at everything from the start. Discovering your medium is a process that takes time.

You also don't have to choose just one medium. If you limit yourself to only one medium and don't allow yourself the flexibility to explore others, you may end up feeling stuck when your projects don't come together in the way you envisioned. Instead, let your creative mind wander and let your medium shift, change, and grow as necessary. This way, you'll be able to express yourself the way you need to.

The process of finding the right artistic medium is like playing with different toys. See what's the most fun for you and what feels the most natural. If it feels right, it probably is. Your medium of choice will become a safe place for you to experiment, allowing you to let your skills develop over time. Regardless of whether you want to design sets, create paintings, or play music, try accomplishing whatever it is you desire with the mindset that it isn't just about finding the right medium—it's also about what you're trying to convey. Once you understand that, the right medium will follow pretty quickly!

WHAT MEDIUMS ARE YOU DRAWN TO?

Here's a simple way to start the process of finding the right medium:

> Review your inspiration list from Chapter One, brainstorm more on the ideas you've written down, and try to figure out what it is you're trying to convey creatively.

> Think about what you are naturally good at or drawn to, and keep that at the forefront of your mind.

> Walk around your space. What do you already own that you could use to start tackling the creative vision you want to bring to life?

> Grab some markers, paint, paper, or whatever it is you have, and dive in. Don't worry about making something perfect. This is for experimentation purposes only.

> After you've made something with the materials you already own, reflect on how it felt. What other materials would help make your vision come to life even more?

> Buy cheap versions of materials that you think could help take your creation to the next level. Try creating a similar piece, this time with new materials you've purchased. When you finish, compare how the two pieces differ. Which one do you like better?

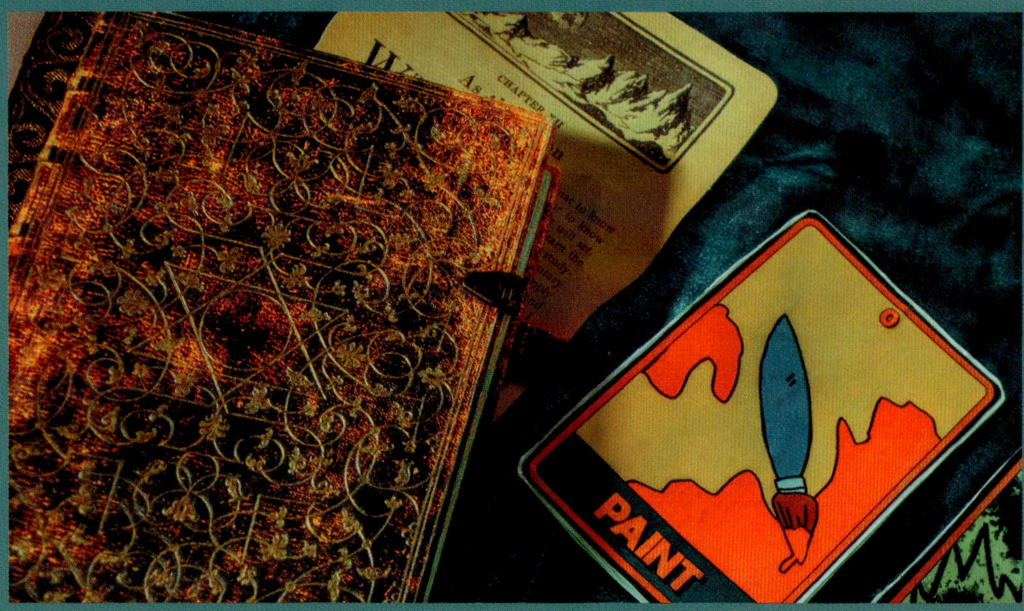

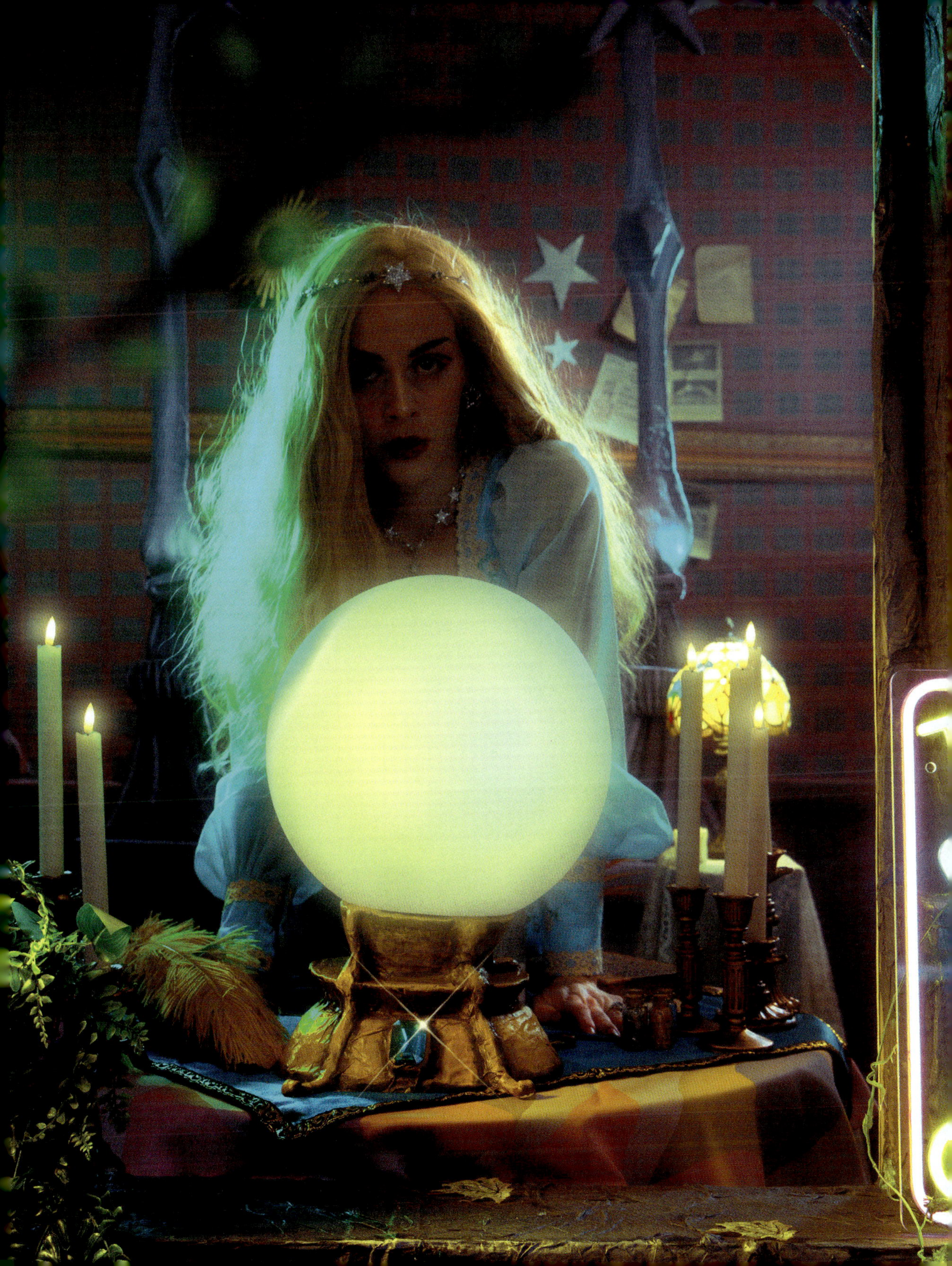

MEDIUMS ACROSS DISCIPLINES

Mediums for art: Think about artwork you already gravitate toward. What are they made with? Do you like them because of the medium or for some other reason? Sometimes realizing what you are already drawn to might be a helpful indicator of what type of materials you like. Are there mediums you have already tried that you had a knack for? What have you always wanted to try but never have? Try combining mediums you are already comfortable with and new ones you are drawn to. It might help you come up with something new and exciting! Are you trying to sell your work? If so, you might want to consider the quality of the material so it lasts. Archival materials are key for preservation.

Mediums for everyday creation: What have you always imagined making? What materials can you use to create that vision? Try to also think about the cost of products. Budget is a big factor in mediums as well; there are always cheaper alternatives that may lead you somewhere new! Do you have a space you can get messy, or would you rather be contained in your creation? I started off using products like watercolors for that reason—the mess was minimal and my space was small.

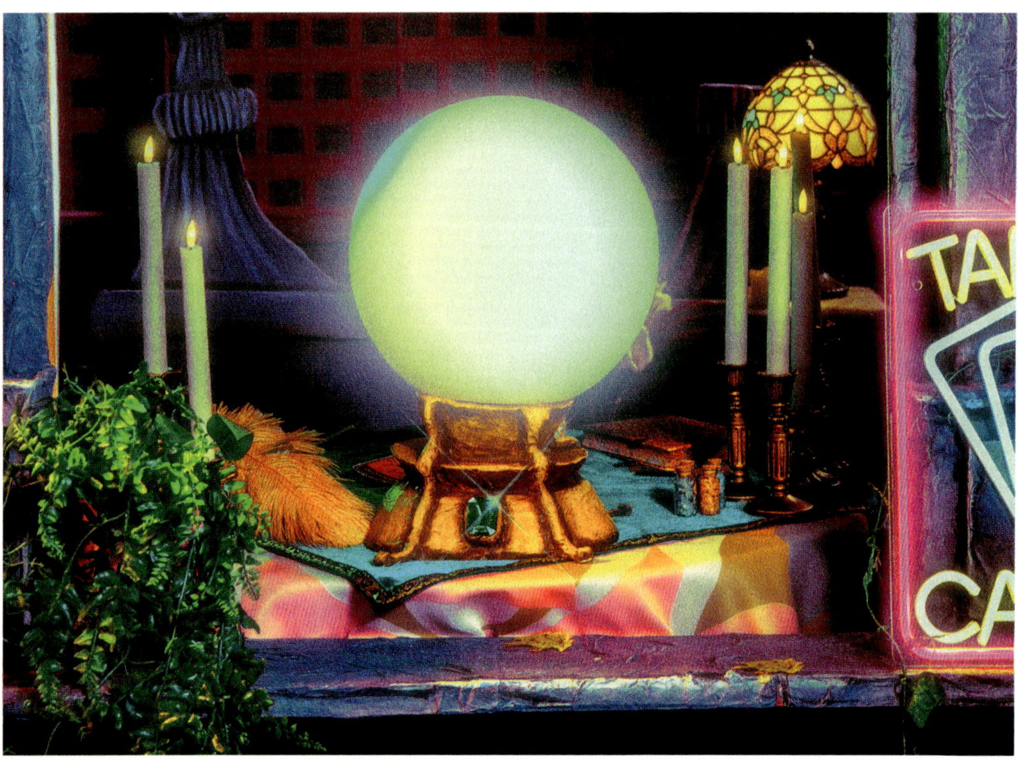

Building Blocks

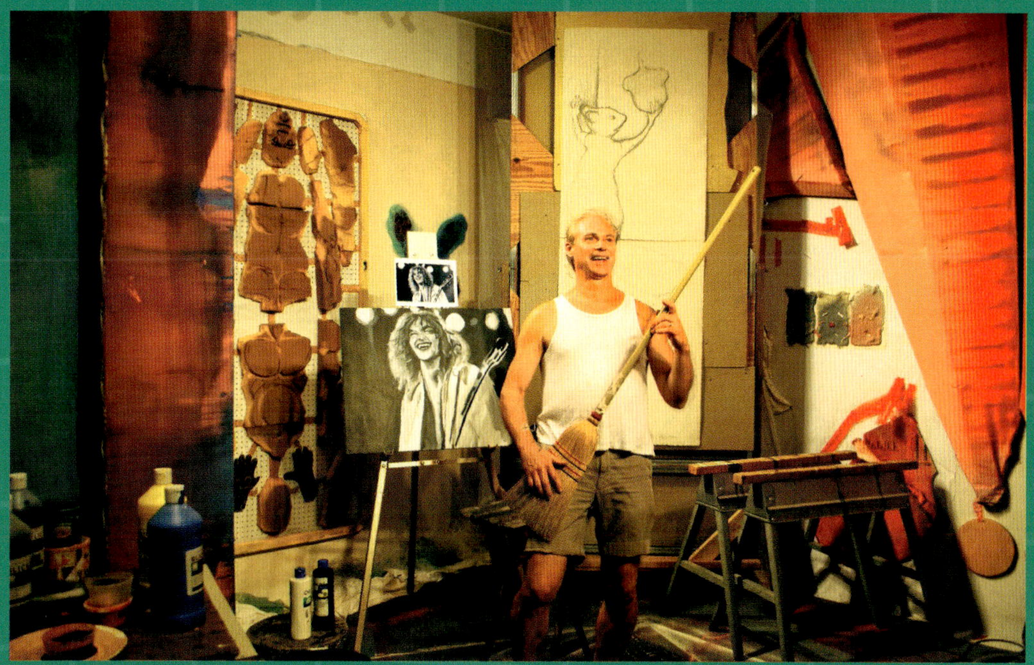

KARL JONES
Installation Artist

Classic children's book illustrations and cartoons were early inspirations for me, and I have memories of striving to draw and copy them, eager to make my draftsmanship match.

Other passions included music, plastic model kits, and fishing. Dad built model aircrafts and fished. Mom kept her hands busy with painting and drawing. During my school years, my discipline physically evolved; normal-size oil paintings became large-scale acrylics, huge painted fish were suspended from ceilings, and monofilament fishing line fleshed out portraits of disturbed critters.

I worked in demolition, eventually taking on carpentry, masonry, and the plastering trades. It was a solid fit since it allowed me to use leftover materials: straight lumber made large stretchers and galvanized wire used in stucco became the skin of the fish.

Found objects kicked off numerous pieces and tile trowels gave structure and decoration to my work. The discarded monofilaments, plastic model kits of my youth, physical labor, and 3D painting laid the groundwork for my preferred mediums to work with as I found my footing as an art constructionist.

CHOOSE YOUR OWN MEDIUM ADVENTURE

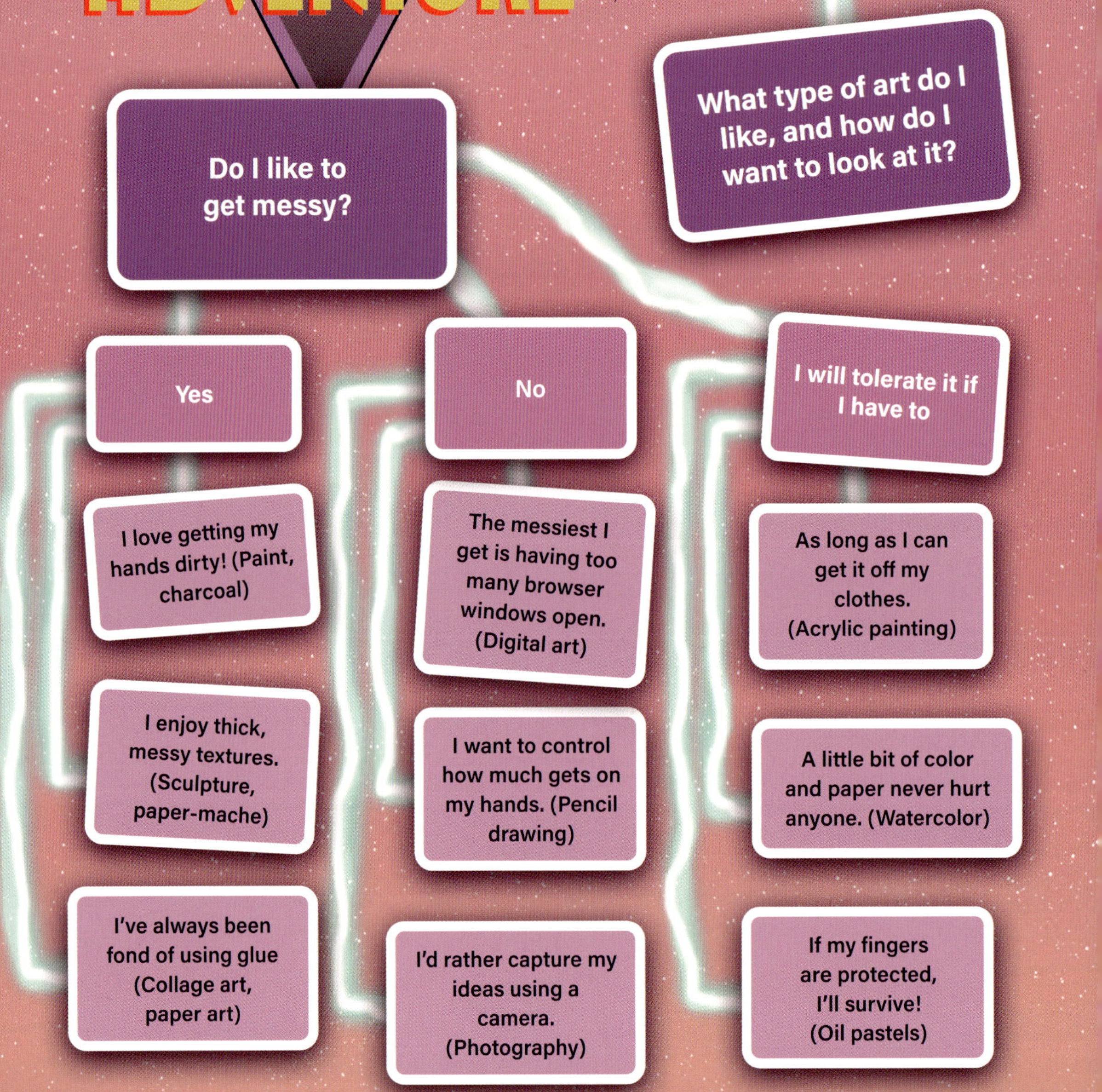

Do I like to get messy?

What type of art do I like, and how do I want to look at it?

Yes

I love getting my hands dirty! (Paint, charcoal)

I enjoy thick, messy textures. (Sculpture, paper-mache)

I've always been fond of using glue (Collage art, paper art)

No

The messiest I get is having too many browser windows open. (Digital art)

I want to control how much gets on my hands. (Pencil drawing)

I'd rather capture my ideas using a camera. (Photography)

I will tolerate it if I have to

As long as I can get it off my clothes. (Acrylic painting)

A little bit of color and paper never hurt anyone. (Watercolor)

If my fingers are protected, I'll survive! (Oil pastels)

Traditional art that can be found on display in museums	**Digital art that can be viewed on a screen**	**Art that can be found or made anywhere**
Large classic paintings or anything hung on the wall in an art museum	Creating work digitally	Combining elements and inspirations
3D art that takes up more space in a gallery	Editing work digitally	Intangible or performance art that shifts in form
Paper-mache, installation art	Photography	Slam poetry, spoken verse, singing
Clay sculpting, plaster	Filmmaking	Theater, improv, musicals
Oil paint, charcoal	Digital illustration	Mixed media that uses various materials
Paper art, collage, printmaking	Graphic design	Found objects, turning random items into something new

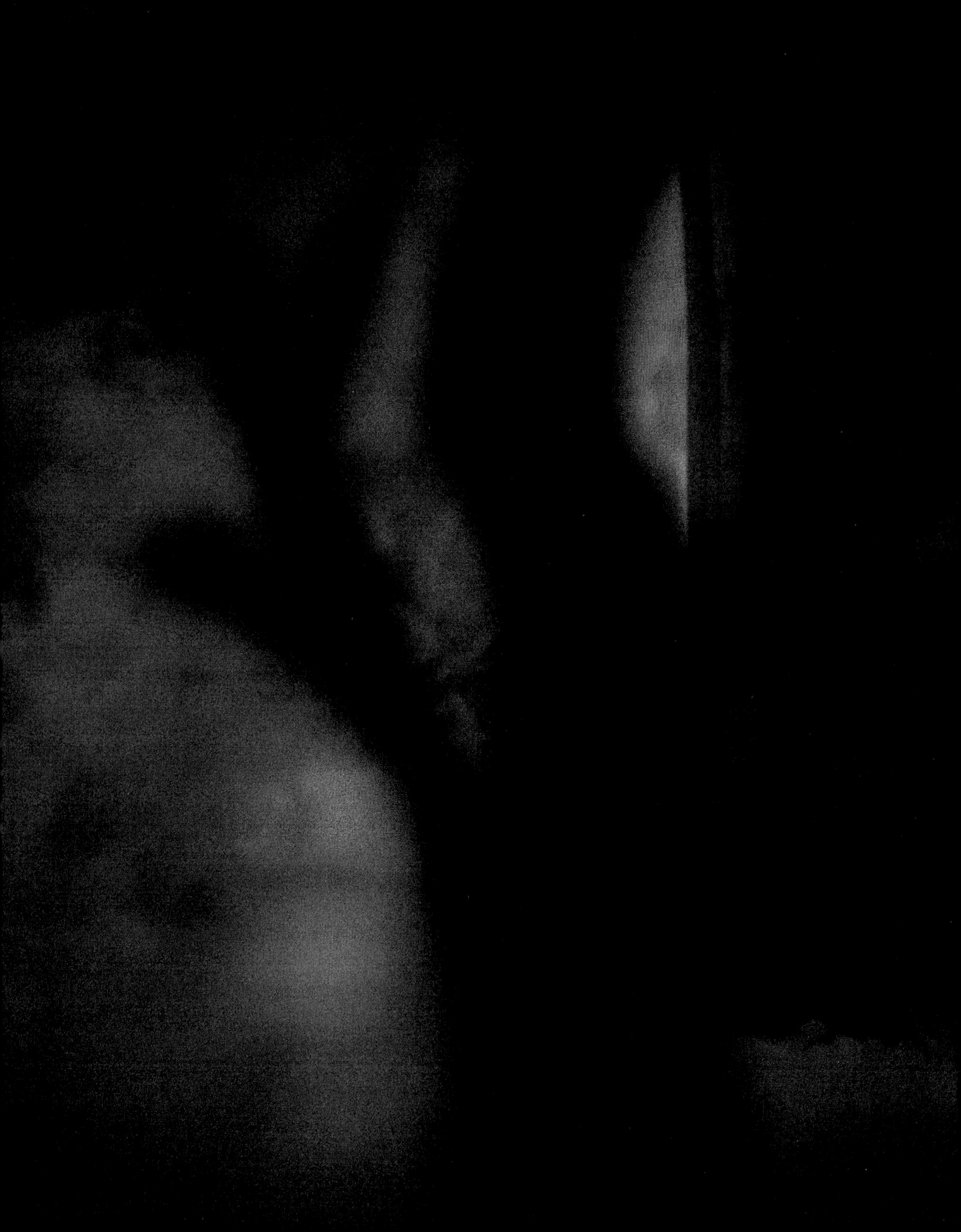

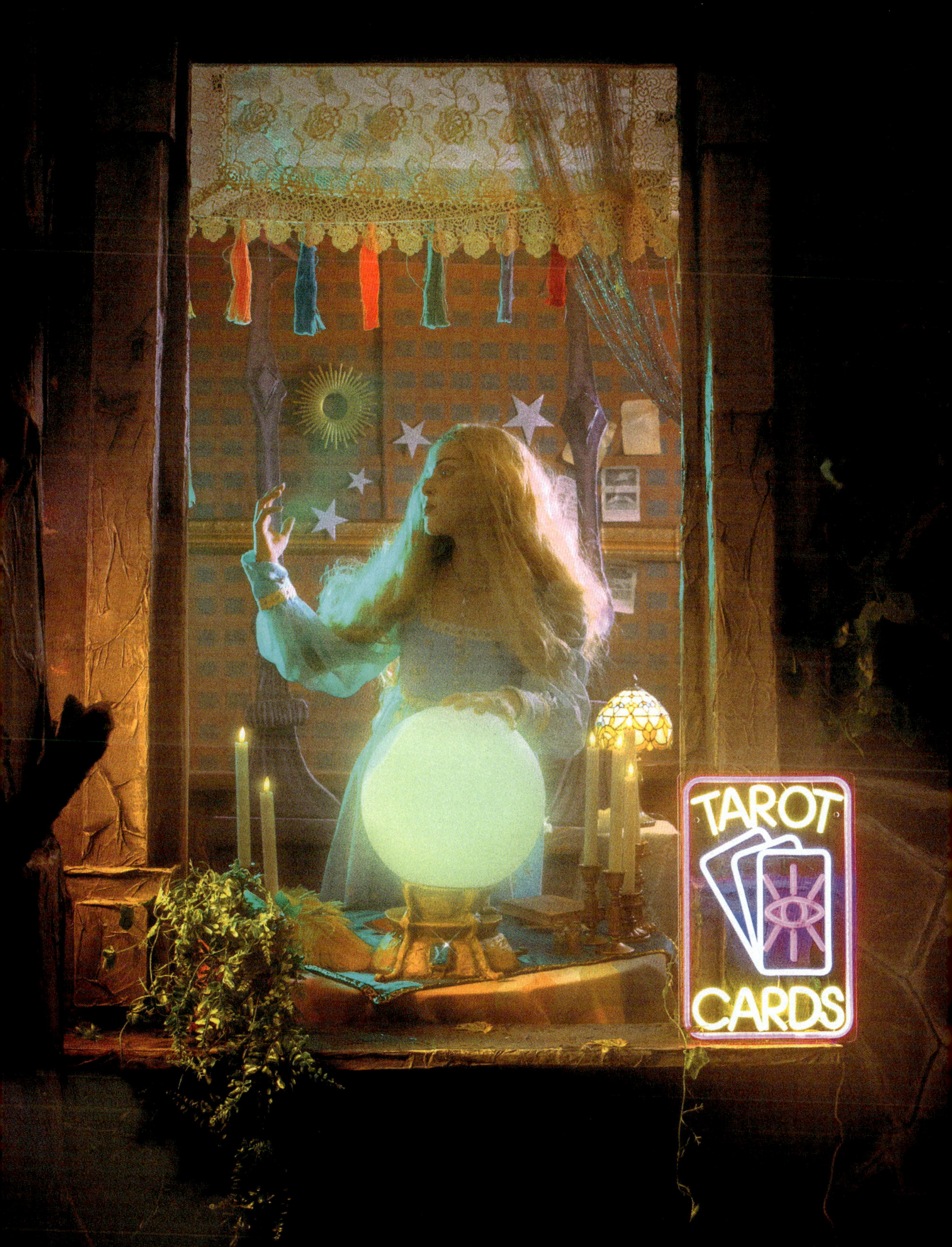

TAROT
CARDS

MEDIUM EXERCISES

> Now that you have selected a few elements from your list, try to create something using a few different mediums and see what feels the best. Try drawing something, painting something, sculpting something, collaging something, etc. You can make a new piece with each of the mediums you try out.

> Try creating the same thing with different mediums. For example, try painting a cat, drawing a cat, sculpting a cat, and creating a cat by collaging materials together. Compare and contrast how your creations vary across mediums and think about which one feels like the best representation of you as an artist.

> Walk around your space and look at the materials you have that you could use to create something new. What mediums do you have that you can start creating with right now? Try making something without buying any new materials.

> Use a medium that you have never worked with before and see how it feels. If you typically only draw or paint, try your hand at creating something new in three dimensions through sculpture or a miniature model. If you usually create videos with movement, sound, and lots of visuals, try distilling these various elements down into one static piece. How does it feel to switch between a medium you're used to and a medium that's new?

> Write down at least five different things or objects on small pieces of paper and put them in a hat. Now write down at least five different mediums on small pieces of paper and put them in another hat. Select one thing/object at random from the first hat, and one medium at random from the second hat. Create the thing/object in the medium you've picked. Once you're finished, think about how satisfied you are with what you've created. Over the next few days, try to work through all the rest of the items in the hats. Are you surprised by how any of these random combinations have turned out?

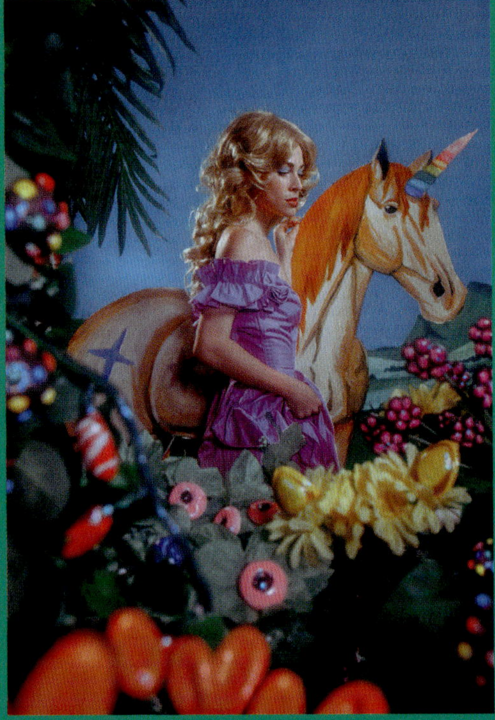

Building Blocks

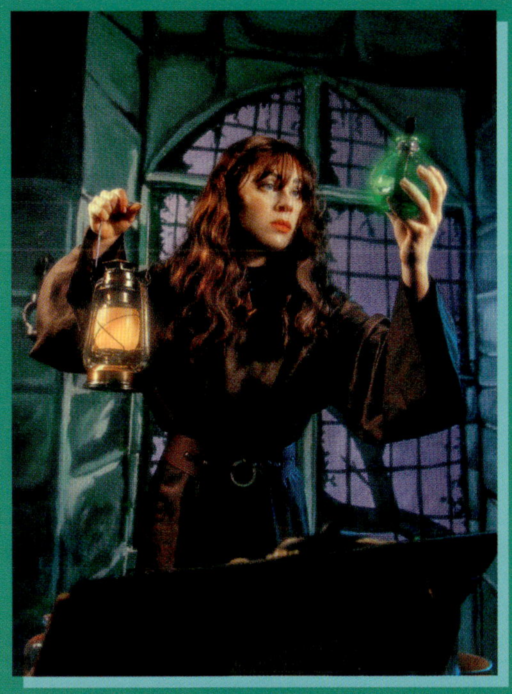

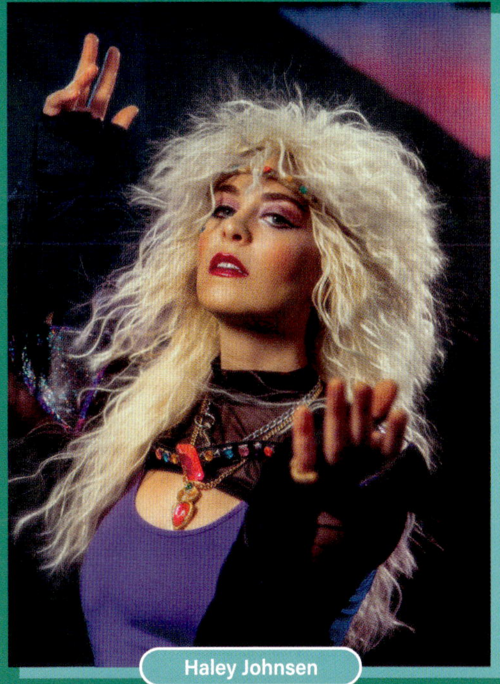

Haley Johnsen

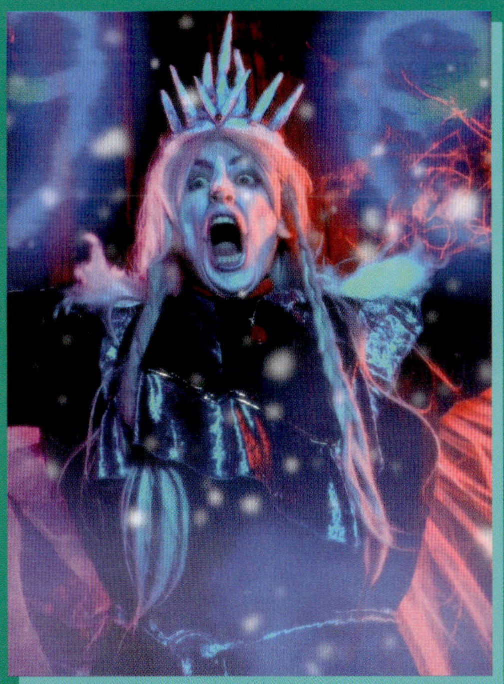

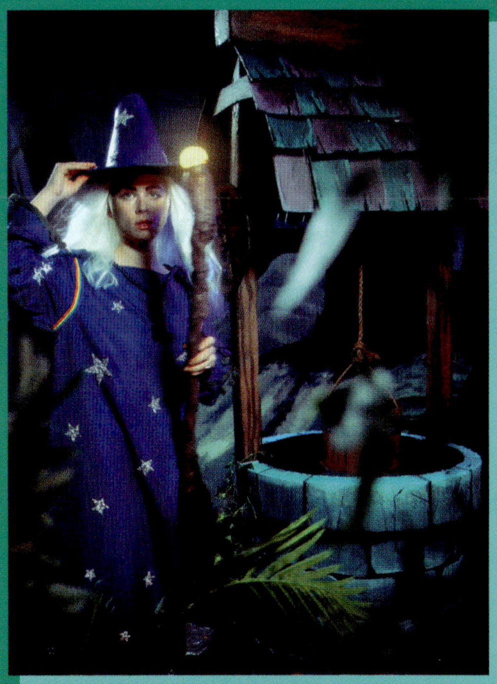

QUESTIONS TO CONSIDER

> What type of artwork are you drawn to most? Are your favorite pieces created using the same medium or many different mediums?

> What types of mediums have you always wanted to try out but haven't yet? What has stopped you from using them up until this point? Is there a way for you to overcome this obstacle and try out this new medium for your next project?

> What type of medium are you already good at using? How long have you been actively using this medium? Do you remember what it was like when you first started using this medium? Did it take you a while to get good at it?

> What's a medium that you used to play around with a lot, but have stopped using? Why did you stop using it? What do you think could convince you to try picking up that medium again?

> What are some of your favorite hobbies outside of the creative realm? Can you apply aspects of some of these hobbies into your creative process? Could you use an element of one of your hobbies as a new, perhaps unusual, medium?

> How much space do you have to create in your home or studio? Is there anything you could change about where you regularly work to give yourself more room to create freely? If space isn't an issue, is there anything else about your workspace or the materials you have available that are limiting you from trying out different mediums?

> If you're scared to try out a certain medium because it seems intimidating or too difficult, are there online tutorials or local classes you could try out to become better versed in using this medium? Are there books you can read about this medium to learn more about it before you try tackling it on your own?

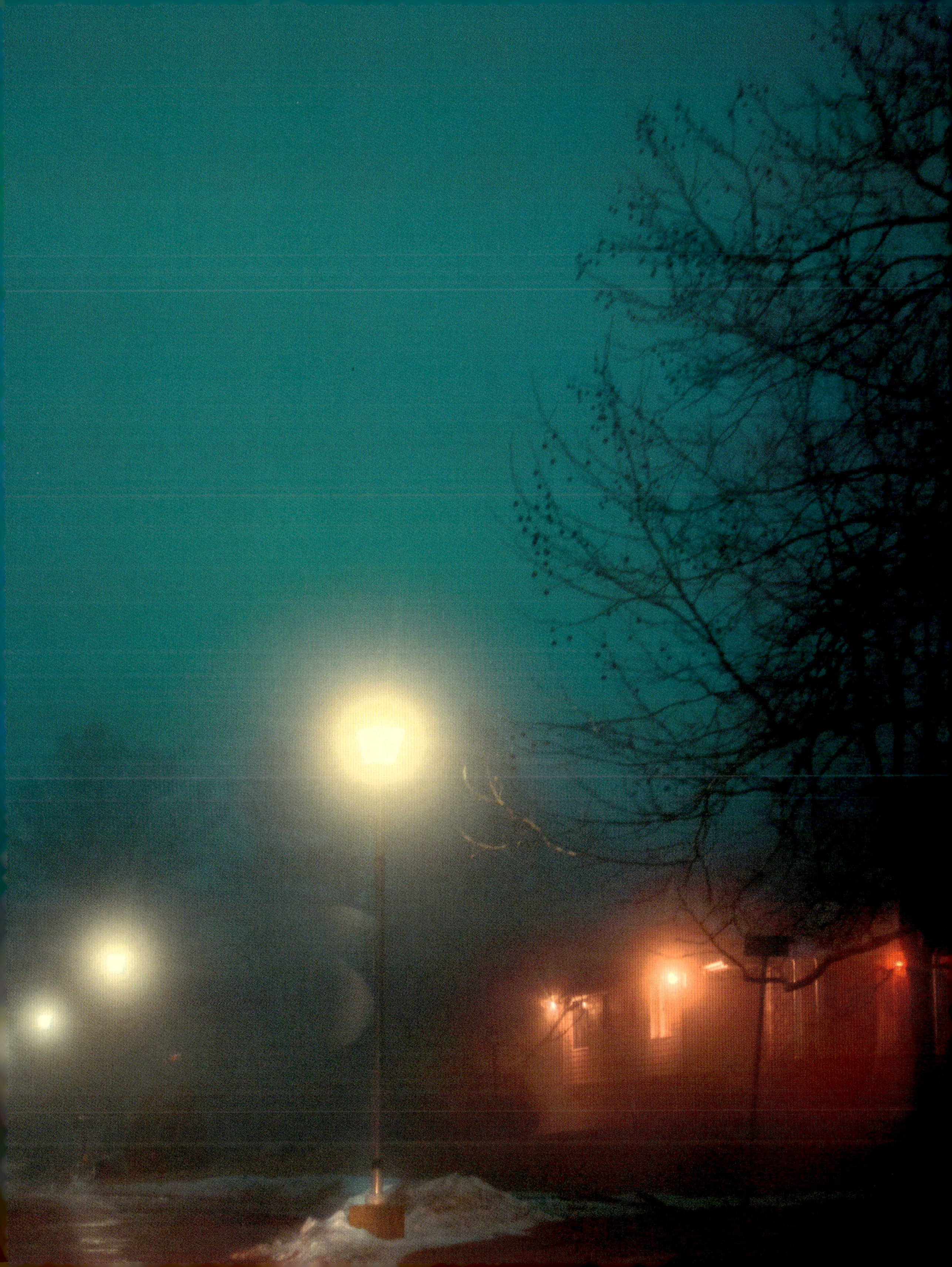

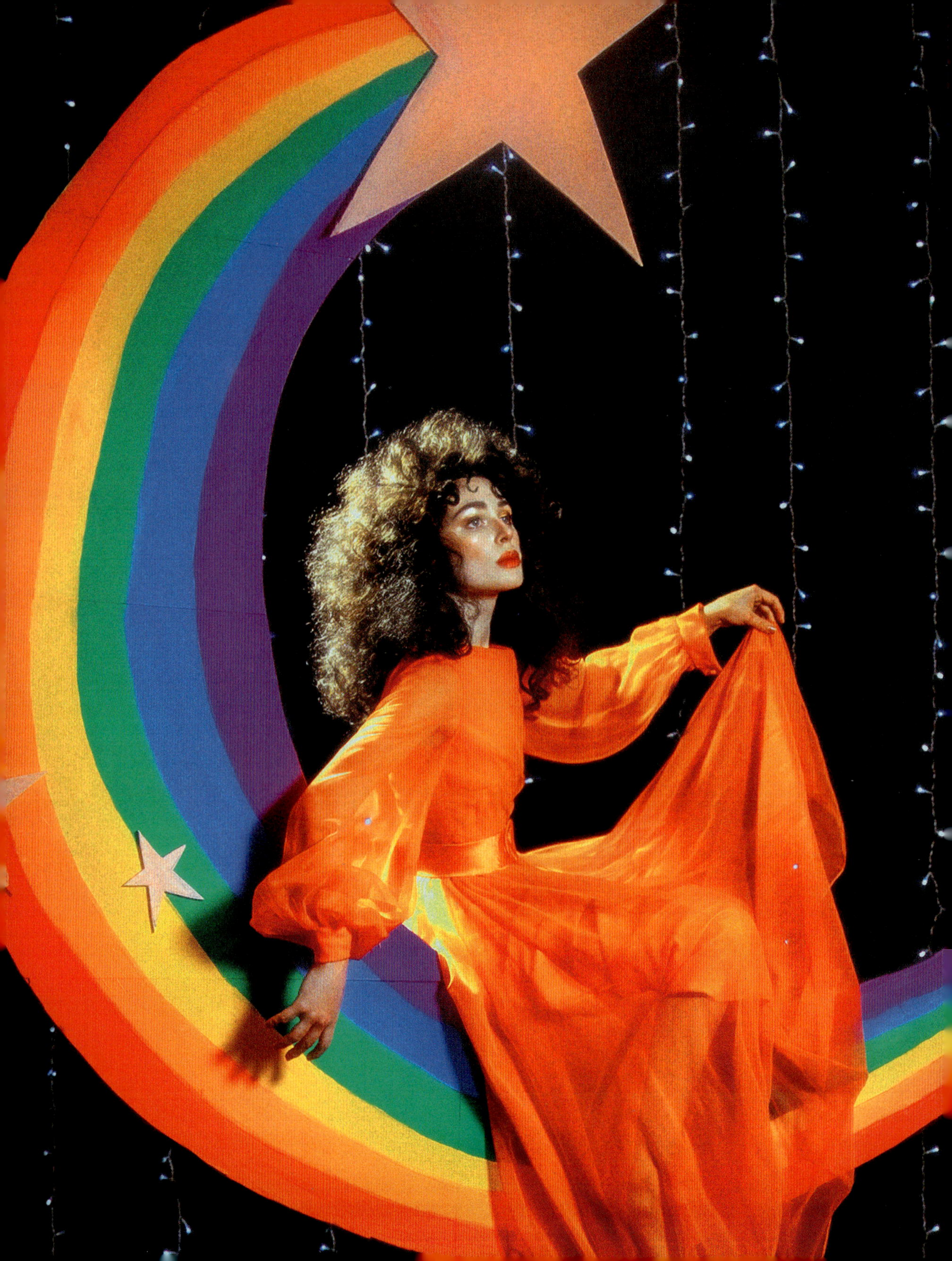

CHAPTER FIVE

A WORLD OF COLOR

VIBRANT & BRIGHT

Colors include a range of thousands of different shades, tones, and pigments that each convey unique and special emotions. Color can help pull a viewer in, make someone feel empowered, or even express a specific emotion. But how do you find the right colors to fit a certain project or lifestyle?

When it comes to color, it can be tricky to have so many options. But with a simple understanding of how colors work, you'll likely find some clarity on the right hues for you.

This chapter will highlight the magnificent vibrancy of color and weave in some simple color-theory tricks to help you find the perfect shade for whatever it is you're creating.

COLOR THEORY

I didn't actively think of color as a child. But as I got older and became a teenager, I realized that my bedroom was my own personal domain. To ensure it reflected me, I decided to paint the walls a different color.

I told my mother I wanted a pink bedroom. She didn't handle this well at the time. Our whole house was painted in darker shades of greenish-yellows that I really disliked. According to her, my idea was in terrible taste. However, she soon caved and let me paint my walls bright pink. I loved it at first, but over the next few years, my mom's opinion replayed in my head, boring down on me until I decided to let her paint my room blue.

I regret letting her paint my walls blue. As I write this, I am in my first real adult apartment and I'm surrounded by pink. Pink is a color that is core to my being. It's never a bad idea to have a base color that you love. It can be your go-to color for projects—one that can be easily incorporated into most of the things you create.

Remember, you don't have to just stick to one specific set of colors across your work. You can always try out new palettes and color combinations! I've found that limiting myself to a set of specific colors restricts my composition. There are so many different shades and hues of any single color that even your go-to pigment can shift. To this day, I still don't have a signature color palette that I stick to when creating or presenting to clients, and it's not because I don't know what colors I want to use. I usually shape what I'm doing around one color I love and mold the rest around it.

Before you can get to picking a color though, it might be a good idea for you to understand some basic rules of color.

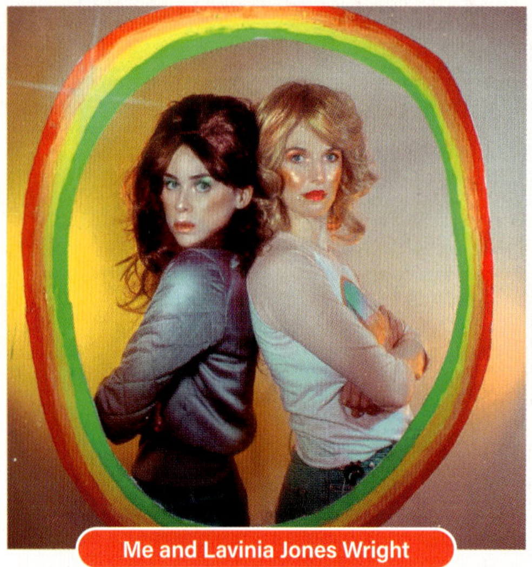

Me and Lavinia Jones Wright

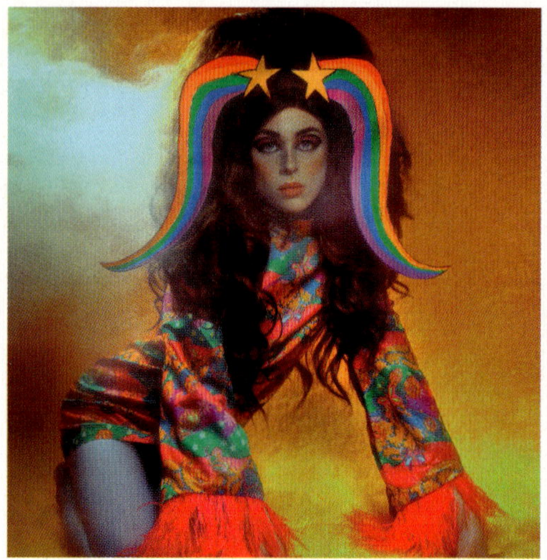

PRIMARY COLORS

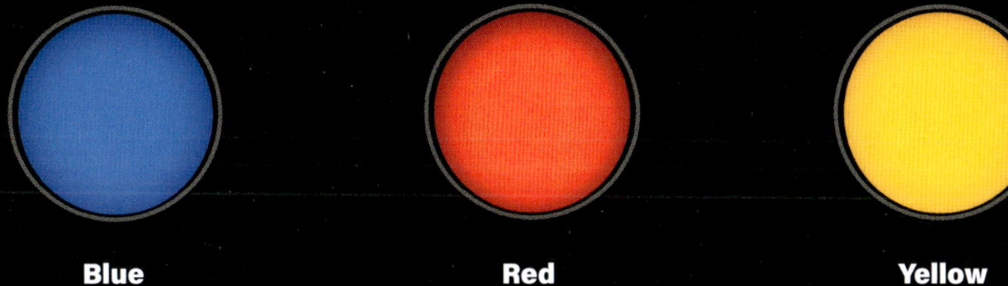

Blue　　　　　　**Red**　　　　　　**Yellow**

Think of the primary colors as the three main ingredients that can be used to make all kinds of recipes. With blue, red, and yellow, you can make all kinds of dishes, depending on the amount of each color used.

SECONDARY COLORS

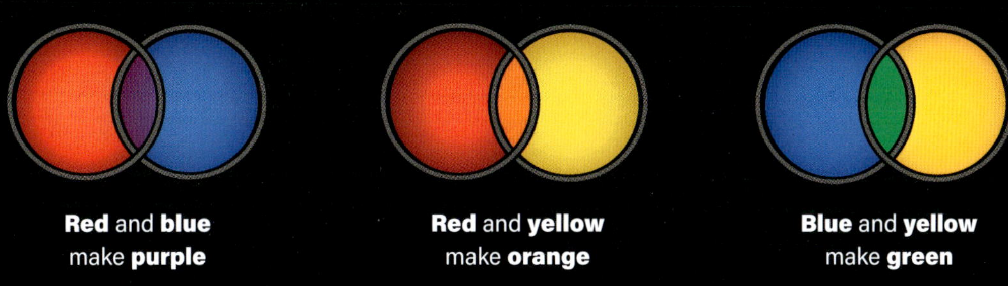

Red and **blue**
make **purple**

Red and **yellow**
make **orange**

Blue and **yellow**
make **green**

The new colors that are created from two primary colors mixed together are called secondary colors. These six colors make up the majority of the rainbow.

TERTIARY COLORS

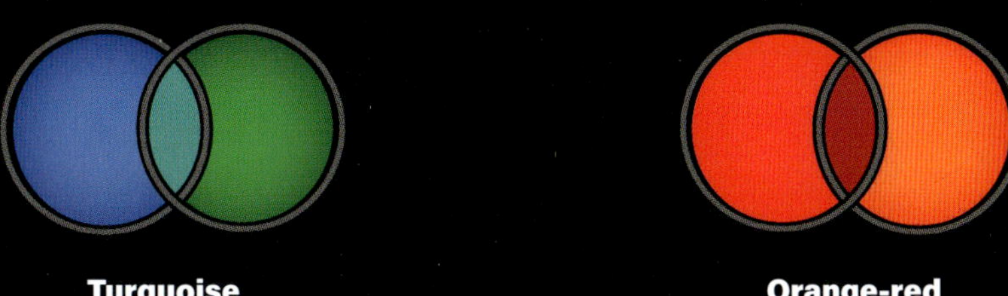

Turquoise　　　　　　**Orange-red**

These are made when you mix a primary color with a secondary color. For example, if I mix the primary color **blue** with the secondary color **green**, I get **turquoise**. Mixing **red** with **orange** creates a sunset **orange-red**.

COMPLEMENTARY COLORS

Some colors just seem to go really well together. Complementary colors are two colors that are opposite each other on the color wheel, but work harmoniously together. Using complementary colors is a perfect way to make something stand out.

Examples of complementary colors:

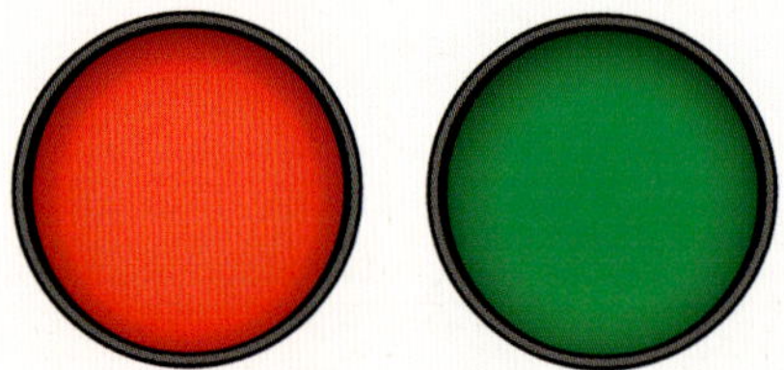

Red and **green**

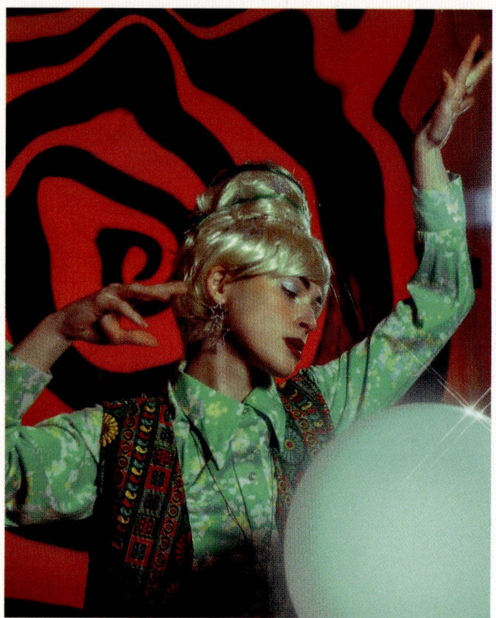

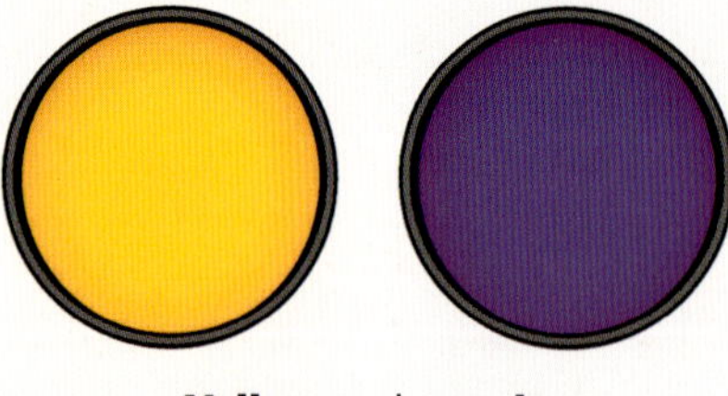

Yellow and **purple**

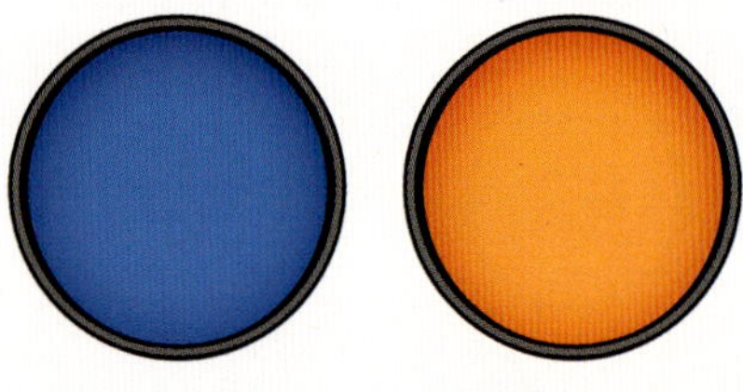

Blue and **orange**

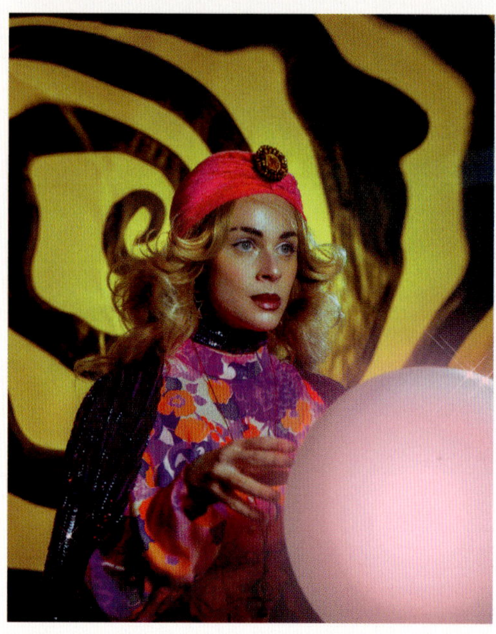

ANALOGOUS COLORS

These are the colors that are directly next to each other on the color wheel. When you put them together, their similarities create harmony. Think of them as family members that actually get along.

Examples of analogous colors:

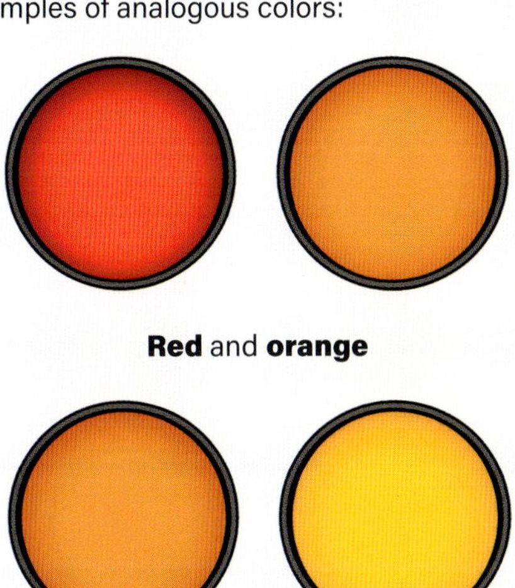

Red and **orange**

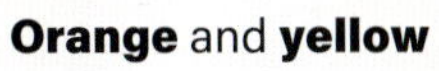

Orange and **yellow**

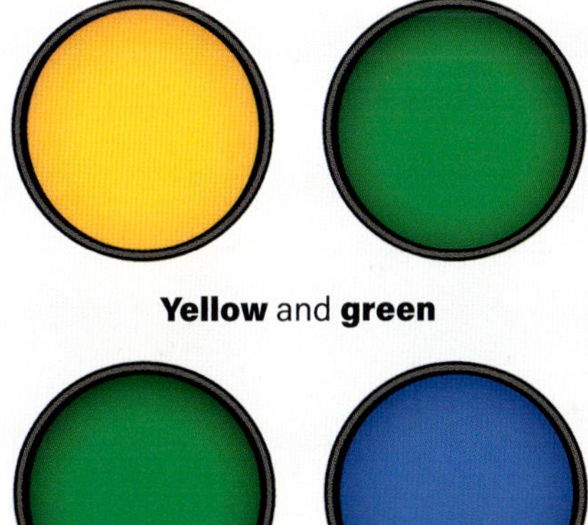

Yellow and **green**

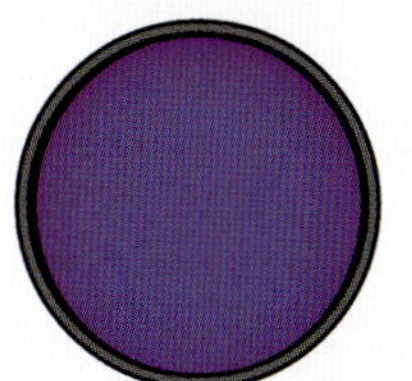

Green and **blue**

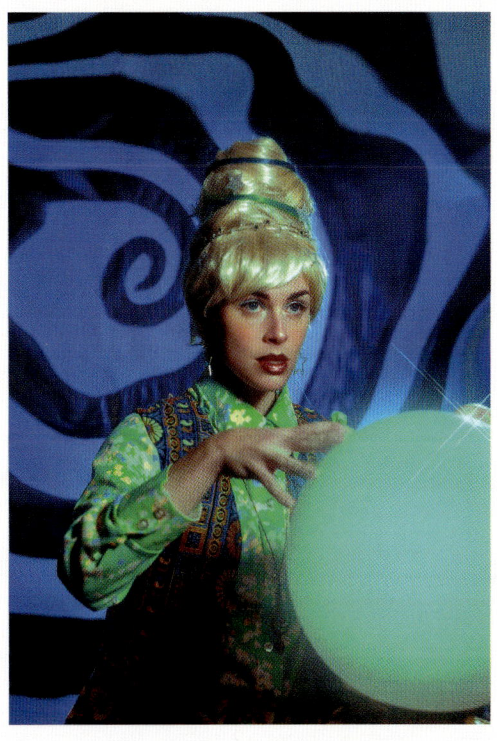

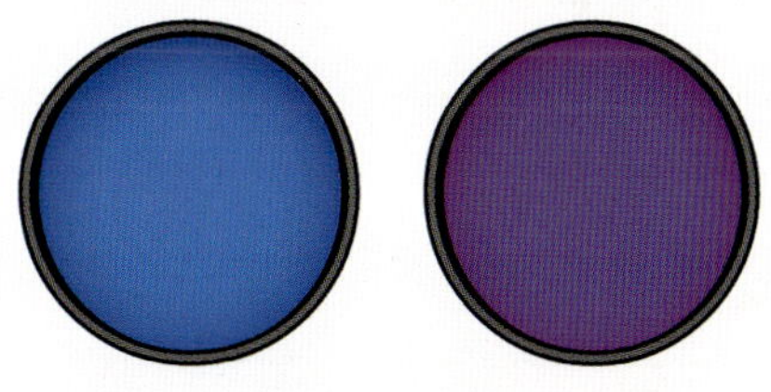

Blue and **purple**

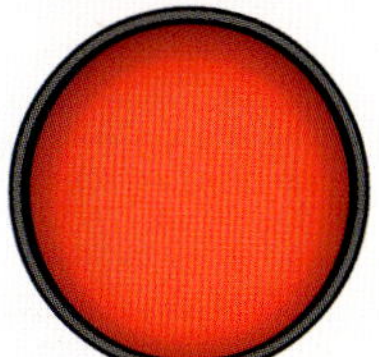

Purple and **red**

WARM VS. COOL COLORS

Another thing to think about when searching for colors is how warm or cool they are and how they work together.

Warm colors are associated with heat, summer, the sun shining, autumn, leaves falling, etc. These colors are **red**, **orange**, and **yellow**.

Cool colors are associated with water, raindrops, the ocean, chilly winters, the night sky, etc. These colors are **blue**, **green**, and **purple**.

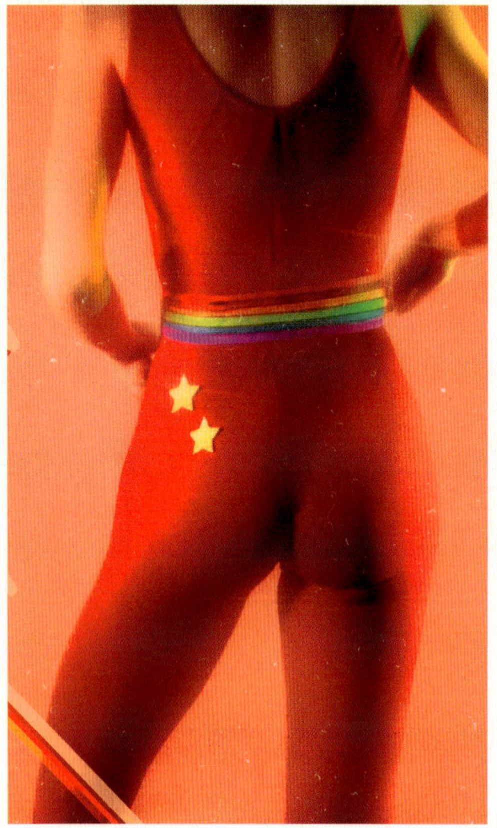

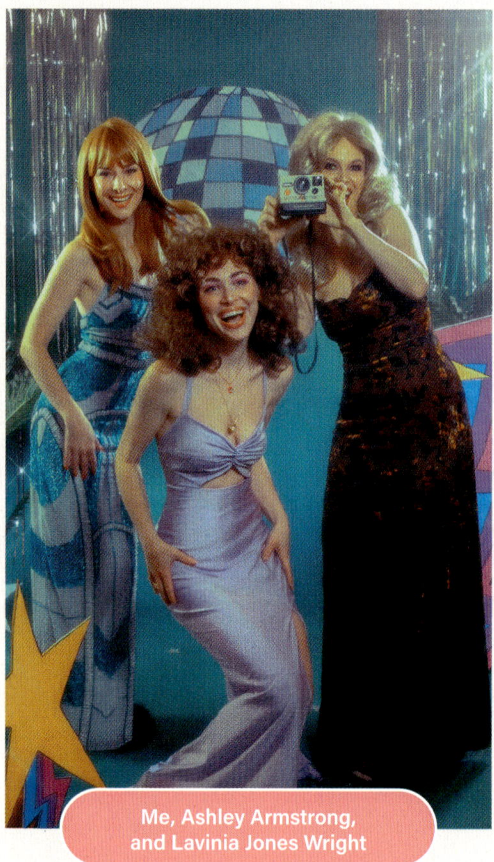

Me, Ashley Armstrong, and Lavinia Jones Wright

When you're creating something new, it's important to think about what type of feeling you're trying to convey. Be sure to consider the temperature of a color, as it can say a lot! Adding contrasting warm and cool colors alongside each other in a piece can also create a really engaging dynamic.

MONOCHROMATIC COLORS

A monochromatic palette focuses on one color and its different tints, shades, and tones.

For example, if I was creating an outfit with a **red** monochromatic palette, I could include **pink**, **scarlet**, **maroon**, and **salmon**.

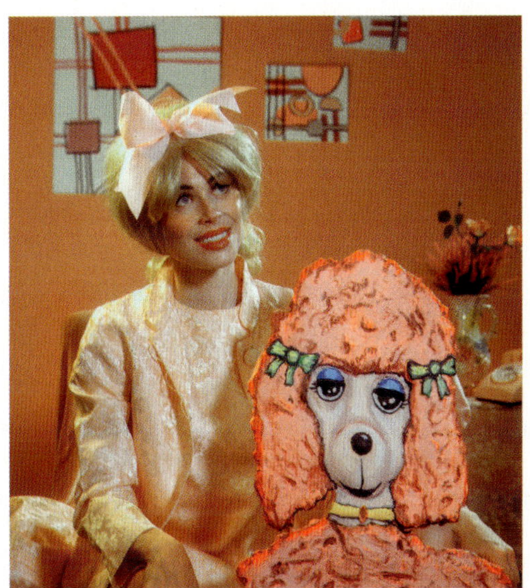

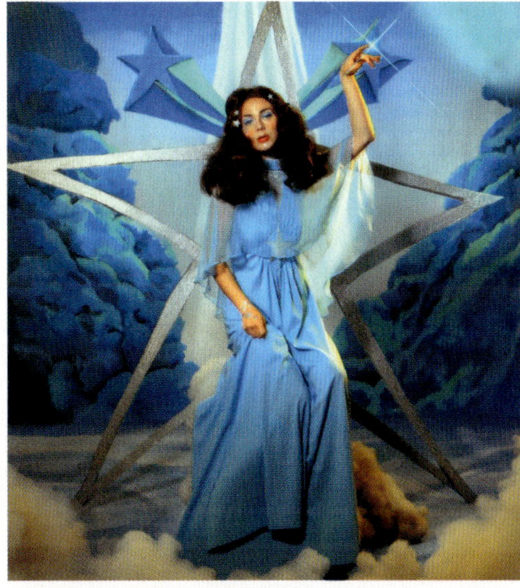

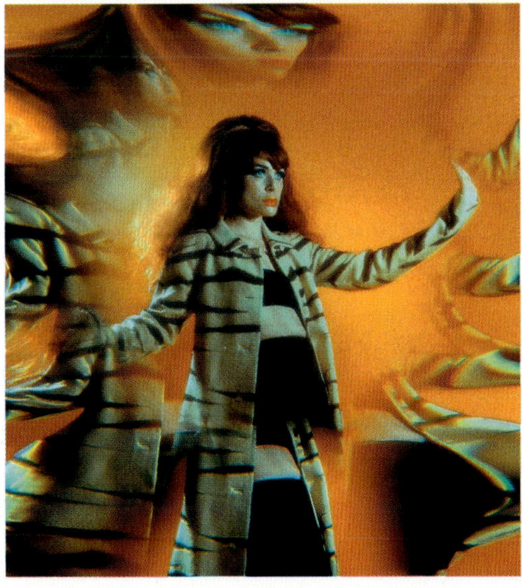

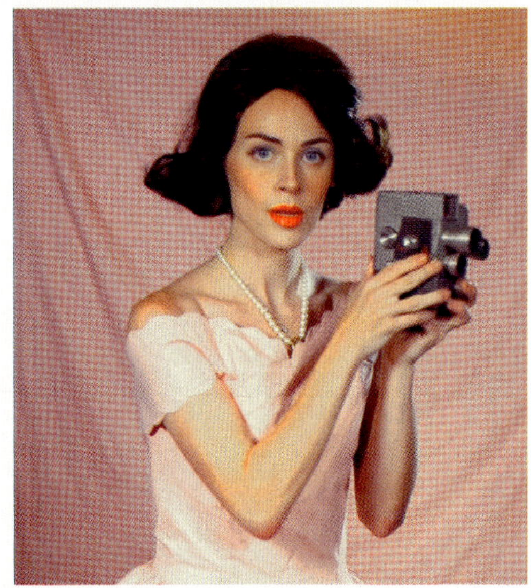

OTHER COLOR RELATIONSHIPS

So what about colors like pink and lavender? These are considered **tints**, or lighter varieties. If you add white to a base color, you're adding white to that **hue**. A hue is the pure form of a color that hasn't been altered. **Pink** is a tint of **red**, and **lavender** is a tint of **purple**.

And what about colors like **maroon** and **navy**? These are considered **shades**, as they are darker forms of an original hue. **Maroon** is a shade of **red**. **Navy** is a shade of **blue**. These shades can still be called red and blue, but their value is darker because of the addition of **black**. The **value** of a color is how dark or light it is!

Here's a checklist for how to search for the right version of your favorite color:

- ✔ **Hue:** The base color in its purest form.
- ✔ **Shade:** Adding black to a hue to make it darker.
- ✔ **Tint:** Adding white to a hue to make it lighter.
- ✔ **Value:** The lightness or darkness of a color.
- ✔ **Tone:** Adding gray to dull the hue down.
- ✔ **Saturation:** The intensity of the hue itself.

At the end of the day, you can make almost any colors go together, but it's critical to ensure that value, tone, and saturation align.

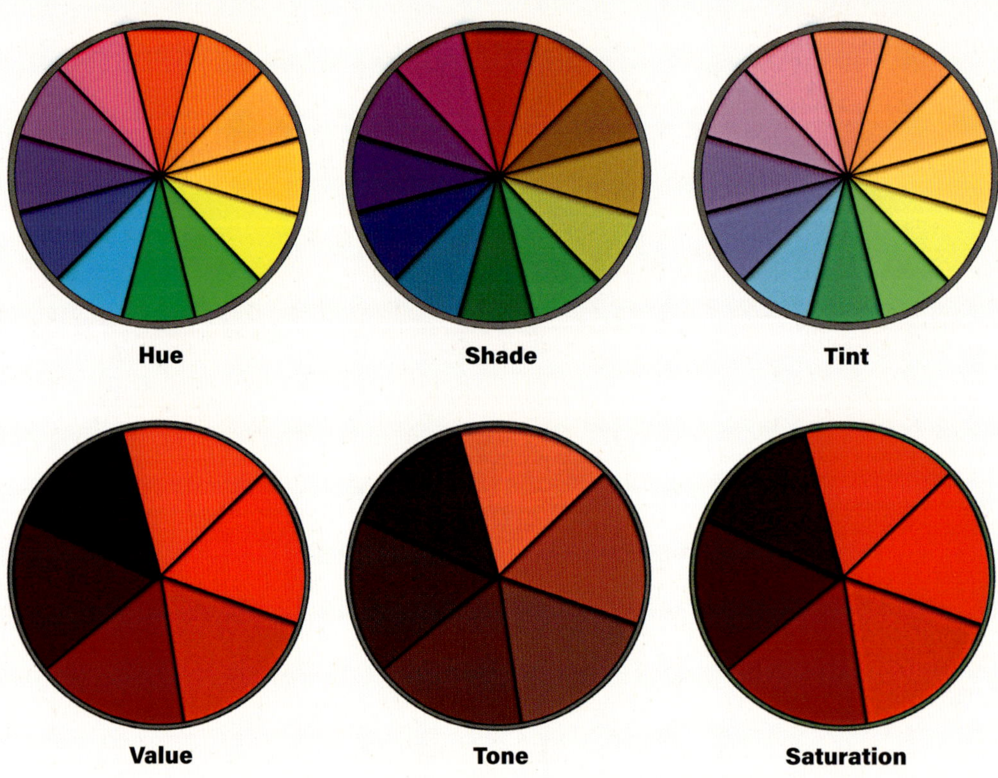

Hue

Shade

Tint

Value

Tone

Saturation

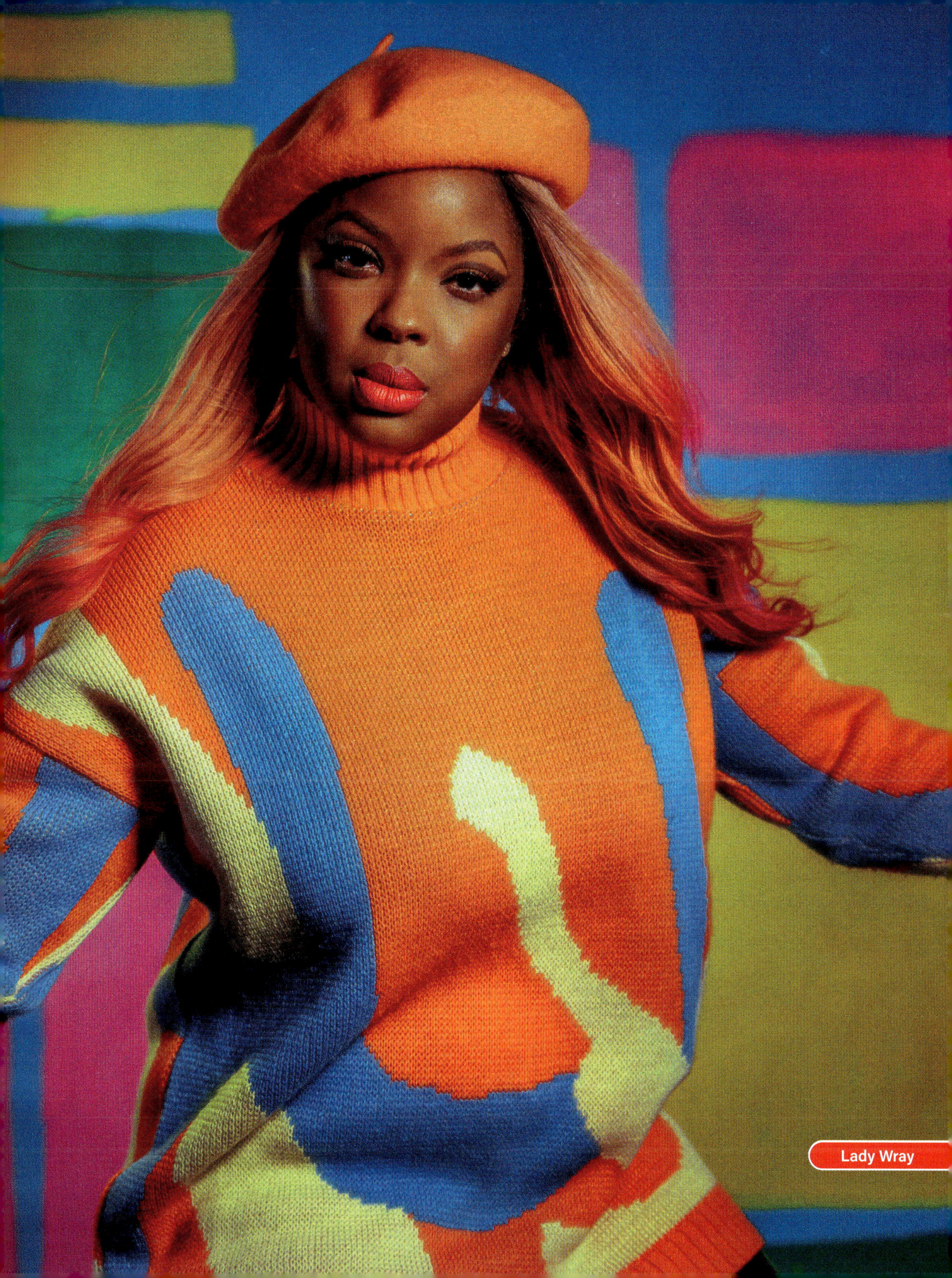
Lady Wray

MAKING MEANING OF COLOR

Whether we realize it or not, color carries a whole bunch of psychological significance. Using colors to shape someone's emotions is a powerful tool to get your point across. Don't forget about this!

Remember, if you change the value, tone, or saturation of these colors, the emotional meaning behind them can change as well. If you consider the emotional story behind the colors you're picking, your color palette will soon come into focus. Think about the main point behind your project. Are you decorating a space for positivity? Putting together a moody outfit? Or making art when you're feeling contemplative?

Common colorful emotions:

> **Red:** Anger, anxiety, energy
> **Orange:** Reflective, hopeful, casual
> **Yellow:** Sunshine, bright, cheery
> **Green:** Prosperity, greed, wealth
> **Blue:** Peaceful, calm, sad, lonely
> **Purple:** Royalty, elegance, exclusiveness

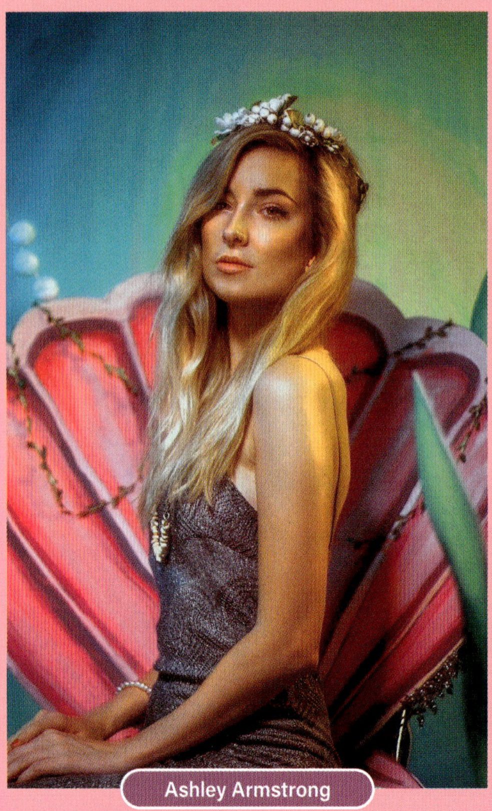

Ashley Armstrong

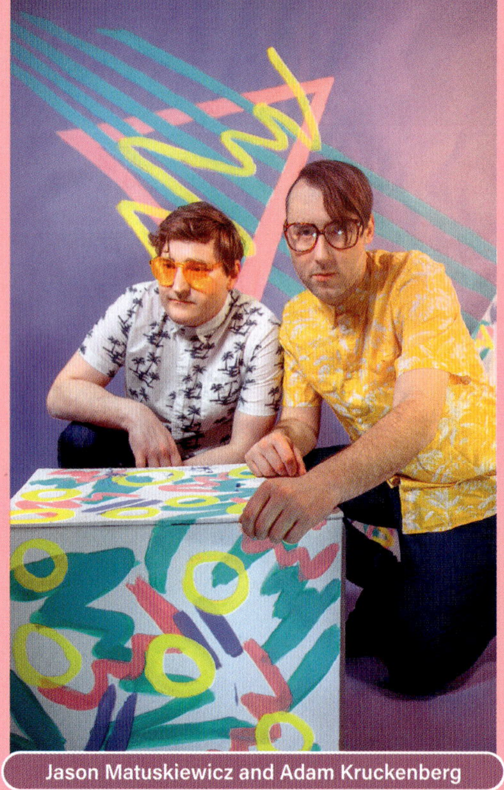

Jason Matuskiewicz and Adam Kruckenberg

CREATING A PALETTE

You can create a palette just by selecting your favorite hues and playing around with shade, tint, tone, and saturation to find the perfect combo. Let's give it a try.

Choose a hue—pick the color that you love at its purest form or the color that suits an emotion you are trying to convey. Be sure to only pick a base color, not a shade or tint. For example, I will choose the color **red**.

Think of a shade and tint that draws you in the most. I like my **red** a bit more muted, so I would tint it to a pure **pink** because adding **white** to anything turns it into a pastel version.

Now, I want a darker value, but I don't want to add black as that would achieve a **blue-pink** while I prefer an **orange**-**pink**. To accomplish this, I would add a bit of **yellow** to create an **orange**, almost coral-like **pink**.

Even though I've turned my base of **red** to **pink**, I can still think of my **pink** as a type of **red**, so it will be easier for me to know what other colors complement it based on everything else we've learned about color.

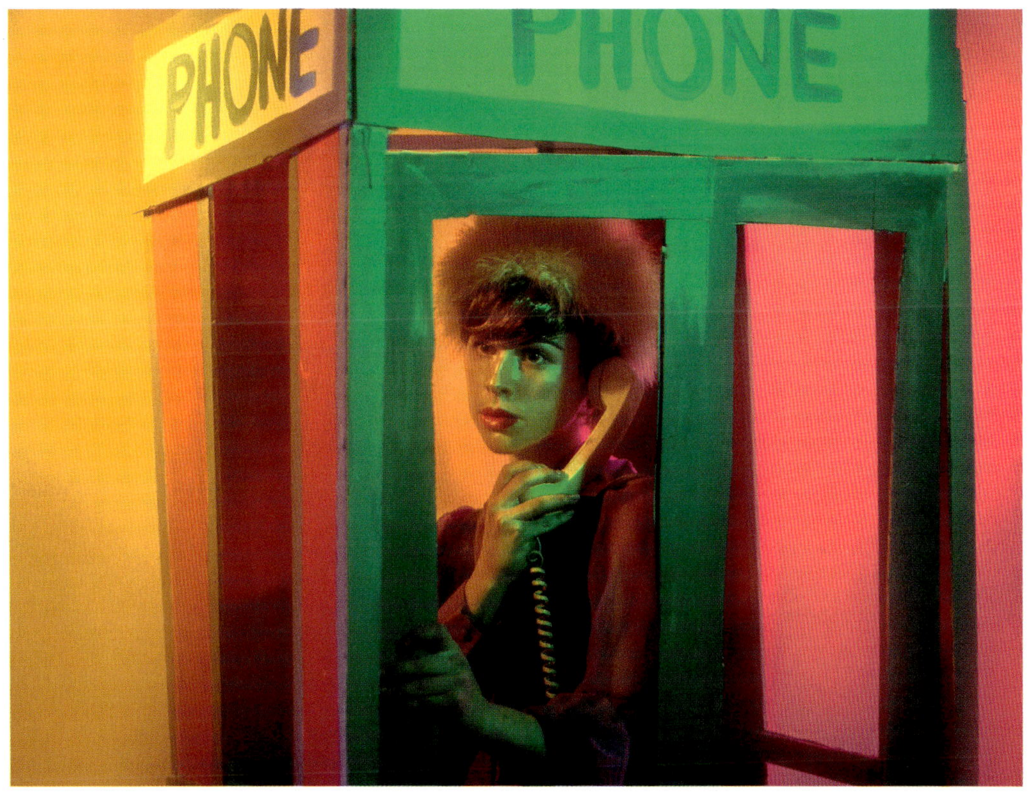

COLORS ACROSS DISCIPLINES

Colors for art: Think about the emotion you are trying to evoke with your work. Start there and build a color palette around that color. By using colors that form a complementary palette, you can use a number of different colors in your piece that work together to make something unique.

Colors for content creation: Find the one color you feel is aligned with who you are as a person and as a creator. It's important for people to recognize you and your vibe instantly with this color. Once you have figured out this autobiographical color, decide what other colors go well with it, so you can incorporate them into your content.

Colors for fashion or interior designer: Find a piece of furniture or an article of clothing that you'd like to build a story around. What color is it? Now see what other colored elements would work well with this piece. Objects, accessories, and entire outfits depend so much on color, as each piece is often identified by its color just as much as any of its other attributes.

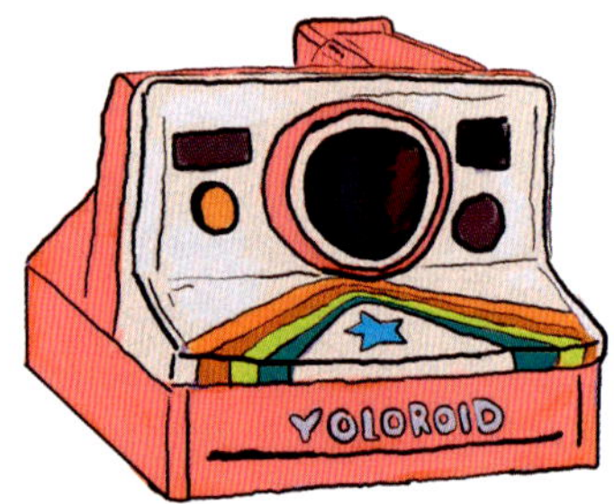

NICOLE BRIDGEFORD
Makeup Artist & Hair Stylist

Color has directly impacted my work as a makeup artist and hair stylist for TV and film over the years in endless ways. Beyond conveying a mood or emotion, color has the power to tell a story and create change. From starting off working at a hair salon, moving to fashion and print, then Broadway, and now television and film, I find that color can establish a connection with a single person or an entire audience. Color is endlessly inspirational when it comes to creating characters, both on- and off-screen. It is an integral part of self-expression.

Whether it's changing an individual's hair color or makeup, color can completely shape a story or a person's everyday life. For me, color becomes a powerful tool. It can enhance or withdraw, create chaos or harmony. Changing someone's hair color and then seeing the incredible impact it has on them and the way they view themselves in real time is a spectacular feeling.

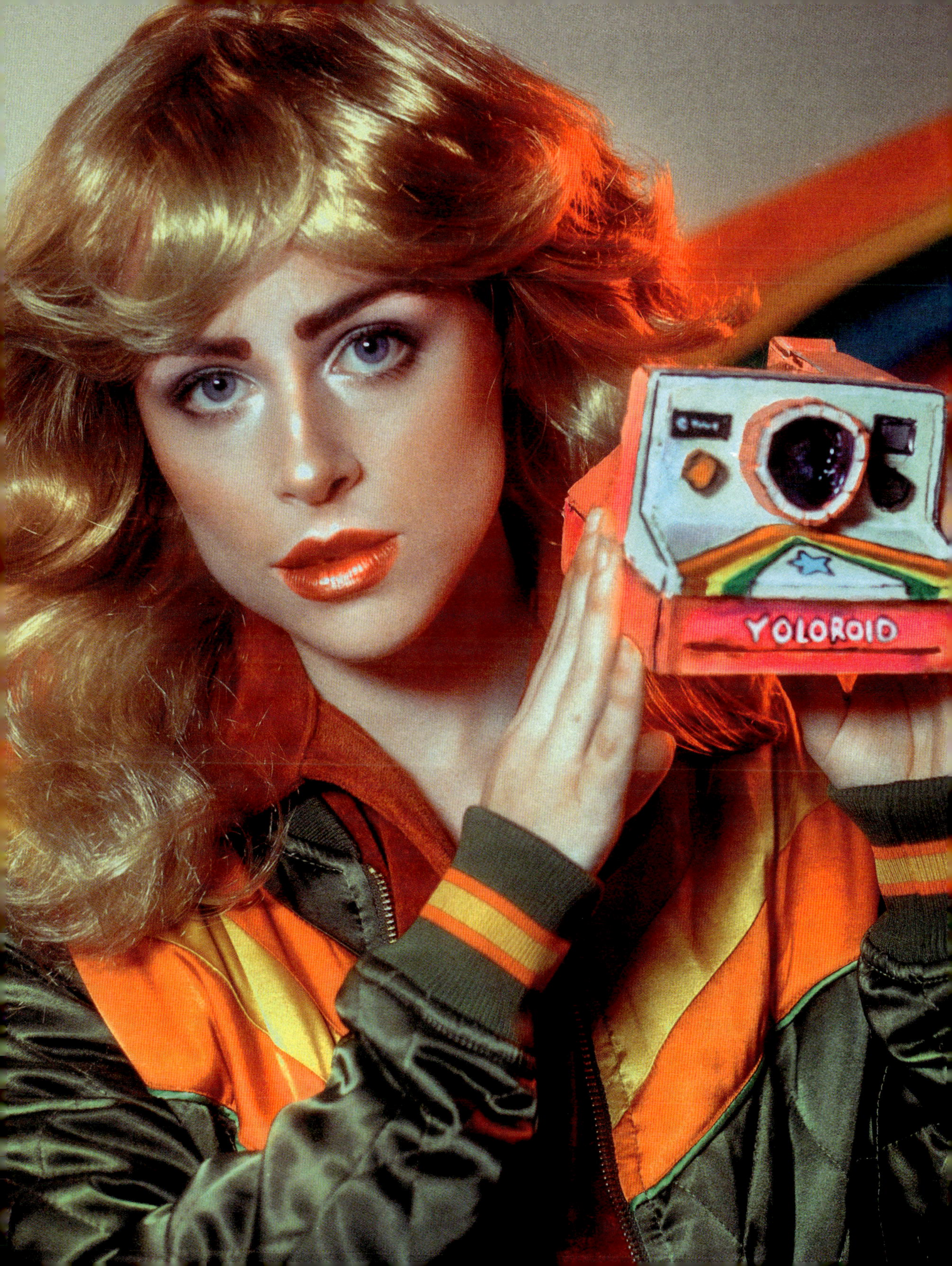

YOLOROID

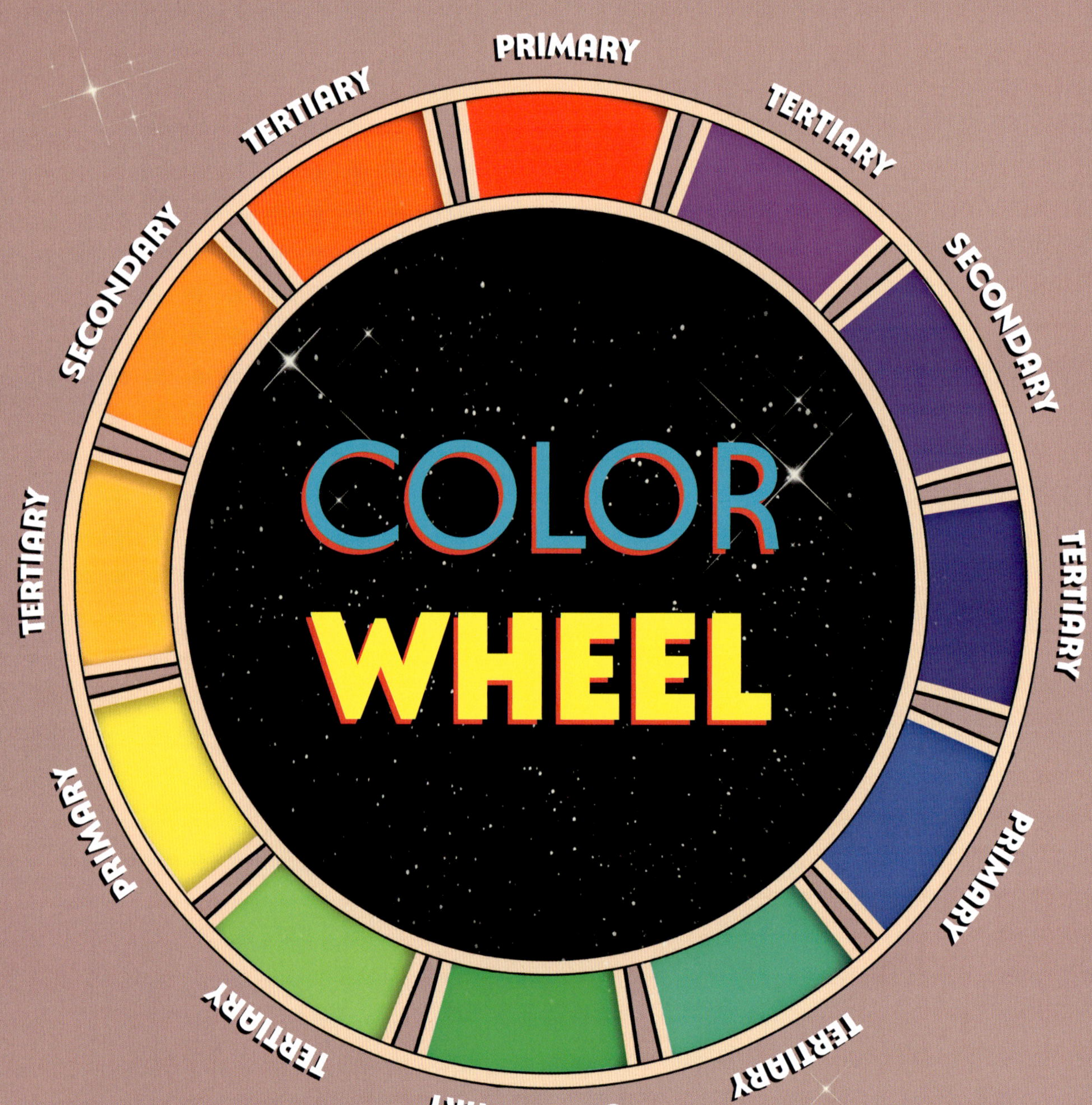

COLOR
WHEEL
PRIMARY
TERTIARY
SECONDARY
TERTIARY
PRIMARY
TERTIARY
SECONDARY
TERTIARY
PRIMARY
TERTIARY
SECONDARY
TERTIARY

COLOR TEMPERATURE

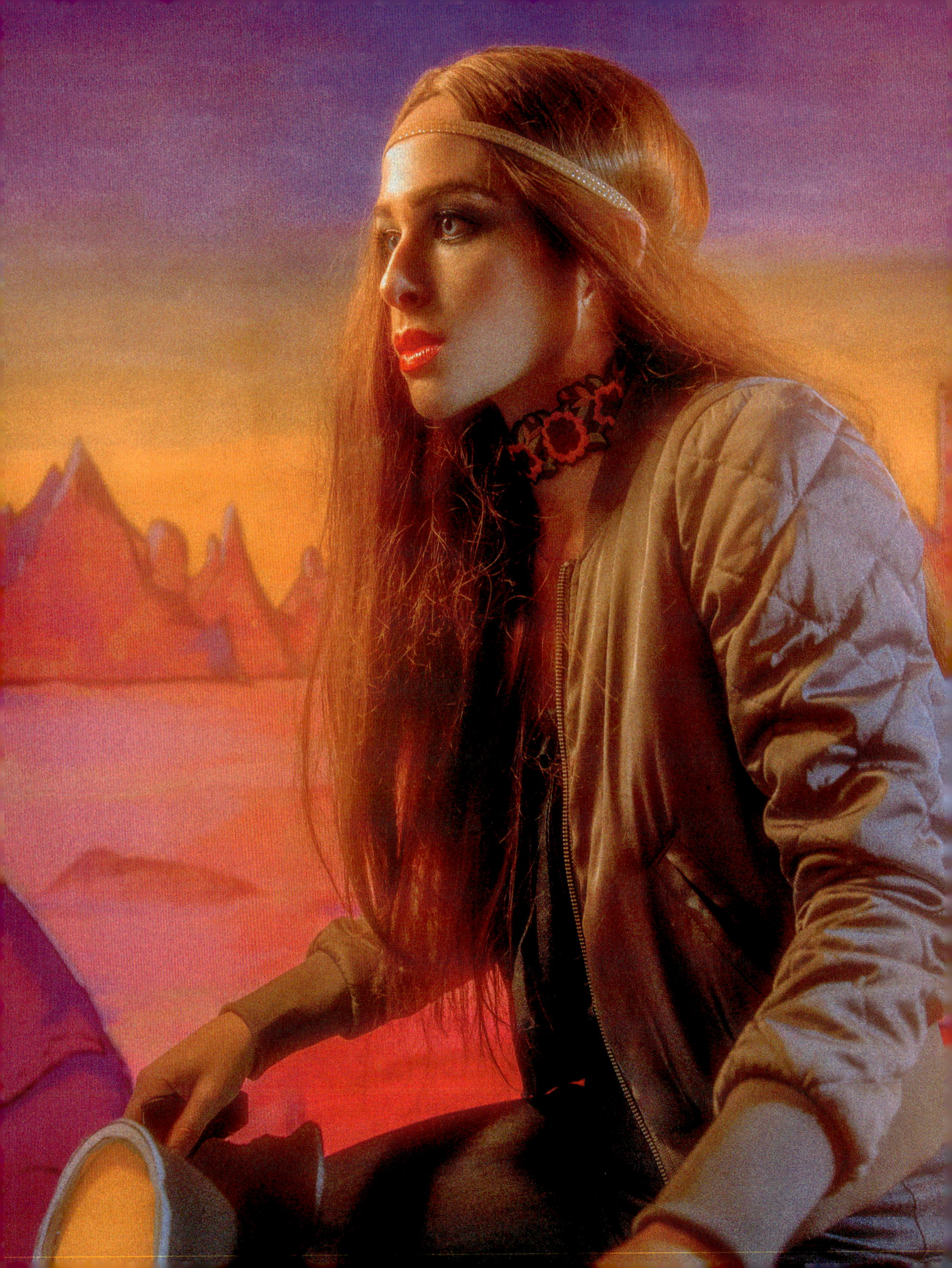

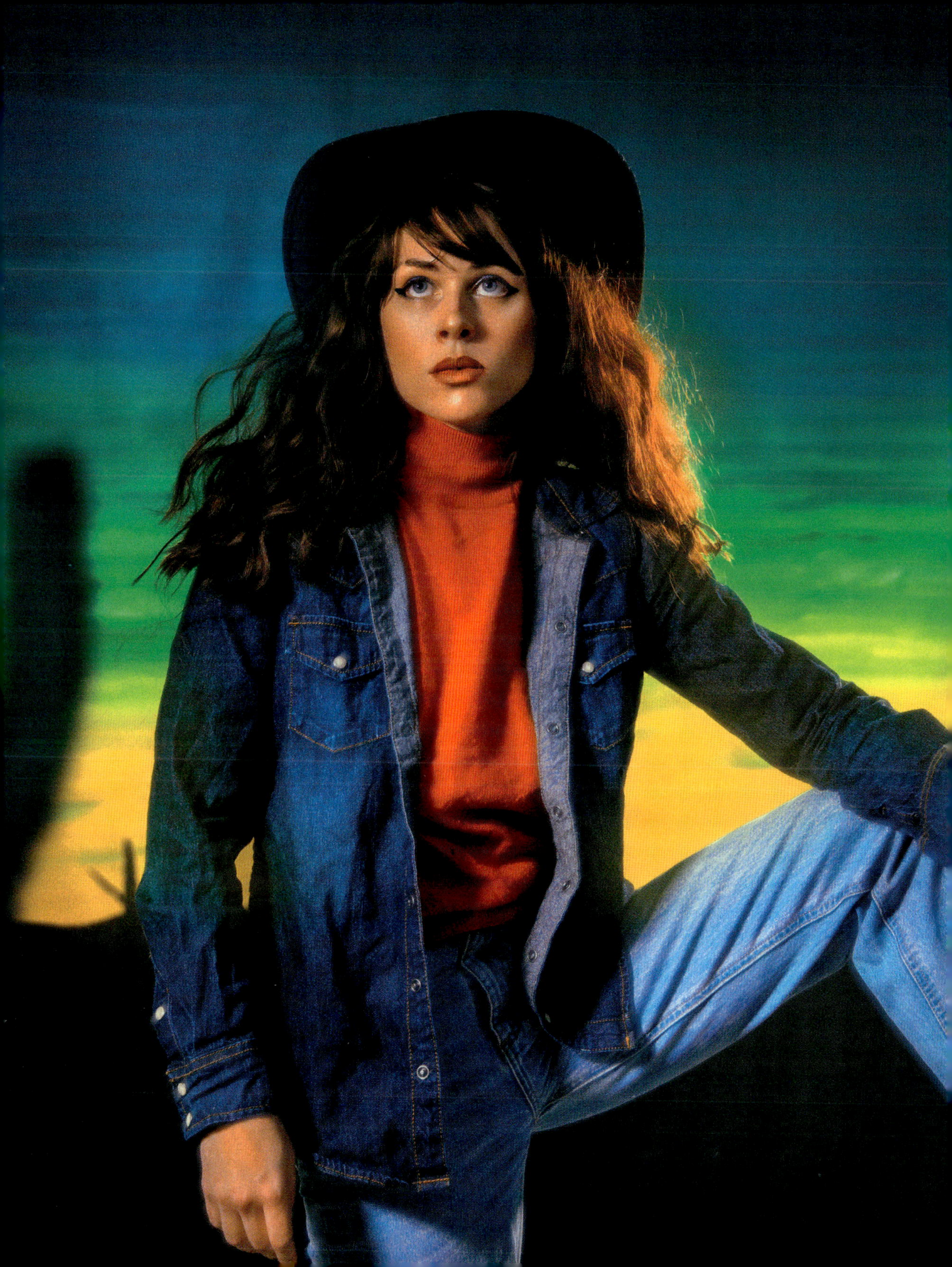

COLOR EXERCISES

> What is your favorite color? Try to reverse engineer it to see what this color is made up of. What type of color is it? Is it a combination? Primary, secondary, tertiary?

> If you are making a piece of art, what emotion are you trying to project with the work? Start with a color that evokes a specific emotion and build a color palette around that.

> Look around your space. Do you notice any reoccurring colors appearing? Do you see a color that you love? Pick one color and try building a color palette around it.

> Create a monochromatic still life in your space by finding objects that share a similar base color.

> Open up your computer and find a simple paint program (if you don't have something like Photoshop or Illustrator), select a color, and make a little swatch on a page. Then, start picking other colors you like. Place them next to that first swatch to see what works best to create a cohesive palette.

> Find a few images online and create color palettes based on them. Are there similarities between the images you're selecting and the color palettes that are being created?

> Find an object around your space and try to color match it using paint. This means starting with at least one primary color and either adding another primary color to it, or adding black/white to create the closest paint color to the object you're trying to match. Refer to the color theory section to learn how to best adapt your color to match what you're going for.

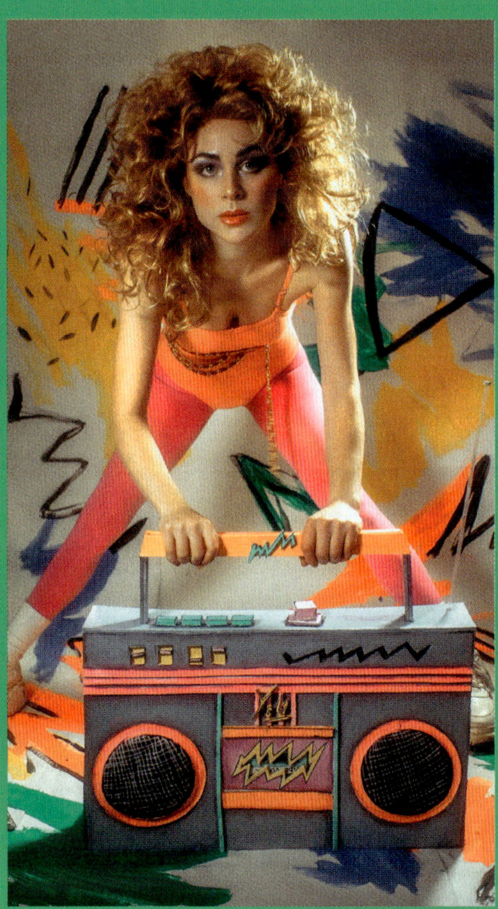

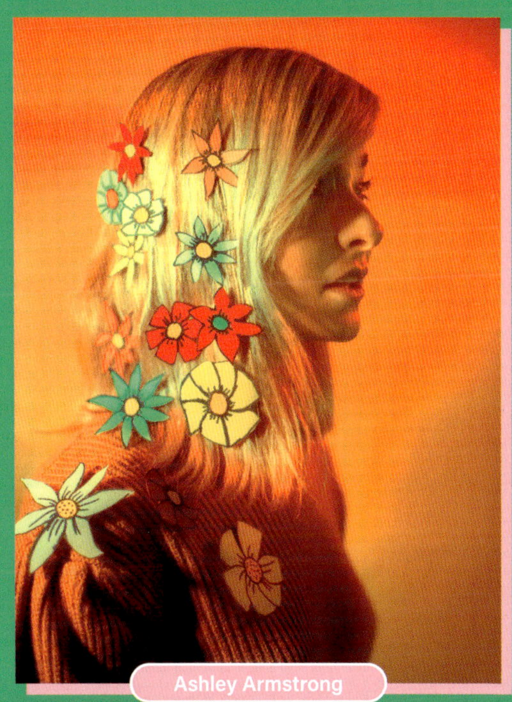

Ashley Armstrong

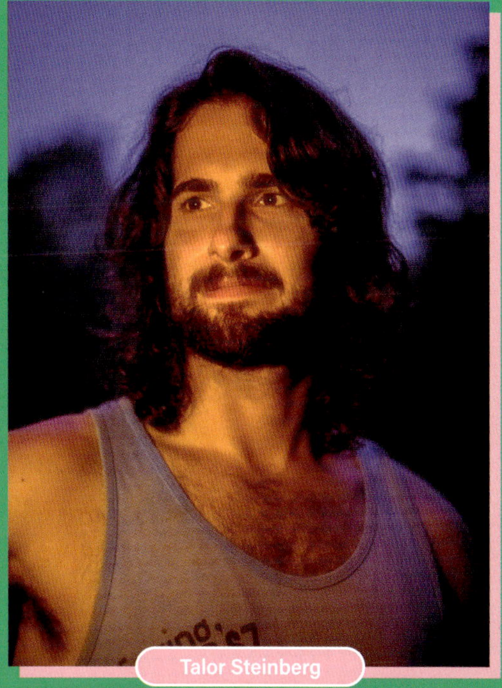

Talor Steinberg

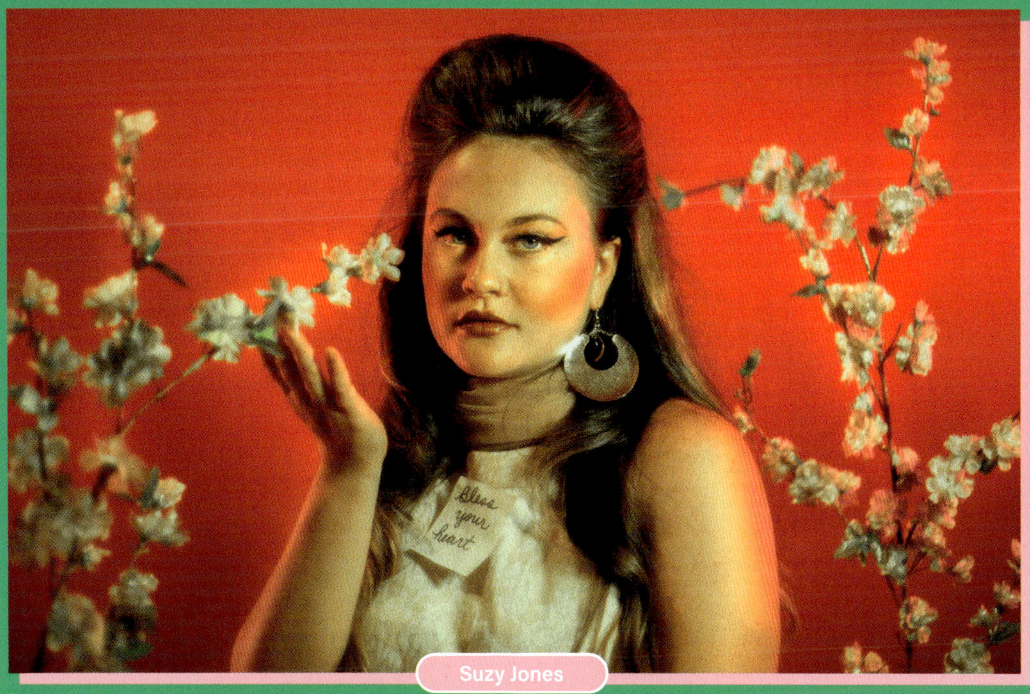

Suzy Jones

QUESTIONS TO CONSIDER

> What are your absolute favorite colors? Why do you feel drawn to them?

> Is your favorite color different now than what it was as a child? If so, why do you think it has changed?

> When scrolling online, what colors make you stop and look longer at a piece of content?

> What kind of mood are you trying to create with your piece? Which colors do you think would help exemplify that mood, and why?

> What color combinations are your favorite when paired together? What about these pairings do you find appealing?

> Do you find yourself drawn more to tints (lighter colors) or shades (darker colors)? Does it depend on the hue of the base color, or is it consistent across all colors?

> Is the work you're creating something that should be highly saturated and bright? Or would it work better if the colors were muted and dull?

> What color do you dislike the most? Why do you feel an aversion to it? Could you try incorporating it in your work just to see how it feels?

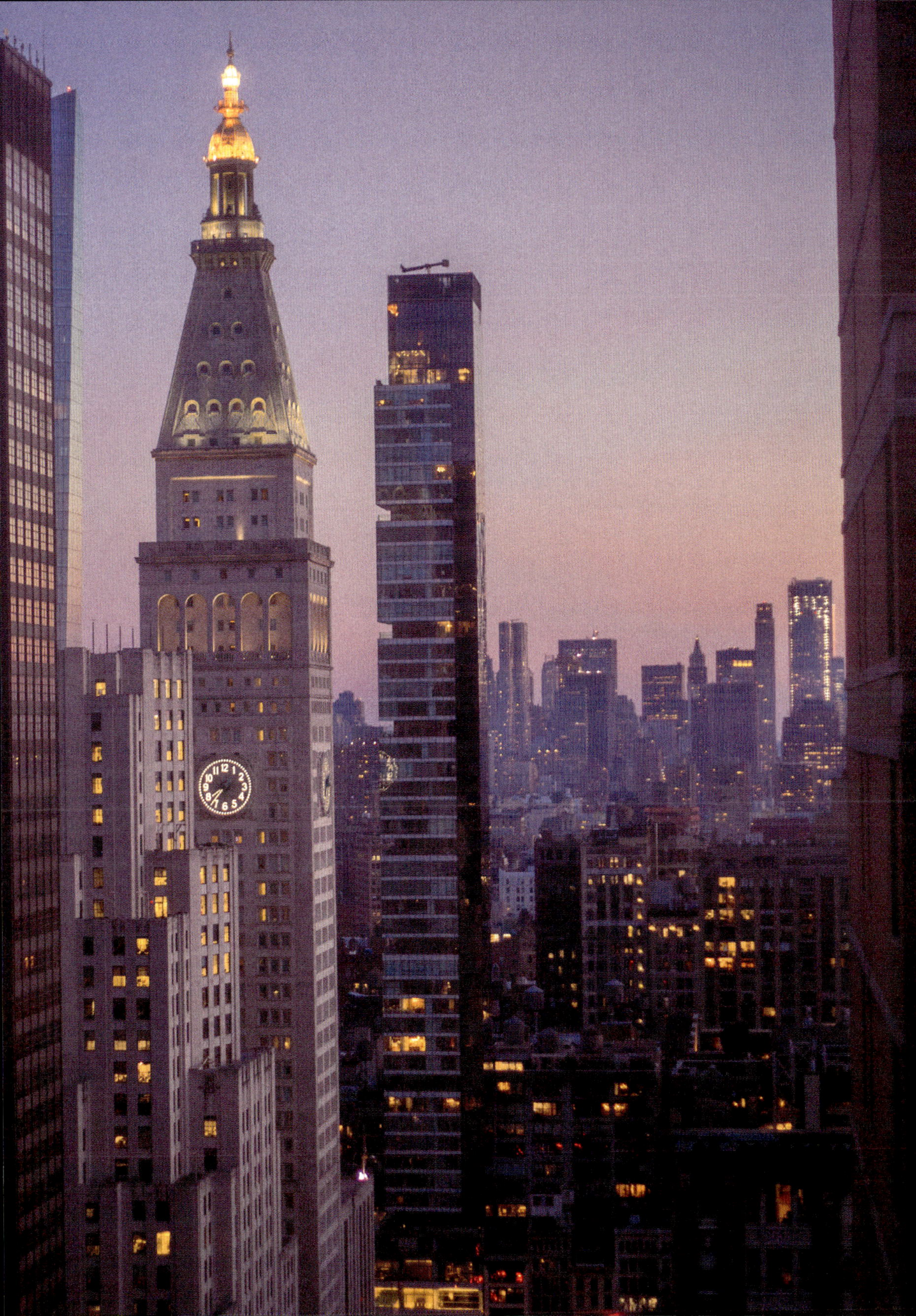

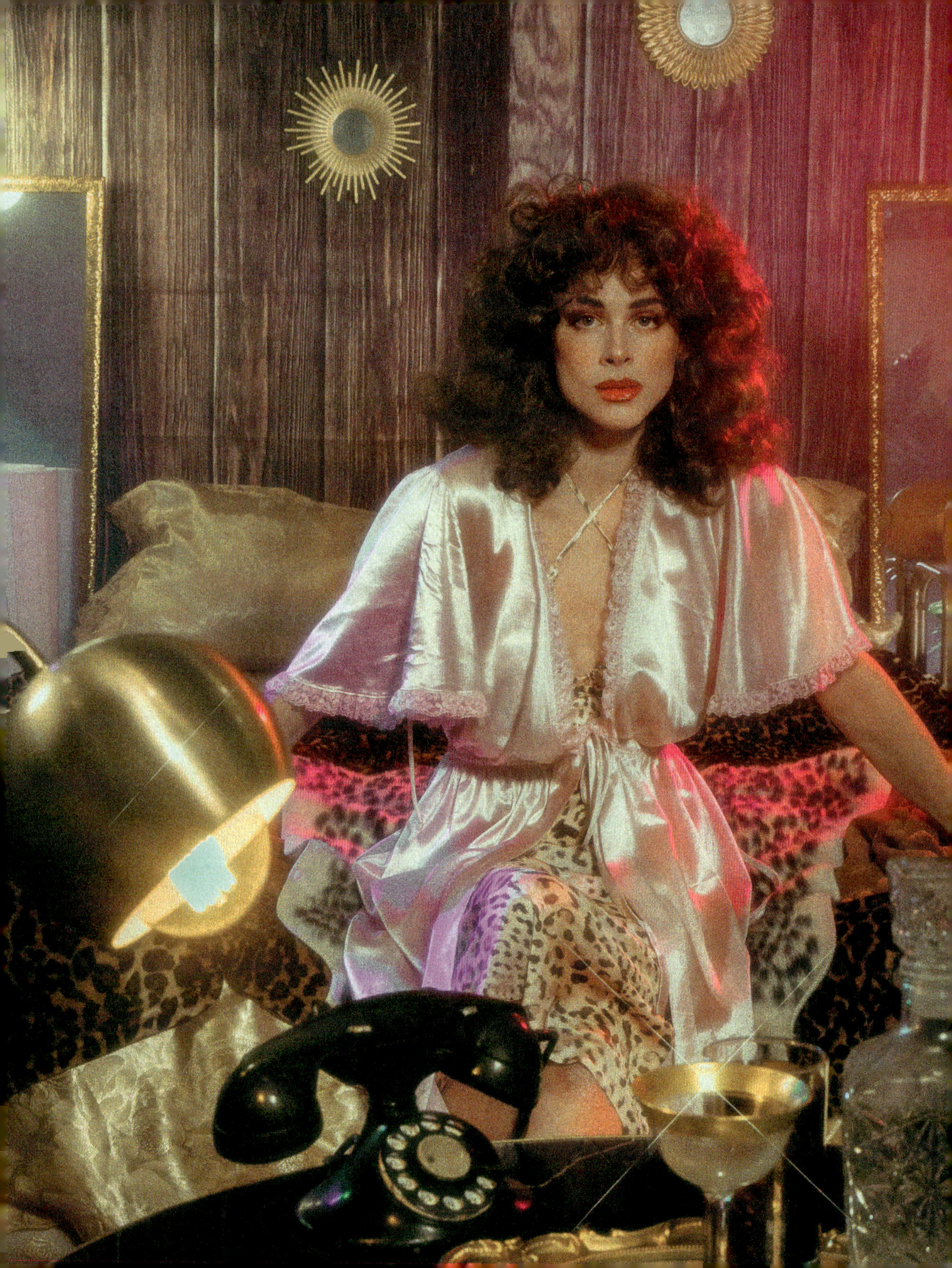

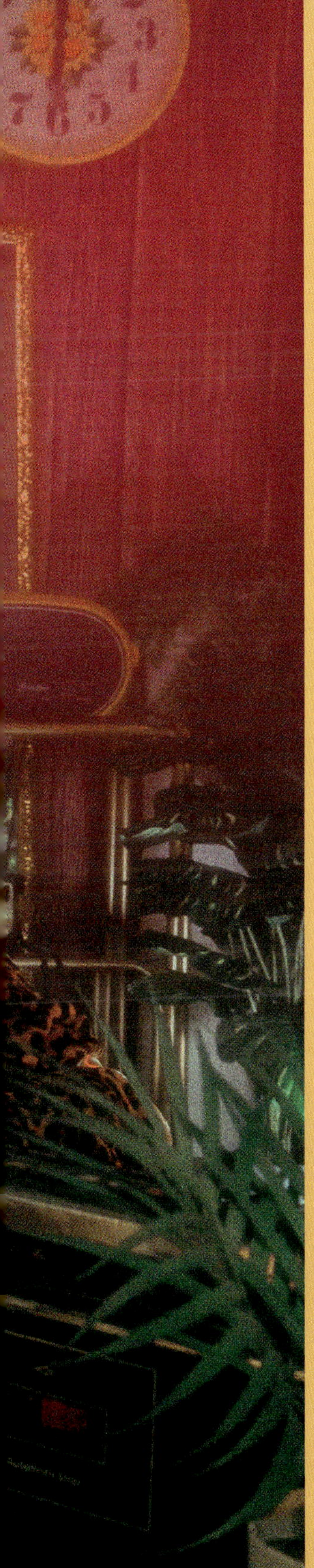

CHAPTER SIX

SETTING, ATMOSPHERE & TIME

FILLING OUT YOUR SPACE

Whether you're a photographer, a fine artist, or just designing a room in your home, if you don't consider the atmosphere or setting you're going for when you add pieces to a space, the final result is going to fall flat. This is why it's so important to consider the individual elements that provide meaningful accents to the room or piece of work you are creating. By using certain objects in thoughtful ways, you can imbue a space or an artwork with the right kind of atmosphere and even make the objects work together to be evocative of a certain time or decade. This chapter is meant to help you think critically about the more ambiguous elements that bring a project to life: setting, atmosphere, and time.

SETTING UP THE ATMOSPHERE

Setting and atmosphere act as the pulse of any project. These elements must be crafted with care to convey the right kind of vibe. Imagine if someone is making a movie and they just decided to randomly place items without considering what the objects might signify to the viewer. No matter how nice the items are, we would have no idea what time period the scene is set in, what the mood is supposed to be, or what the scene should be making us feel. The same applies for scenes created for paintings, drawings, collages, or other mediums.

Growing up, my parents didn't have many lights in our house. They preferred to sit in natural light. This lack of light played into the atmosphere of our home, creating a dark, moody space. My friends called our place the vampire house; I really disliked this. I always knew that when I got my own place, I'd want the lighting and atmosphere to feel very different. I am someone who adores bright pops of color and warm light.

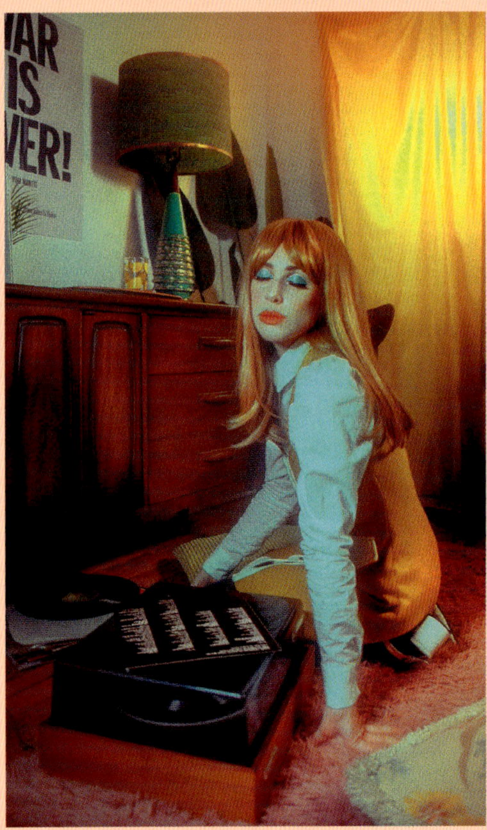

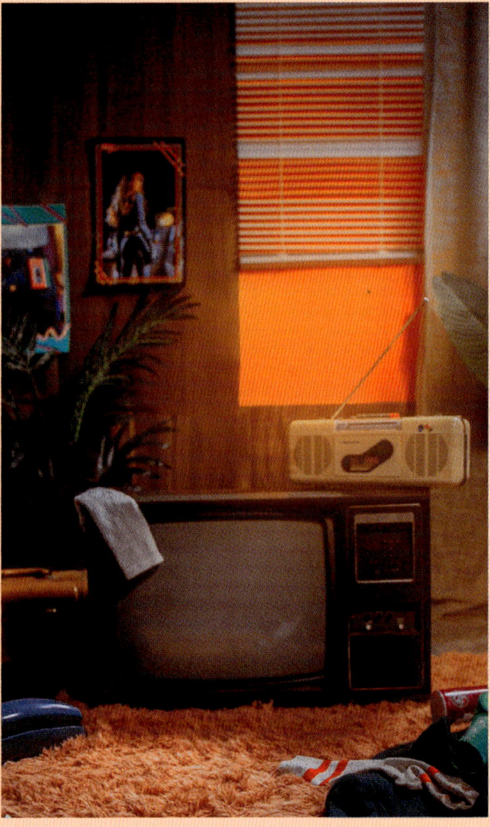

So what makes up an atmosphere? Well, it depends on what context you're referring to, but the main elements to keep in mind include the following:

Temperature: Should the space be warm or cold? Temperature goes hand in hand with the seasons, tones of light, and times of day.

Energy: The sun provides us with powerful energy that can radiate over your work. Energy can also be added to a piece through the depiction of movement.

Gases and dust: These particles exist in our atmosphere, generated from other sources. These elements are what can really shape a space. A messy person's home may be covered in dust, while an otherworldly scene could have strange visible gases in the air.

Playing with light to create a specific atmosphere:

Think of light as an element that exists on a scale ranging from warmness to coolness. We feel the presence of light more often than we may consciously realize. Warm light is like a sunset or a candle burning in a dark space. Cooler, more subdued light signifies darkness and the night.

Using color: Depending on what the weather is like or where light is shining onto or through, light can come in an array of various hues. To imbue light with specific colors, you can pick up lighting gels at photography stores or online. Alternatively, you can place colored cellophane over light sources to change the color they emit. You can even find fun-colored light bulbs to use.

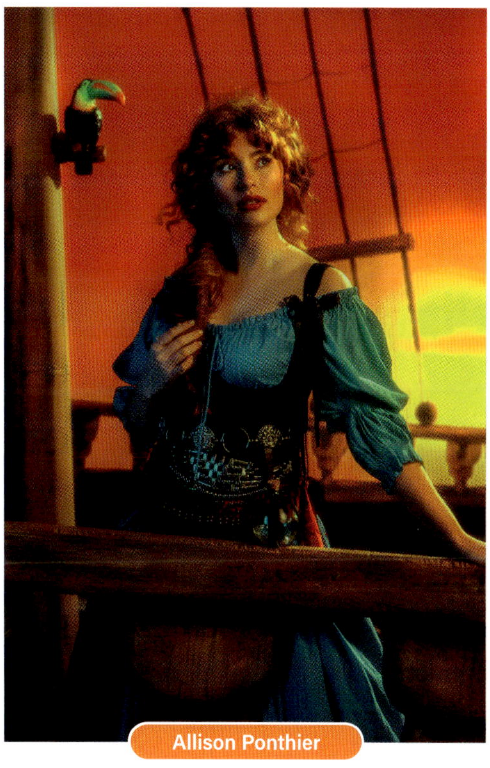

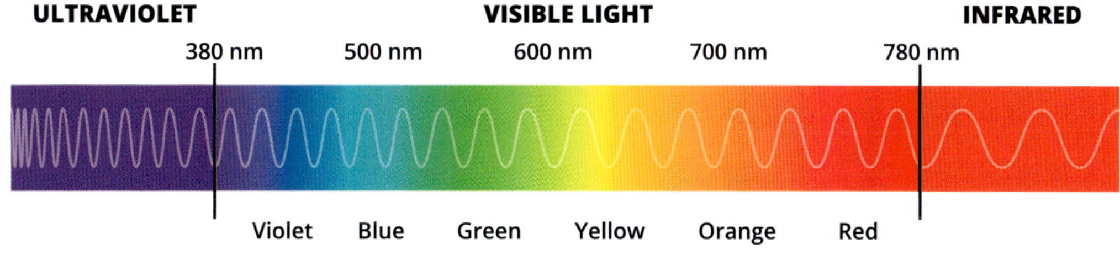

I often tend to throw orange gels over my directional light to play up the sunbeam look. If I want to play into a dark-blue night, I put blue gel over my lights. If I want to create the impression of a colored light or neon sign out of frame, I toss pink gel on a light to create superficial light sources.

Using cucoloris or "cookies": In theater and film, flat boards with cutouts of shapes are placed over lights to cast shadows. Imagine that you are looking through a window at night. The moon is lighting your face, but a tree blocks the path of light between you and the moon. A shadow of the leaves is then cast onto your face. Cookies create the same illusion, with a famous example being Batman's bat symbol.

Ambient/accent lighting: This is lighting that hardly gives off any actual light but adds dimension to a space. I find that accent lighting is an easy way to indicate a specific period of time. I also like how, under accent lighting, pieces of furniture let off a little sparkle for the eye. Whether you are redecorating or creating a scene, accent and ambient lighting are super helpful ways to tie a space together. Even though LED strips, lava lamps, candles, lanterns, and table lamps give off little to no light, they still shape a space's atmosphere.

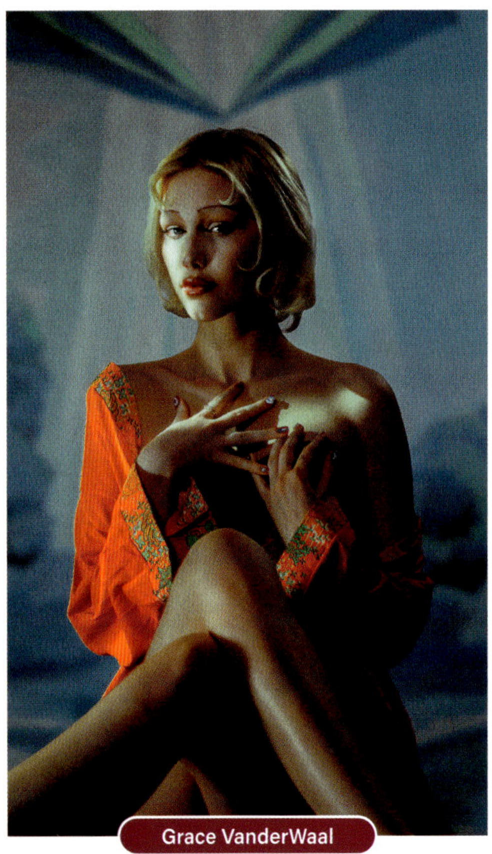

Grace VanderWaal

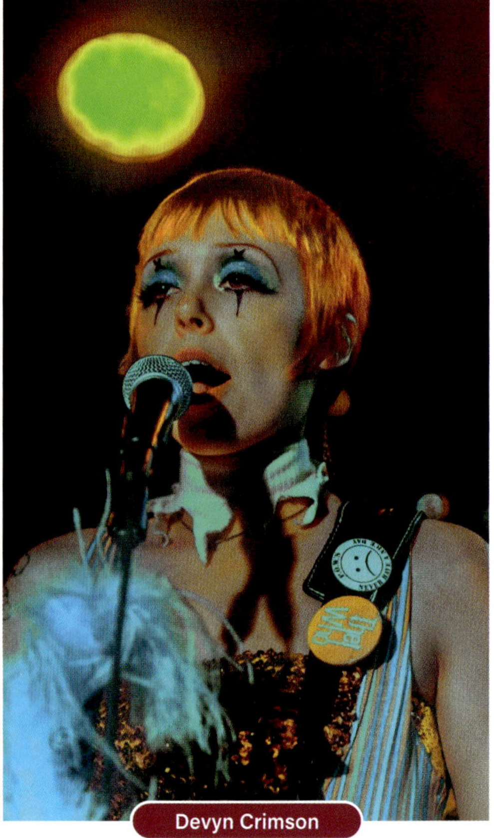

Devyn Crimson

Other tools to help create atmosphere:

Fog machines or **atmosphere spray** are extremely helpful tools to shape atmosphere. Fog machines can be found at party supply stores and can create a thick, hazy vibe. Atmosphere spray can be found at photography stores and is great to use with directional beams of light. Using atmosphere spray in the direction of a light beam can make it look as though the air is filled with dust, like in an old, dusty attic or basement.

Candles and **incense** add natural ambience to your space with smell and smoke.

Fans can really help create atmosphere by highlighting weather and outlining motion. Throw a fan into a space to get subtle movement from a subject's hair or a window curtain.

A **subject's appearance** can also be a good indication of a scene's air quality. If it is hot and humid, spray your subject's face with water or cover them in baby oil or Vaseline.

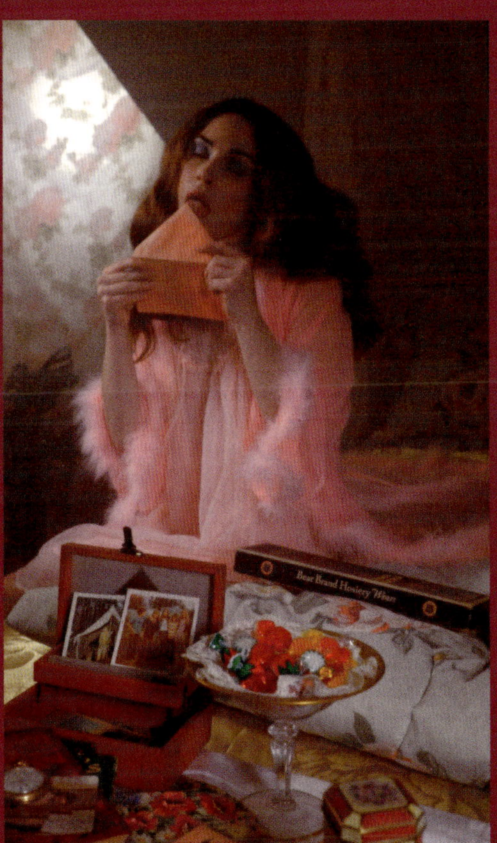

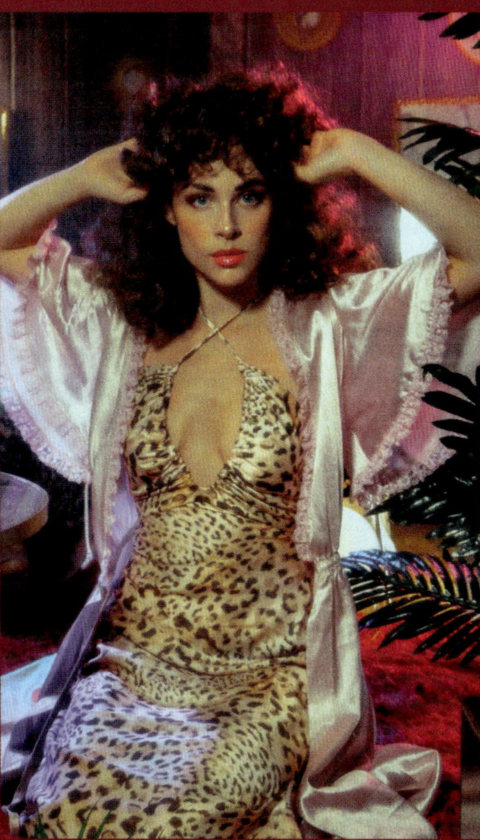

CREATING A SETTING

So how would I use all these tools to build a setting? Let me show you! But first, let's go over what a setting is. A setting is where the action takes place, acting as the landscape to your story (or life). A setting is a combination of three different things:

1. **Location:** *Where* the piece you're creating is happening. It can be a specific place, like a city or a castle, and can include geographic details.

2. **Time:** *When* the piece you're creating is happening. Time often impacts a setting's context. For instance, if the time period takes place in the past, the setting might include references to certain historical events.

3. **Environment:** *What* the piece you're creating looks and feels like overall. The environment is made up of the weather, architecture, nature, surroundings, and the people present. It includes the location's sensory details.

Thinking about all three of these elements when creating a setting will add extra depth to what you are trying to create. For example, when I made my video on the evolution of bedrooms across time, I didn't just stop at the design of the bedrooms themselves. For each decade, I also added various environmental and atmospheric elements to bring each room to life.

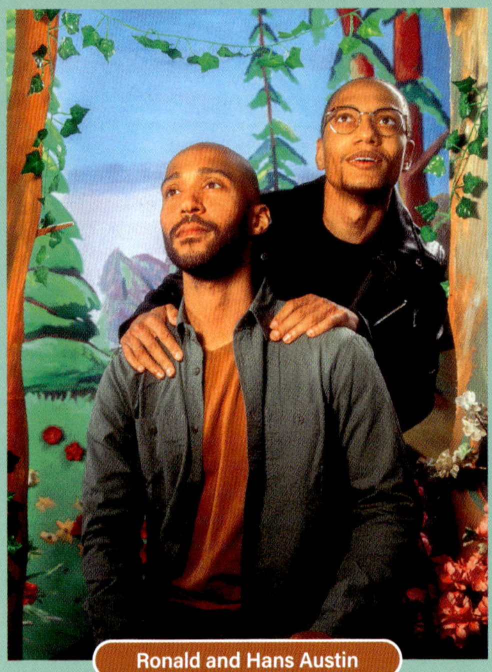

Ronald and Hans Austin

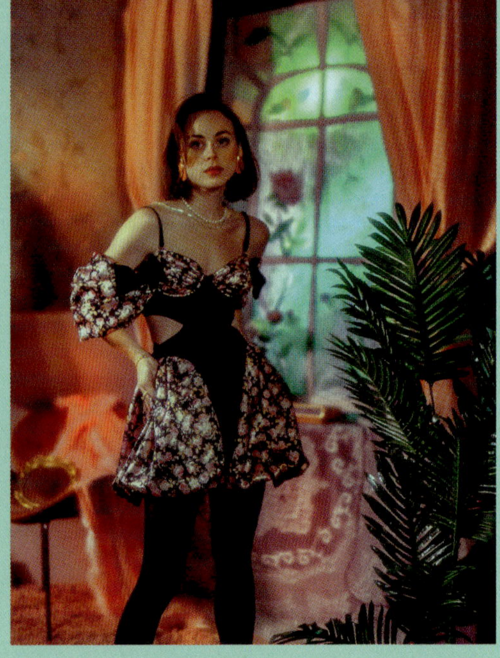

Building Blocks

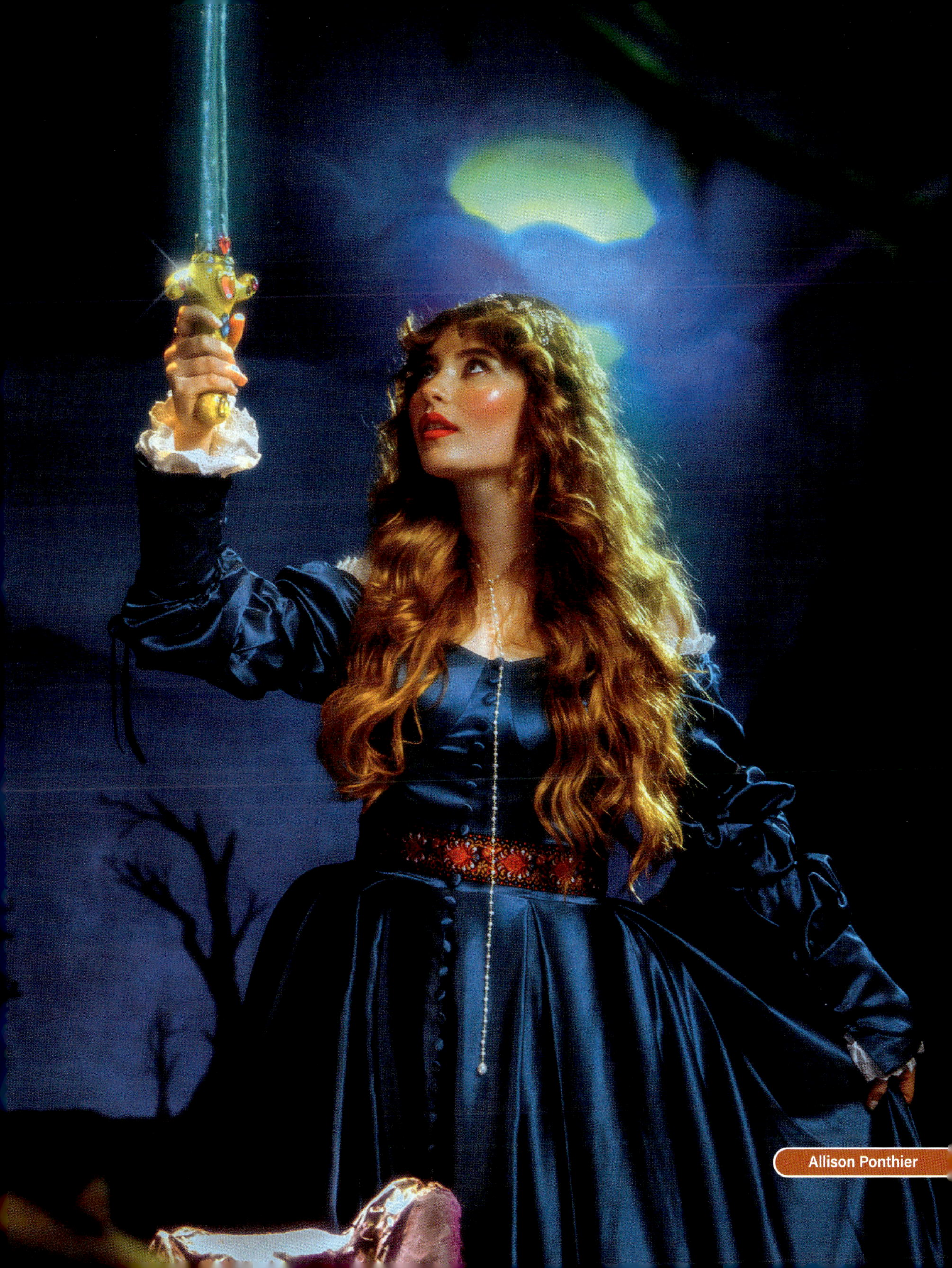
Allison Ponthier

BEDROOMS ACROSS TIME

For this project, I decided to keep the bedroom setting constant. The feature that changes throughout the video is time. But how do I bring my vision to life? While planning, I think about the time periods I want to include and the vibes that existed then. Next, I start figuring out who would live in each bedroom. What type of character are they? What do they like? What have they been doing? What time of day is it? These are the questions that help shape atmosphere.

The 1950s

Setting: A bedroom in the mid-1950s, midday, sunny spring, in a little suburb

Atmosphere: Soft light coming out of a window, very little ambient light because of the time of day. Overall look is cheerful, crisp, and colorful. Background sounds include ambient noises of rustling trees in the wind.

The 1960s

Setting: A bedroom in the mid-1960s, early evening, winter, in a little suburb

Atmosphere: Minimal light spilling in through the window, warm light coming from the lamps, giving a cozy atmosphere. Crisp air with some shadows mimic a room at night. The sounds include a suburban street and crickets chirping.

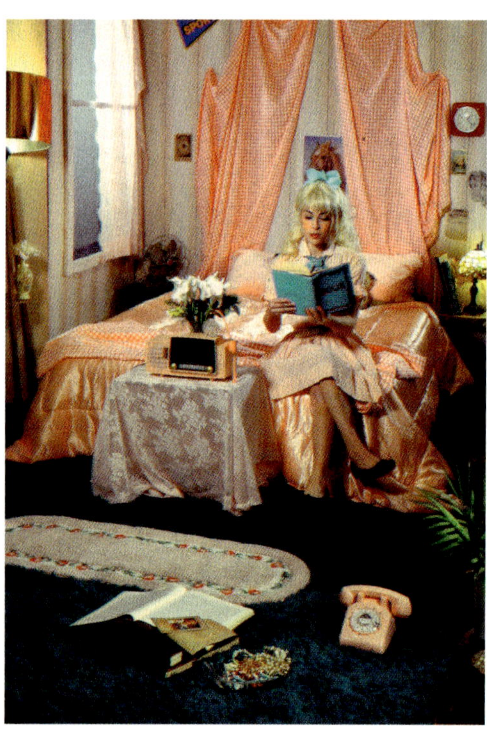

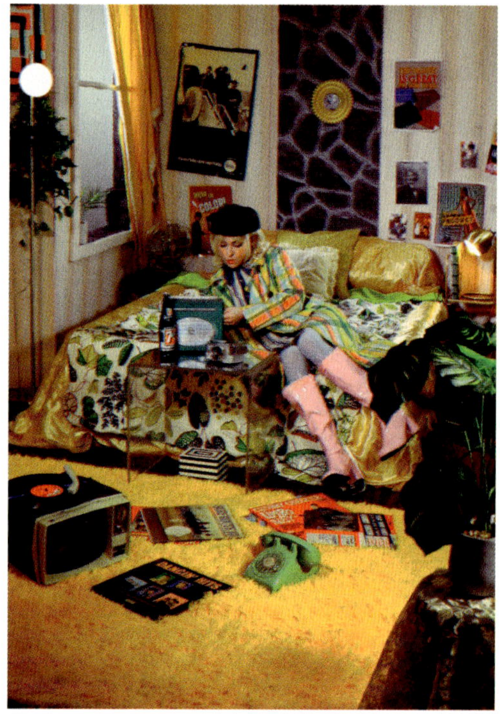

The 1970s

Setting: A bedroom in the late 1970s, late afternoon, muggy spring, in a little suburb

Atmosphere: That feeling of muted sunshine, budding florals, and mist. Warm light keeps the mist diffused, emulating the idea there might be rain clouds in the area. Since there are rain clouds, I add some ambient light to give off a warm glow. Applying a haze effect will also make the air seem thick with humidity and candle smoke. Overall, it looks ethereal. Sounds include the faint suburban ambience of light rain stopping and starting, with the occasional boom of thunder.

The 1980s

Setting: A bedroom in the mid-1980s, 7:00 p.m., dry summer, in a little suburb

Atmosphere: Sun low in the sky, but still light out. A soft pinkish glow comes from the window. The air is thick from all the hairspray that the woman has used in her hair. The last hours of natural light dance into the room. One lamp is switched on to add some warmth and to show that it is in fact getting darker out. A neon light hanging on the wall adds some colorful light to the room. Sounds include music playing from a boombox and the laughter of kids laughing outside.

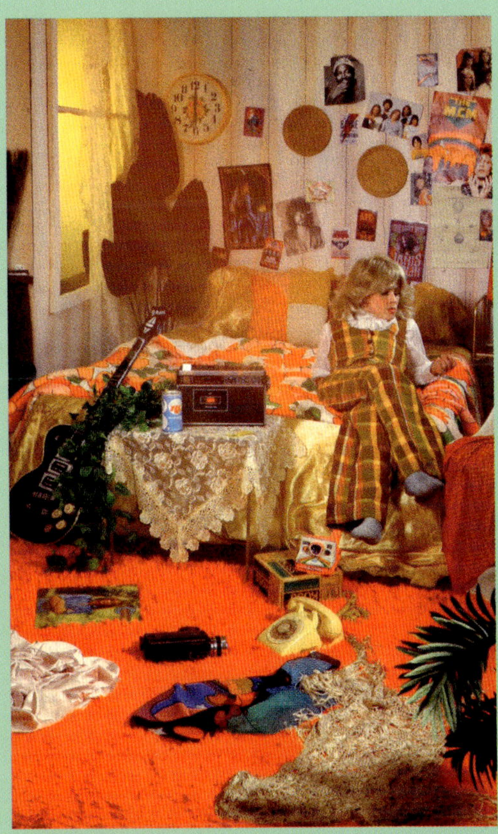

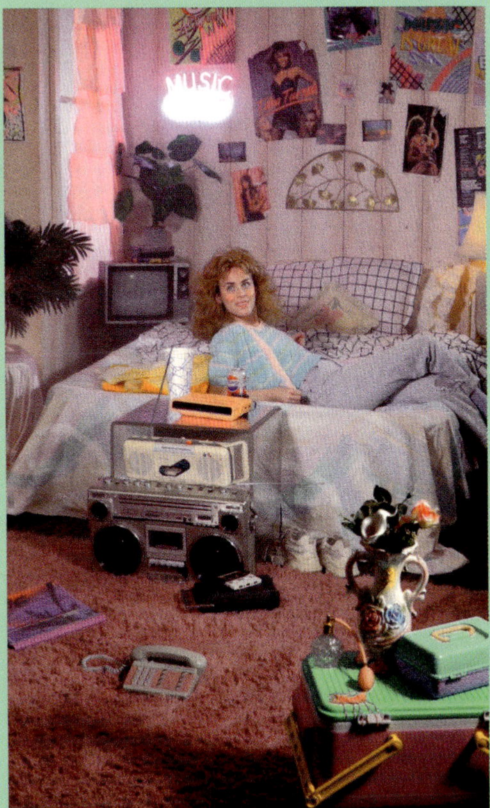

The 1990s

Setting: A bedroom in the mid-1990s, late night, crisp fall, in a little suburb

Atmosphere: Sun has already set, no light coming through the window, only darkness shows. Since it is close to winter, the interior lights have been turned on to add some warmth and to keep the space illuminated. Simple overhead lighting helps create some subtle shadows. Background sounds include cars driving by outside and the hum of a girl singing as she listens to one of her favorite new songs.

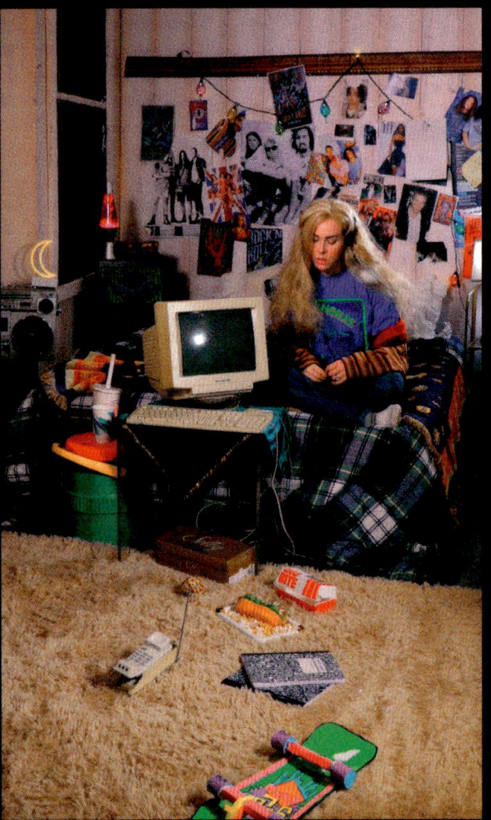

The 2000s

Setting: A bedroom in the early 2000s, after dinnertime, early summer, in a little suburb

Atmosphere: Warm light coming from a colorful floor lamp with multiple bulbs. The window is closed and the curtains are drawn since it's getting dark outside. Shadows show up due to where the lightbulbs spread their glow, with the plastic lamp shades creating light that varies slightly in color and tone. Sounds include the television playing a comedic laugh track from a sitcom downstairs, as well as the faint sound of wind rustling outside.

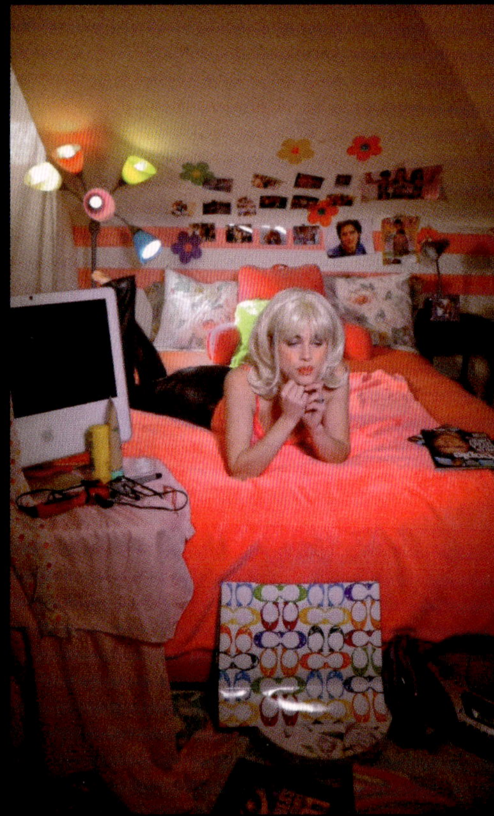

The 2010s

Setting: A bedroom in the early 2010s, daytime, summer, in the city

Atmosphere: Natural light spilling in from the window through a sheer curtain, with a few strings of lights glowing that are hung on the walls. The character is looking at a cell phone to give the viewer a clue that we are in the modern era. The subject is well lit, most likely from an overhead light. The overall vibe is an industrial technological age with a hint of glitz. The sounds we observe are the beeps of the cell phone and the soft sounds of a lively downtown outside the window.

The 2020s

Setting: A bedroom in the early 2020s, midafternoon, spring, in the city

Atmosphere: A few funky accent lights add a fun flair that feels almost organic. The bright lights mimic the look of a bright sunny day where we can imagine birds chirping outside the window. A soft haze effect circulates the room to give an almost dreamlike vibe that matches what it feels like to be living with the constant presence of social media. The sounds outside are buzzing bees, people passing by on the sidewalk, and the sound of the earth reawakening after winter.

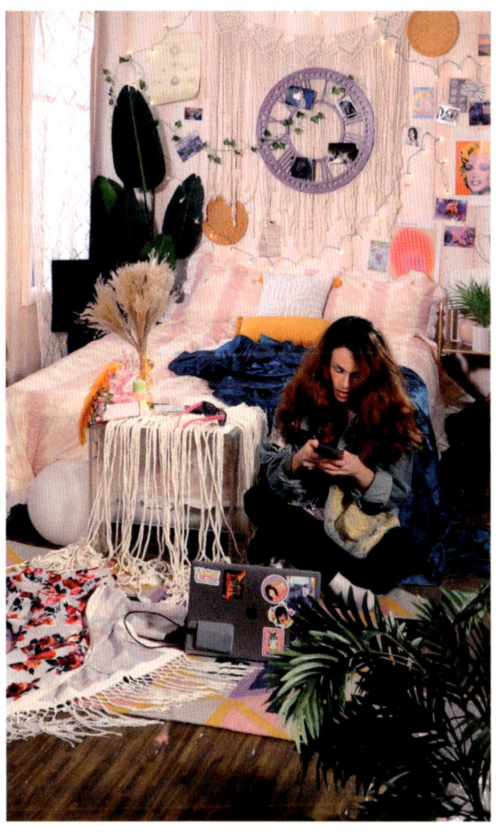

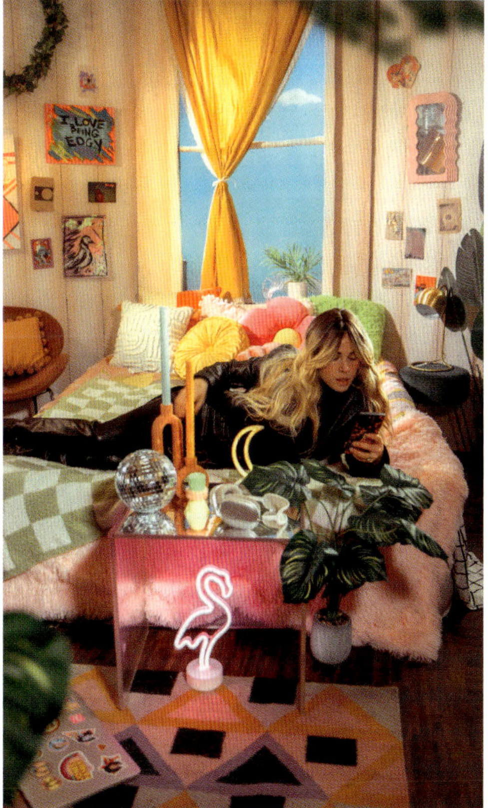

SETTING, ATMOSPHERE & TIME ACROSS DISCIPLINES

For art: *Setting:* Try thinking of places either you or your character like. Sometimes it is also fun to think of an environment and then reverse engineer it to create a narrative or theme that supports it. *Atmosphere:* Avoid limiting the atmosphere to lighting elements. I always like to ask myself, "Is it a rainy afternoon or is it a sunny afternoon?" Think about the air and how it feels. *Time:* Consider what periods you are drawn to and if you have a favorite time of day.

For interior design: *Setting:* Just because the space you're decorating is in a specific location doesn't mean it has to reflect that place. Think about where you like to spend your time. *Atmosphere:* When designing, I like to think about what I want the air to feel and look like. You can shape the air with candles and lighting for softer ambience. *Time:* Furniture styles usually have a time period attached to them, so you can select your furniture first if you don't want to start with a time period.

ALLISON CRAIG

Illustrator

Animation is a medium of motion. A series of twenty-four drawings are put in a timed sequence to form one second of life, brimming with kinetic energy. We all think of our favorite animated characters and what they do, but sometimes it's their surroundings that tell their stories best.

Setting can make all the difference with how well characters' emotions come across. A desolate city street at night can express a character's loneliness. A storm can enhance the chaos of a dramatic chase scene. Even changing the overall color tone to red can exaggerate anger.

I was once leading a team on an episode of a kids' cartoon in which two best friends start out on a sunny vacation but by the end are fighting an evil force. At the final stage of production, we realized the two besties were fighting evil in a bright, beautiful setting. The emotion of the sequence was completely muddled! We quickly got our painters on the task and fixed the atmosphere to be dark and broody, then recomposited the assets. Like magic, the battle felt epic and perilous.

Take all the potential elements of weather, location, and atmosphere at your disposal and pair them with your character's actions. The setting is no longer static, but is a piece of the moving picture. It builds the framework for the emotions of your characters. This is what makes an engaging piece of animation.

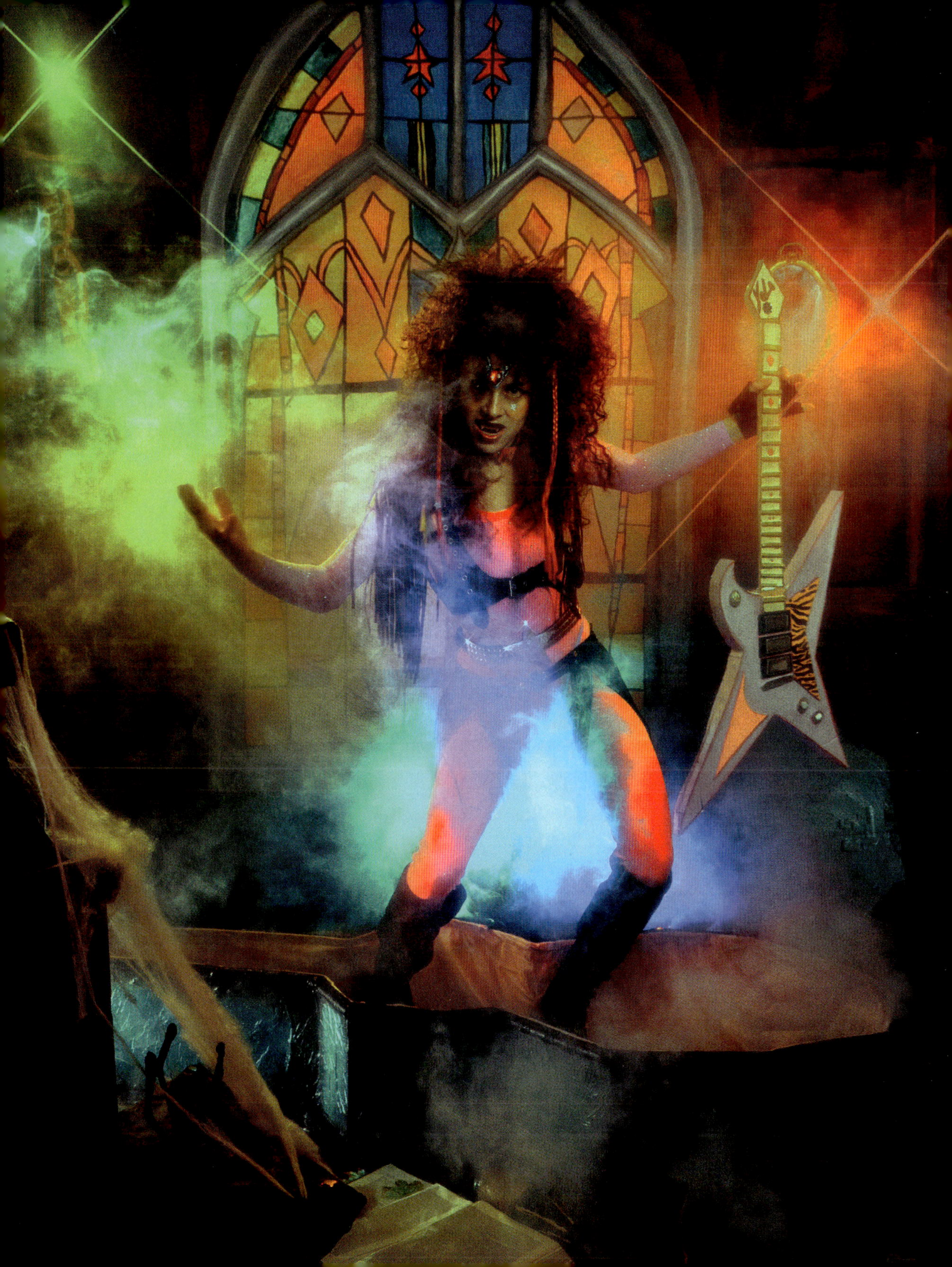

CHOOSE YOUR OWN SETTING ADVENTURE

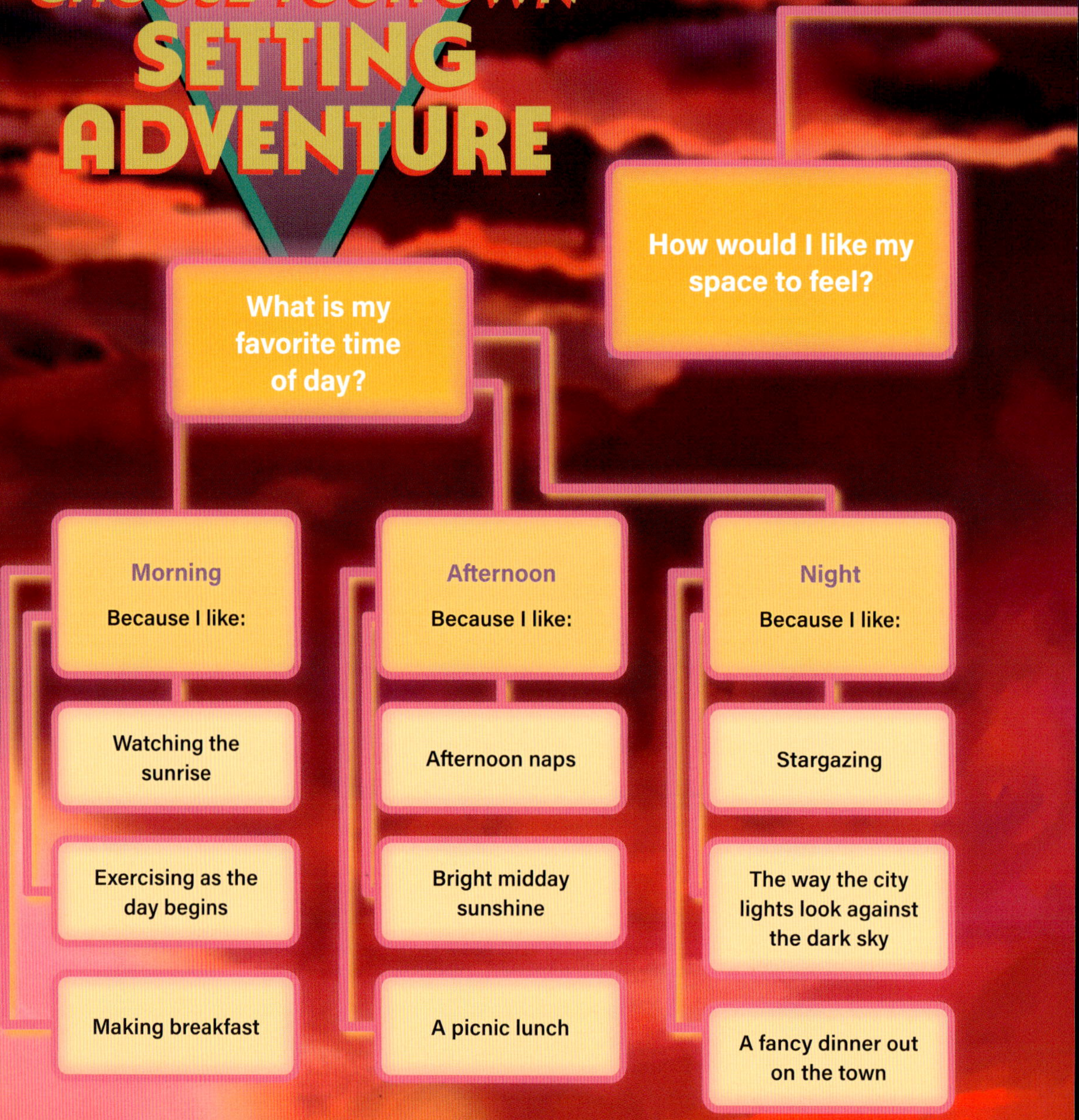

What is my favorite time of day?

How would I like my space to feel?

Morning

Because I like:

Watching the sunrise

Exercising as the day begins

Making breakfast

Afternoon

Because I like:

Afternoon naps

Bright midday sunshine

A picnic lunch

Night

Because I like:

Stargazing

The way the city lights look against the dark sky

A fancy dinner out on the town

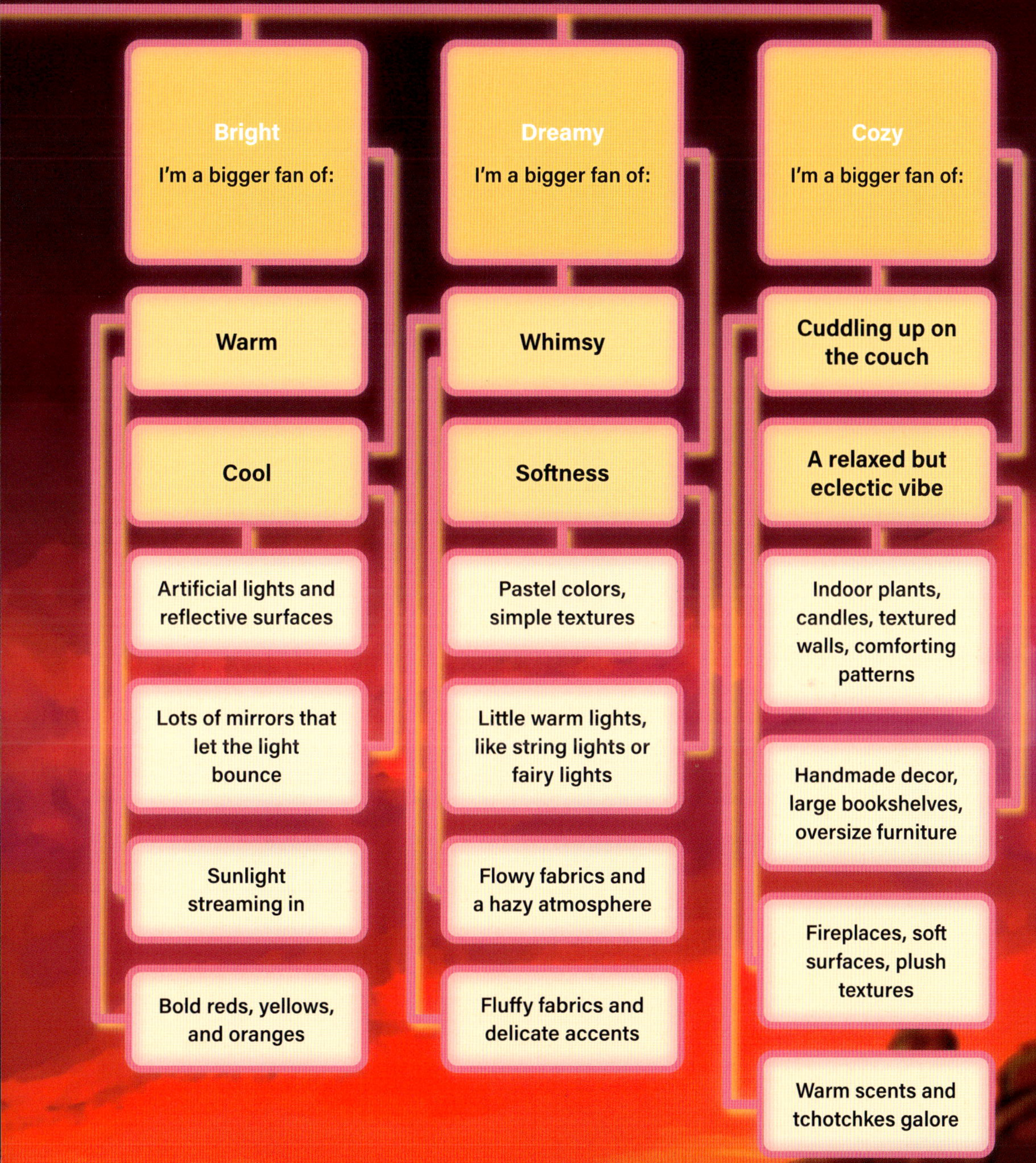

Bright

I'm a bigger fan of:

- Warm
- Cool
- Artificial lights and reflective surfaces
- Lots of mirrors that let the light bounce
- Sunlight streaming in
- Bold reds, yellows, and oranges

Dreamy

I'm a bigger fan of:

- Whimsy
- Softness
- Pastel colors, simple textures
- Little warm lights, like string lights or fairy lights
- Flowy fabrics and a hazy atmosphere
- Fluffy fabrics and delicate accents

Cozy

I'm a bigger fan of:

- Cuddling up on the couch
- A relaxed but eclectic vibe
- Indoor plants, candles, textured walls, comforting patterns
- Handmade decor, large bookshelves, oversize furniture
- Fireplaces, soft surfaces, plush textures
- Warm scents and tchotchkes galore

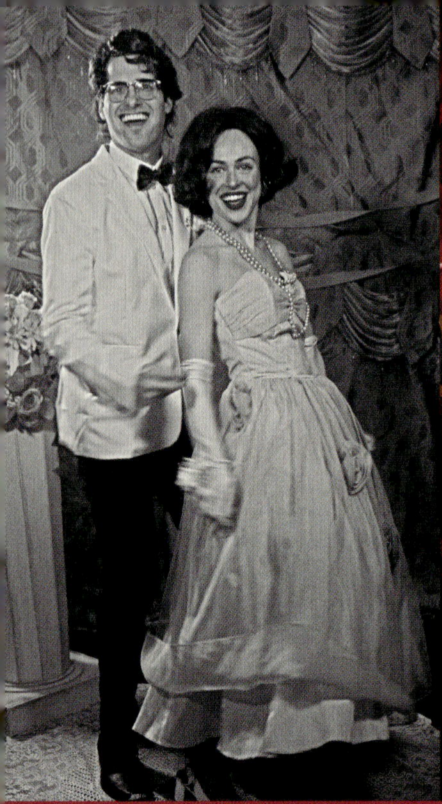

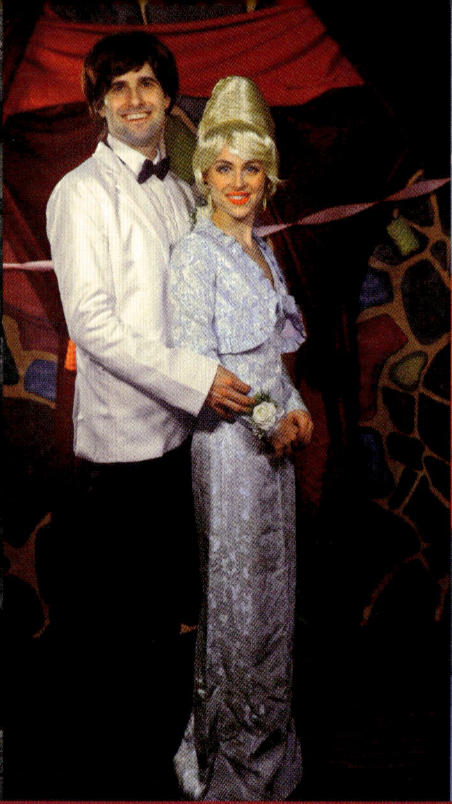

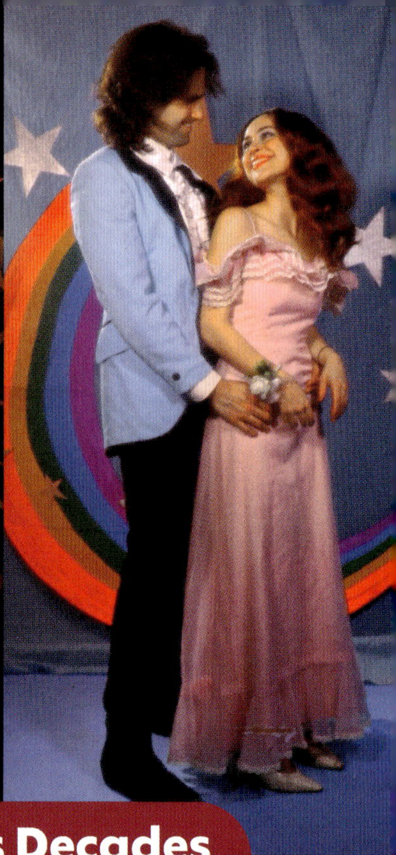

Prom & Wedding Couples Across Decades

(Me and Talor)

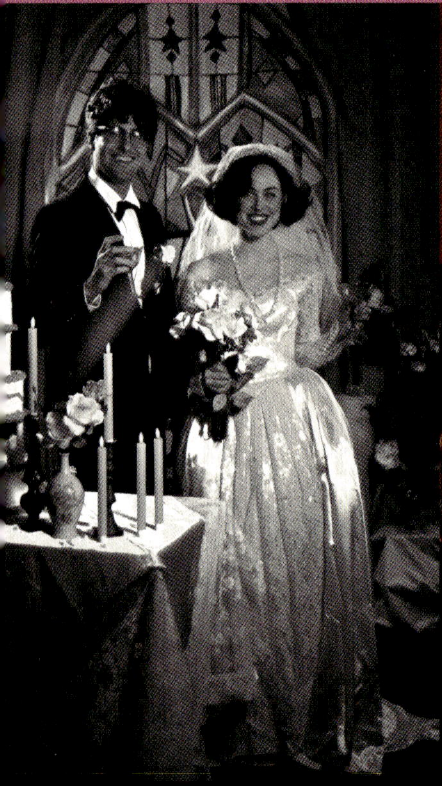

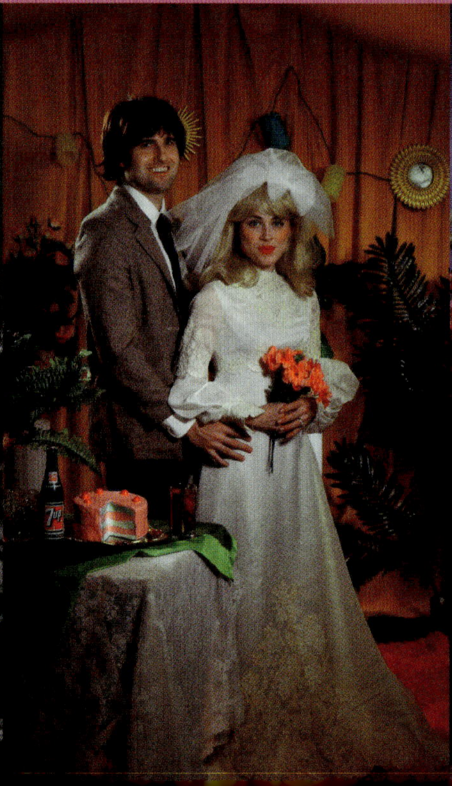

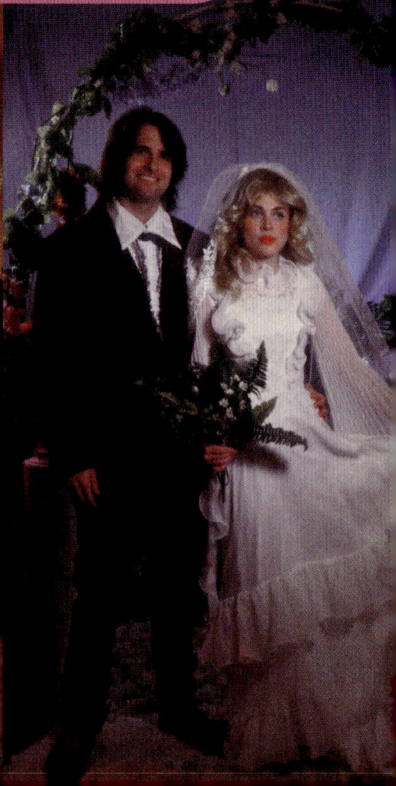

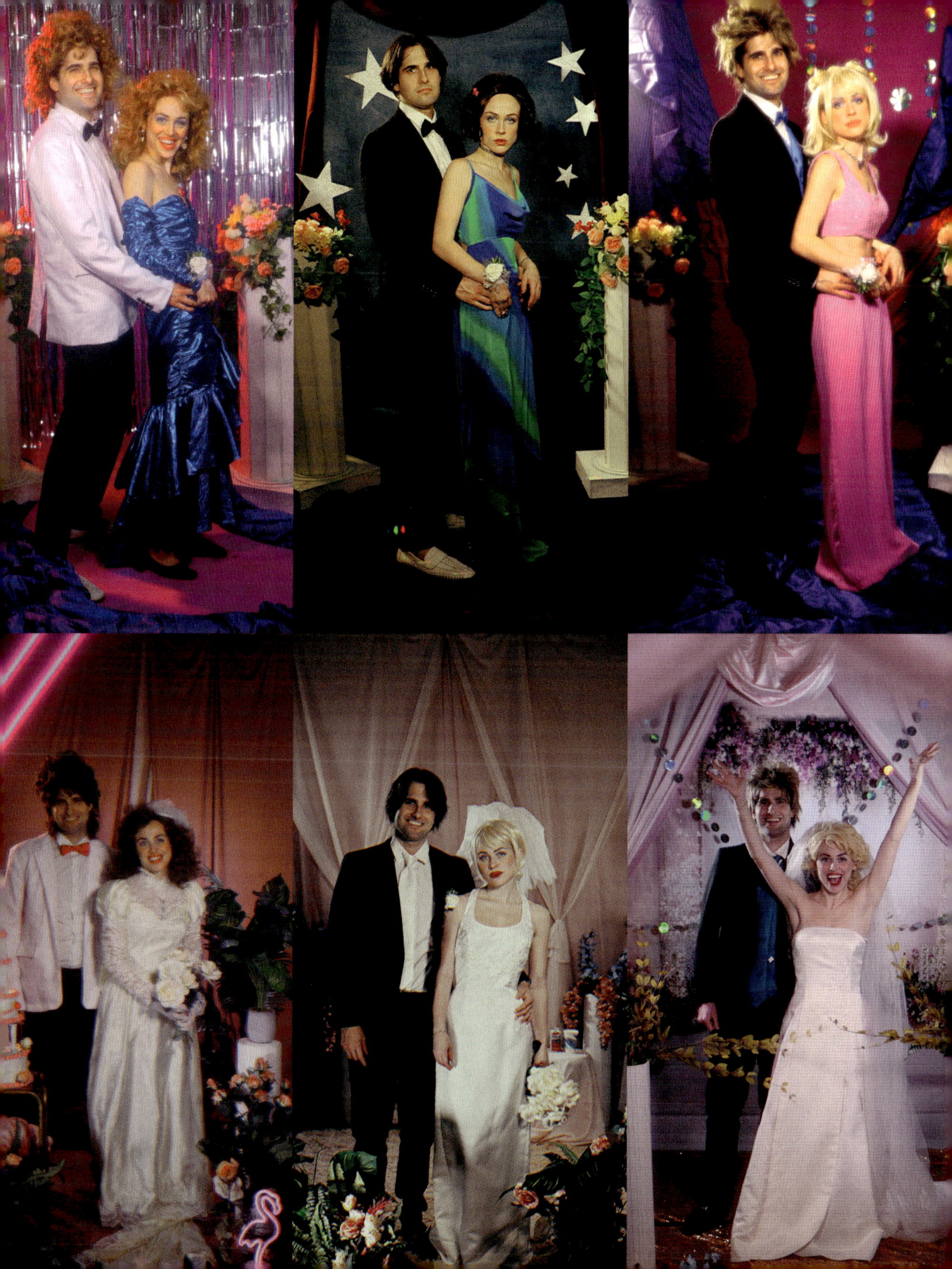

SETTING, ATMOSPHERE & TIME EXERCISES

> Think of an environment that you like. If you are unsure, you can always refer to your list from Chapter One. What kind of environment would work well to depict some of the things on your list in a cohesive piece? Once you've decided on an environment, try to create a story that will take place there.

> If you're filming something or taking photographs, find a corner of your living space and build a little set to capture videos or stills in. What is the time, setting, and atmosphere of the environment you've created?

> If you need to create an environment for a painting, drawing, sculpture, or other medium, think about what you want the piece's story to be. Try using atmospheric elements to uncover who your character is, if one factors into your creation.

Now, let's have you try adding your own unique vision and details to specific settings. Below, I've provided an example, starting with the setting, thinking of the time, and then building out the atmosphere around the first two points.

Example:

Desert at sunset

Time: 8:45 p.m., the height of summer, 1974

Atmospheric elements: dust clouds that make the air seem thick, light dry wind, beams of light peeking through the horizon

---

NOW YOU TRY!

Spooky forest

Time:

Atmospheric elements:

Sunny beach

Time:

Atmospheric elements:

Fancy candlelit restaurant

Time:

Atmospheric elements:

Spaceship cockpit

Time:

Atmospheric elements:

<table>
<tr><td>

Mountains at night

Time:

Atmospheric elements:

</td><td>

Apartment in a crowded city

Time:

Atmospheric elements:

</td></tr>
<tr><td>

Countryside in the morning

Time:

Atmospheric elements:

</td><td>

Suburban street in the fall

Time:

Atmospheric elements:

</td></tr>
</table>

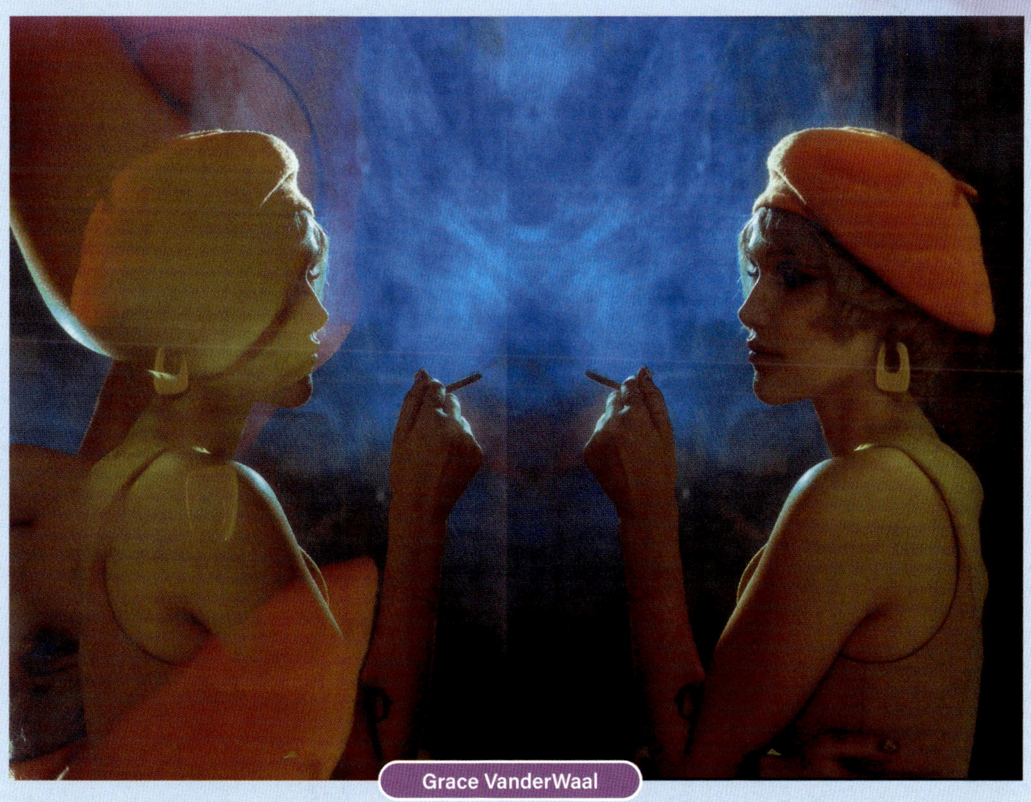

Grace VanderWaal

QUESTIONS TO CONSIDER

> What kind of settings do you envision for your creative works? What about these specific settings can help bring your projects to life?

> Do you like setting most of your pieces in interior or exterior settings? If you prefer one more than the other, why do you think that is?

> What time of day do you feel the most like yourself? Do you feel more alive in the sunshine or in the dark of night?

> When you imagine your perfect day, what is the weather like outside?

> What time periods are you drawn to? What do you find to be the most fascinating decade, and why?

> Do you consider yourself someone who is fond of nostalgia? How do you intend to incorporate nostalgic elements into your work?

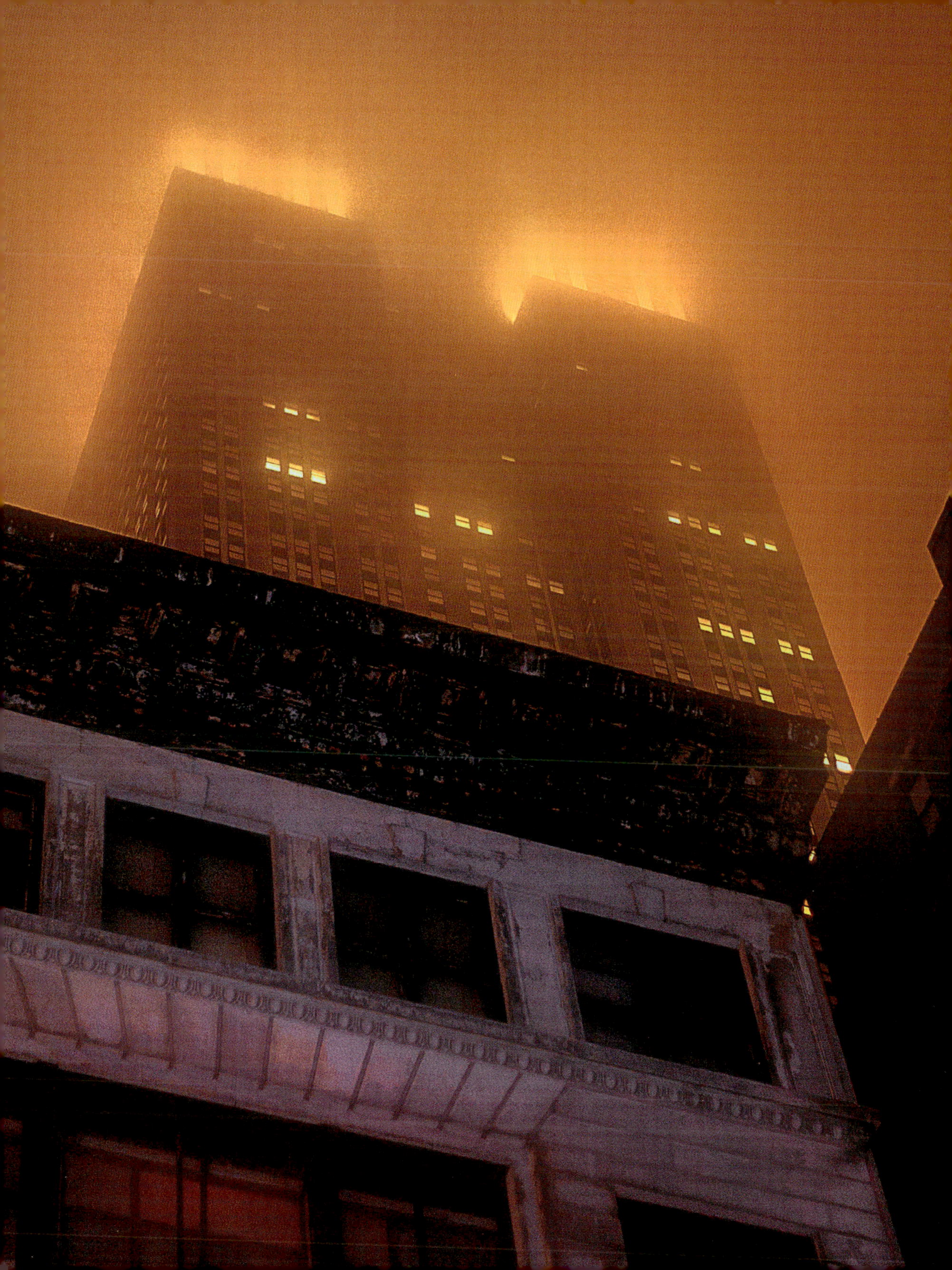

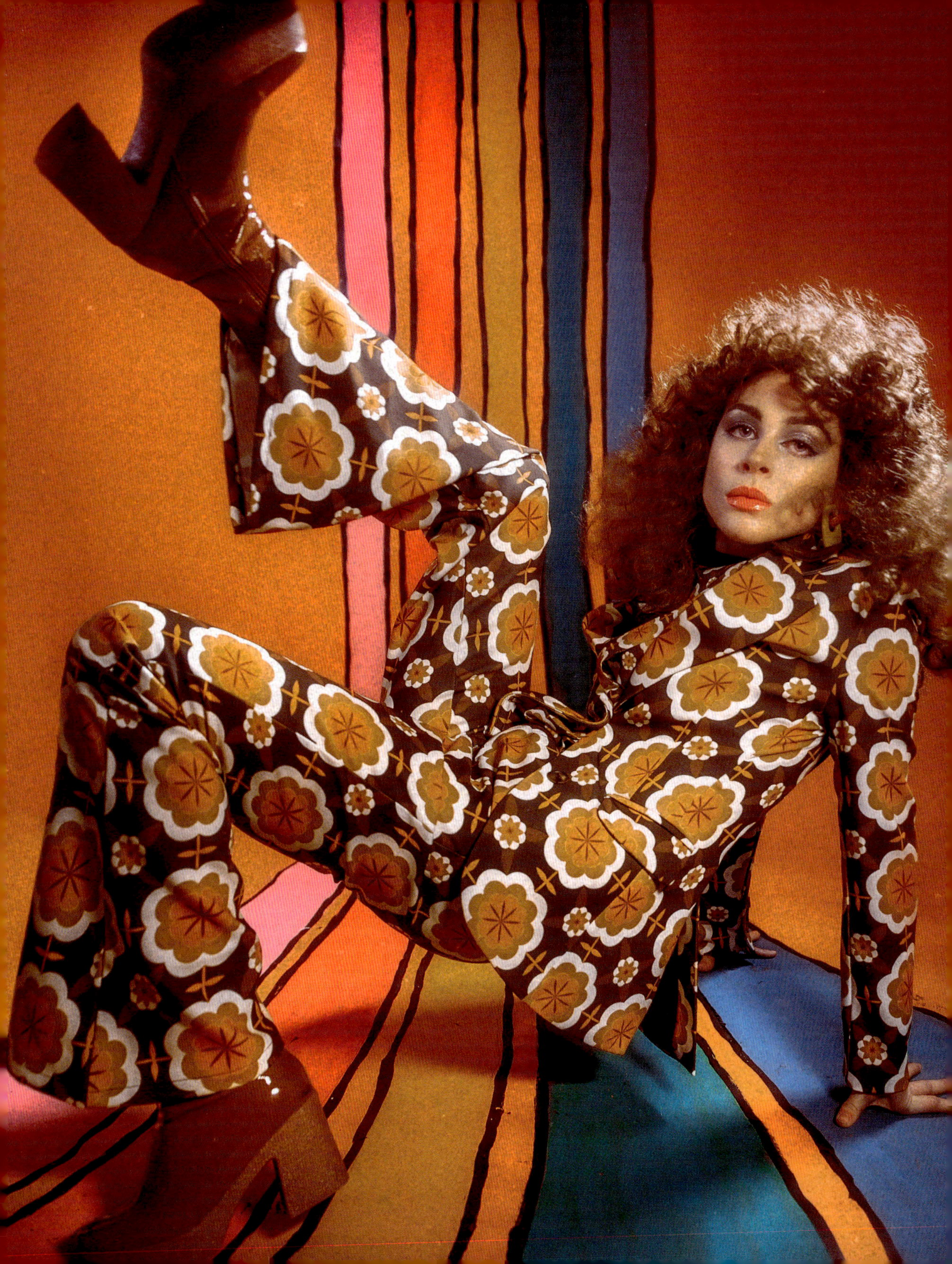

PART III

VIBING OUT

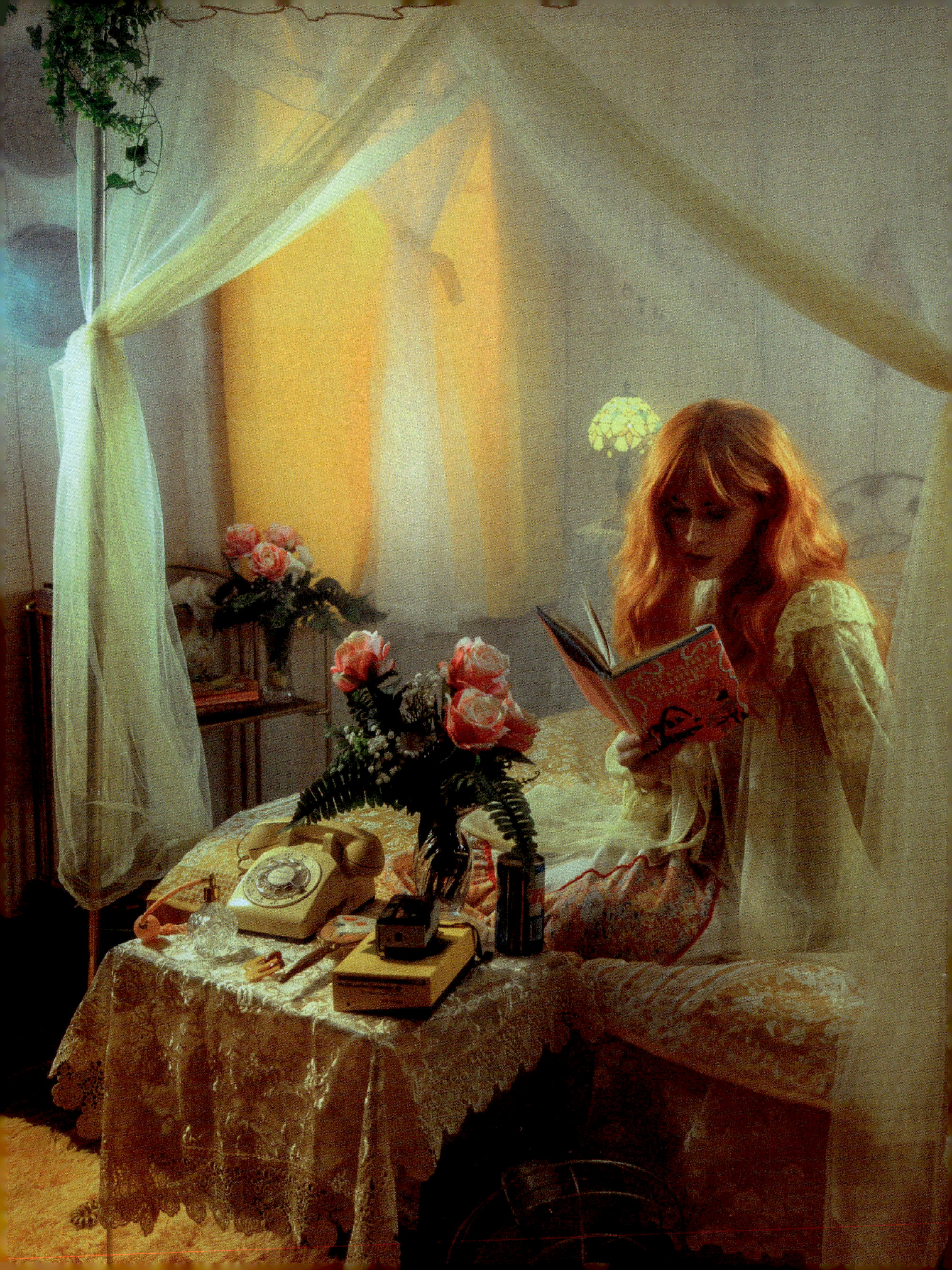

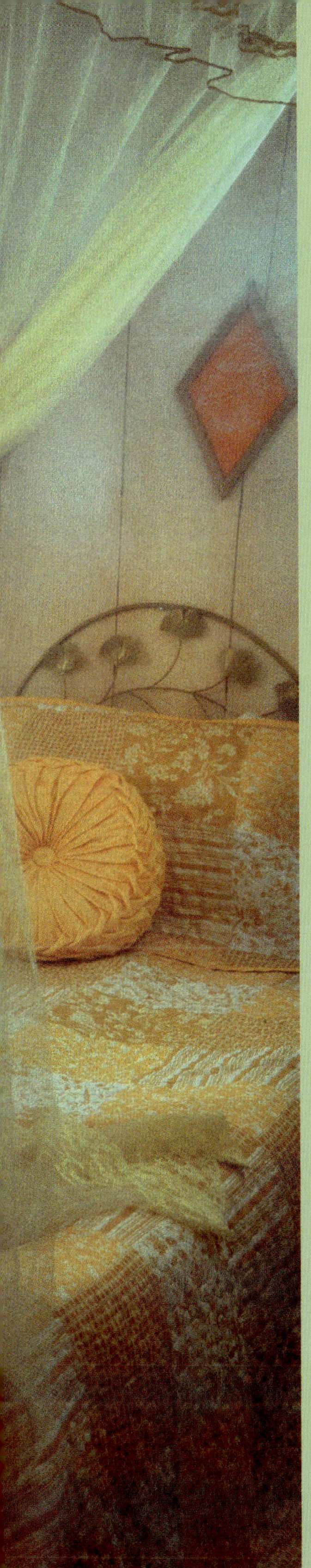

CHAPTER SEVEN

TEXTURES, PATTERNS & STYLES

THE ELEMENTS OF DESIGN

Whether you're creating something for your house or your art or simply putting an outfit together, textures, patterns, and styles will add dimension to your work. Not only do textures and patterns make things more interesting to look at, they also add to the story you're telling by placing features in context. Adding a specific texture, pattern, or style to your design also brings in certain historical and geographical associations. This can help spark intrigue for people—encouraging them to realize the perspective behind your work and fortifying the narrative you wish to communicate through your art.

Everything we create is derived from a different style movement. Every pattern and texture has a place in history, and everyone borrows inspiration from what has come before. I highly suggest you do the same. Let's create something new by pulling stylistic pattern-and-texture elements together in a way that speaks to your personal aesthetic.

ADDING TO YOUR FOUNDATION

Creating a design or artistic composition is like fitting puzzle pieces together—you start with one focal piece and then build around it. This can help take away the pressure of following a curated idea. Instead, you get to experience something new by building out one part at a time. As you get started, be sure to consider how you will find the right balance, negative space, and contrast in your design.

Balance: When designing a space (whether it's in real life or on paper/canvas), balance refers to arranging furniture, colors, and decorative elements in a way that makes the space feel stable and comfortable. There are two types of balance to consider: asymmetrical and symmetrical.

Negative space: Think of this as the breathing room in a physical space you're designing or a piece of art you're making. This space is absent of textures, patterns, and styles. Using negative space can help make certain things stand out more or help with the overall balance of a design.

Contrast: Using different colors and textures helps create a strong emphasis that leads to eye-catching design. Pairing dissimilar elements can have a positive impact on the overall look and feel of a space or piece of art. You can pair contrasting elements in size, color, texture, and shape to help draw a viewer's eye in. Contrast often creates another level of focus. Different textures paired together add a unique experience that play with our senses in an exciting way—adding another level of depth that you won't have otherwise!

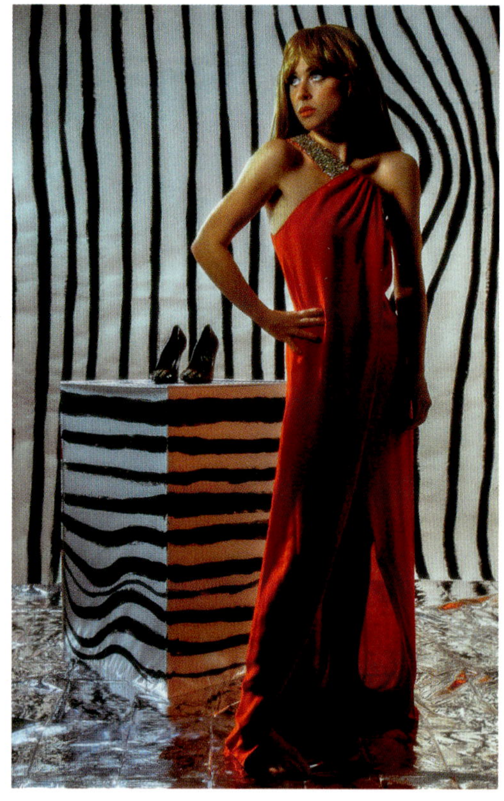

When beginning a new design, you should have at least one item that you want to start with. Once you've identified this item, think about what else it could be paired with. Analyze the item's texture, pattern, and style. What do you associate with these elements you've identified? Thinking about this primary item's design components will allow you to come up with ideas on how to build and create your new space or artwork.

Let's take a look at how this works . . .

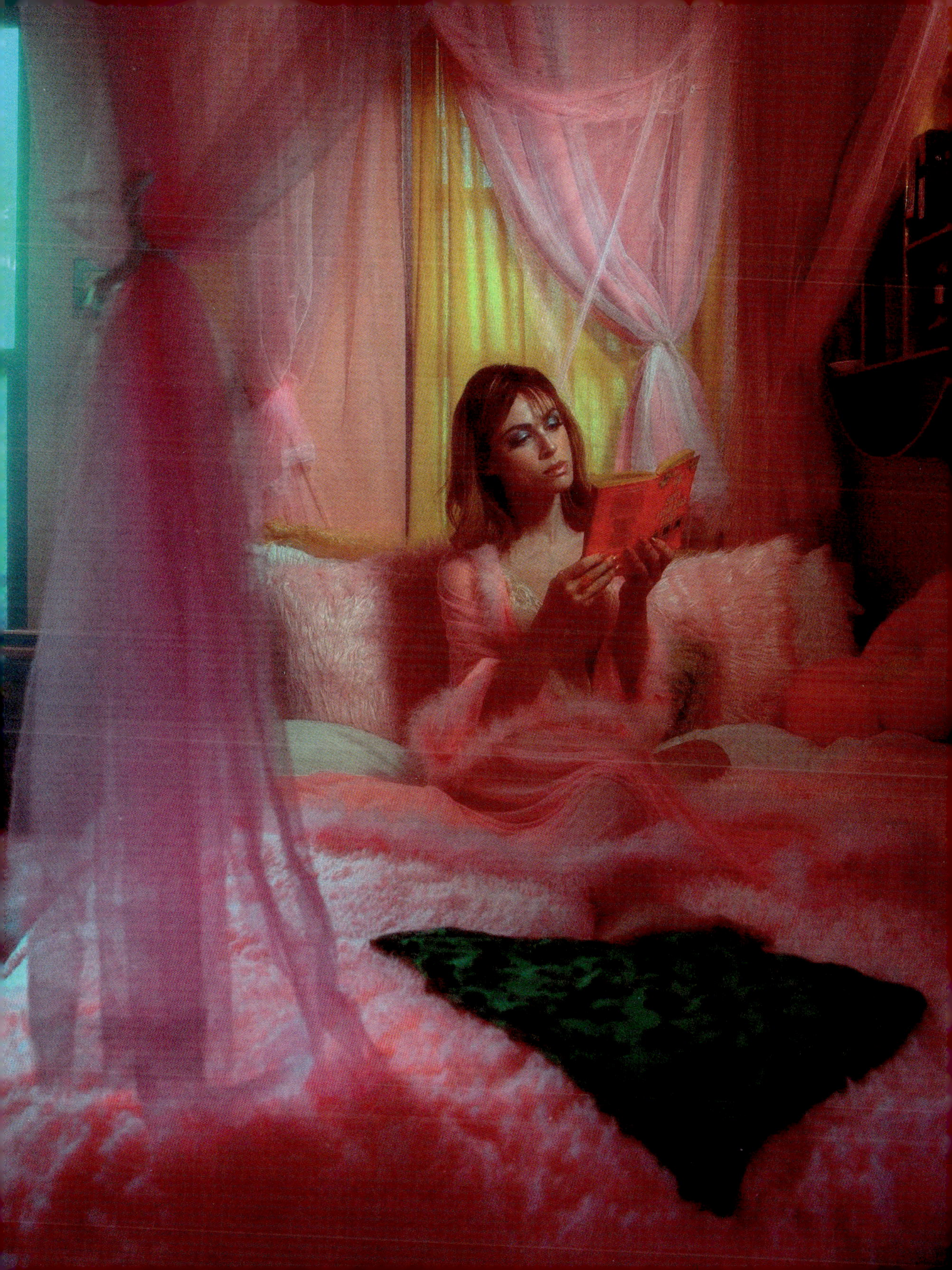

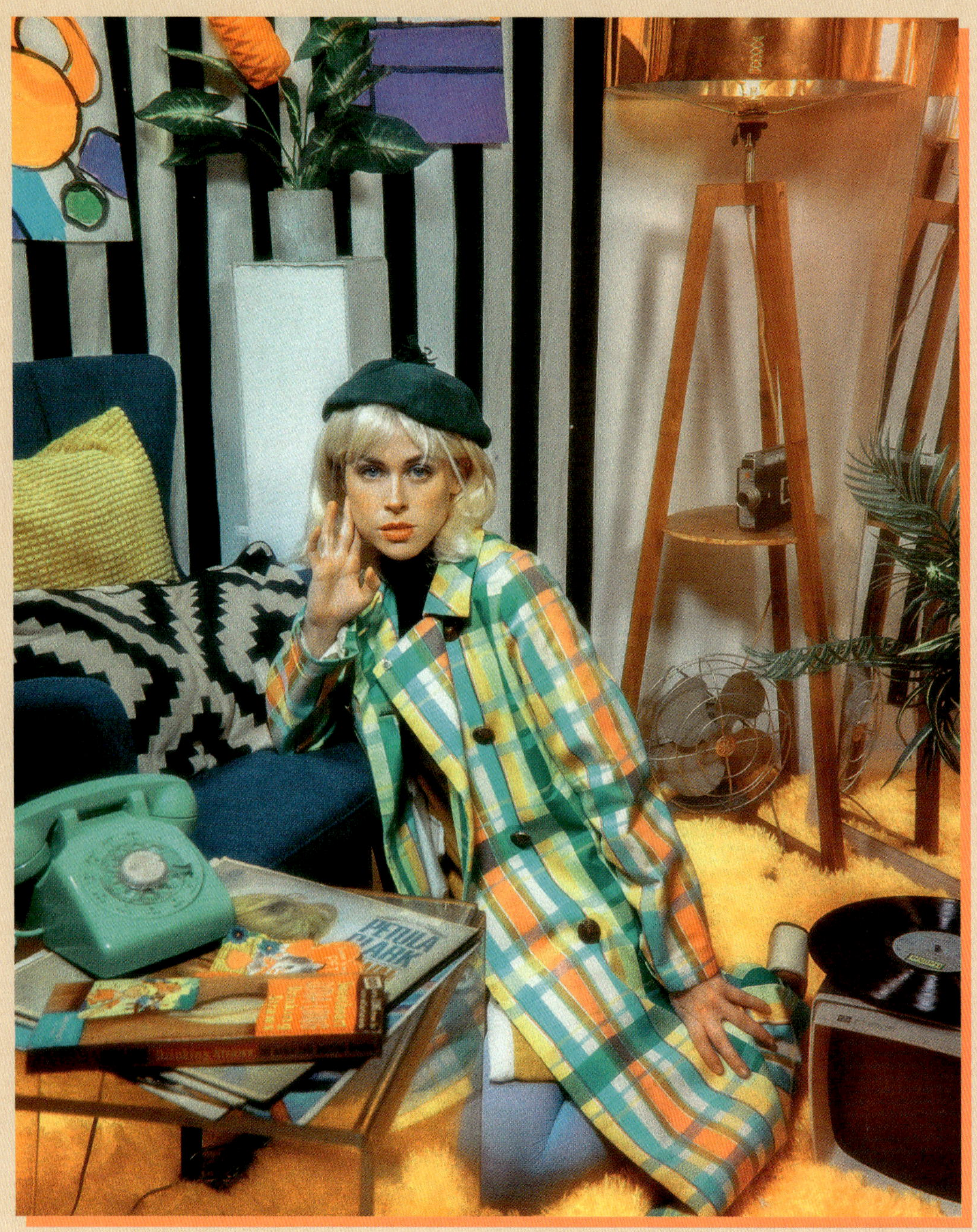

I've identified my curtains as my main item:
(i) my curtains are very geometric, (ii) they are pastel, (iii) the design of the curtains is Art Deco, and (iv) both the pattern and color feel very '80s.

The '80s was a time of Art Deco resurgence. The Art Deco movement was founded in the 1920s. Yet in the 1980s, people copied all the curvatures and angles of the style, then filtered it through pastels to make it into something new. The '80s Art Deco style implements arched angles and often showcases gold accents, but I don't just want an '80s-themed apartment. Instead, I want to create a new style for myself by combining what I like from others.

I can use things in the style of the '80s and Art Deco—and things from late '70s disco too—that are closely related to my curtains in terms of the shapes and materials. The curtains are loud and geometric, so I know I want to keep the harshness and the drama to a minimum (unless I want to go for a whole eclectic maximalist vibe). Furthermore, since the curtains have yellow, pink, and white elements, I can add gold as a complementary color. It's all about balance.

While color tends to be more connected with emotions, textures and patterns are more sensory. The textures and patterns you choose can tell a story, so it's always important to be deliberate when choosing what to add to your space. If I were to design a sleek room with a dark color palette and fill it with stone and metal furniture, you'd get a pretty good idea of the type of person I am. This setting would probably remind you of a classic movie villain who's plotting something devious. It might also indicate that I'm intense and moody. And what

if I dressed the space with wooden walls and flannel textures? It might indicate I'm into nature, invoking a warm, cozy, and simple cabin atmosphere. I might choose to utilize resources around me and care less about material items. What about a polka-dot-and-lace room? What are these materials telling someone about me? Maybe I'm into kind, soft, and romantic vintage styles?

Remember, you can always pair opposite things to create a unique vibe. Let's use fashion as an example. You start with one piece you know you want to wear; maybe it's a white button-down shirt—preppy or business casual, signaling a sort of refinement. Say you decide to pair that white shirt with a leather jacket—this turns the outfit into something edgy, something you see worn by people who ride motorcycles. A leather jacket is an article of clothing that announces boldness. When you pair these two contrasting elements of style together, you craft a more complex storyline: you've created a character who works a boring office job by day and rides a Harley by night.

When you're thinking about textures, patterns, and styles, it's a good time to revisit the aesthetic list you created in Chapter One. On my list, I have big, puffy sleeves, princess dresses, King Henry VIII, the Renaissance, and David Bowie. I'm able to create my own aesthetic by combining a lot of the elements from my list's items, and you can too!

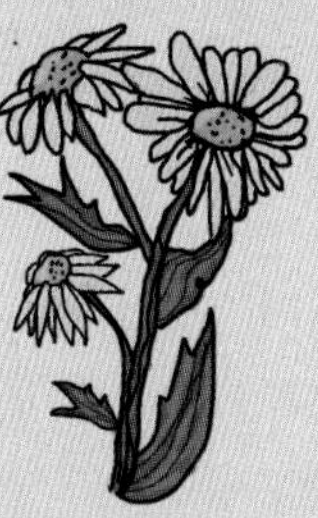

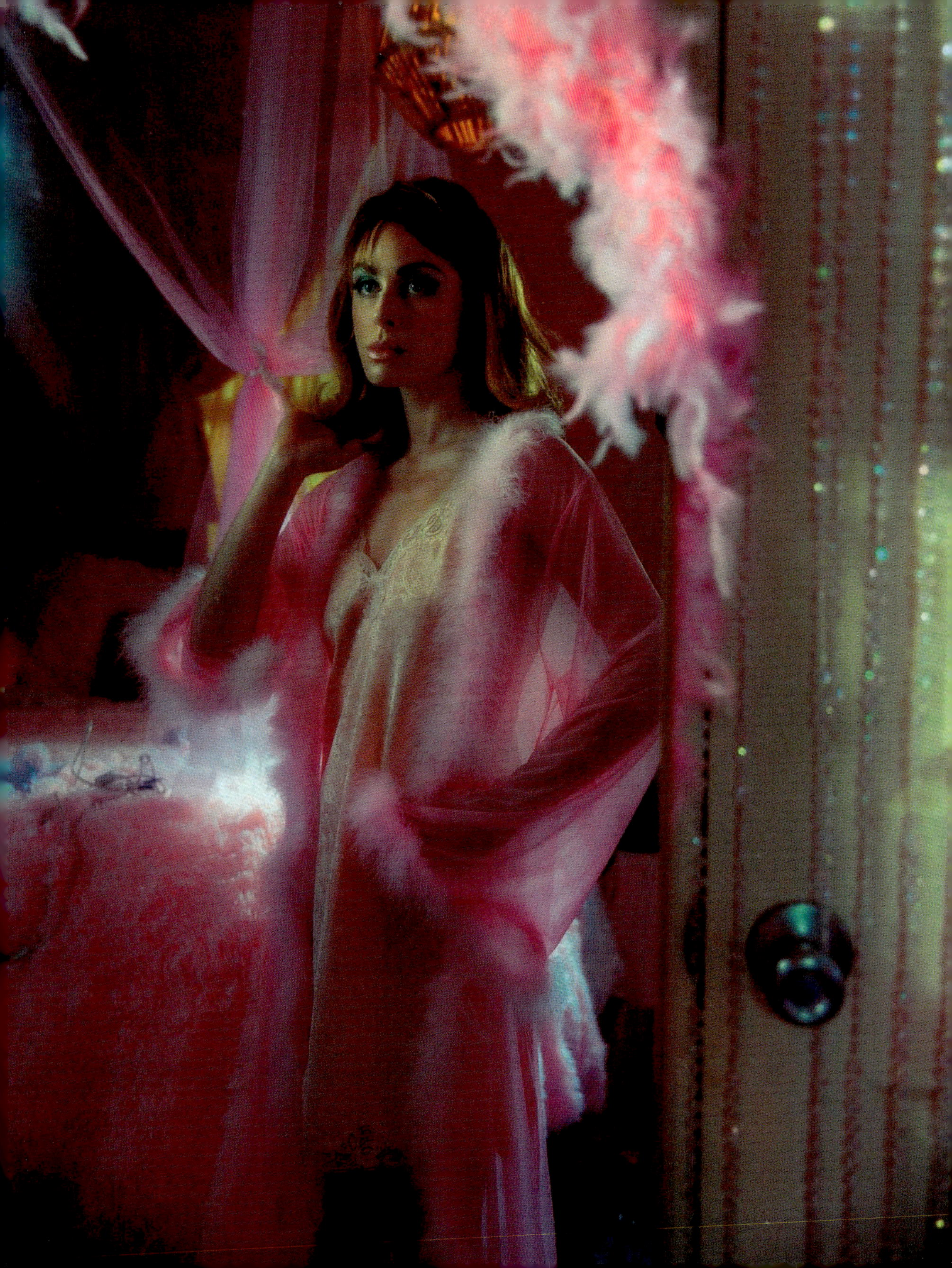

CONSIDERING DIFFERENT TYPES

So what kinds of textures, patterns, and styles are out there? The list is endless! To find the elements that will accentuate your space or artwork with the right kind of vibe, it's important to brainstorm some of the different options out there. I've listed some of my go-to choices as examples below. I encourage you to read through and see if any of these could be a good fit for your work. Try thinking of a few personal faves for each category that isn't on my list and briefly expand on them using bullet points. Where do they come from? What do they signify? What can they bring to your piece?

TEXTURES

> **Fluffy:** fur, wool, cotton, polyester, feathers, or down. Fluffy textures usually signify comfort and coziness and sometimes even luxury. The fluffier the material, the more likely someone spent money on it. Fluffy textures are reminiscent of clouds—don't you just want to snuggle up in one and drift off to sleep?

> **Smooth:** sleek surfaces with no cracks or holes. Smooth textures include laminated or stained wood that's been sanded down, fabrics like leather, and even transparent, flat surfaces like glass. Smooth textures usually signify modern living and are associated with cleanliness, simplicity, and formality due to their uniform look. Smooth textures also help balance light and often brighten up a space.

> **Bumpy:** surfaces that have uneven textures. Bumpy textures are found on natural stones, uncured wood, and even quilted fabrics. This texture is associated with spaces or people that are into a natural or rustic feel. Since bumpy textures are typically in their natural state, they remind us of someone or something that likes the natural state of things. They love the organic nature of our world.

> **Velvety:** known for having a rich, smooth, and luxurious feel. Velvety textures usually come from various types of velvet. The most traditional types are from silk, but less-expensive versions can come from polyester or cotton. When a space is covered in velvet, it usually signifies luxury and opulence to the highest degree because of the cost of velvet. Someone who loves velvet might be a bit decadent and dramatic. It conveys elegance and warmth as opposed to smooth textures, which offer more of a cold elegance. Velvet's soft surface brings out warmth.

> **Feathery:** light airiness and a delicate feel, often with an unusual shape. Real feathers come from birds, but less expensive artificial feathers are also available. Feathery textures can signify many things, depending on how they are used. They can depict luxury when used as a trim or accent, but their unique visual component can also be used to signify quirkiness and whimsy.

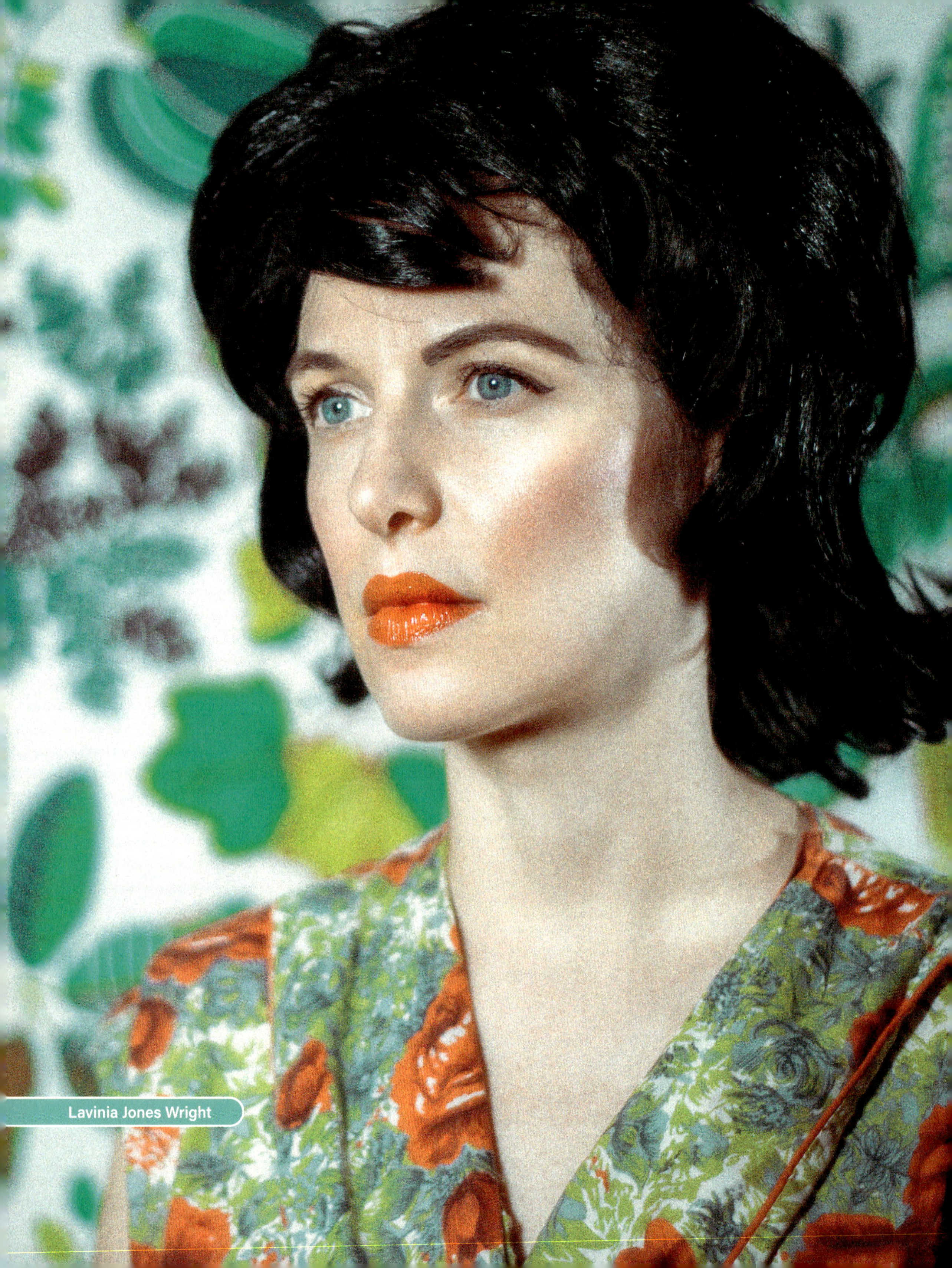
Lavinia Jones Wright

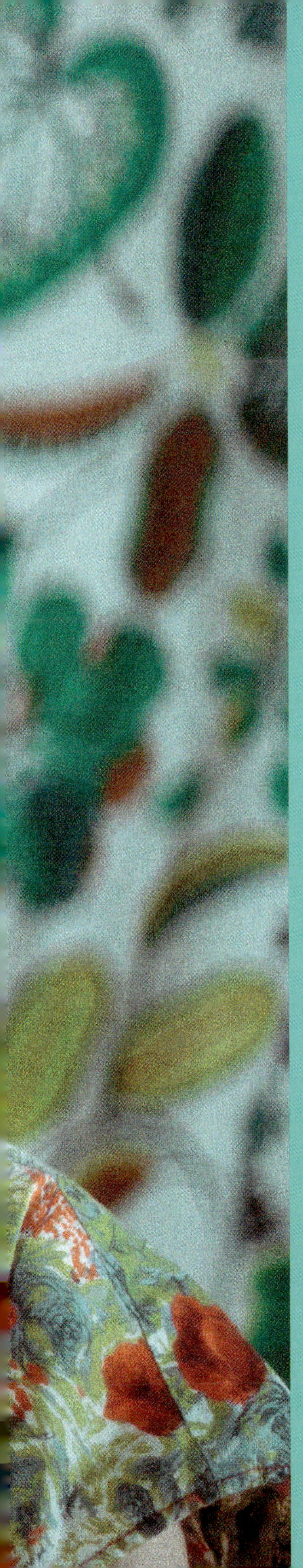

PATTERNS

> **Geometric:** various shapes and symmetrical lines. Signifying symmetry and balance, these versatile patterns are often used to depict an element of playfulness. Geometric patterns can be used to showcase a bit of a retro look. The clean lines give this pattern an element of simplicity, while the various shapes add a bit of spontaneity.

> **Stripes:** includes many parallel lines in a row, can be made from lines of all different sizes and widths. Often categorized as classic and versatile, this pattern is attention grabbing due to its bold and deliberate style. Stripes can be used to make a statement while also inspiring a more classic vibe. Due to their repetitive nature, stripes can be connected to uniformity and order. Often associated with the mod movement of the '60s, where striped designs were used to play into the growing aesthetic of psychedelia.

> **Floral:** depicting flowers and various foliage. Although florals can signify many things, the most common association is soft romanticism and femininity. If a space uses florals, we often link it with delicate beauty and vintage styles. Prior to the boom of midcentury modern, many designs featured floral elements on them.

> **Gingham:** a checked pattern that utilizes white and another contrasting color. Gingham is often associated with cottage- and country-home styles. It is a bit rustic and nostalgic. If someone utilizes gingham, they might prefer life's little simplicities.

> **Paisley:** a busy pattern that centers around a curved teardrop shape. Stemming from Indian textiles, paisley is now closely associated with the bohemian movement of the '60s and early '70s. If someone utilizes this pattern, they are often seen as a free spirit who enjoys being unconventional.

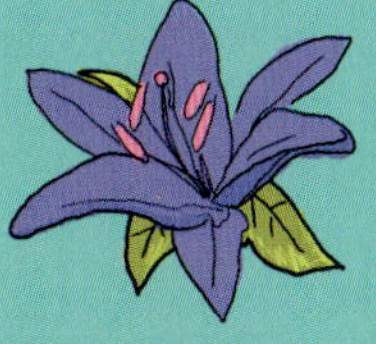

> **Gothic:** originated in the Middle Ages. The architectural style is categorized by pointed arches and stained glass windows. We often associate it with horror since the design of many historical castles where potentially scary things live were built in this style. The gothic fashion style (which is separate from the architectural style) tends to include dramatic black and white pieces and intense makeup.

> **Preppy:** originated in the United States. This style is usually associated with old money and the elite. It derives from the culture of prep schools—expensive, upper-class private schools. Often, when we see prep styles, we think of East Coast money and activities such as boating or skiing. It has become a mainstream look but can still be used to signify the vibe of old money and extravagance.

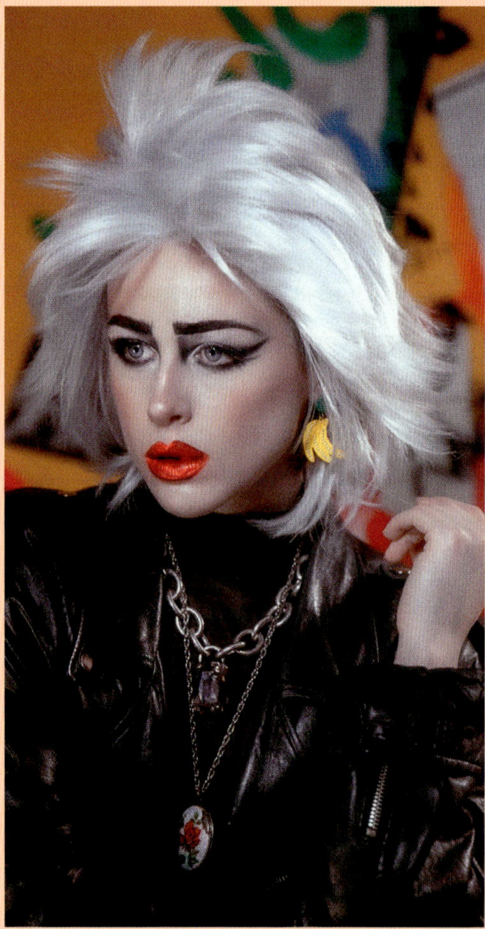

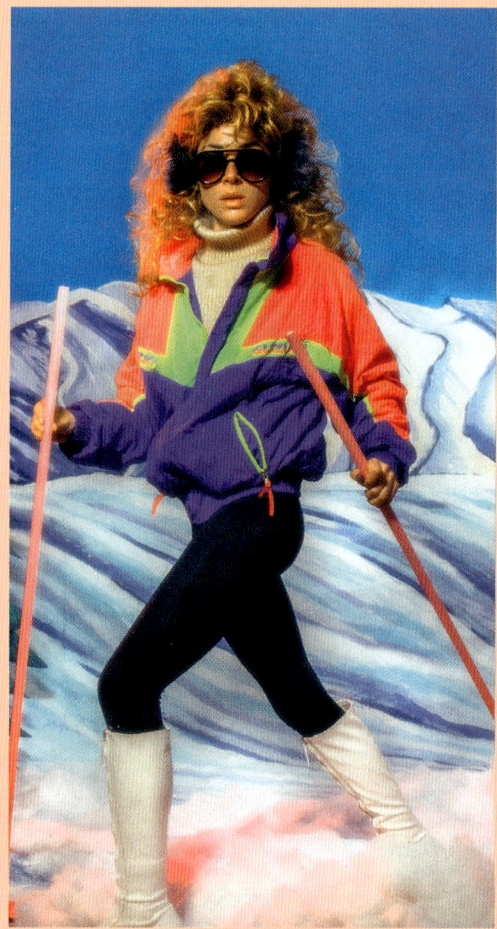

> **Bohemian:** characterized by its artistic and eclectic nature. The origins are vague, but it comes mostly from the French bohemian movement in the 18th and 19th centuries, which was comprised of various intellectuals and creatives. The bohemian style had a resurgence in the '60s and '70s and is now associated with the hippie movement. People who use bohemian elements in their homes or for their outfits are usually seen as free-spirited, quirky, and artistic.

> **Bold:** a simple and clean style. It utilizes monochromatic color palettes which usually have one big, bright pop of color to draw the eye in. This style is related to minimalism in some ways, and usually becomes popular every time a more decadent design movement loses its luster, serving as a reaction to its busier predecessors. Bold styles are very deliberate and are often associated with simplistic elegance and carefree sophistication.

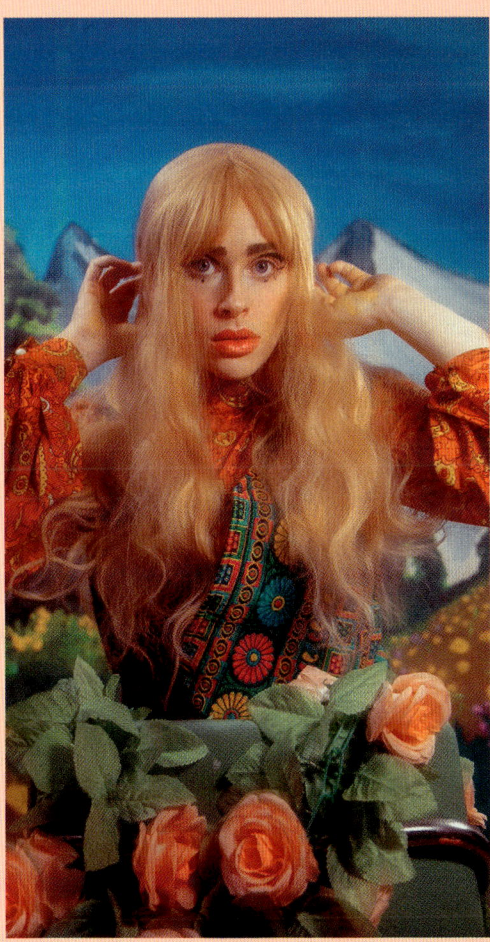

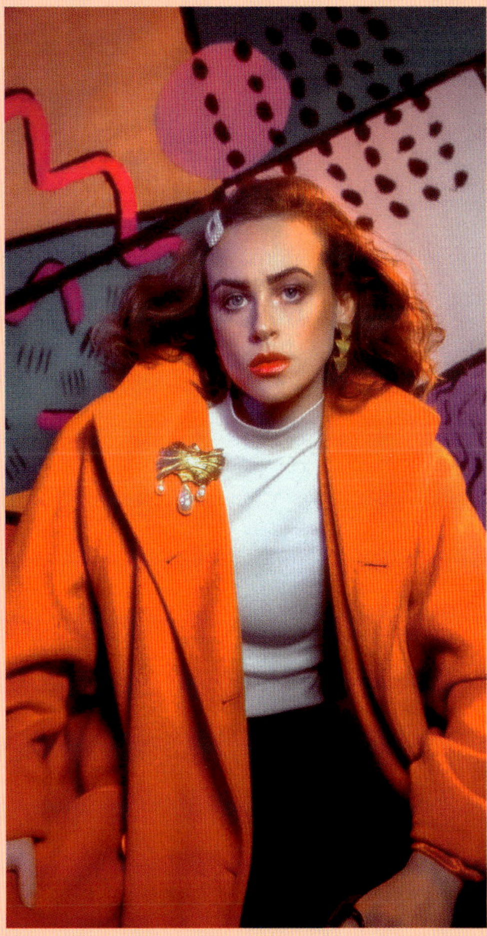

TEXTURES, PATTERNS & STYLES ACROSS DISCIPLINES

For art: If you're working on a physical piece of art, do you want it to feel a certain way when you touch it? This alone can be a deciding factor as to what type of textures you should use when creating the work. When using patterns, you should try to consider if you want to create an obvious pattern or if you want to hint at one subtly through reoccurring shapes or colors. Patterns can often be used subliminally to hint at deeper themes. You should think of the style of a piece based on your personal touch and how your hands can create distinct lines that are added to the canvas in a free-flowing way. Style is the unique ingredient that makes a piece yours.

For set design: Using different textures can add depth to a set and help make the scene you're constructing more believable for an audience. Creating elements with texture will help bring the scene to life and convince the viewers that they're truly looking at a stone wall, even if the stones aren't real. Adding texture can bring the illusion to life, even if you're not using the real thing. Using patterns can be a way to hint at themes or the emotional state of a character. The style of a set is often decided on or guided by the director, but it's still important to use your own creativity as you build a set so it results in a cohesive space for your story to unfold.

STEFFY DEGREFF
Fashion, Home Decor & DIY Influencer

As a content creator who focuses on interior decorating and fashion, my goal is to coherently place different pieces together to make spaces or outfits feel complete. Finding a stopping point, or a point of completion, is always subjective since the process is a nuanced balancing act of textures, patterns, and colors. While some might find a design to be "too much" or "too maximalist," others might think it's too sparse and unexciting. I see my role as finding balance between my own personal aesthetic and a style that can appeal to the masses.

I usually begin by finding a pattern that feels unique and adds some excitement, and then I build around that color palette. Mixing patterns can add a lot of interest to a space. To achieve balance, mix and match patterns that are different in scale and complementary in color, such as pairing a boldly striped rug with curtains that have a more subdued pattern in the same color palette. Complete the space by adding layers of texture, like covering a couch with pillows made from different fabrics. Completing an outfit can be as simple as mixing a crocheted top with a silky scarf.

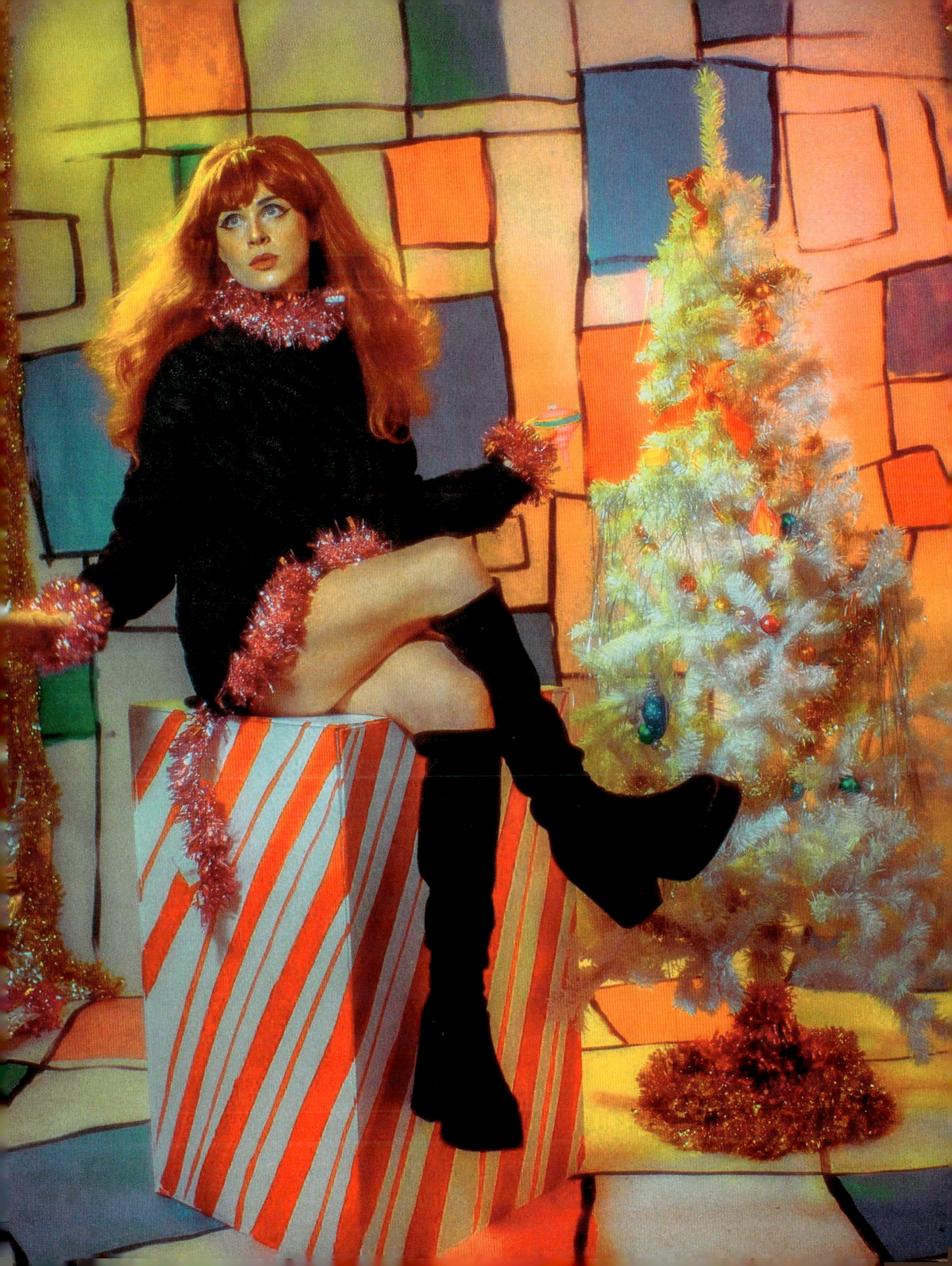

WHAT ARE YOU DRAWN TO?

TEXTURES

WOVEN
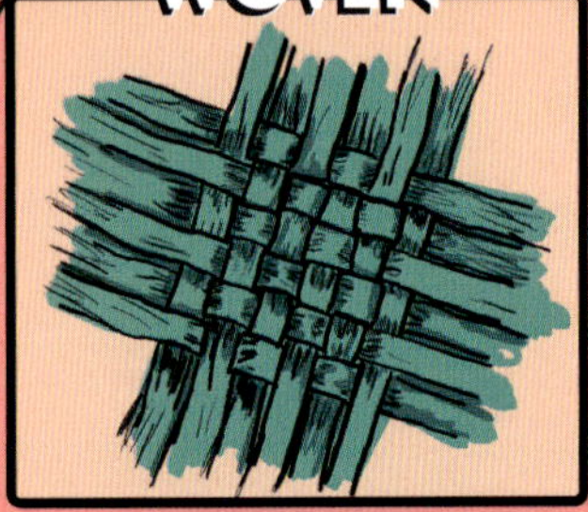

SMOOTH
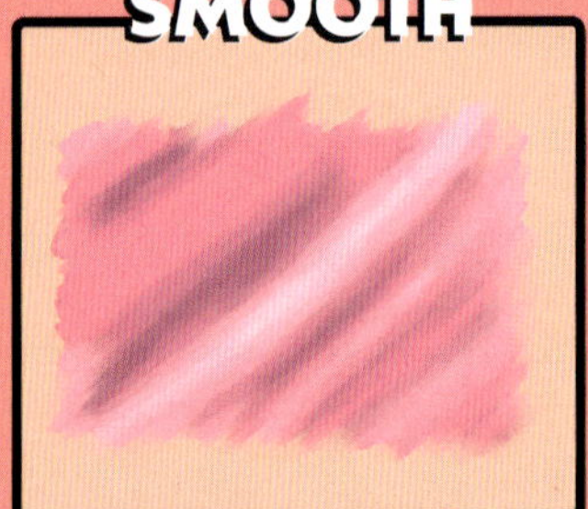

FLUFFY
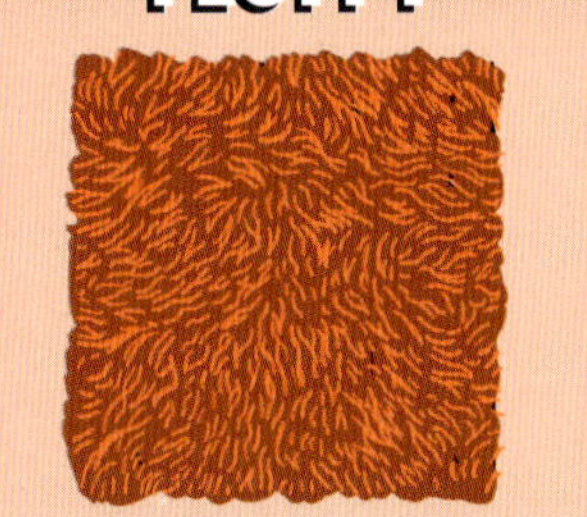

SILKY
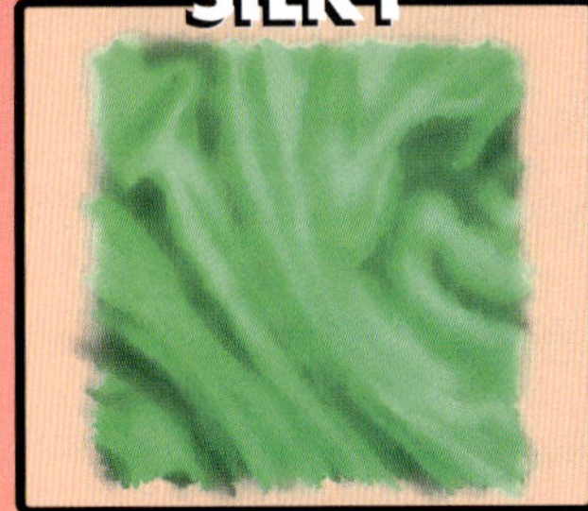

GRITTY
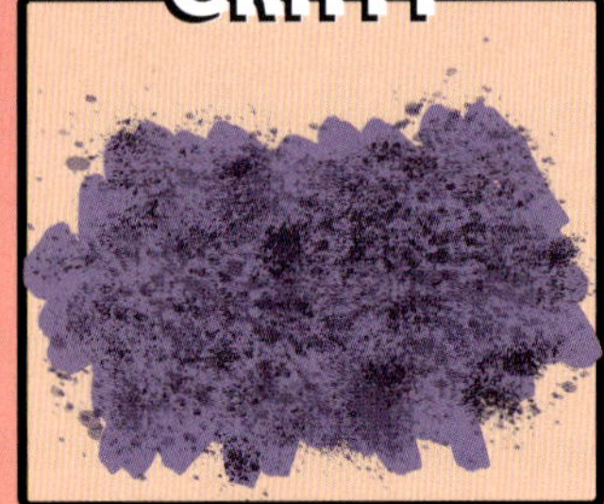

PRICKLY
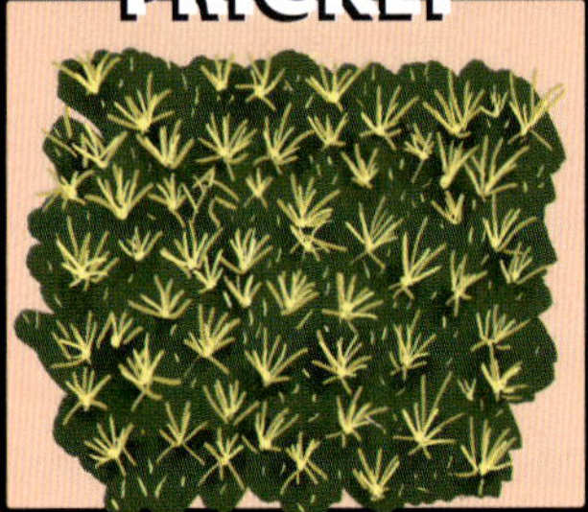

ROUGH
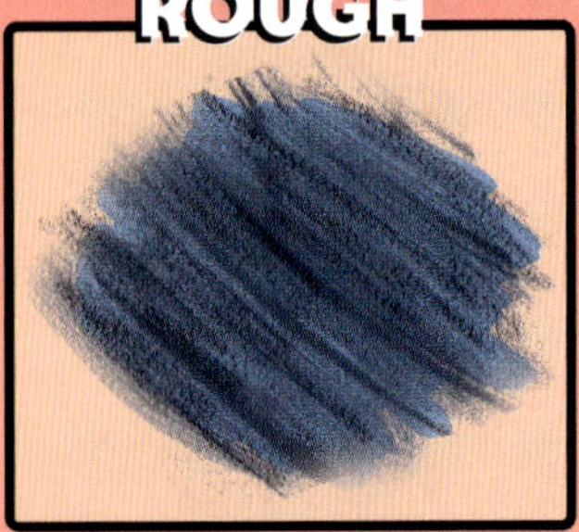

WRINKLY
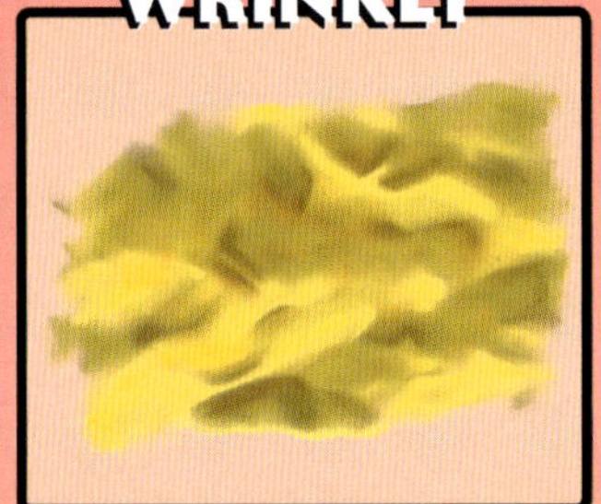

BUMPY
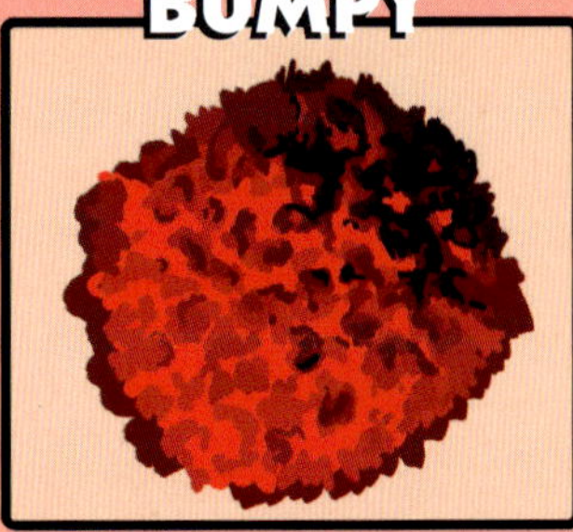

PATTERNS

CHECKED
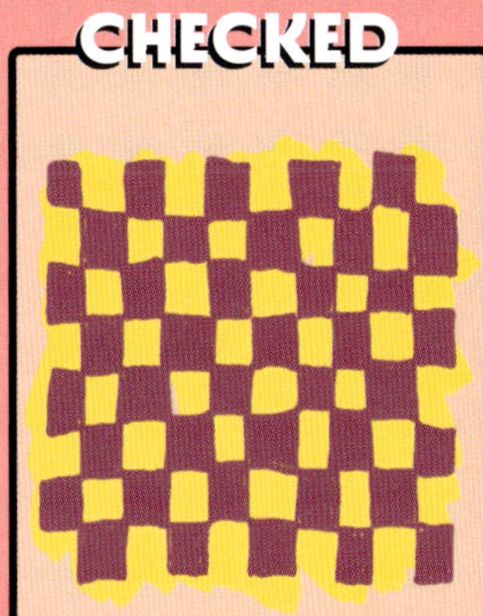

STRIPED
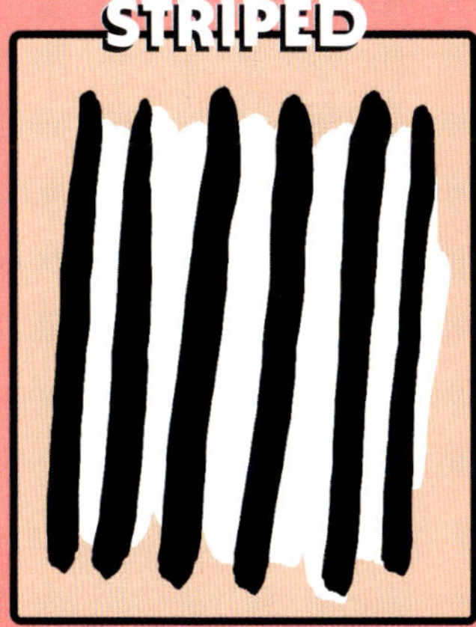

POLKA DOTS
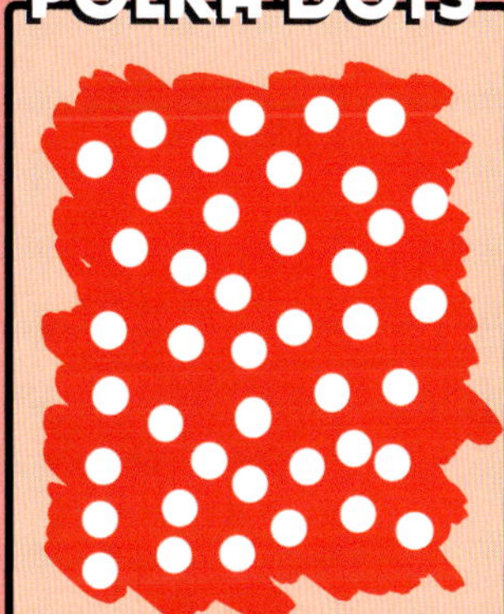

CHEVRON
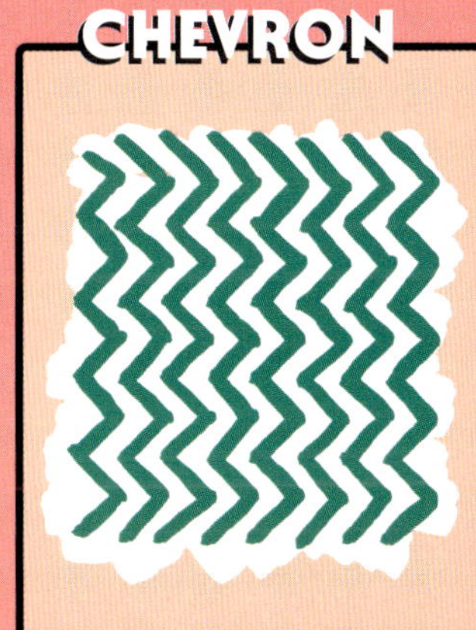

GINGHAM
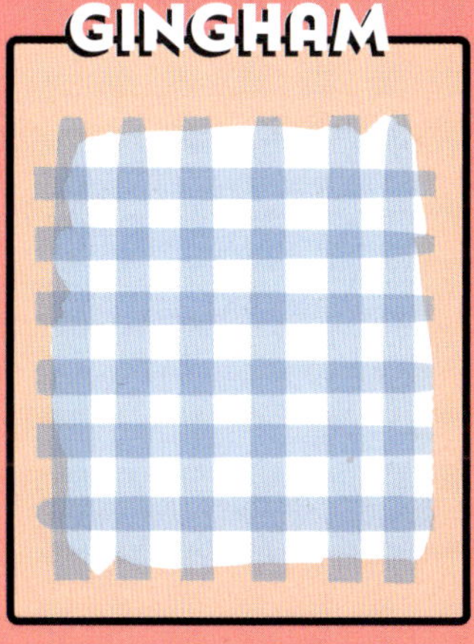

ZEBRA
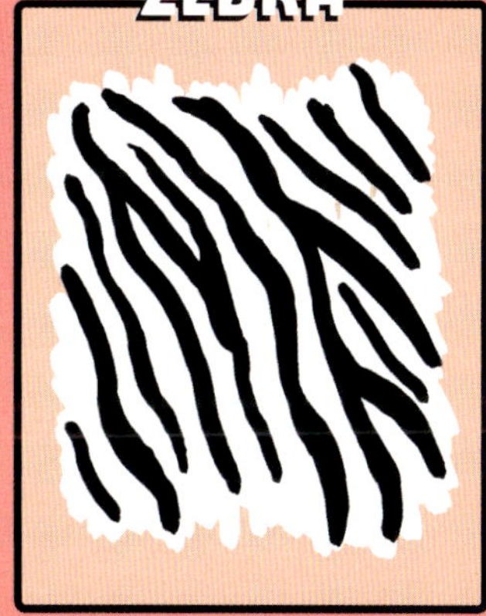

ARGYLE
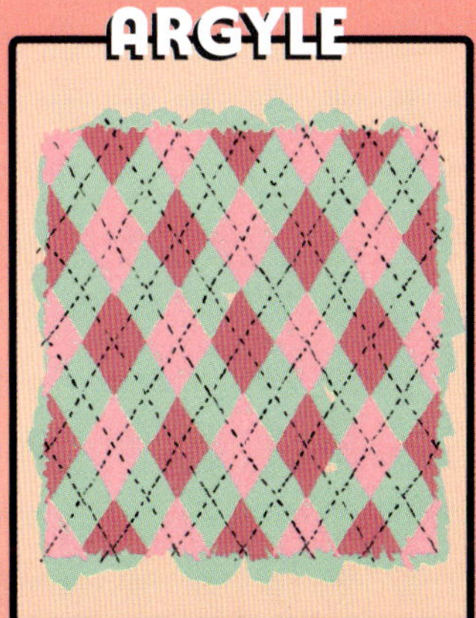

FLORAL
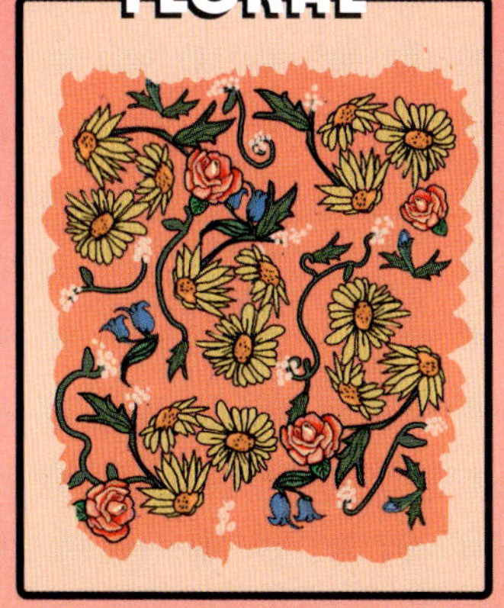

PLAID
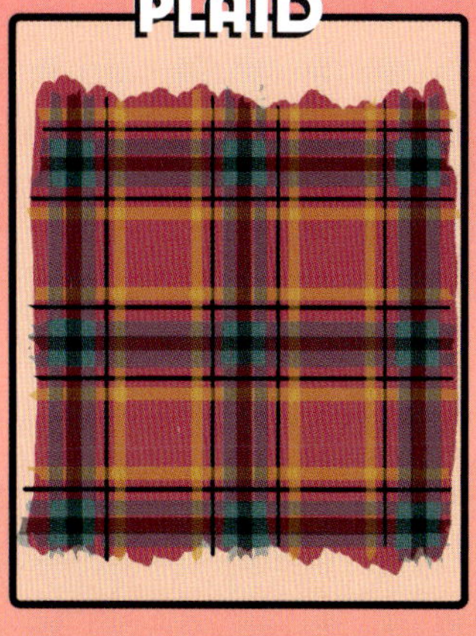

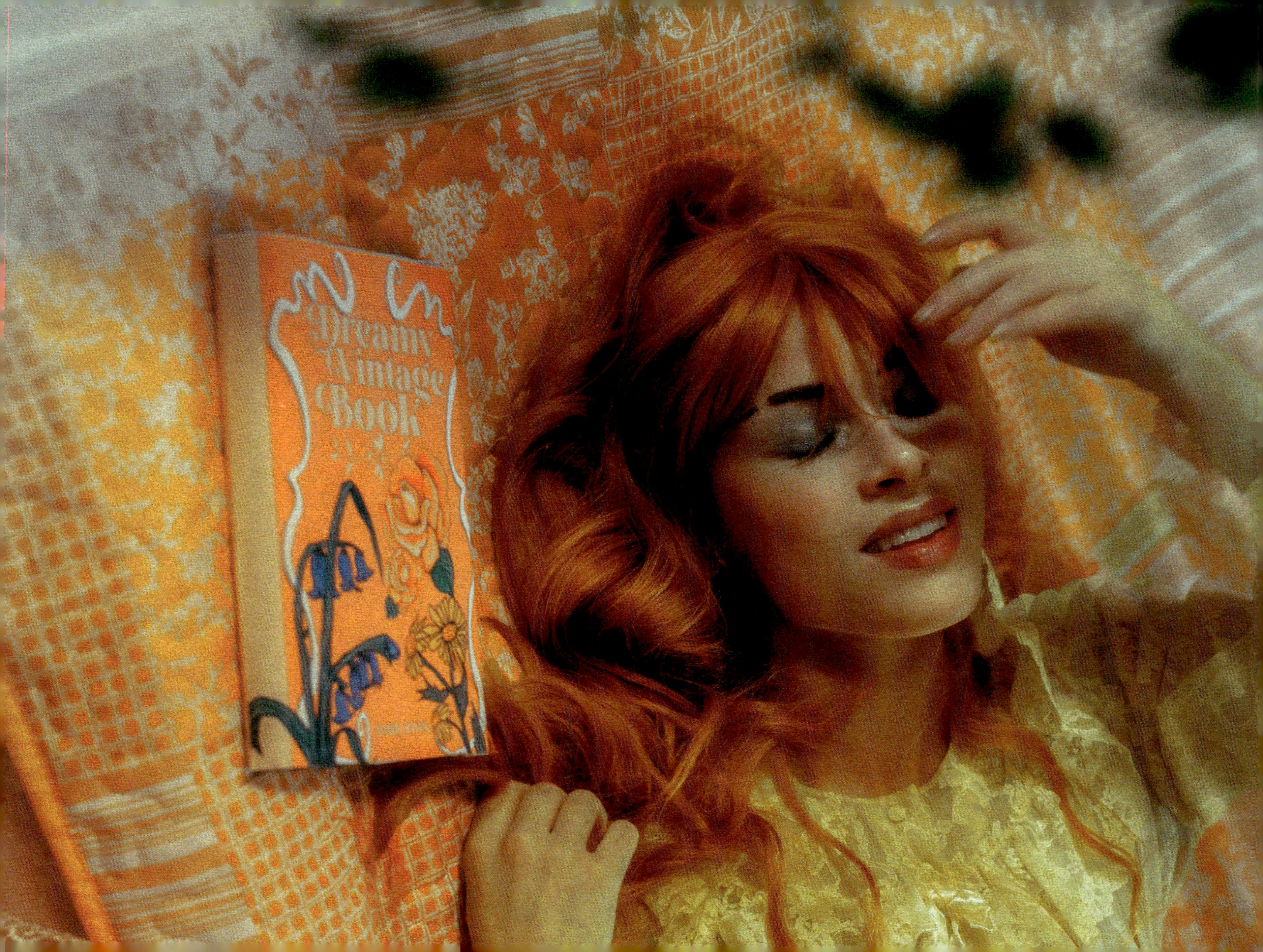

Dreamy
Vintage
Book

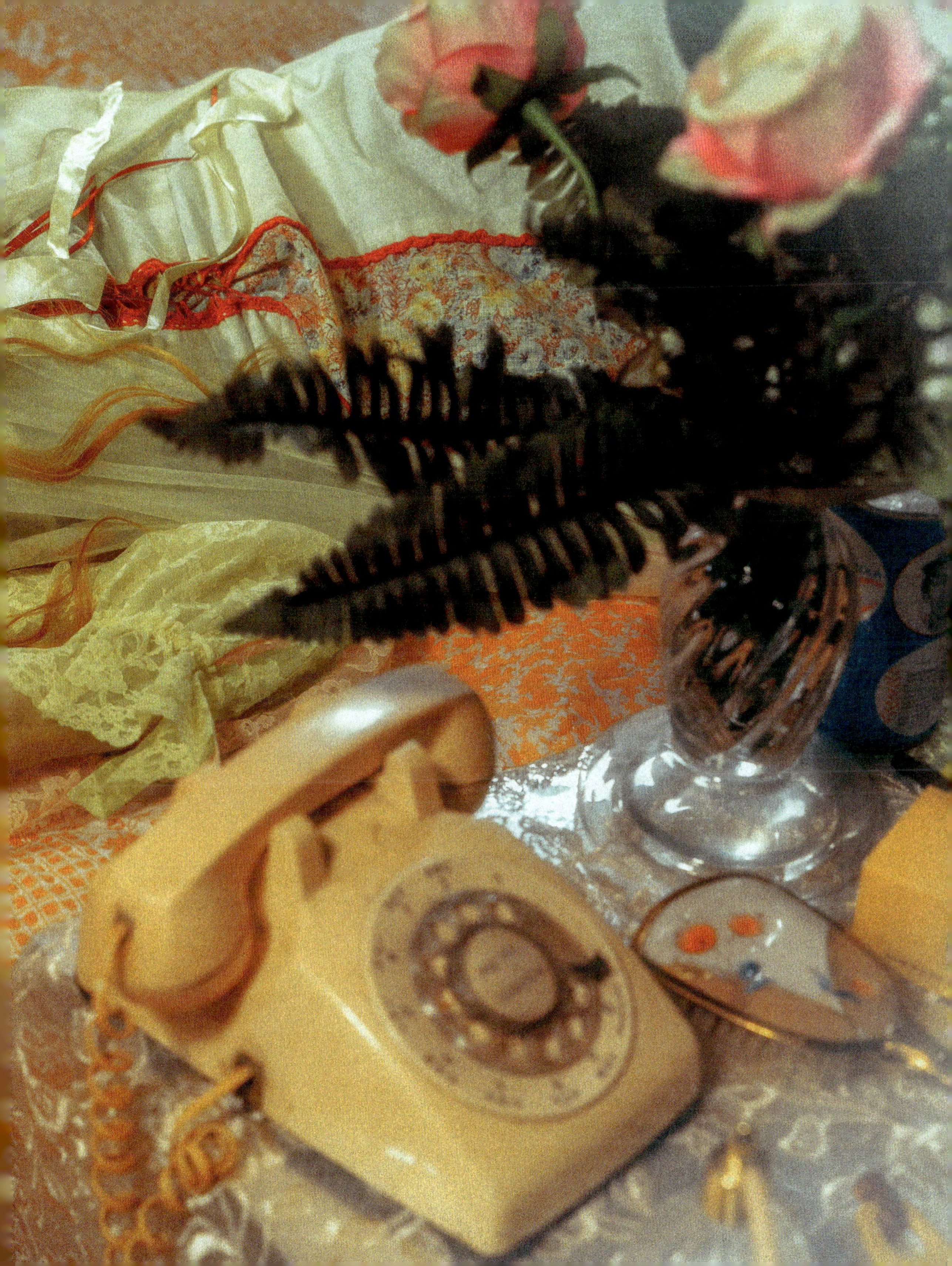

TEXTURES, PATTERNS & STYLES EXERCISES

> **How to build a space using patterned fabrics and textures:**

- Quite often when designing a space, I don't have what I truly need to give it a certain look. I often turn to fabrics (or even shower curtains) to disguise the fact that I don't have enough to fill a space entirely. Start by finding a base layer of fabric you like. (I like to keep the base more on the simple side usually.) And then throw the base fabric on the wall.

- Bring in main pieces, such as furniture or objects that you wish to use in your design. Next, try adding some fabrics and elements that have more apparent textures and patterns, such as pillows, blankets, and carpets.

- You can even drape other fabrics on top of the base fabric to create contrast. Play around and have a good time switching up the textures in the space. See what your brain likes best. These same ideas work if you're creating a space in a drawing or a painted scene too!

> **How to design a space using a particular style without breaking the bank:**

- Are you trying to create a specific style for your space and you don't quite have the money to bring it to life? Try these tricks to help get your desired result:

1. Match similar colors and patterns that are associated with the particular time period you're trying to represent. These colors and patterns can be on anything; they don't have to be fancy items or expensive pieces!

2. Narrow down the number of elements you're trying to include to just the most important ones. Sometimes, less is more.

3. For each piece you want to include, focus on the specific criteria that makes it an important component. How does it bring out the right vibe in your overall design? Once you've identified what these criteria are, try searching online for cheap things that have the same elements.

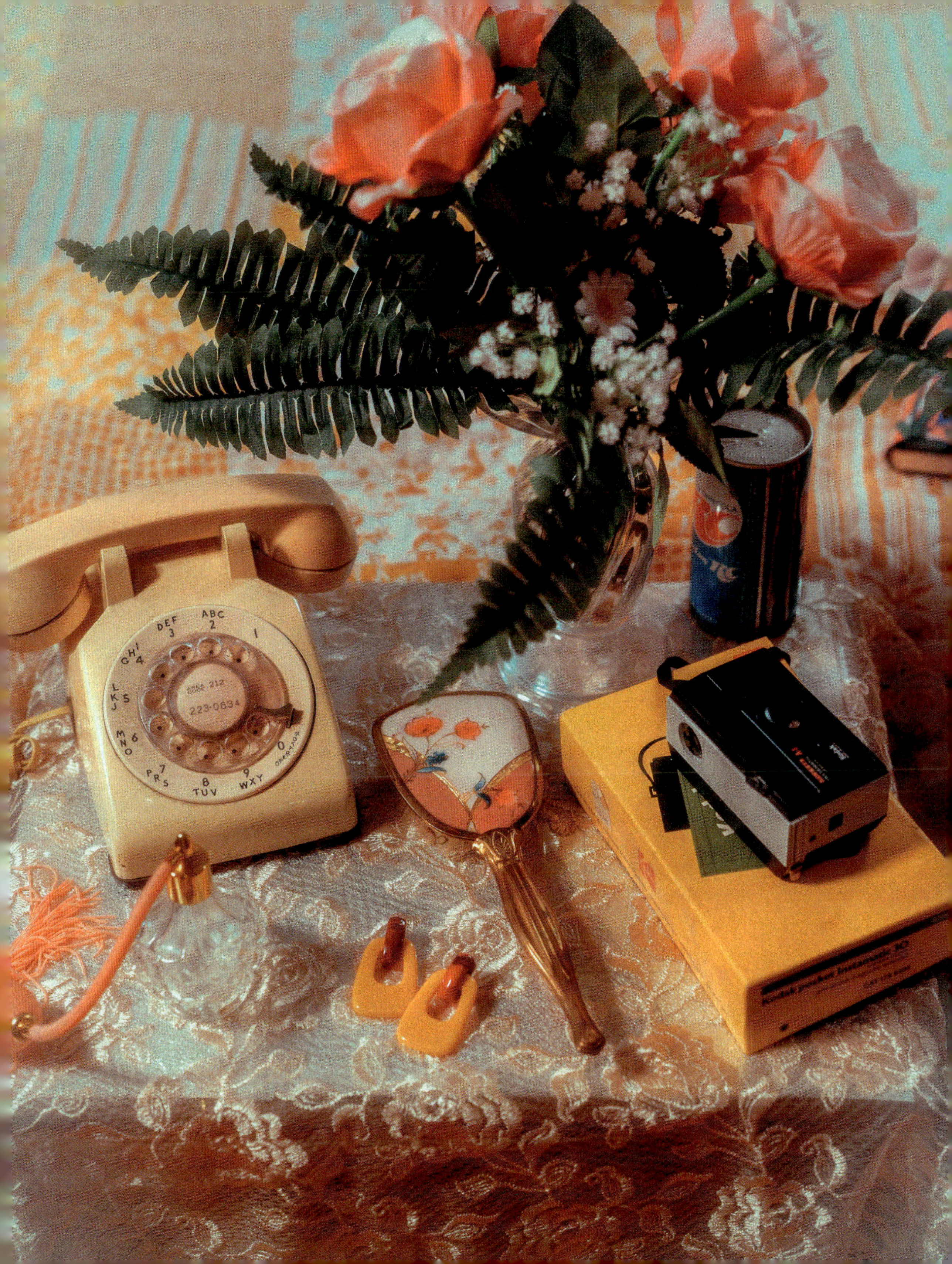

QUESTIONS TO CONSIDER

> What kinds of textures are you drawn to the most? Why do you think that is?

> How do you feel when you touch a coarse texture, like sandpaper, versus a soft texture, like velvet?

> What patterns do you wear the most? What patterns do you see showing up the most in your home decor? Are they the same or different?

> What are two different patterns you like that you think could work well together?

> What are two different patterns that you think contrast too much or maybe even clash? Could you try finding a creative way to pair them together anyway?

> How would you describe your sense of style when it comes to fashion? What about home decor? And art?

> Do you find that your stylistic choices when creating artwork align with your fashion and decor style choices? Or are they at odds? Why do you think that is?

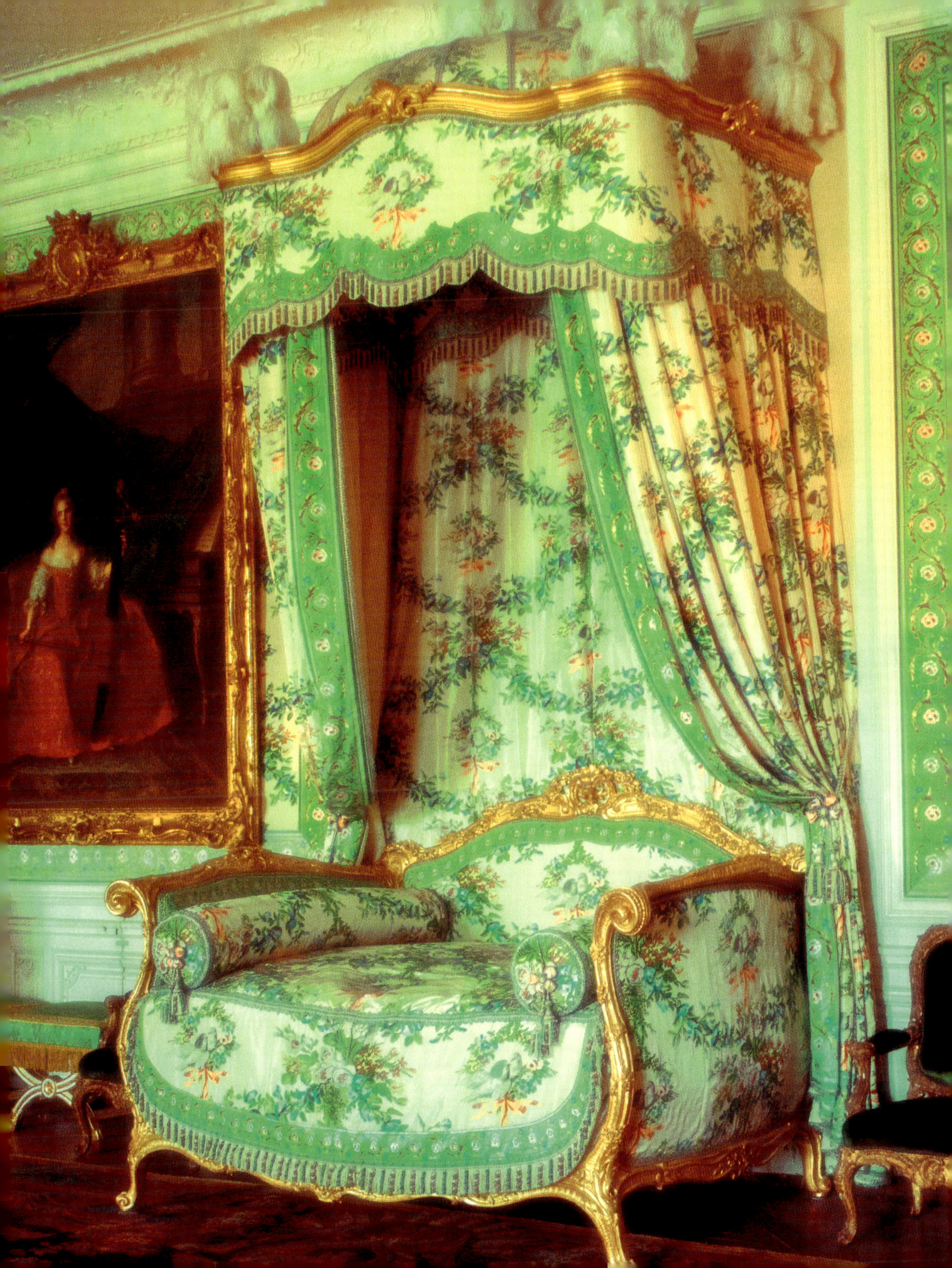

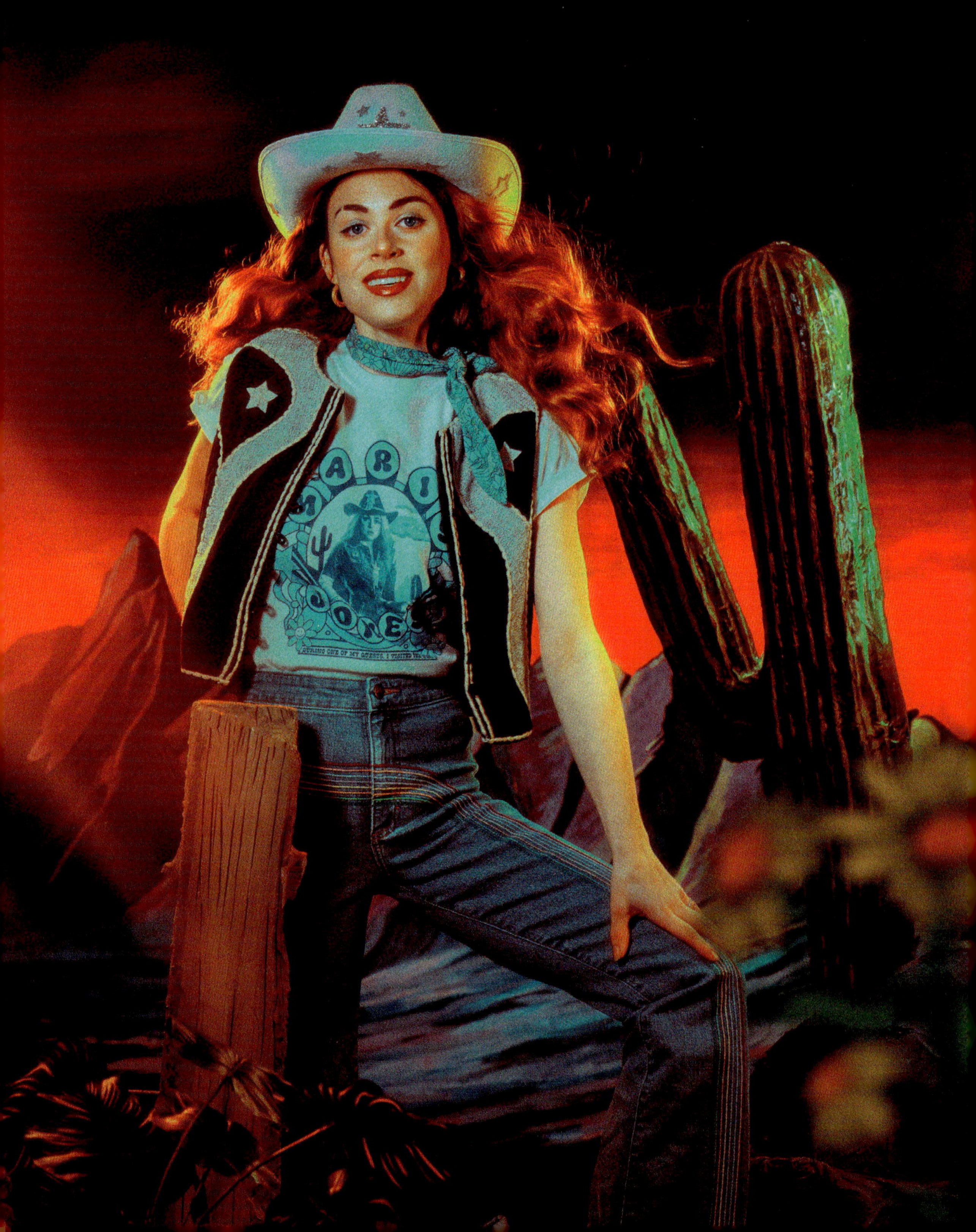
MARIE JONES
DURING ONE OF MY QUESTS, I VISITED THE

CHAPTER EIGHT

FIT CHECK!

WHAT TO WEAR

You have to wear clothes—it's the law, and society is weird about not wearing them. There's good news though: fashion is a tool you can wield to express yourself. Clothing offers an additional dimension to add complexity to the character you wish to create. I use clothing as a nonverbal channel to showcase a side of myself that often remains quiet in social situations. If I didn't dress to impress, I'd likely fade into the background. I derive a sense of empowerment and sophistication from the clothing I choose to wear, and you can too. You can choose any kind of outfit to convey what you wish—the options are endless!

It's essential to embrace what you wear. Fashion is fundamentally about confidence. When you feel good in your attire, you feel more self-assured. It's crucial to wear clothes that genuinely make you feel good, and you should pick outfits that help your creative subjects shine. Fashion shapes how you and your characters see the world, just as they shape how the world sees you and your characters.

The beauty of fashion lies in its flexibility. There are few rigid rules when it comes to what you can wear, but ultimately, it's more about how the clothes make you feel. Your clothing can mirror your emotions and amplify your mood when you step out into the world. It doesn't matter what others see; you elevate your inner self. The same goes for the clothes you choose to dress your characters in. You can pick the outfit you want to collage or paint to signify who your subjects are and what they're aiming for.

When assembling an outfit, consider how it feels to wear it. What message do you want to convey? What's the centerpiece or focal point? Much like designing a space or selecting furniture, I typically start with one defining element—a beloved item I know suits me well. It can be either a simple piece or an extravagant display, as long as it serves as the foundation for the rest of your outfit.

Remember, fashion is not static. It's constantly evolving. Every new day presents a fresh opportunity to express your emotions and personality through clothing. Chances are you're already choosing your outfits based on how you feel—even if you're not consciously aware of it.

PUTTING A LOOK TOGETHER

Let's start your style journey with something you're intuitively drawn to. I've always had a fascination with big sleeves and dramatic shoulders. It's something I keep in mind when putting together outfits. If you're completely stumped when it comes to creating an outfit, whether for yourself or a character, you should ask yourself, "What's something I'm consistently drawn to?" Then explore different ways to incorporate that element into your outfit. I'm drawn to fun and decorative elements, bold jewelry, a vibrant color palette, and a sleek edge. Looking at my lifelong preferences, I've always been captivated by costumes—'70s glam rock, musicals, and puffy sleeves reminiscent of Dorothy's in *The Wizard of Oz*. For me, it's all about the theatrical, and I like creating outfits with a bold style in mind.

When working with a character, consider who they are, since clothing often communicates information to viewers. Actively think about how you assign ideas and symbolism through the clothing. For example, a character you've created walks into work wearing sweatpants and a T-shirt. This combination of clothes says something about who this character is or what they're currently going through. It might signify they have an active lifestyle, or a hectic day ahead they want to be comfy for, or perhaps they just prefer soft, casual clothes. Fashion choices are laden with meaning.

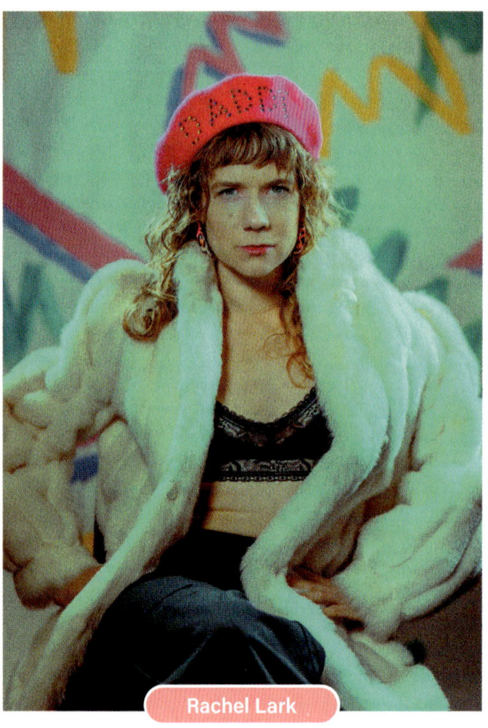

Rachel Lark

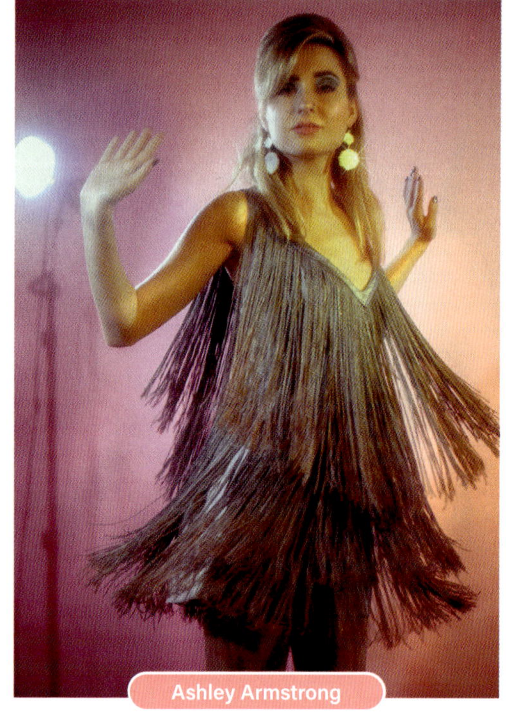

Ashley Armstrong

I often lay out items that I adore and think, "I want to create an outfit with these pieces." After starting with my favorite items, the ones that make me feel fantastic when I wear them, I incorporate other objects and accessories to bring the look together.

Experiment with different combinations, and don't just evaluate how the outfit looks; pay attention to how it makes you feel. Your facial expression often reveals your true feelings. When you're looking at an outfit in the mirror, examine your emotions and how they're coming across on your face. I recall a recent evening when I was getting dressed to go out and every time I looked in the mirror I despised what I saw. Although the outfit probably looked fine, it didn't make me feel fine. Fashion is all about highlighting how you want others to perceive you and making your innermost self feel incredible.

Consider your proportions (or that of the character you're creating) and the parts of your body you like best. Factor in this physical appearance when thinking about building a look and decide what you want to emphasize. Understanding your proportions can be incredibly valuable. For instance, I have broad shoulders. Since I can't conceal them no matter what I wear, I decide to exaggerate them with my clothing. I don't have very wide hips, so I occasionally incorporate extra fabric or hardware to create the illusion of fuller hips. Think about how you want to play with your proportions and focus on the silhouette that resonates the most with you. Craft a silhouette for yourself, not for standardized beauty norms.

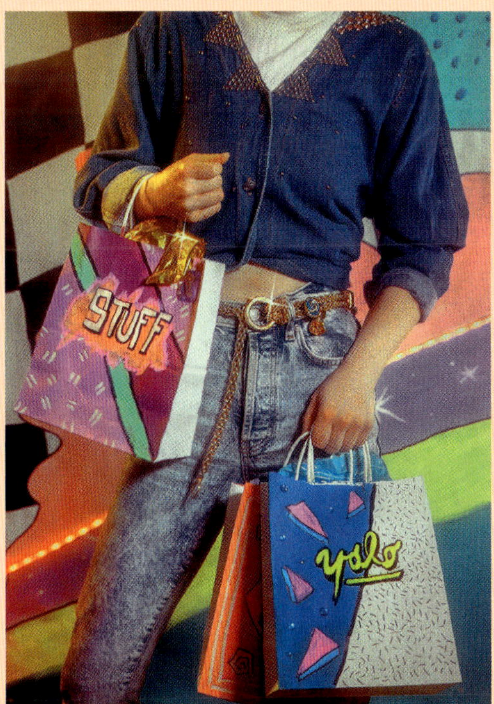

Putting the right look together is all about balance, akin to designing a space where balance and proportion matter. For example, if I choose a strongly structured shoulder piece, I'd choose to pair it with simpler pants, like tapered jeans. I love outfits with bold, structured shoulders, but it doesn't mean everything else has to be exceptionally structured. To avoid resembling a Pixar movie villain, I might balance out the dramatic shoulders and simpler pants with oversize chunky shoes. The shoes reinforce the outfit's overall concept, punctuating it.

Remember, when it comes to fashion, various factors come into play that aren't solely about personal style. Consider how much time you have, your destination, and the weather conditions. But no matter how you decide to put your outfit together, make sure it's communicating the messages you wish to convey, while also portraying a sense of balance.

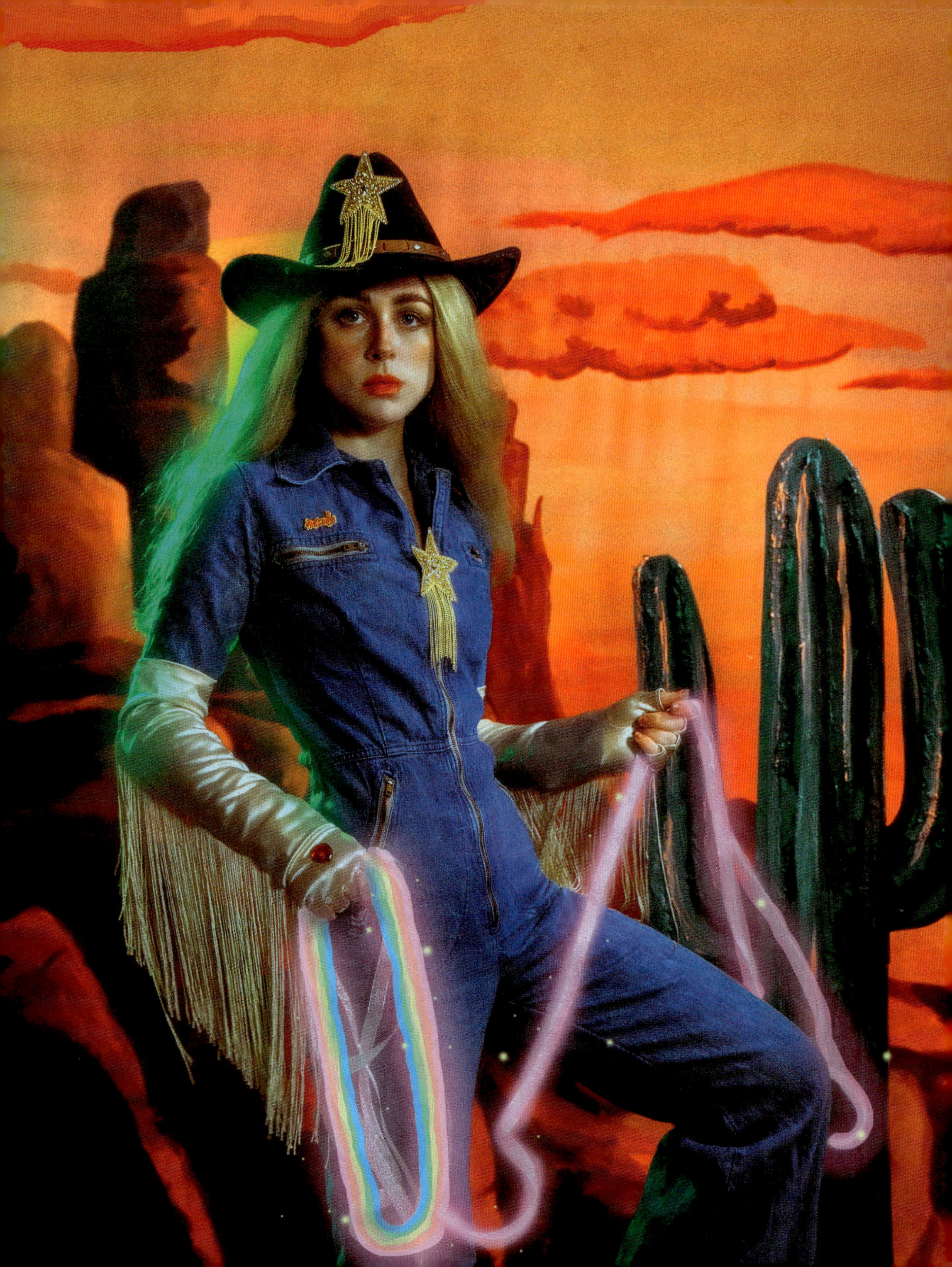

POPULAR FASHION STYLES

If you're looking to create an outfit based on popular fashion trends or styles, you can start by using what you already have and building on top of it to create a unique look.

1. Begin with the base layer of your outfit. This tends to be pants and a shirt, a dress, or a skirt and blouse, etc.
2. One piece at a time, add other items, focusing on finding the right balance. If your base look is very structured or has a loud print or color, you might want to pair it with cleaner or simpler pieces. If your base look is very simple, try adding a pop of color or a statement piece to accentuate it.
3. Once you've found the right balance, complete the look by adding some fun accessory elements that pair well with what you've put together.

Check out the popular fashion-type examples on the next page to create a look that's inspired by specific styles.

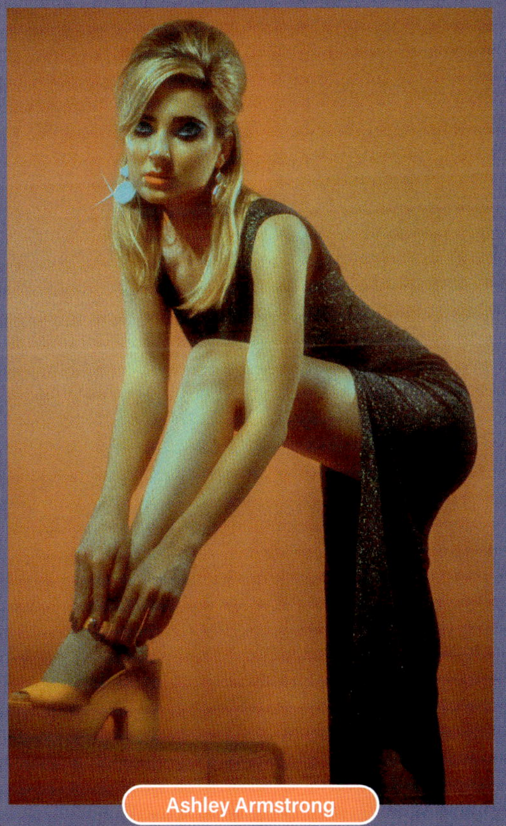

Ashley Armstrong

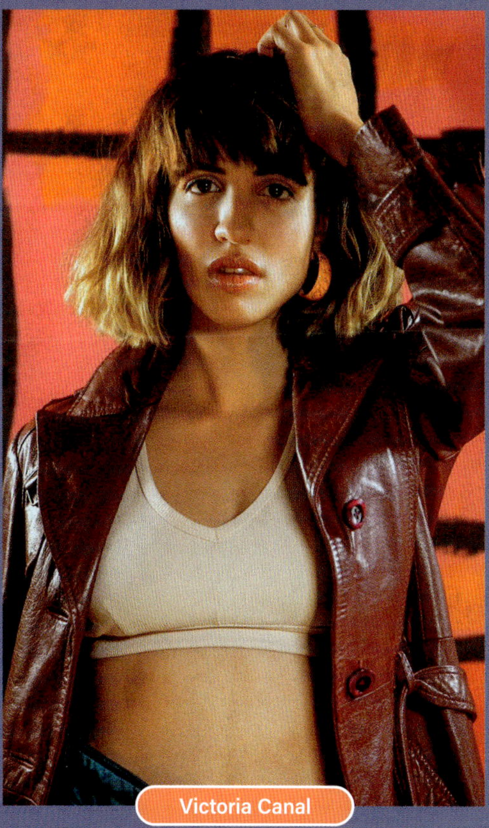

Victoria Canal

PREPPY

Fabrics: seersucker, linen, tweed, cotton

Patterns: argyle, plaid, nautical, stripes, madras, checked, tartan

Colors: navy, beige, white, salmon, light blue, black, maroon, army green, nude, camel, cream

Clothing: button-down shirts, polos, Henleys, blazers, chinos, khakis, sweaters, neckties, bow ties, little scarves, rugby shirts, belts, quilted jackets, sweater vests

Shoes: boat shoes, loafers, wedges, tennis shoes, flats

Accessories: headbands, pearls, sunglasses

Silhouette: clean and sharp

PUNK

Fabrics: leather, denim, mohair

Patterns: stripes, houndstooth

Colors: black, white, red

Clothing: sweaters, leather jackets, skinny jeans, denim jackets, button-down shirts, embellished items like spray-painted shirts or metal-studded items, vintage band tees, leather pants

Shoes: chunky black boots, platform shoes, black sneakers

Accessories: studded belts and jewelry, skinny black ties, safety pins, silver chains, chokers

Silhouette: fitted and tight

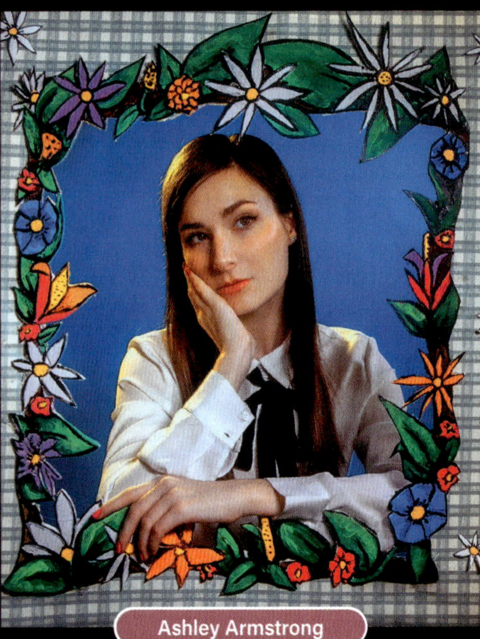

Ashley Armstrong

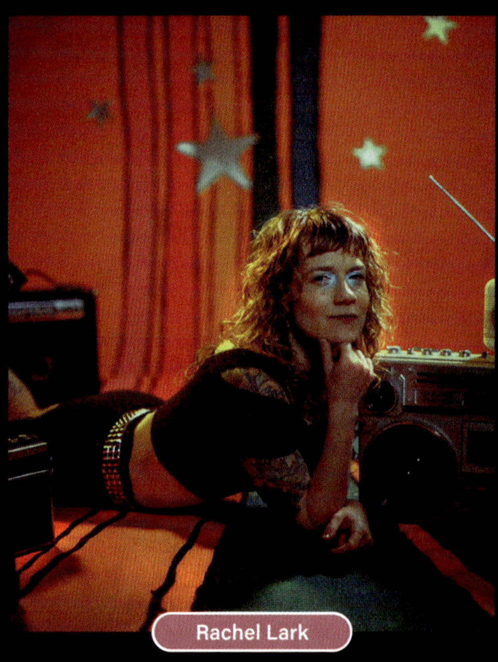

Rachel Lark

BOHO

Fabrics: woven and knitted cotton, linen, velvet, silk, suede, leather, fur, beaded

Patterns: floral, paisley, tie-dye

Colors: beige, brown, earthy red, white, burnt yellow, orange, dark green

Clothing: shawls, maxi dresses and skirts, kimonos, bandanas and scarves, sarongs, long-sleeve shirts with prints, wide-leg jeans

Shoes: clogs, ankle boots, cowboy boots

Accessories feather earrings, bangle bracelets, shell and stone jewelry, oversize sunglasses, wide-brimmed hats, floral crowns

Silhouette: loose and flowy

MODERN

Fabrics: cotton, denim, linen, wool

Patterns: solids, pinstripes, small polka dots, monochromatic and subdued prints

Colors: earth tones, grey, beige, brown, black, white, cream, blue

Clothing: white button-downs, straight-leg blue jeans, simple trench coats, black slip dresses, turtlenecks, blazers

Shoes: flats, white sneakers, simple heels

Accessories: neutral scarves, simple leather belts, plain baseball caps or fedoras

Silhouette: well-tailored and relaxed

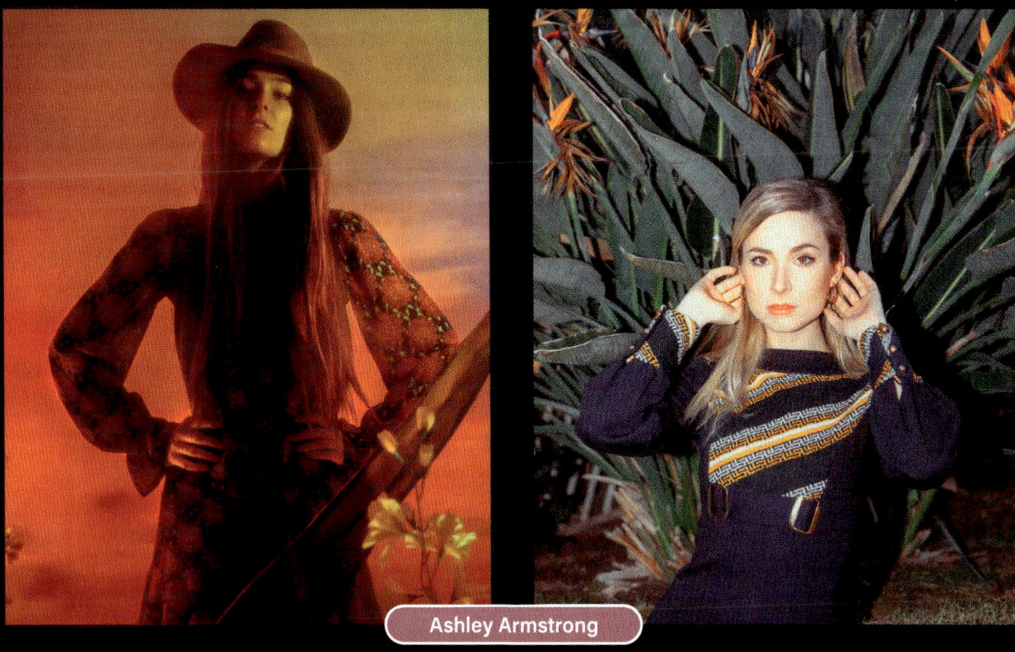

Ashley Armstrong

FASHION ACROSS DISCIPLINES

Fashion for art and content creation: When making art, incorporating fashion into your piece can follow a different process. Art often capitalizes on lighting. Rather than focusing on the specific items of clothing, it's important to consider how the fabrics move or look with certain light sources. The clothes should reflect light and be in conversation with the scene you are creating. This same idea also applies when putting together a clothing display, as the designer will most likely be thinking of what fabrics will look best under light and what textures and pairings can be selected to catch the eye of passersby.

Fashion for everyday: Before getting dressed, I try to figure out how I'm feeling and what kind of outfit will best accentuate or help my overall mood. Fashion is a way of expressing yourself, and the outfit you're wearing can be used to indicate to others how you're feeling. The key to a successful outfit is ensuring you have a good read on your emotional state and what you'd like to convey. Once you have this figured out, you can select a few items that will bring this look to life. I always make sure I have good pairs of jeans, yoga pants, leather pants, and a few solid shirts that I love in my arsenal—that way, I always have the basic items I need in case I am not feeling creative!

MONA MAY
Costume Designer

As a costume designer, I design and build costumes for characters outlined in a script. My job is super creative and an instrumental part of storytelling. When you first see a character on-screen, you know who they are by the clothes they wear within seconds, even if they haven't said a single word. Clothes and fashion express a character's personality, mood, economic status, physiological state, and much more. This is also how audiences can relate to the authentic characters we are portraying, and perhaps see themselves in them or even emulate them. That's the power of costume design.

Designing is an intense but fun process. It's like being a detective. I have to dive into the psychology of each character, analyze and understand them, then create how they should visually look. The inspiration can come from anywhere: nature, art, architecture, books, emotions, spirituality, day-to-day life, or even people I see walking down the street. There is creative inspiration all around us! And when it comes to getting in touch with your creative side, I believe in opening our minds, sitting quietly, and listening to our inner hearts. It guides us to new ways of experiencing ourselves and the world around us.

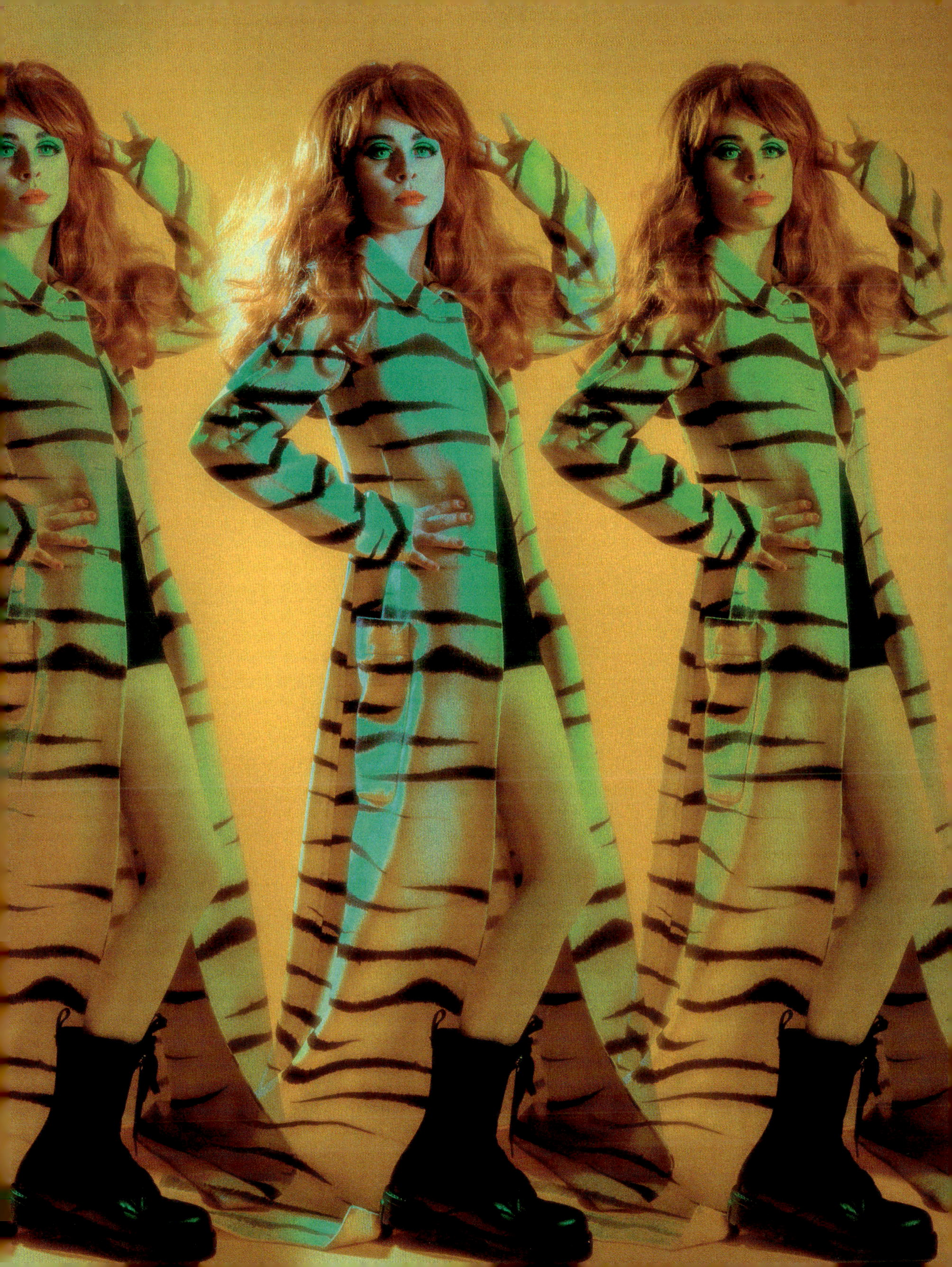

CHOOSE YOUR OWN OUTFIT ADVENTURE

Where am I going?

How do I want to feel in my outfit?

Party
How fancy is the event?

Work meeting
What do I want to signify to my colleagues?

Nowhere in particular
What vibe do I want my outfit to bring to my day?

Mega glam, black tie, red carpet

Professional, business mogul vibes

Adventurous, athletic, and ready for action

Family event, wedding, sit-down dinner

Creative and cool energy

Cozy—I want to stay in and do my own thing

Casual hang with friends

Everyday casual and laid-back attitude

Incognito, a.k.a. leave me alone

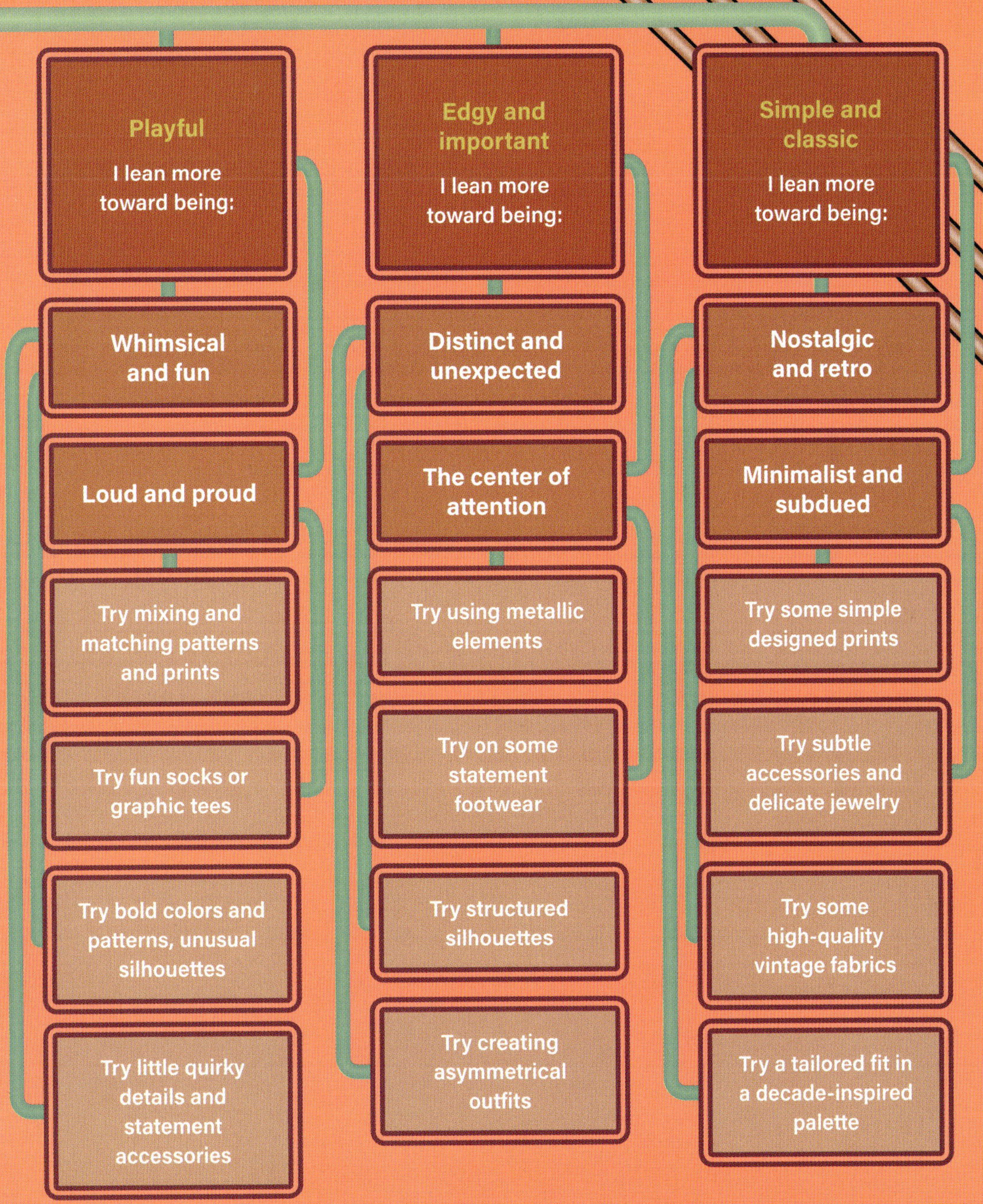

Playful	Edgy and important	Simple and classic
I lean more toward being:	I lean more toward being:	I lean more toward being:
Whimsical and fun	**Distinct and unexpected**	**Nostalgic and retro**
Loud and proud	**The center of attention**	**Minimalist and subdued**
Try mixing and matching patterns and prints	Try using metallic elements	Try some simple designed prints
Try fun socks or graphic tees	Try on some statement footwear	Try subtle accessories and delicate jewelry
Try bold colors and patterns, unusual silhouettes	Try structured silhouettes	Try some high-quality vintage fabrics
Try little quirky details and statement accessories	Try creating asymmetrical outfits	Try a tailored fit in a decade-inspired palette

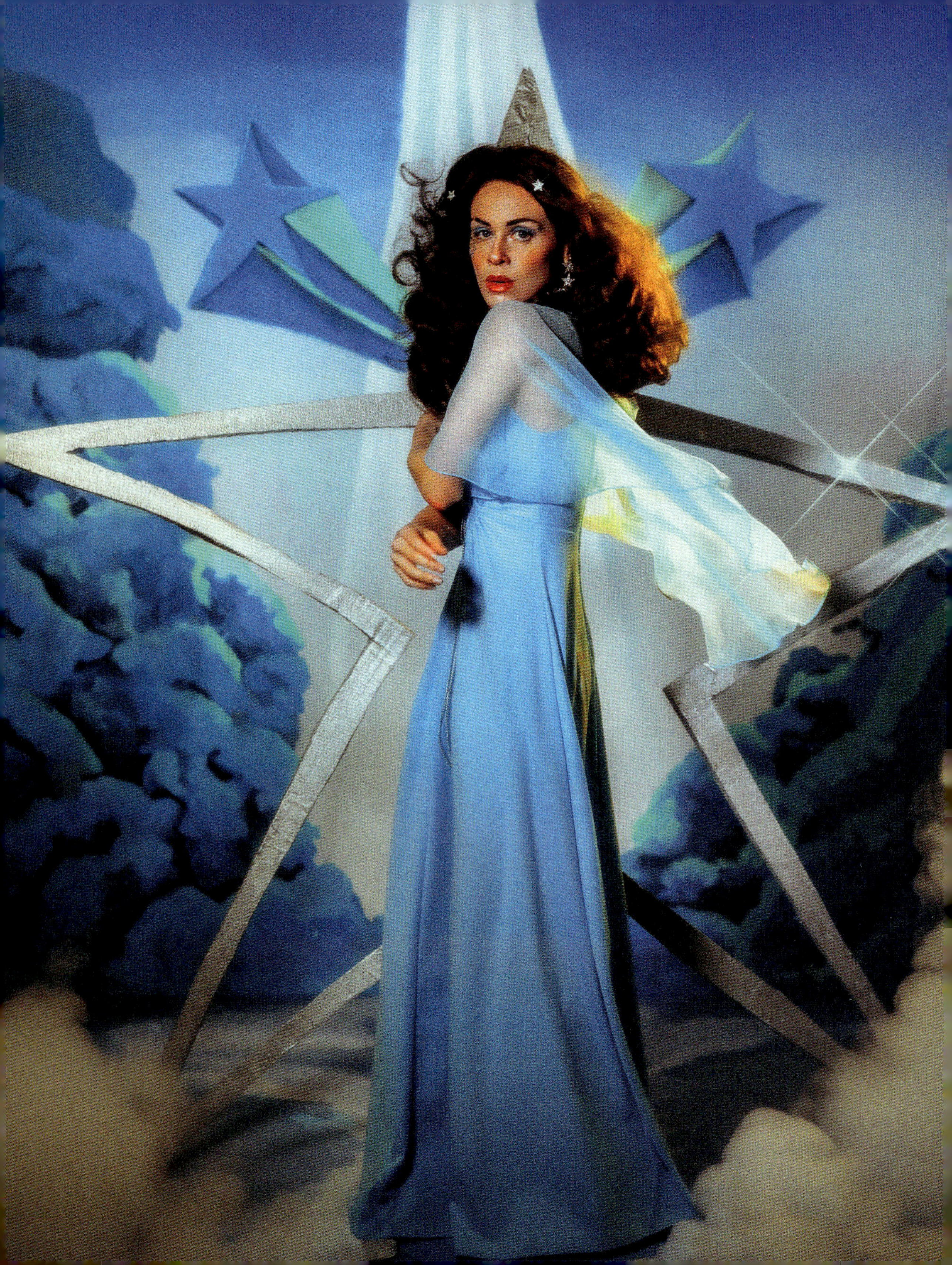

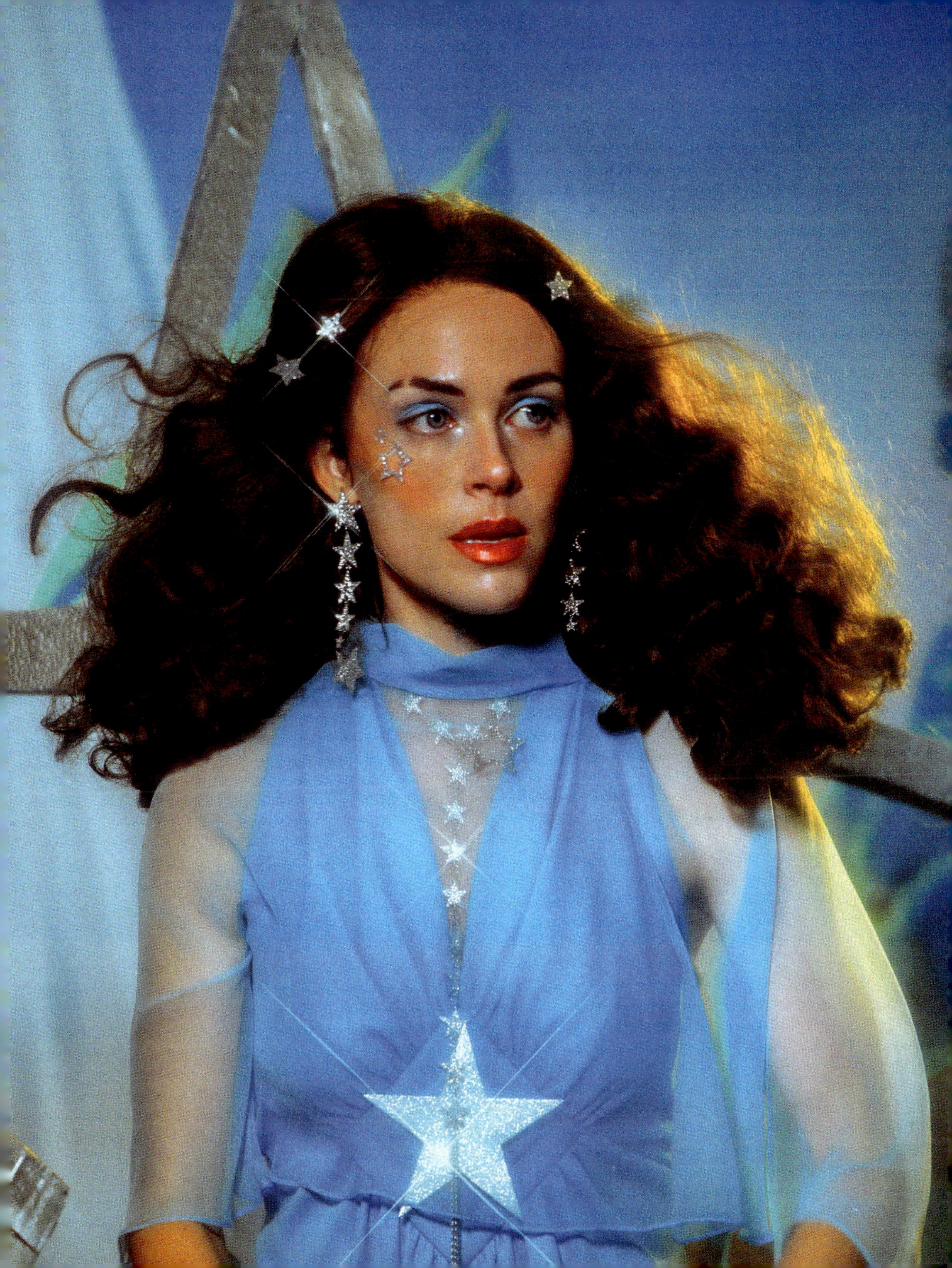

FASHION EXERCISES

> Browse through your wardrobe and identify the pieces you wear most often. List the characteristics you like about these items and see if you notice a pattern that ties them together. Next, identify the items in your wardrobe that you rarely ever wear. List the characteristics you aren't crazy about for these pieces and see if you notice another pattern. How do the items you like compare with those you don't like as much?

> Take a photo of your outfit each day for a full week. Write down how the outfit makes you feel after you take each photo. When the week is over, look back at all seven photos. Think about which ones made you feel the best and rank your top three favorite looks. Why do you think these three appeal to you the most?

> Choose a few of your favorite fashion icons or stylish celebrities. Write down their names and what you like best about their senses of style. See if you notice any similarities showing up across your lists. Try to recreate some of their outfits or create a look that is inspired by them.

> Create a photo mood board of different fashion items—include everything, from clothing to accessories! Put together a new look that pulls inspiration from the collage you've created. Try to pair items that you've never worn together before.

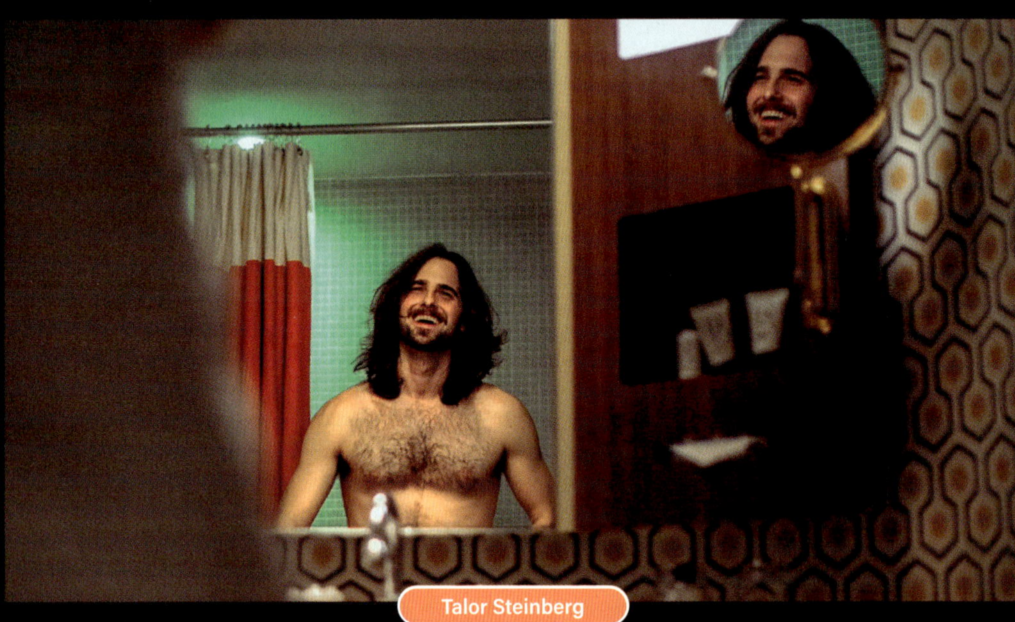

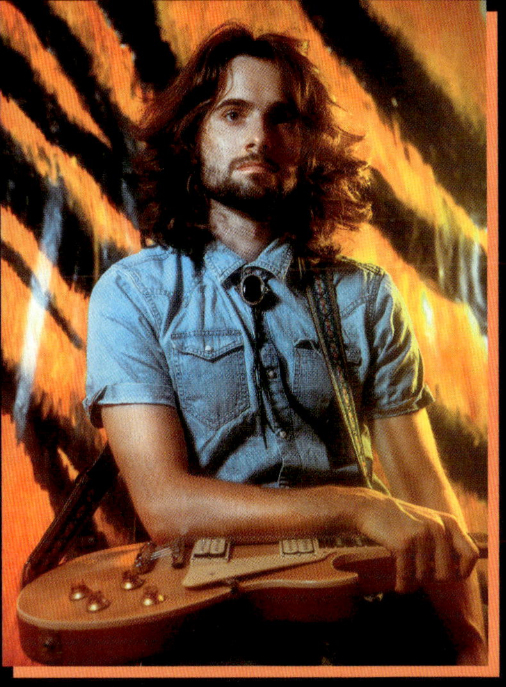
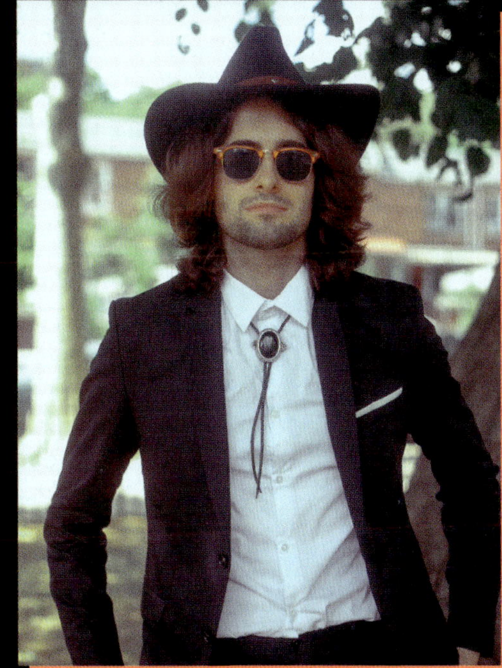
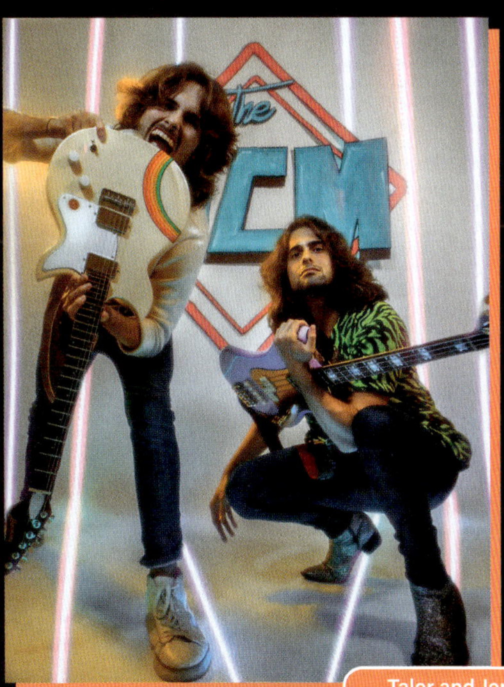

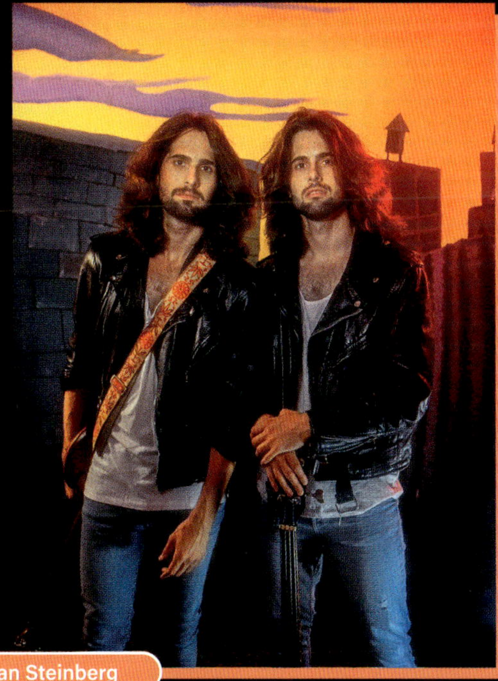

Talor and Jordan Steinberg

QUESTIONS TO CONSIDER

> Refer to your aesthetic list. Are there any people or characters on it? What outfits do they wear? Could you imagine yourself wearing an outfit like what they're wearing? Could you use their looks as inspiration to create a new outfit?

> What parts of your body do you feel the most comfortable with? How could you accentuate or draw more attention to them?

> What parts of your body do you feel less comfortable with? How could you choose pieces to highlight them in a way that makes you feel more confident? Or what other body parts could you highlight to draw attention elsewhere?

> What are your favorite colors to wear? Does wearing a certain color affect your mood in one way or another? What colors do you feel happiest wearing? What colors do you feel least happy wearing?

> What's a go-to clothing item that you always feel good in? What about wearing it brings you comfort?

> Is there a bold piece of clothing you've wanted to try out but have been too nervous to do so? What if you paired it with one of your go-to pieces to help bring a sense of balance to the outfit?

> What are you trying to convey with your personal style? What are you trying to convey with the style choices you apply to the characters or human figures in your creative works? Do you think it's working? If not, what changes could you make?

> Do you want to feel more confident or comfortable? Do you want to feel edgy, or do you want to feel timeless?

> Look at what your favorite celebrities and trendsetters are wearing for inspiration. What outfits of theirs do you like the most? What about these outfits attracts you?

> Are there any designers that you like? If so, can you try to make a more budget-friendly recreation of their looks?

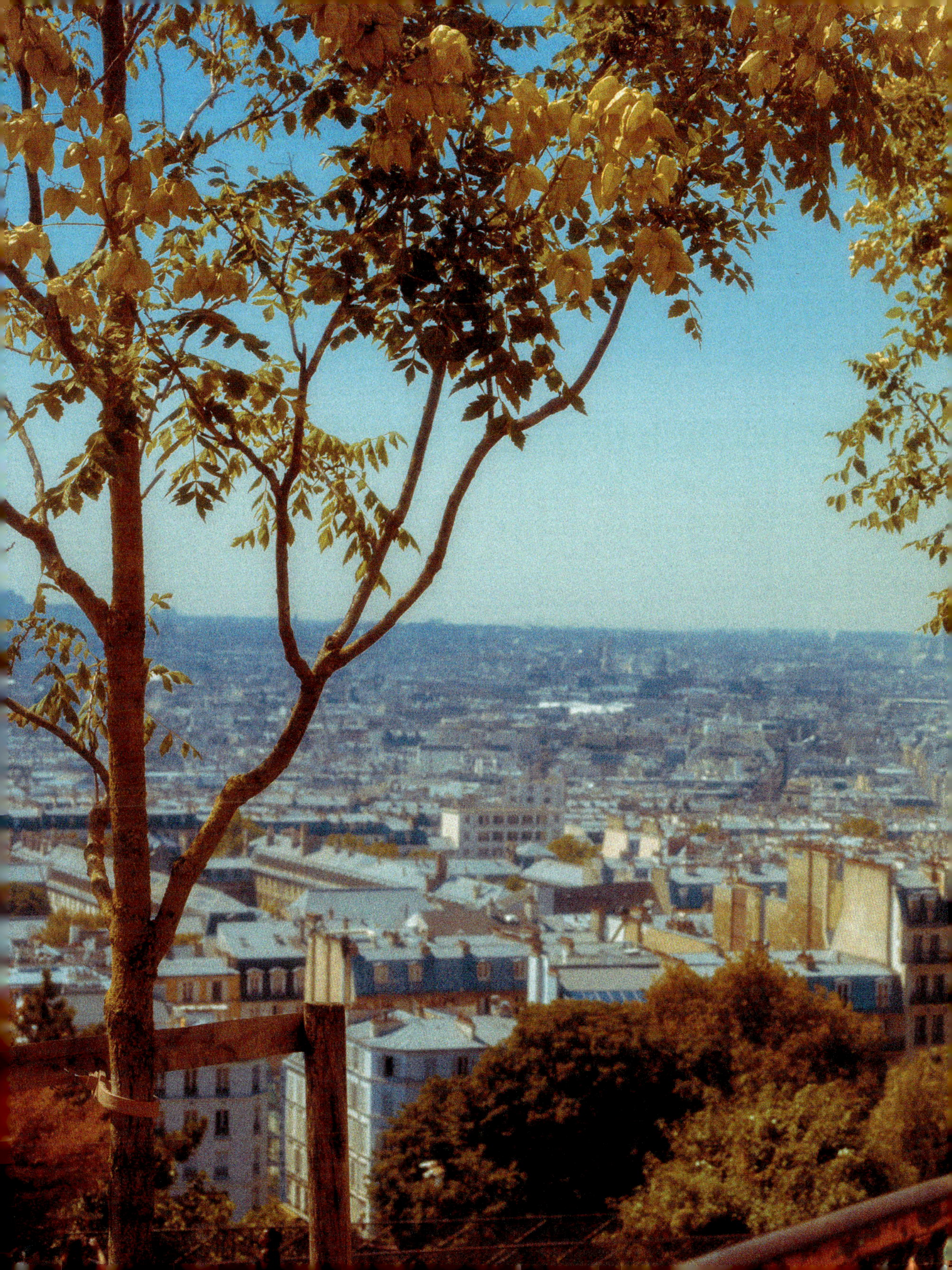

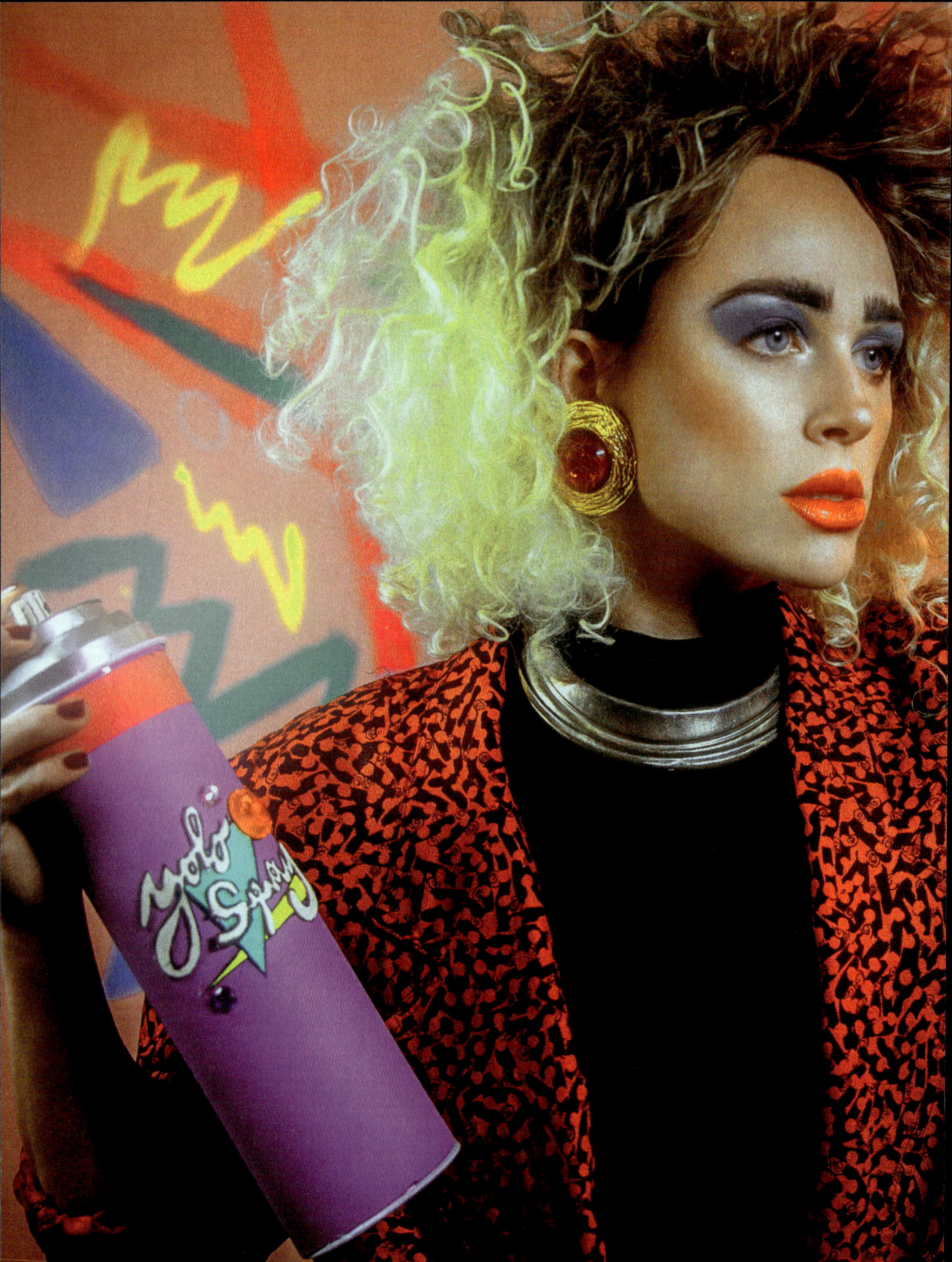
Yolo Spray

CHAPTER NINE

OBJECTS & ACCESSORIES

ITEMS THAT SHARE STORIES

Objects and accessories can be storytellers, each with their own unique tales to share. They're the keepers of memories, witnesses to life's adventures, and often even companions on our journeys. In the world of design, they can bring an intimate and personal touch to a space, adding unexpected charm and a touch of vulnerability into the mix.

I believe the objects in a space often function as visual character descriptions, hinting at the personality type and aesthetic preferences of whoever placed them. Objects and accessories are the real, physical elements that breathe life into our surroundings and styles. If paired together right, they can solidify the specific character traits you are trying to get across to the viewer.

When I'm creating a scene, I always ask myself questions like: What items are lying around? What book is the character reading? Do they have any personal photographs, awards, or accolades on display? What kind of art do they have on their walls? Each of these elements contributes to the narrative of an aesthetic, adding layers of depth to what I'm trying to convey. It's all about those extra touches that bring the story to life. For example, if a baseball bat is leaning up against a character's bedroom wall, you could assume they like sports. If the character is also wearing a baseball cap as an accessory, it would be safe to say they love the game more than anything else.

The objects and accessories in your space are like personal snapshots. They silently convey a wealth of information about you and your surroundings. Whether you're styling your home or picking out an outfit, objects and accessories have a big say in your personal style.

PLACING WITH PURPOSE

Whether you're crafting a video or sprucing up a living space, the objects you choose to add to the room bring a sense of vitality. They can work as allies to your storytelling, offering a deeper glimpse into the narrative you wish to create.

When you're engaged in a creative project, such as making a movie or painting a scene, the objects you choose to display are pivotal to character development. If the scene you're creating feels bare, add in some objects to the background or bring in more accessories for your character to wear. Experiment with placement and see what feels best.

When I'm setting up a scene for a video, I first arrange all the furniture and then think about who inhabits this space and what they use it for. Once I've come up with a direction, I begin placing objects. I'll move around the space and ask myself questions like: Would this person have this item? Why? Where would they keep it? It's all about capturing the essence of the character and the story; feel free to use any kind of object that fits into your vision.

For example, even though my "Dreamweaver" Valentine's Day video is meant to be set in the '70s, I decided to bring in a lot of Victorian and soft, romantic objects. I envisioned this character as someone brimming with excitement about an upcoming date, her thoughts lost in a dreamy reverie of romance. She's a character with a fascinating blend of influences, the kind of person who's enthralled

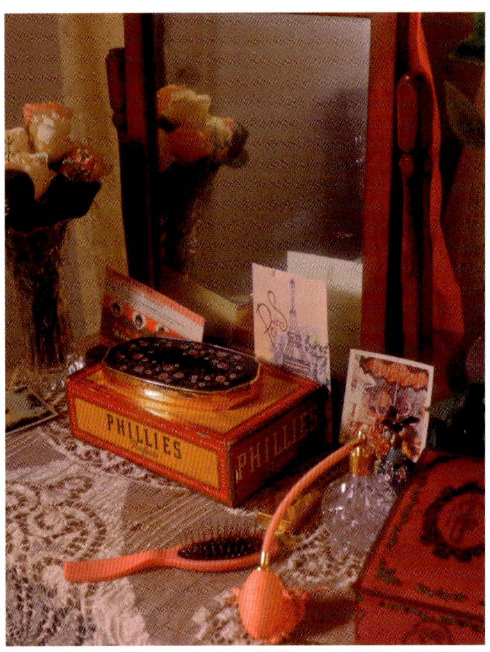

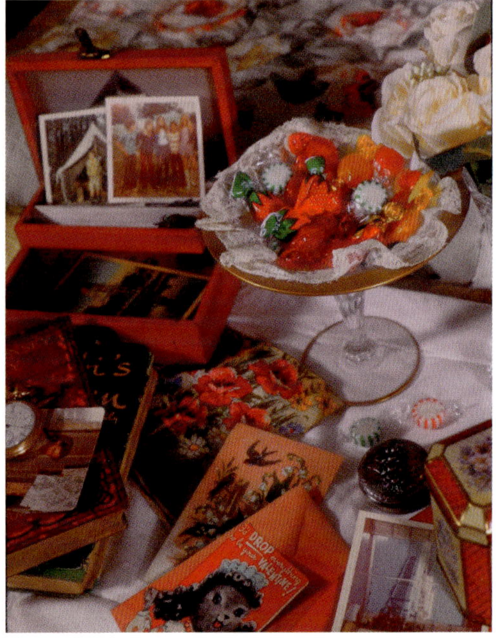

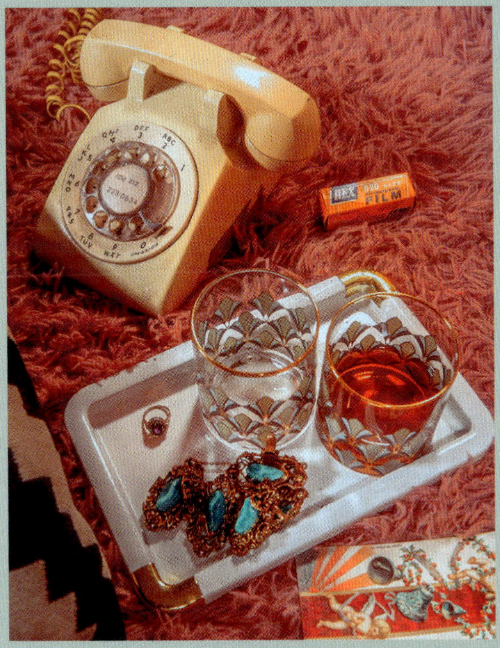

aspirations. The robe acts as a free-flowing swirl of romanticism because of the movement it brings to the scene as she gets ready. She eventually changes out of the robe and into a ruffly romantic dress. The dress is paired with a beautiful vintage beaded bag—completing the look while also highlighting that this character wears accessories that are in direct conversation with the Victorian-era objects in the room.

Imagine if I had included a pizza box or a skateboarding magazine in the scene. It would have sent a vastly different message! Even altering the photographs, artwork, or substituting another object or accessory could completely shift the character's identity. It could suggest that the character is putting on a front, forcing a dreamy facade that doesn't reflect her true self.

by ethereal notions of love but who also has a penchant for rock and roll.

Making these character decisions allowed me to select objects that would bring this vision to life. I adorned the tables with delicate objects like little candies, jewelry, tin boxes with photographs, and assorted romantic trinkets. These objects played a pivotal role in shaping the persona of the character I was creating and helped me achieve the aesthetic I wanted— evoking the characteristic '70s resurgence of the romantic Victorian trend.

I considered the robe worn by this hopelessly romantic character as more of a prop than a costume. It has a flowy quality that enhances the dreamy, sweeping movements I wanted to capture. It also exudes old Hollywood glamour, which echoes the character's glamorous

Objects and accessories are more than just adornments or decorations—they are storytellers. When you're choosing items, keep in mind that their stories may evolve and intertwine with your own, enriching the tapestry of your aesthetic journey. In the real world, the longer an object lives in a space, the more meaning becomes attached to it, allowing the story it signifies to change and expand. These items can reveal the essence of who we are and what we value most. So whether you're crafting a scene, styling a room, or putting together an outfit, remember that these seemingly inconsequential details play a vital role in shaping your unique aesthetic and the stories you tell. Embrace the quirks, showcase the memories, and let the unique additions shine through. In the world of aesthetics, it's the personal touch that leaves the most lasting impression.

LAST BUT NOT LEAST

Objects and accessories are usually some of the last additions to a piece. They are the finishing touches that help bring out personality and character. Before placing objects and accessories to really make the final product shine, make sure the foundation of your room, outfit, or artistic work has already been laid out and that you feel good about it.

Think about what story you are trying to tell with your room, who might wear this outfit, or what the character in your painting is trying to achieve. Once you're able to come up with answers, you can begin to place items to make these goals even clearer to the viewer who will see your finished work.

Objects and accessories have endless possibilities to tell stories. It all depends on how your characters interact with them and how they are displayed or worn. For example, we can use a map to depict a person who is lost. Maybe they've been on the road for a while, experiencing a long journey of self-discovery. Accessories that would further convey this message could include a backpack, sunglasses, and a wide-brimmed hat.

What if we see an old man sitting alone in his study, a large grandfather clock ticking behind him? The sound and the grandness of the clock could signify that the passage of time is weighing heavily on the man's mind. Maybe he's contemplating past regrets. How could we show this even further? Perhaps one of his accessories is a locket with an old image of a former lover.

We can also take similar objects and attach totally different scenarios to them depending on the context and clues provided. For instance, what if we see a teenage girl sitting in her bedroom, all dressed up and staring at the moving hands of a clock ticking away on the wall? Perhaps she too has a locket with an image of a partner in it. As she clasps it tightly, the viewer may come to understand that she is eager to go on an upcoming date.

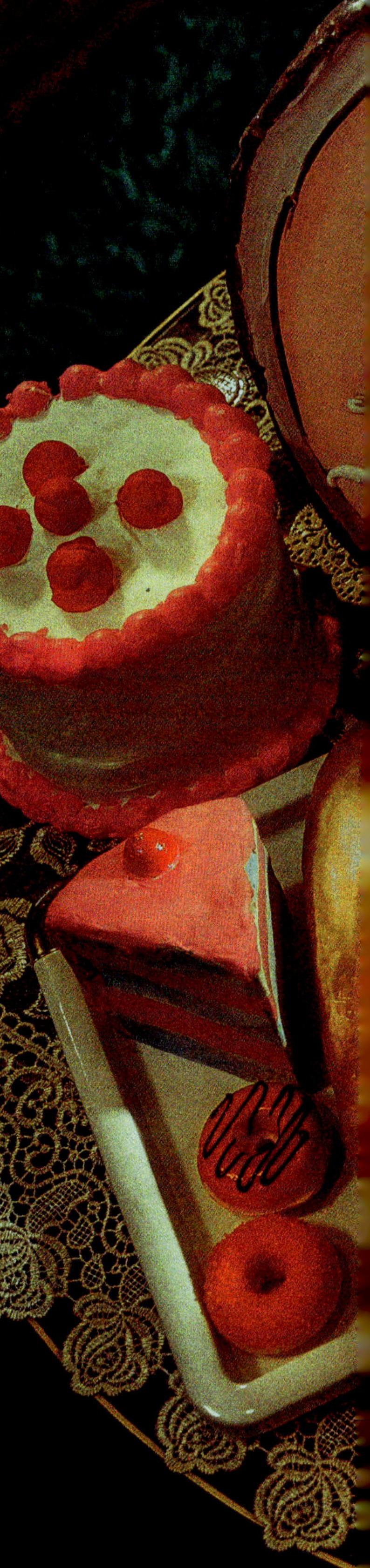

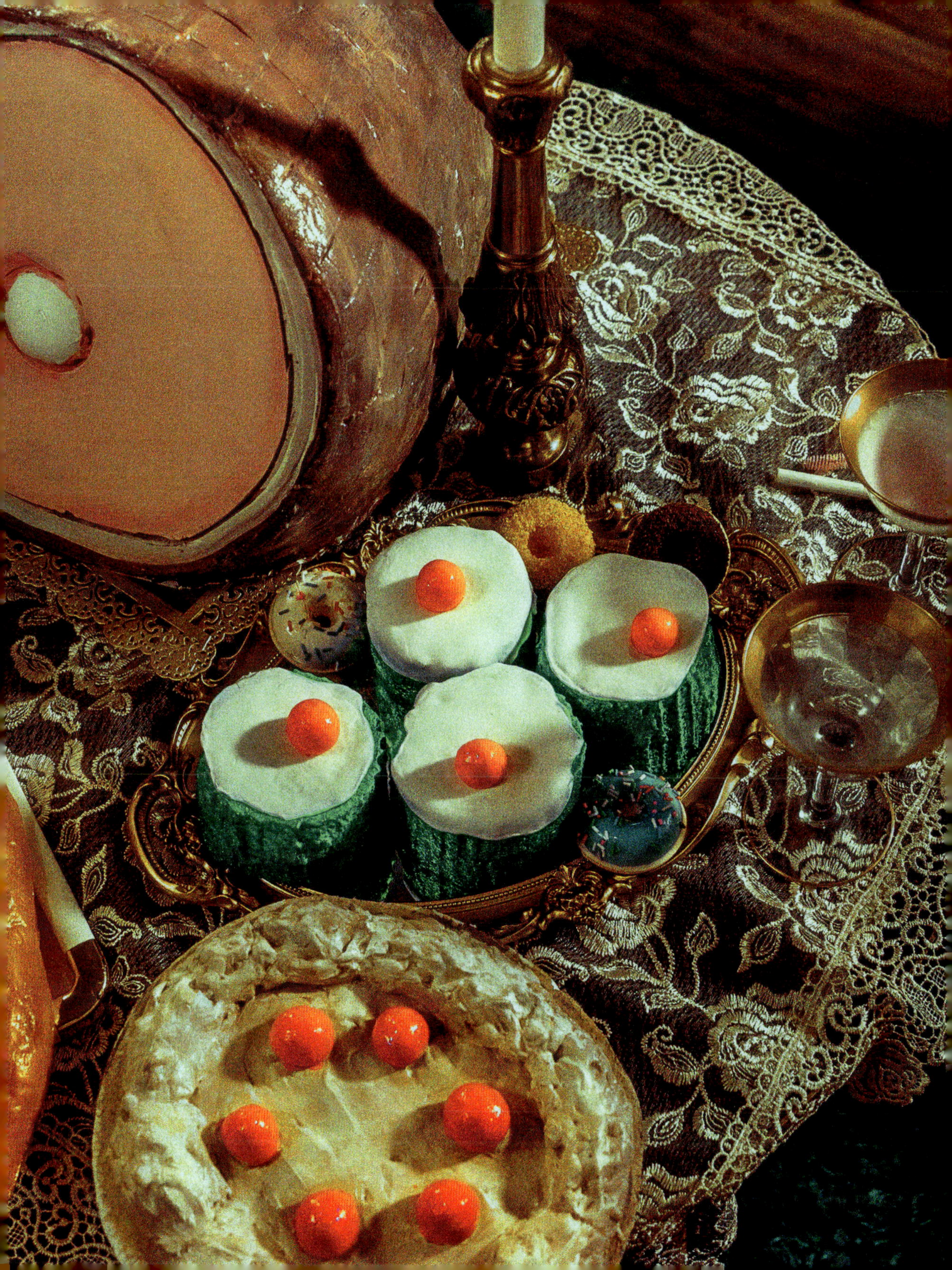

OBJECTS & ACCESSORIES ACROSS DISCIPLINES

Objects and accessories for film design: Objects and accessories can function as story builders. Each item should give insight into the story in some way. The objects and accessories don't all need to have strong roles in the scene or film, but they should add value to the universe the story lives within. Other things to think about when designing a scene include the mood and themes you're going for. Do the objects fit with the overall vibe? You may also need to consider your budget and get creative to save on costs.

Objects and accessories for everyday creation: The items we see and use in our daily lives often come with attached emotional connections that influence how we feel. In our everyday lives, we might approach objects and accessories according to our innate desire for the piece, rather than its use or function. The objects and accessories we select for ourselves don't have to be so absolute in telling others who we are or what goals we're aiming for. Feel free to experiment with a range of different items before solidifying what you truly want to fill your space or accessorize yourself with.

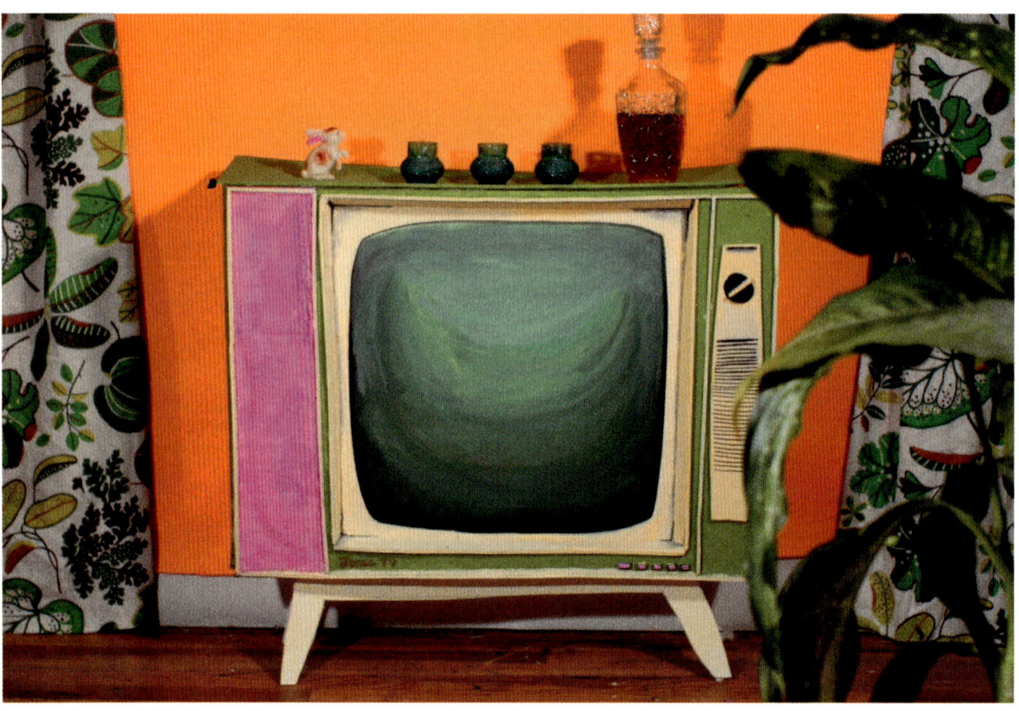

Vibing Out

LAVINIA JONES WRIGHT
Actor & Writer

There's a box of stuff in the closet at the acting studio where I sometimes work. My theater company gets together on Tuesday nights to work on scenes from plays. Every Tuesday, we haul out the box. It's not a ton of stuff: three telephones from different eras, a hot plate, a few plastic wine glasses, coffee mugs, and linens. A few books and magazines. A vase with flowers.

I've seen similar boxes of props in every acting studio I've ever been in. Things that were either brought intentionally to fill out familiar spaces or things that were left behind and forgotten about that became a permanent part of the collection. With slight variations—maybe there's plates, place mats, a tablecloth—and some wild cards: one had a samovar, one had exercise equipment, ours has a cigar box.

It always makes me think about the common threads between the spaces in human lives and the way that interacting with these things is so familiar they can transport us. Every office desk had a telephone (until they didn't!), every house has plates and cups, every fancy restaurant has wine glasses and tablecloths, every coffee table and waiting room has magazines. By placing these things into the hands of actors, they are instantly transported to these spaces. A heavy, black telephone can turn a card table into a mahogany desk; a small, gold alarm clock turns the card table into an elegant bedroom nightstand; and a crisp, white tablecloth and vase of plastic flowers turn it into a restaurant.

It's amazing how much a scene changes when just a few props are added to the mix. When the actor has something tangible to hold onto and interact with, suddenly they are adding behavior to the emotion of the scene. They are nervously folding their napkin, staring at the phone waiting for it to ring, throwing books at the wall in anger. You can enter a scene without a door. You can build a sofa out of four folding chairs. But it's very hard to make a phone call without a phone. Ask people who do improv.

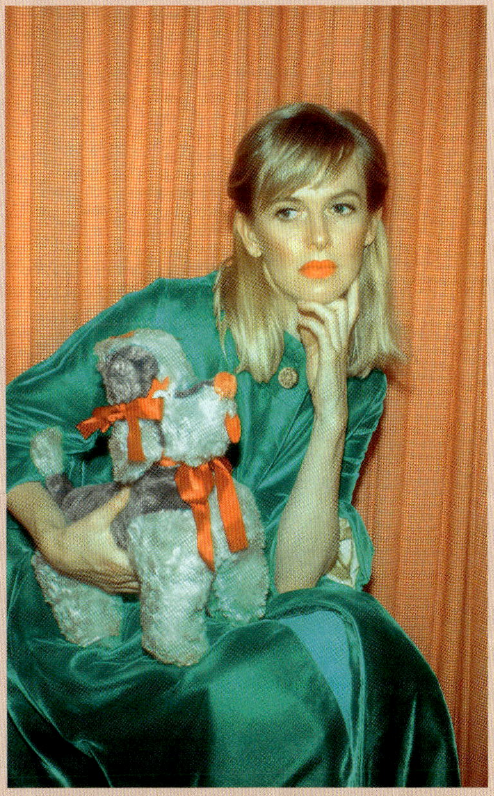

WHAT CAN YOU ADD TO YOUR SCENE?

OBJECTS

LOCK

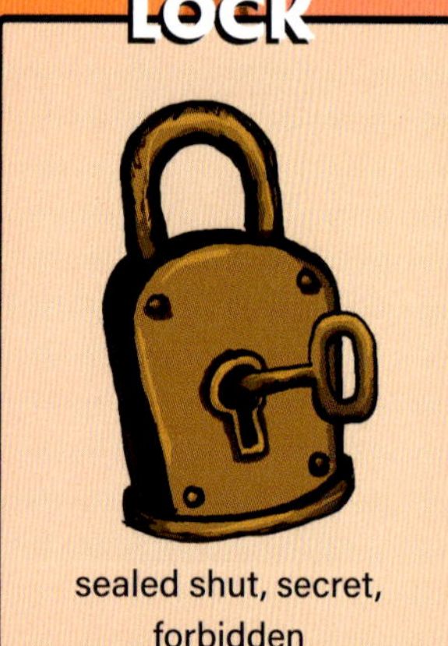

sealed shut, secret, forbidden

MAP

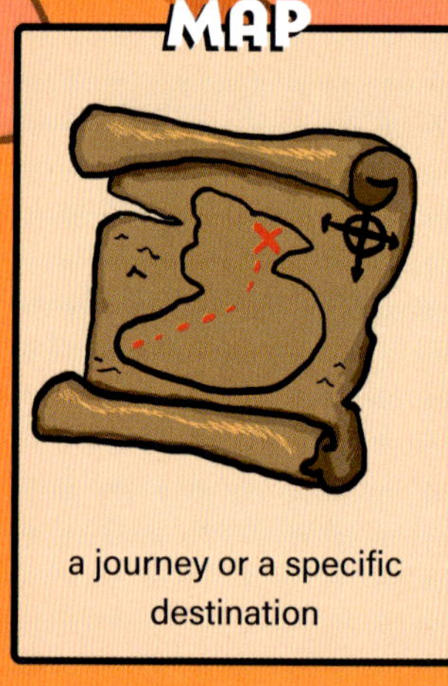

a journey or a specific destination

COMPUTER

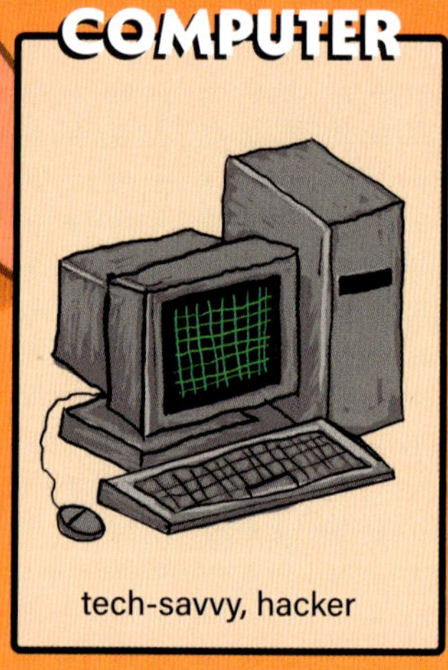

tech-savvy, hacker

HEADPHONES

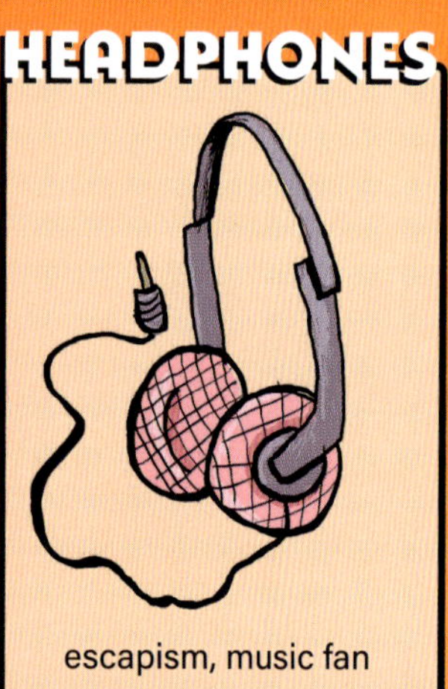

escapism, music fan

GLOBE

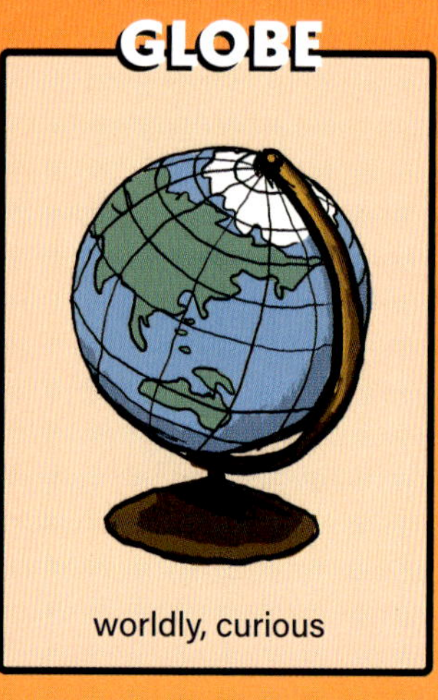

worldly, curious

BOOK

scholarly, smart

ACCESSORIES

BASEBALL HAT

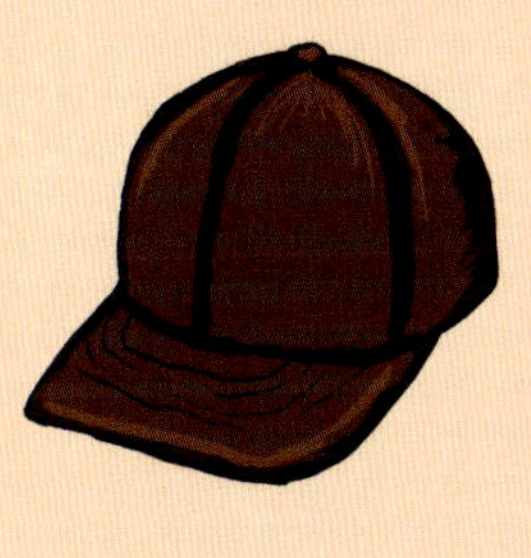

casual or sports fan

SUNGLASSES

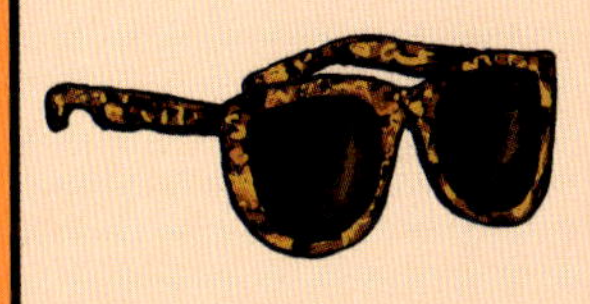

cool and collected

WATCH

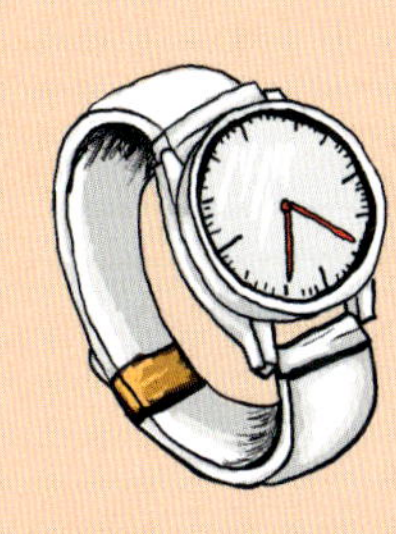

a punctual person

BACKPACK

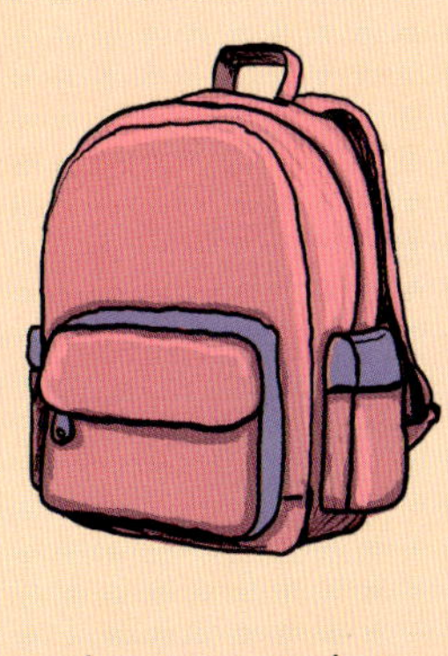

adventurer, student

BOW TIE

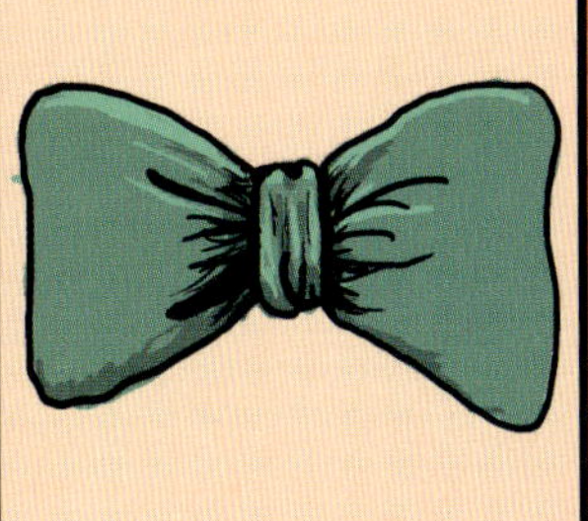

charismatic intellectual

HANDBAG

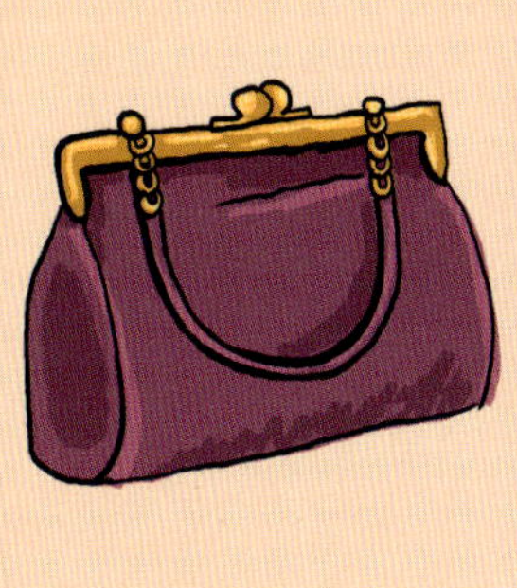

organized elegance

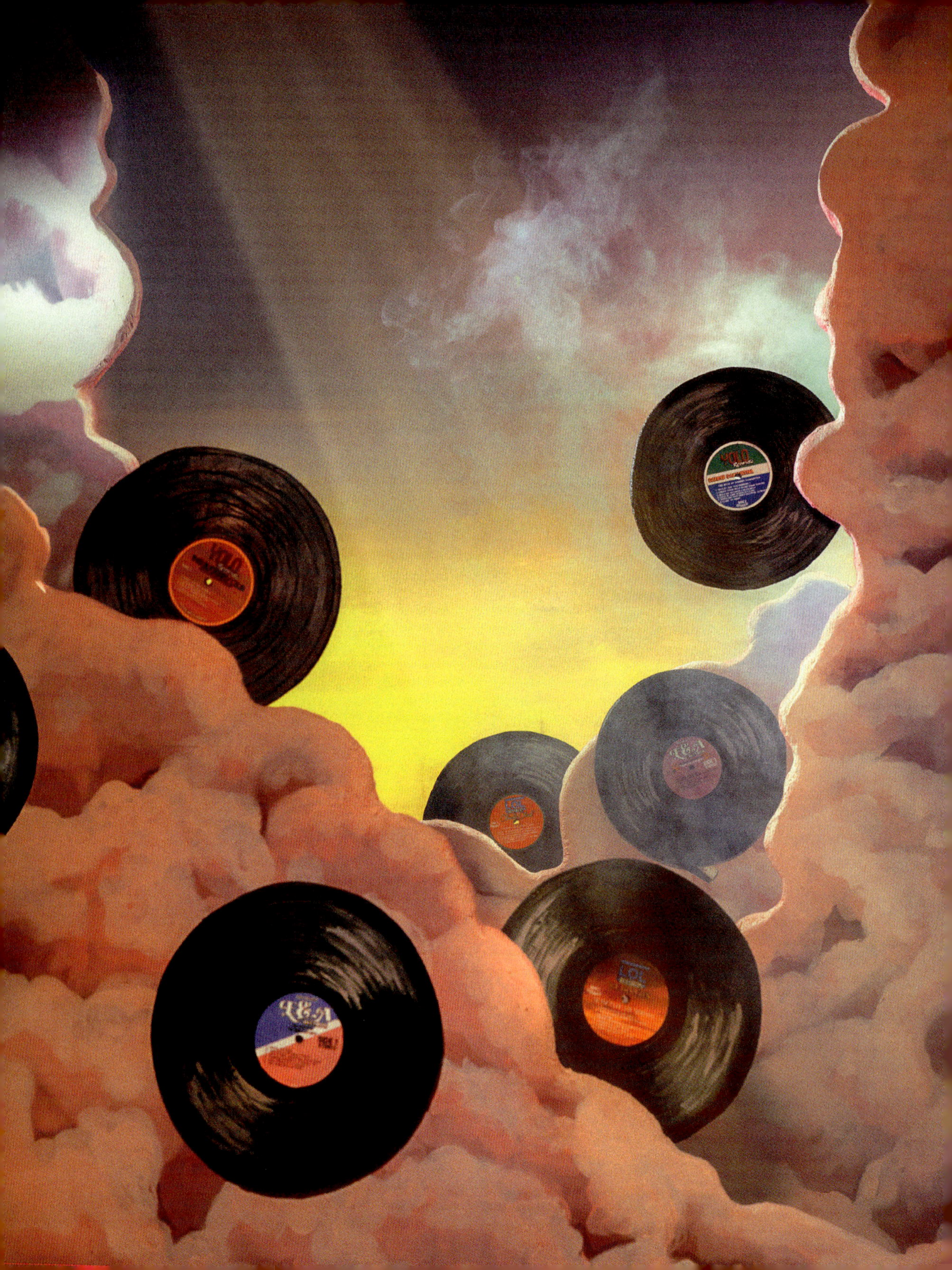

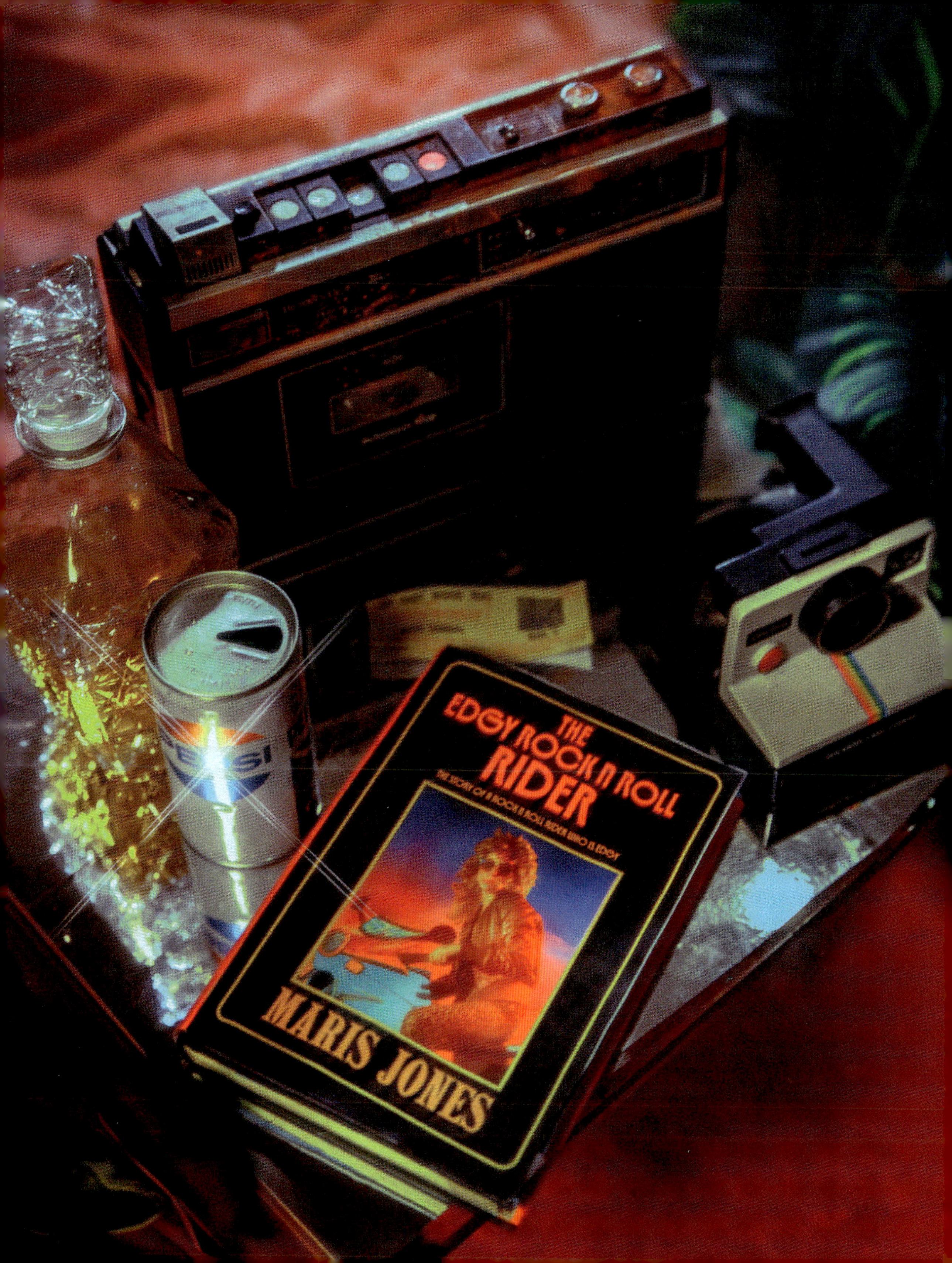
THE
EDGY ROCK N ROLL
RIDER
THE STORY OF A ROCK N ROLL RIDER WHO IS EDGY
MARIS JONES
PEPSI

OBJECTS & ACCESSORIES EXERCISES

> **Place items with purpose:**
Choose a central theme or style for your room, and select objects and accessories that align with it. For example, for a beach-themed living room, incorporate seashells, driftwood, and coastal artwork. Then try adding objects that serve both a decorative and functional purpose, such as storage boxes, stylish bookends, or unique lighting fixtures.

> **Give more information to a story:**
Select objects and accessories that symbolize key aspects of a character's personality, history, or motivations. For example, a character who collects vintage records might indicate that they have a passion for music and nostalgia.

> **Don't be afraid to create contrast with your items:**
Use contrasting objects or accessories to create tension or provide subtle clues about a character's inner conflict. A tidy, well-organized space juxtaposed with a hidden, disheveled corner can hint at secrets.

> **Create change:**
Show changes in a character's life or story arc by gradually altering the objects and accessories in their environment. For instance, as a character develops, their space might become more cluttered or minimalist. Incorporate objects with unique stories or histories that can be woven into the larger narrative you're trying to tell, adding depth and intrigue to the story's world.

> **This idea works with accessories too:**
As your story progresses, try making the character's jewelry louder and bigger or maybe make the pieces more delicate and smaller. Try telling a story through your character's accessories, where a piece changes in appearance from the beginning to the end. At the start of a story, a character could love wearing a large feather boa because they want to feel decadent and bold. But by the end of the story, their feather boa has lost half of its feathers and is covered in dirt. What could this signify?

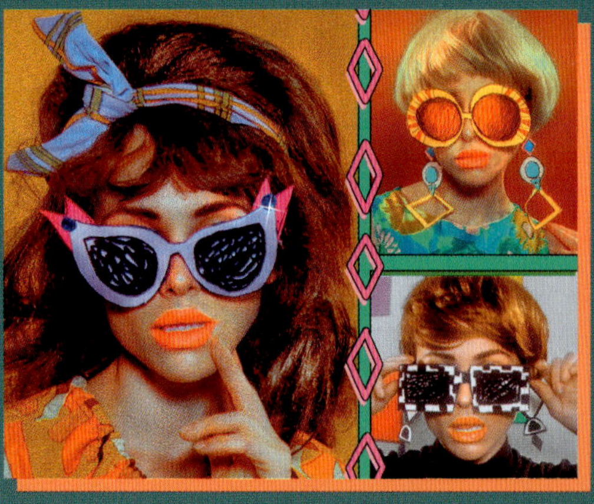

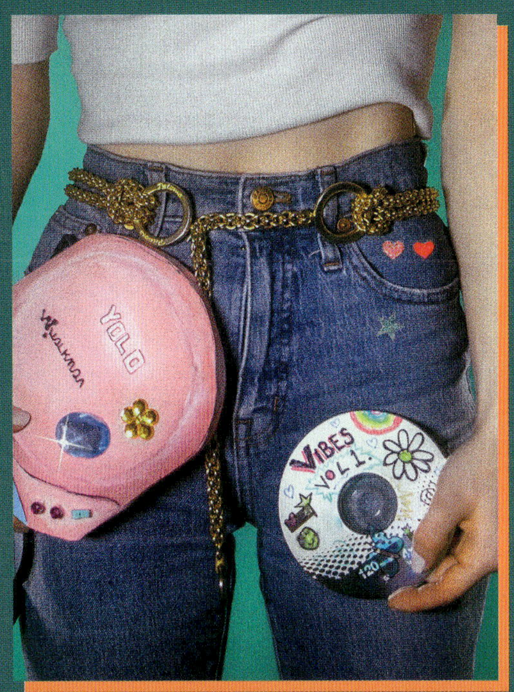
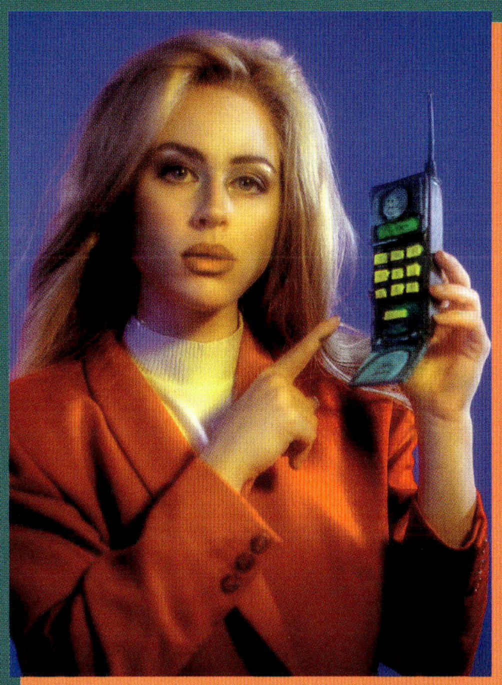
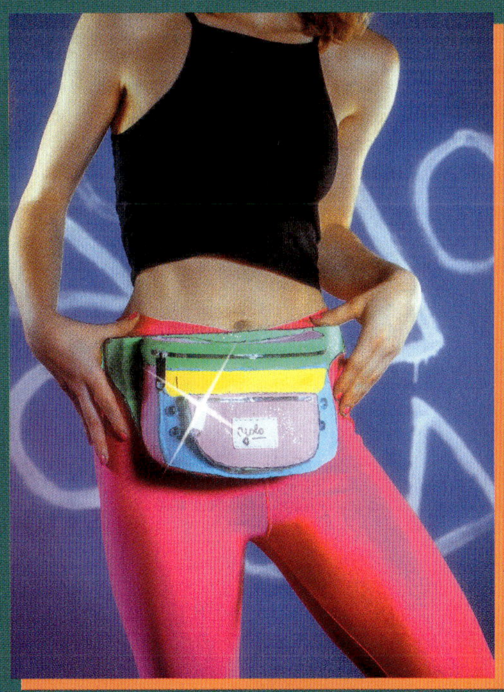
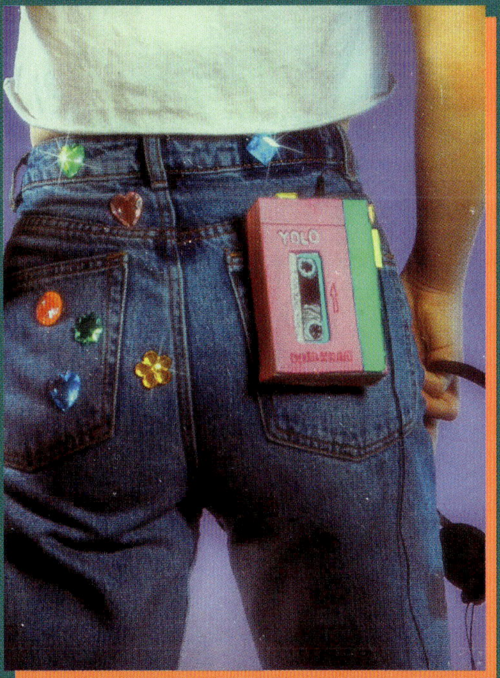

QUESTIONS TO CONSIDER

- What type of objects are you naturally drawn to?

- What are some of your favorite objects in your home? Where did you get them? Why do they mean so much to you?

- What are some of the objects you use the most in your space? What is their purpose?

- If you're working on a painting, drawing, or other piece of artwork, are there any objects in the scene? Could you add any to help get the story you're trying to tell across in a more obvious manner?

- What is the overall style or vibe you are going for with your project? What kind of objects or accessories could you add to it to help complement and strengthen this vibe?

- What are some of the accessories that you use on a regular basis? Are they something you add to an outfit or something that you carry around with you for a functional purpose?

- Is there a certain piece of jewelry that you wear regularly? What do you think it signifies to others who see you wearing it?

- Do you own any accessories that you wear only on very specific occasions? What are they? Could you try incorporating them into your regular attire more often? How could that change the way you are perceived?

- Could you add an accessory to your character's outfit that would totally change how others view them? What would this accessory be, and how would it change things?

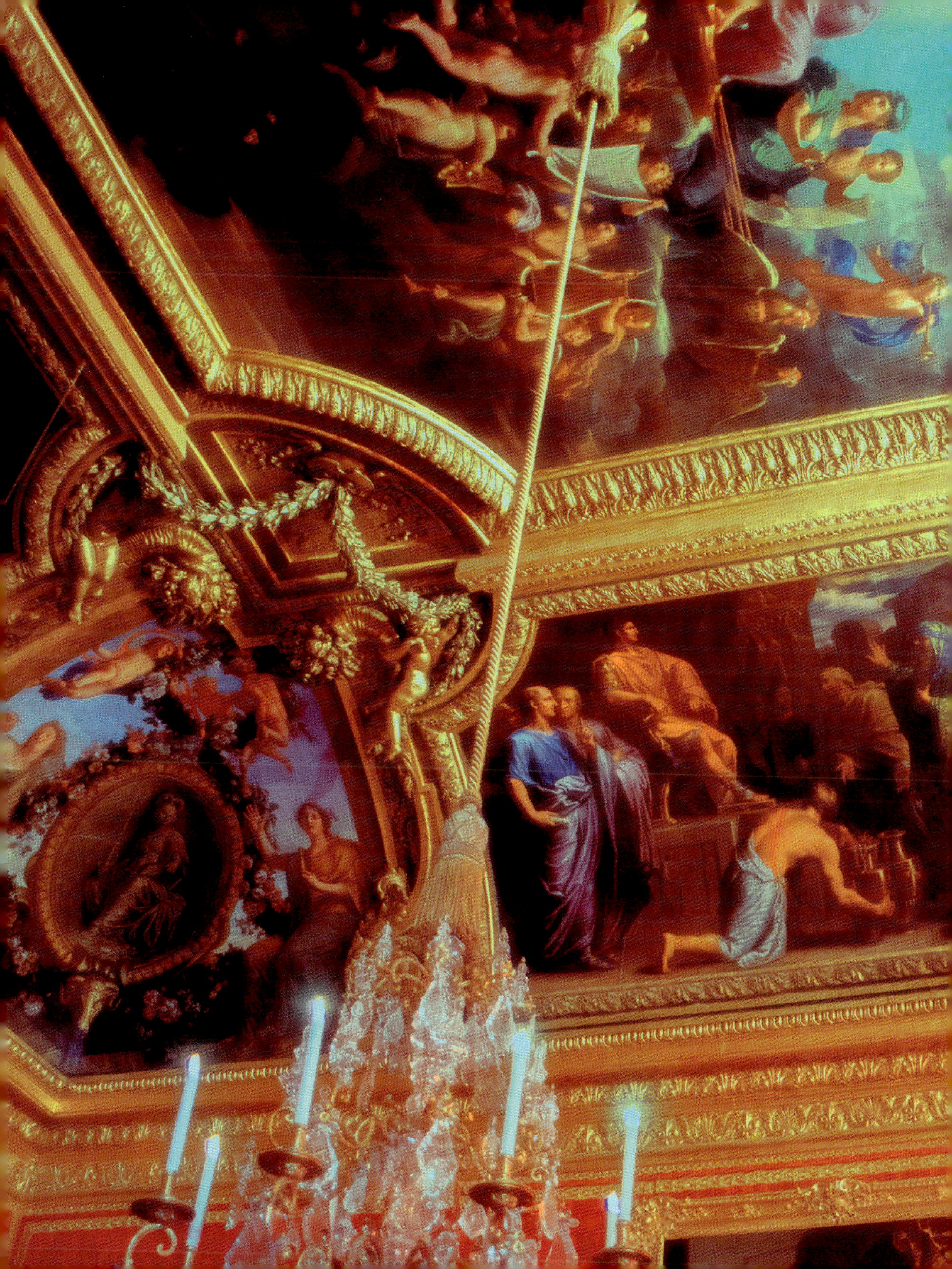

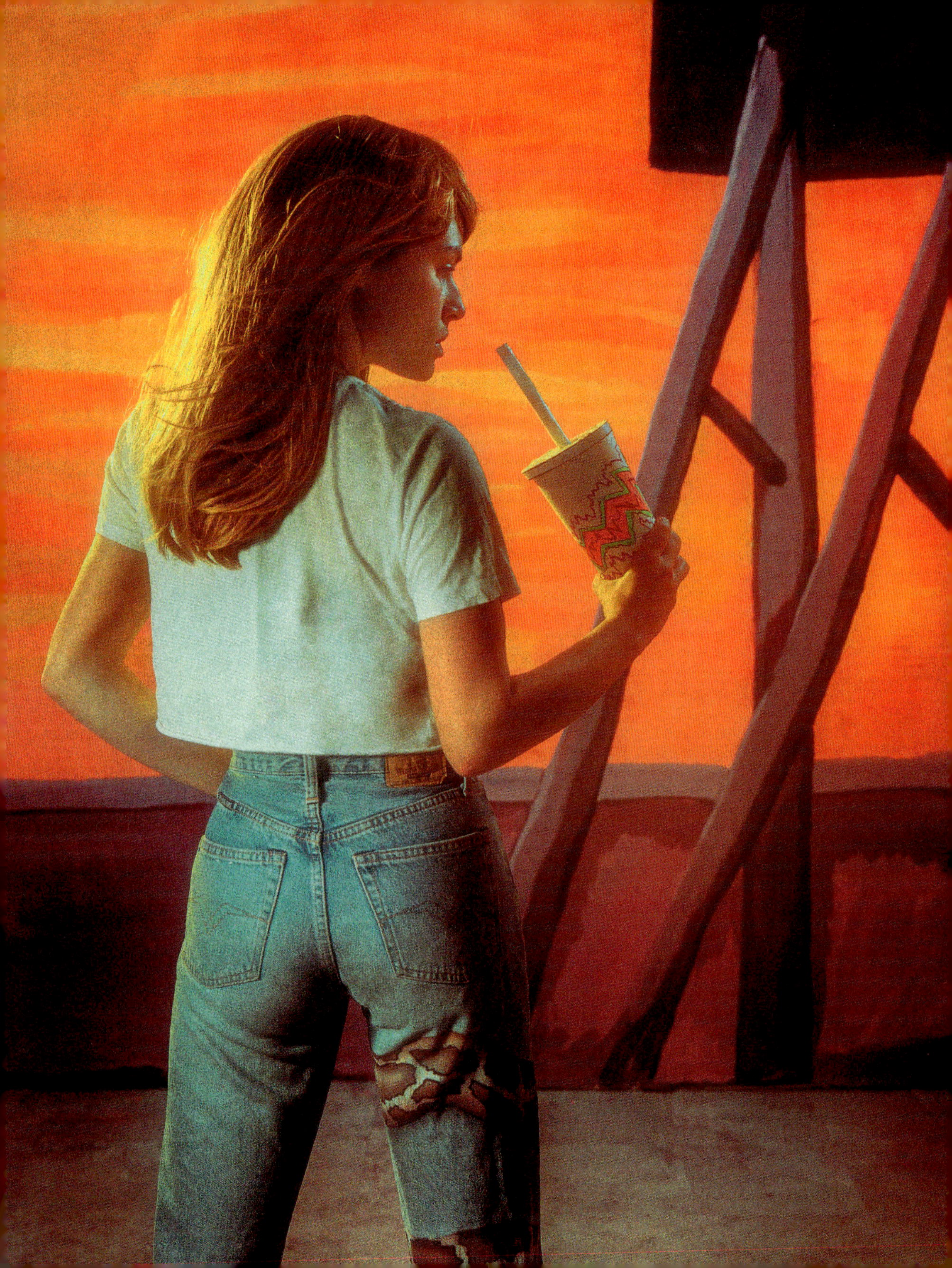

PART IV

FINISHING TOUCHES

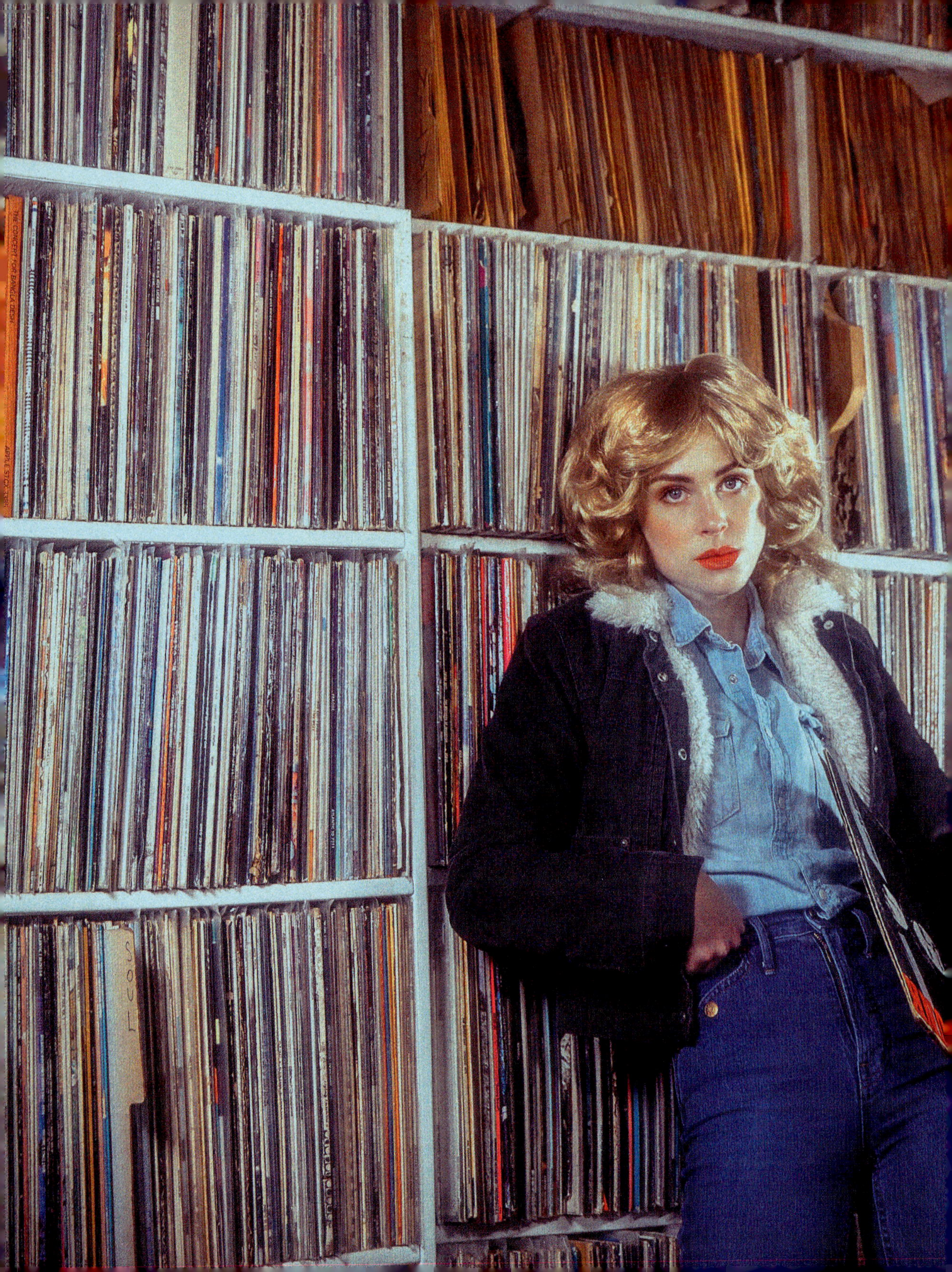

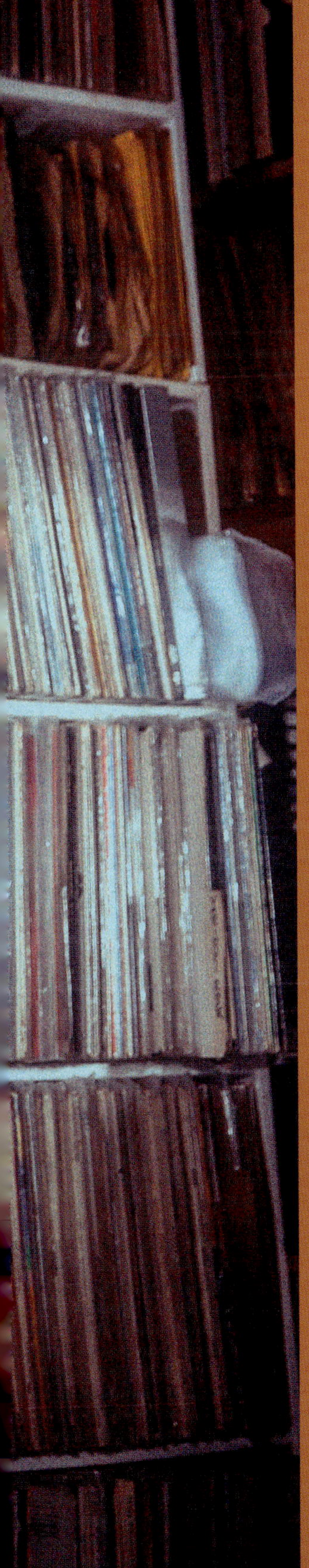

CHAPTER TEN

LISTEN TO THE MUSIC

THE SOUNDTRACK OF OUR LIVES

A single chord can elicit an immediate emotional response, and the addition of a carefully chosen song can utterly transform a creative project, infusing it with the specific theme or atmosphere you are striving to convey. Music works like a key to unlock our emotions. Music can come into play if you're crafting a score or soundtrack for a film, curating a rockin' playlist for your morning commute, or adding some rhythmic grooves to your social media content. Regardless of the creative endeavor at hand, listening to music can inspire your artistic process.

What makes music truly remarkable is its profound ability to mold and shape the ambience of any given piece it's paired with. It is without a doubt one of the main keys to unlocking the magic of the human soul, capable of shaping and influencing every facet of our creative work.

I often use music to completely alter the theme and vibe of my creations. While silence can be a deliberate choice to convey a message, this chapter focuses on how music shapes our work, how to find the perfect music for a video or audio project, and how to derive inspiration from it.

THE POWER OF MUSIC

Music possesses a specific, potent ability to shape the atmosphere in any situation. It resonates deeply within our souls and can effectively set the tone for any creative endeavor. With the right music, you can transform a simple setting into an entirely different world.

Our brains associate emotions, feelings, and memories with various elements, including sounds. Certain sounds trigger subconscious emotional responses, whether they make us feel happy, sad, frustrated, or curious. Music, with its ability to evoke specific emotions, becomes a powerful tool to enhance storytelling, even in the home environment.

Consider this scenario: You're creating a playlist for a gathering. What kind of emotions are you aiming to evoke in your guests? Do you want to create a relaxed and mellow atmosphere or infuse the space with high energy for dancing and enjoyment?

Using music as a starting point for your creative endeavors can lead to surprising and exciting outcomes. I often employ this technique as an exercise to spark my creativity. While listening to a playlist, I might suddenly stumble upon a song that resonates deeply with me, evoking a specific emotion. At that moment, I'll pause and ask myself, "What colors come to mind?" Other times, I might hear a song that triggers certain emotions and sparks my imagination, encouraging me to construct a story around it.

If you can pinpoint a song that encapsulates a specific emotion, you can build an entire creative concept around it. This process helps you connect with your audience on a deeper level by conveying your message through a universally understood medium. But how do you begin to select music for your own projects? Start by contemplating the message you want to convey. Music can significantly amplify and direct that message.

While exploring music, I routinely curate playlists, adding songs that evoke emotions and themes relevant to my artistic vision. Over time, these recurring themes become signatures in my work, contributing to its unique identity. If you're uncertain about the themes you wish to convey through your work, take a look at your playlist. What common themes and emotions run through the songs that resonate with you? Reflect on your own experiences and the narratives that have always captivated your interest.

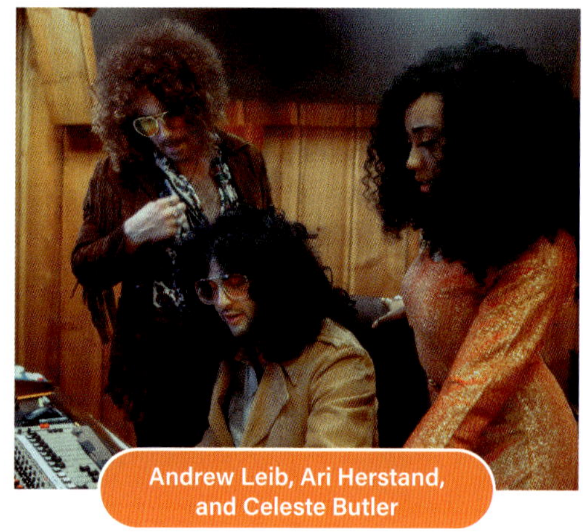

Andrew Leib, Ari Herstand, and Celeste Butler

Finishing Touches

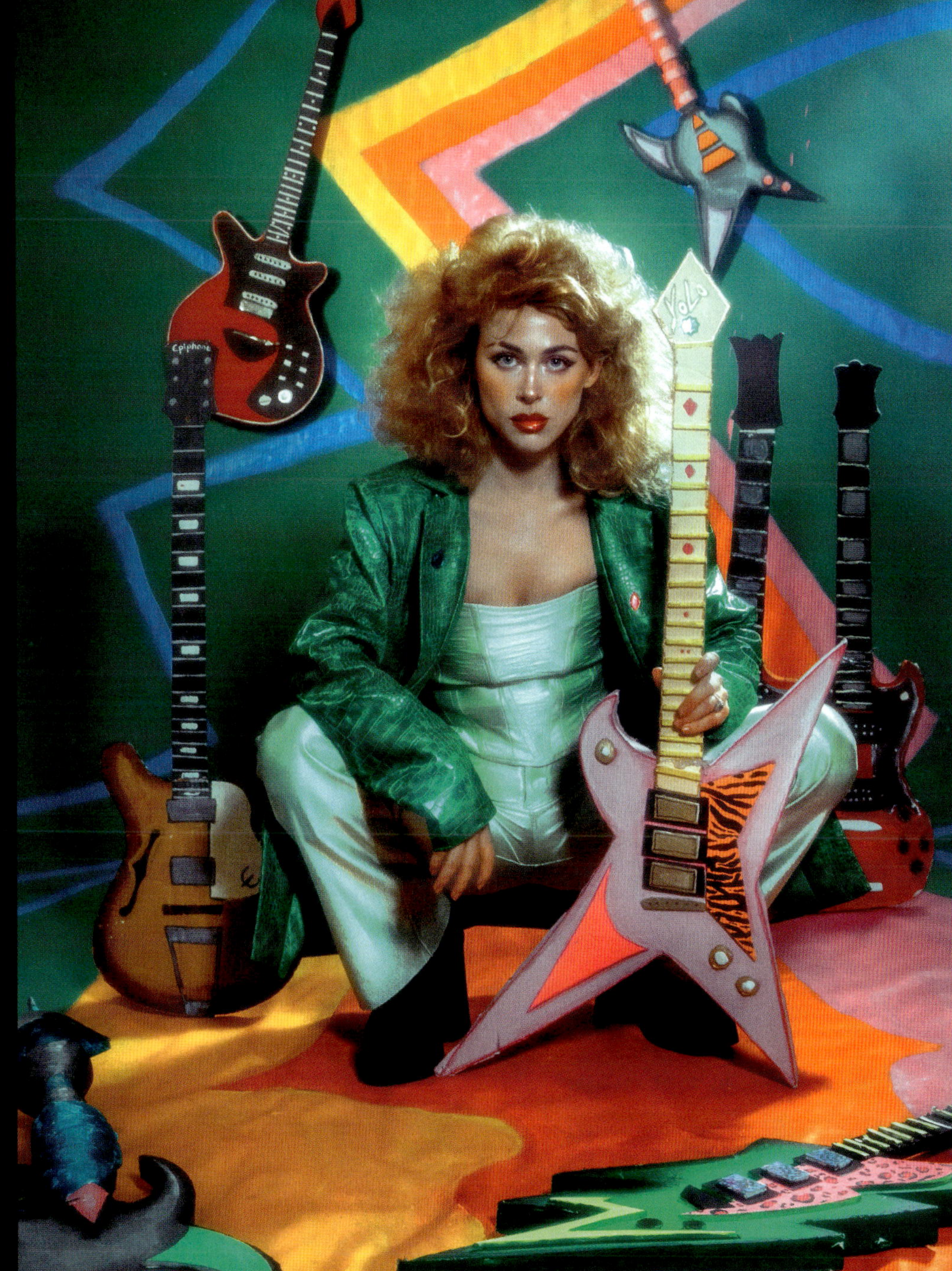

PICKING THE RIGHT SONG

Incorporating music into my creative work, especially in narrative videos, is second nature. I consistently infuse recurring themes by selecting songs that align with the emotions and ideas I wish to convey. These recurring themes become signatures in my work. For example, I am often drawn to triumphant underdog stories, so I tend to seek out songs that capture a similar essence of triumph and power. Understanding the themes that resonate with you allows you to curate a unique musical palette.

The collective memories tied to songs create shared experiences and emotions. People inherently connect with the emotions and cultural contexts associated with specific songs, making them powerful additions to creative projects. These cultural references are invaluable tools for storytellers.

Songs can transport people to specific moments in time. They evoke collective memories associated with the era in which they were popular. You can instantly establish the setting and atmosphere by incorporating well-known songs from a specific period, enhancing the storytelling experience. Consider a scene set during the Vietnam War; iconic songs like "Fortunate Son" or "For What It's Worth" will instantly transport audiences to this era.

Furthermore, specific music genres are also closely tied to certain emotions. Rock music often signifies aggression or rebellion, while pop music can be used to convey cheerfulness. Classical music suggests sophistication, while jazz can evoke various emotions from chaos to introspection. These associations are deeply ingrained in our cultural consciousness.

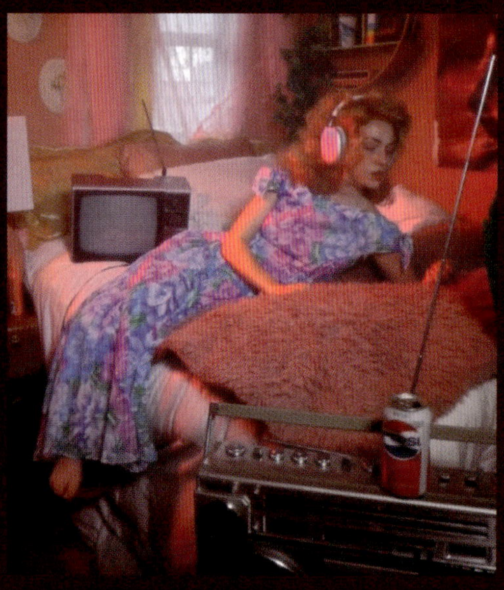 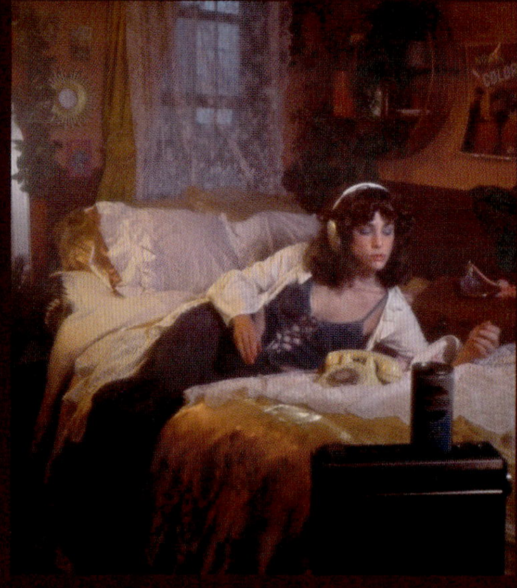

If you've already started a project, you likely have a clear understanding of the message you wish to convey. This emotional foundation provides a starting point for finding the right music. Suppose you're producing a video and have a distinct emotion in mind. In that case, you can search for a song that matches the on-screen energy or the character's persona.

Alternatively, you can use music to create juxtaposition and convey a different meaning. This technique can be quite powerful. For instance, say you're creating a scene set in the 1930s or 1940s with a softer, more traditional aesthetic. Your audience might expect gentle, sweet melodies that fit the vibe. However, what if you want to show that there's more to the character on-screen than meets the eye? You could overlay the scene with an unconventional rock song. This use of music transcends what is visible on-screen, offering insight into the character's inner world.

Music selection is an essential aspect of storytelling, since it shapes an audience's emotional response. By incorporating music into your creative process, you tap into a universal language that enhances your storytelling. Whether you're working on videos, writing, or other artistic endeavors, music serves as a powerful tool to elevate your work and connect with your audience on a deeper, emotional level.

Incorporating music into your creative process can unlock new dimensions of inspiration and enhance storytelling. Consider your target audience and the kind of music that resonates with them most. Songs that are from the era when they came of age will evoke nostalgia and create a deeper connection with your work for them. Whether it's for a video project or a personal endeavor, music serves as a universal language that enriches.

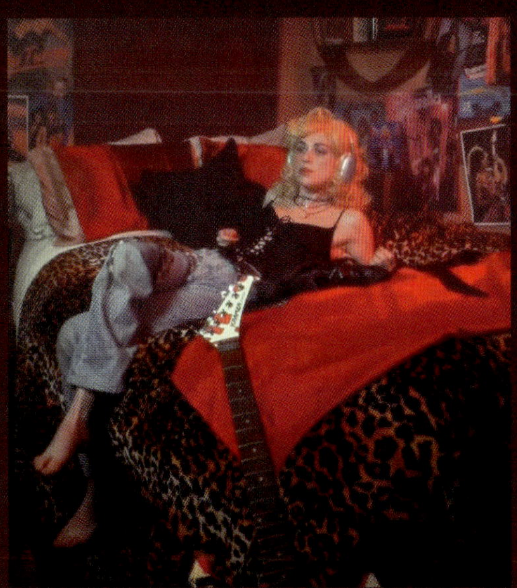

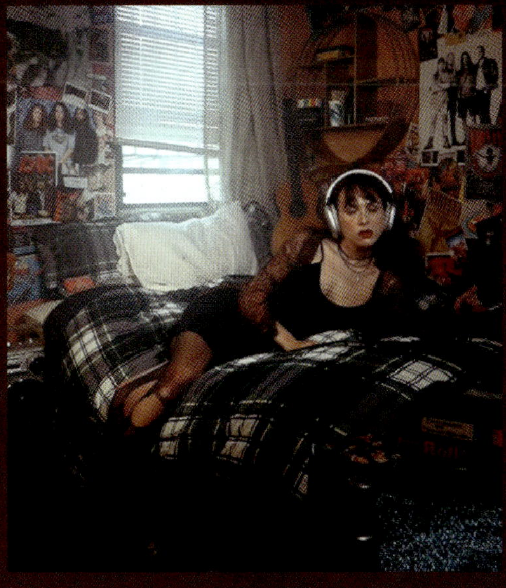

MUSIC ACROSS DISCIPLINES

Music for filmmaking: First, think about the tone of the scene you want to add music to. The music you choose is going to help create that emotional connection from the viewer to the screen. What kind of music shares a similar feel to your visuals? It's also important to find music that has a similar pace to the scene.

Sometimes, if you want to try something totally different, you can use music to create juxtaposition. Experiment with music that's opposite to the tone of your scene. You can try out tons of sounds, placing them over a scene as you see how the overall impression feels.

Having a clear idea of the emotional end goal will help you the most when selecting music. If you haven't identified the emotional themes in your piece, you're going to have a harder time finding the right music. So be sure you have an idea of what you want your work to say!

Don't forget to also think about where the work is going. If the project is just for you, feel free to use any music. But if you plan to put your work out in the world, you might need to find royalty-free music or have someone compose a score for you.

Music for everyday creation: Since how you feel will heavily influence what you want to listen to, it's always a good idea to start with your mood. Do you want something that will hype you up, make you think, or calm you down? If you know what mood you're in but not sure what genre to go with, you can try revisiting past music you've enjoyed to see if any of those tracks spark your interest. If you

want to listen to songs you haven't heard yet, check out the algorithmic playlist that your streaming app makes based on your music preferences. I always like listening to new releases to see if anything excites me. Listening to music throughout your day is a good way to spark inspiration, improve your mood, and come up with new ideas.

Trust your instincts—your mind and body should alert you when you're listening to music that fits your sonic needs. If you're still having trouble, you can walk around while testing out new tracks to see which song energizes you. Once you've found a bunch of tracks you like, try creating a playlist for other people to check out. You can even use the playlist to enrich your next gathering!

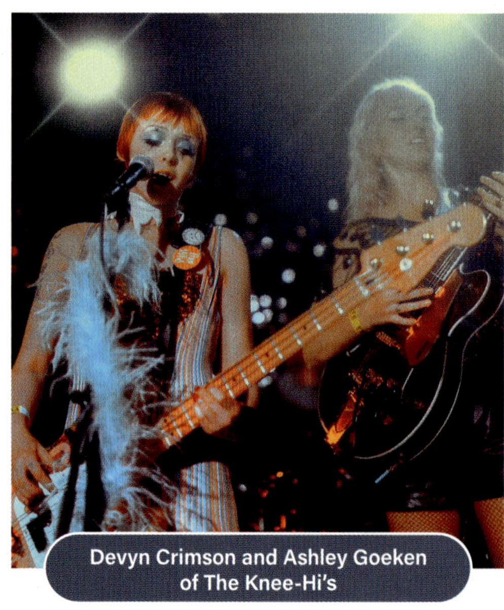

Devyn Crimson and Ashley Goeken of The Knee-Hi's

TALOR STEINBERG
Musician

When I'm not teaching guitar lessons or working as a professional guitarist, most of my creative energy is focused on my band, The Moon City Masters. Growing up, my brother and I were always more excited to write and perform our own music rather than playing other people's songs. Everything I create comes from my love of improvising. I can get lost for hours playing guitar, exploring and trying to play things I haven't before. Honestly, it's no different than doodling. In music, we call it *noodling*.

All my song ideas come from sitting on the couch, improvising for as long as I feel inspired until I hear something that stands out. Maris is often hanging out with me, playing video games or doing something creative next to me while I'm playing guitar. Whenever she stops me and says she likes something I'm playing, I know it's good if it stands out to her. It can even just be a little riff, but the moment I know I have something I'll record it on my phone, then I'll listen to it the next day with fresh ears, and if I still like it, I show it to my brother and we jam on it.

We know it has the potential to be a song if we can come up with a strong vocal melody. Sometimes the song doesn't come together as fast, and the original idea can take a while to build out as we try to write the next part. It's important to not force it and give the idea space, if needed. I remember I wrote the riff to our song "Draw the Line" during a guitar lesson. I just couldn't come up with a melody or another part other than that riff. Then a year later, I put a capo on the third fret of my guitar and played the riff again, and my brother instantly came up with a vocal melody. We wrote the rest of the music in 15 minutes.

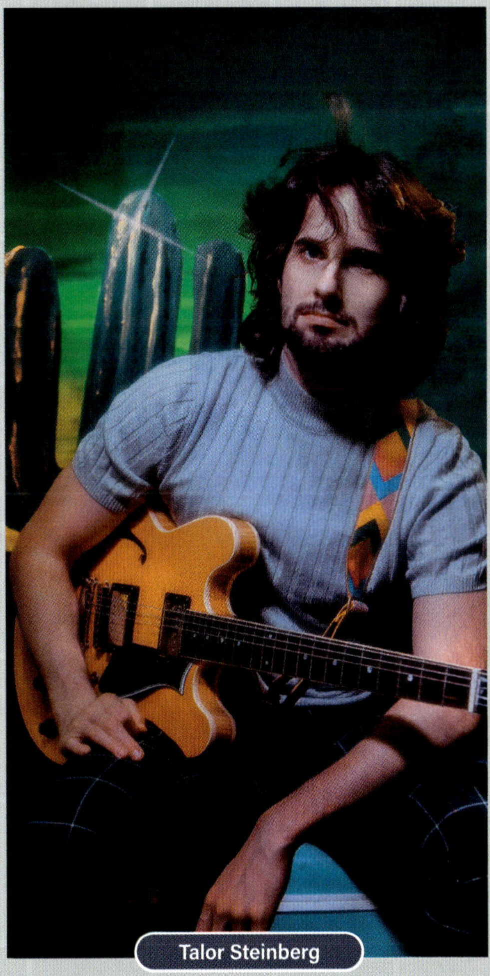

CHOOSE YOUR OWN MUSICAL ADVENTURE
What do I want to convey with my creativity today?
How do I feel today?
Excited
How come?
Nostalgic
How come?
Emotional
How come?
Big life event
Work accomplishment
Just everything
Recalling a fond memory
Thinking of my childhood
Something more recent is on my mind
The weather sucks
Love hurts
It didn't work out

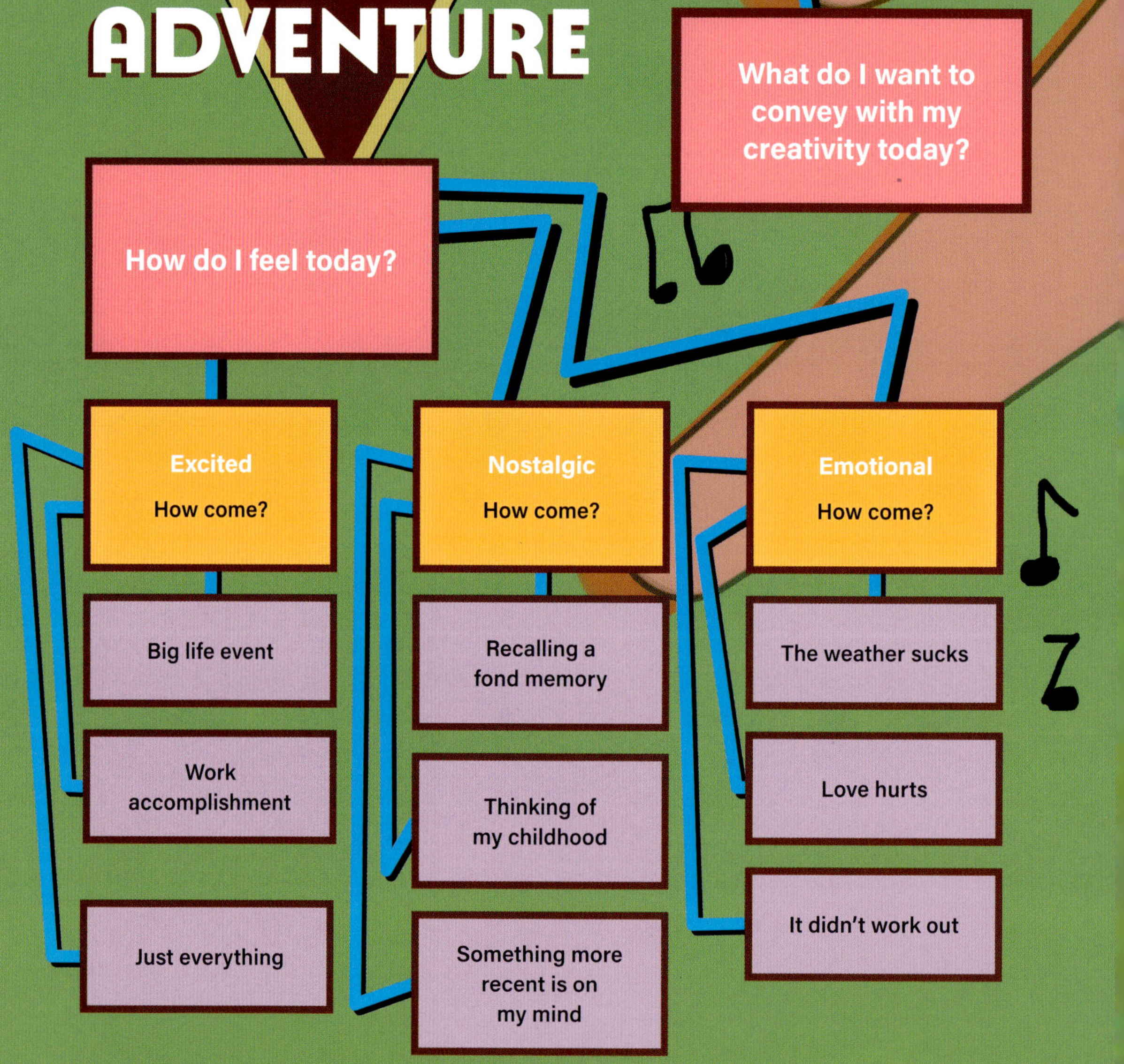

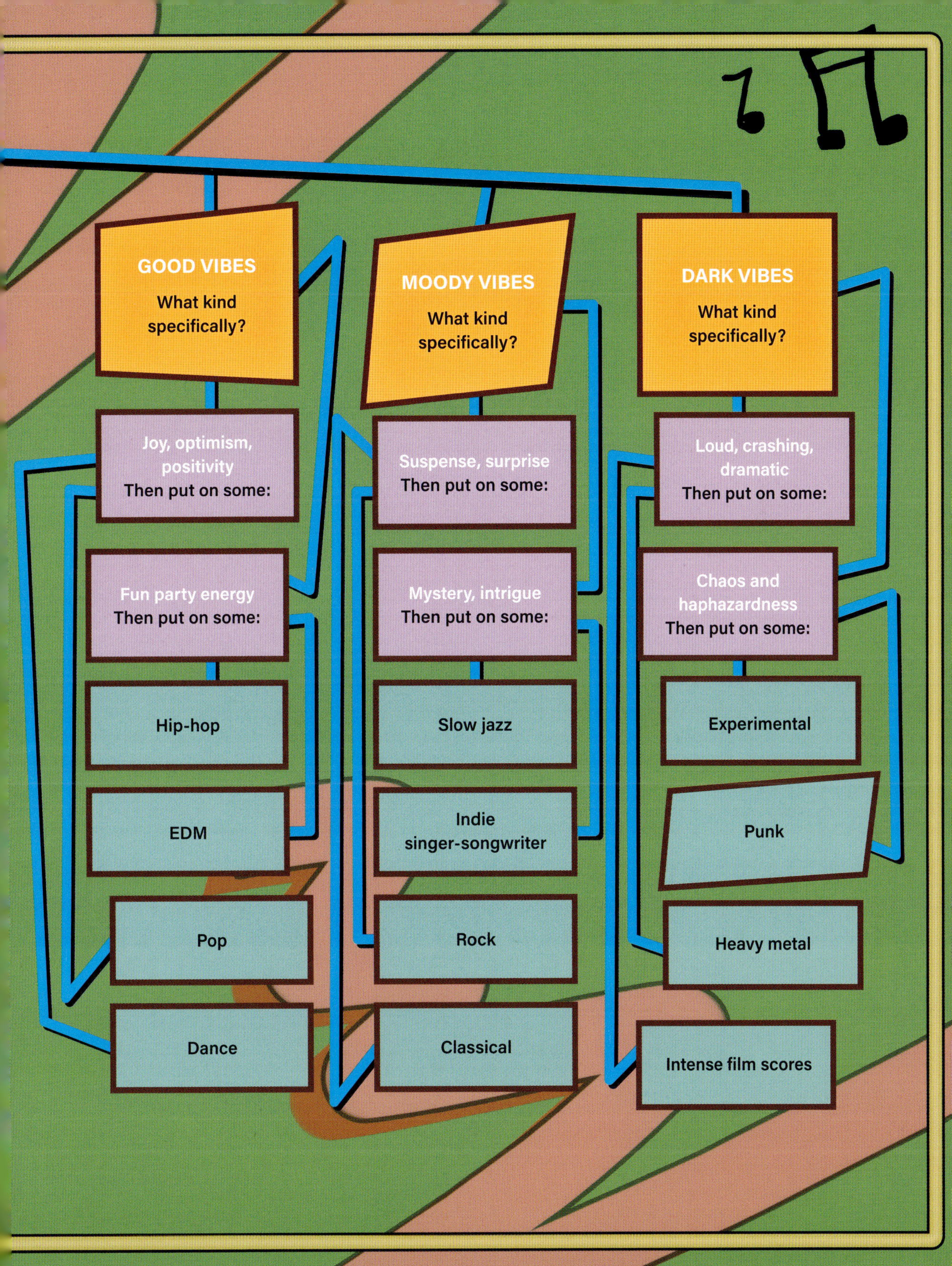

GOOD VIBES
What kind specifically?

MOODY VIBES
What kind specifically?

DARK VIBES
What kind specifically?

Joy, optimism, positivity
Then put on some:

Suspense, surprise
Then put on some:

Loud, crashing, dramatic
Then put on some:

Fun party energy
Then put on some:

Mystery, intrigue
Then put on some:

Chaos and haphazardness
Then put on some:

Hip-hop

Slow jazz

Experimental

EDM

Indie singer-songwriter

Punk

Pop

Rock

Heavy metal

Dance

Classical

Intense film scores

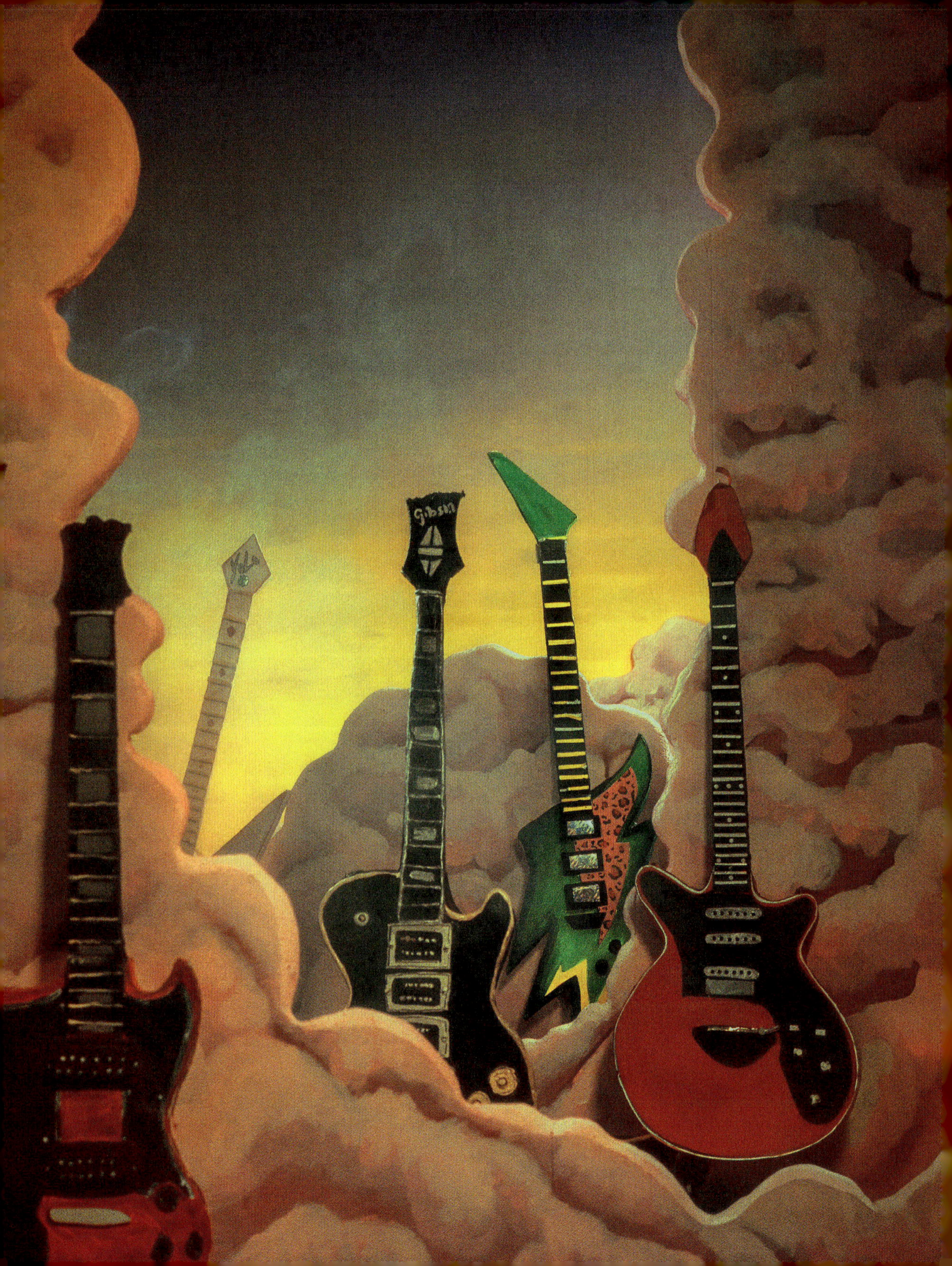
Gibson

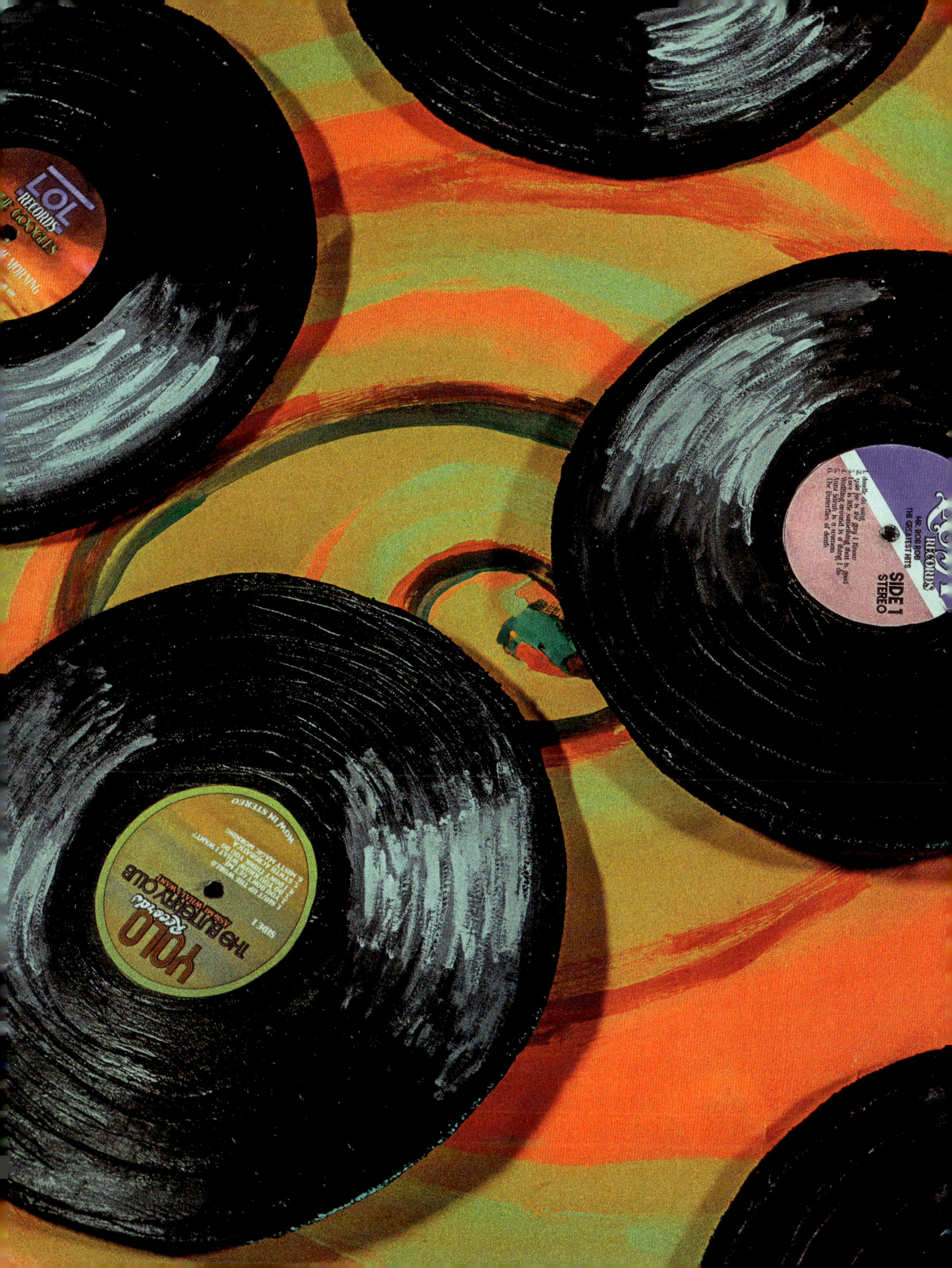
LOL
RECORDS
MR. BOB ROB
THE GREATEST HITS
SIDE 1
STEREO
1. doodle-do-song
2. yolo for is the girl I know
3. Love is life
4. Waiting around is something that is good
5. Aunt Sarah is a woman
6. The Butterflies of death
YOLO Records
THE BUTTERFLY CLUB
ASK ME WHAT I WANT
SIDE 1
1. SHOUT FOR THE WORLD
2. I DON'T GET IT
3. I KNOW WHAT YOU DO
4. GIVE ME WHAT I WANT
5. AUNT SARAH
6. THE BUTTERFLIES OF MORNING
NOW IN STEREO

MUSIC EXERCISES

> Dedicate time to listen to a song without distractions. Repeat listening can help you develop a vivid mental image. Visualize scenarios, shapes, and colors inspired by the song. This process can reveal unexpected and inspiring creative directions. Write down or sketch out any ideas that may bubble up to the surface during or after listening.

> Try taking a walk while listening to music. New environments can stimulate fresh mental imagery, and you may find that your surroundings influence the visuals that come to mind. Pay attention to colors and shapes in the real world that resonate with your music. This exercise can lead to innovative and visually compelling ideas.

> Use music to kick-start a creative project! Often people are thinking about music for a piece after they've already conceptualized the rest of the project. But I find that picking the music first can kick-start your brain to create something that you never thought you were going to create. Try using a song to come up with a story!

> Listen to a playlist. It could be one that you made or one made by someone else. Focus on a particular song, whichever one makes you stop and think, "I love this song!" Listen to it many times, focusing on the different elements of the song. What emotion does it evoke in you? What colors and images do you see or imagine? What era does the song take you to?

> Put on a song you know well and identify the themes and emotions that it conveys. How does the song showcase these themes and emotions within the music and lyrics? Now put on a song that you don't know very well (or at all) and try to identify the themes and emotions it communicates. Is it harder to do this when you are unfamiliar with the song?

> If you've finished putting together a video or audio project, try pairing it with different types of music to see how each song helps accentuate the work. Be sure to keep the themes and emotions you're going for in mind, but also be open to being surprised. You might find a different kind of song works better with the piece.

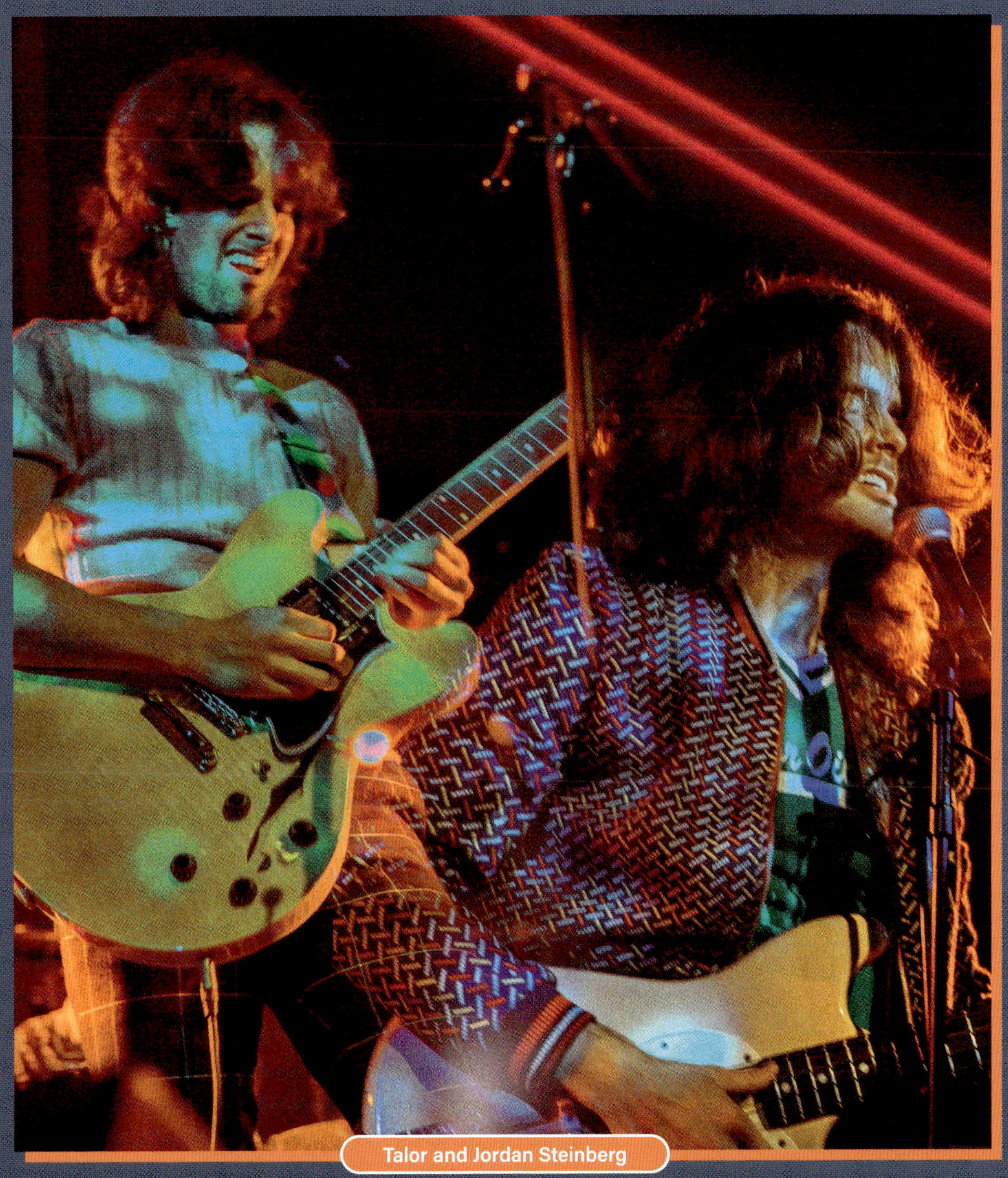

Talor and Jordan Steinberg

QUESTIONS TO CONSIDER

> What type of music are you naturally drawn to the most? What genre would you say is your favorite?

> Who are your favorite musical artists? If you had to pick a top five, who would they be? How are these five musical acts similar? How are they different?

> If you're looking to pair music to a piece, what emotions do you want to convey with the project? How can the right song choice heighten the themes and emotions that you already have present in your work?

> Are there any songs or albums that are attached to a cherished memory? How does that memory make you feel when you think about it? If you put those songs on, does the music transport you back to that memory?

> During what era is your project set? Can you pick a song or piece of music that is evocative of that era to further indicate the time period to your audience?

> Who do you think the main audience will be for your piece? Can you pick songs from a specific era that will appeal to your main audience? Is there a specific song that will bring your audience a sense of pleasing nostalgia?

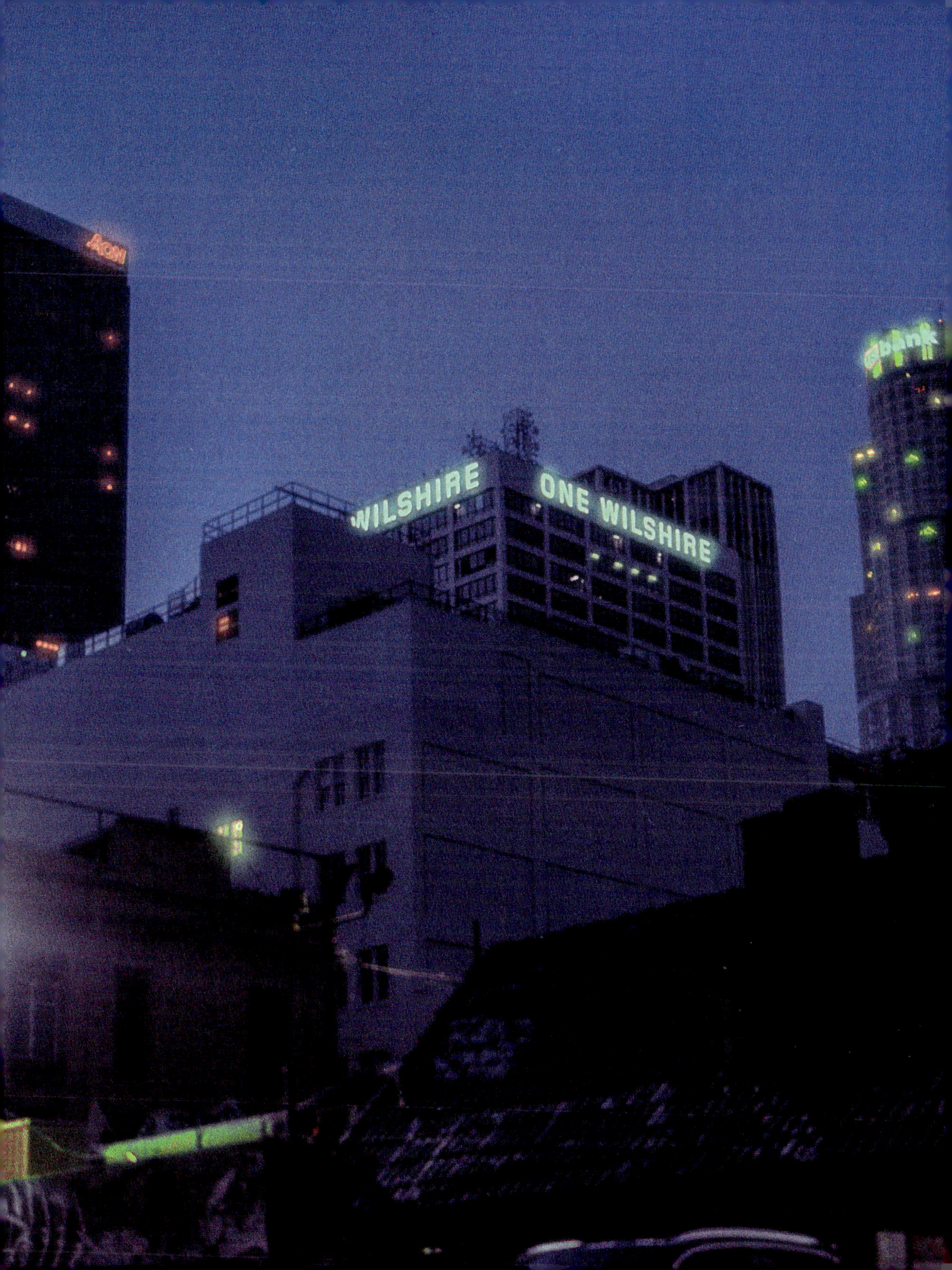

Aon
WILSHIRE
ONE WILSHIRE
U.S. bank

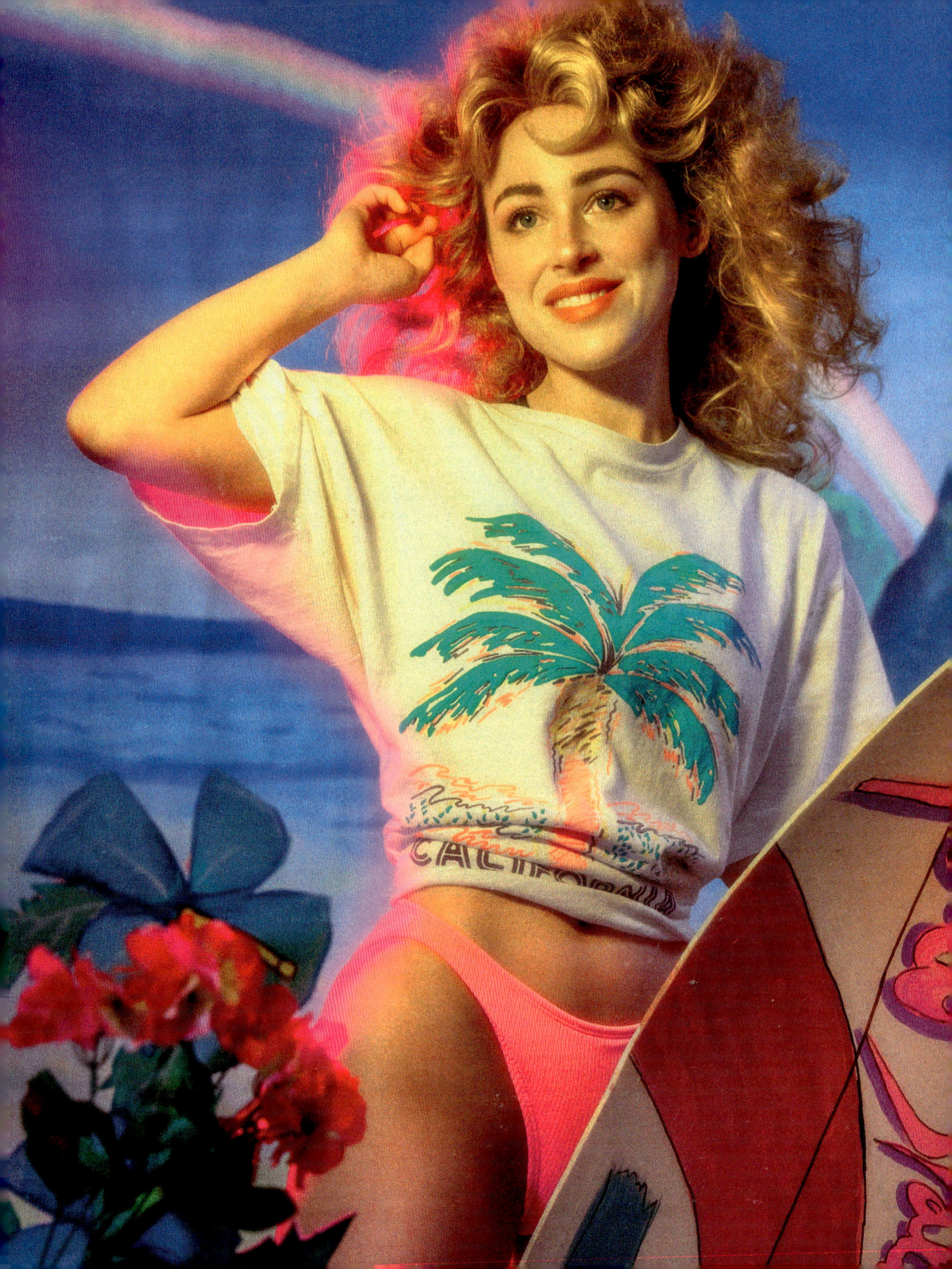

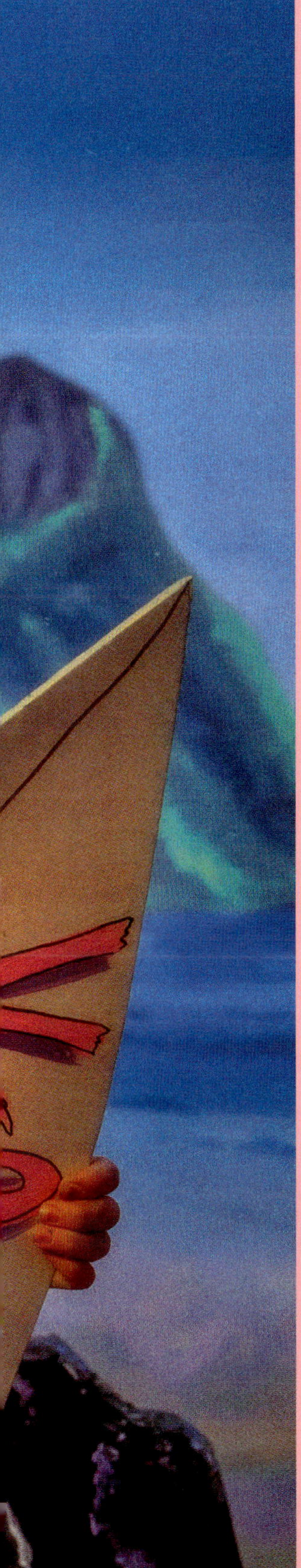

CHAPTER ELEVEN

EDITING & POSTPRODUCTION

THE EDIT

Now that we've discussed how to find inspiration and get creating, let's look at the last step to every creative endeavor: the edit. Editing plays a pivotal role in achieving a polished final product and effectively conveying your intended message or purpose. From a technical standpoint, it involves assembling and organizing the various components you've created into a coherent whole.

Although most people might think of editing as a tool specific to the contexts of film, photography, and writing, it isn't confined to just these realms. Editing is a versatile tool that can be applied to various aspects of our lives.

Since it usually takes place toward the end of a project's construction, editing grants you the freedom to shape and mold your work as you go along, alleviating the pressure of having to figure everything out from the outset.

It's crucial to remember not to edit prematurely. Allow yourself the freedom to be creative, and trust that the editing phase to come will bring everything together seamlessly.

LET YOUR WORK EVOLVE

I rarely begin a project with a crystal-clear vision. I'm both specific and loose in my approach. Take, for instance, designing a room. I don't usually start with a precise layout in mind; I start by adding elements to the design. Then I step back and evaluate what's working and what's not. This is where the magic of editing comes into play.

This principle applies to fashion as well. Let's say I want to put together an outfit with jeans, a turtleneck, and some boots. Along the way, I might decide to incorporate a few more elements, experiment with accessories like earrings, and contemplate what additional touches would make the outfit feel just right.

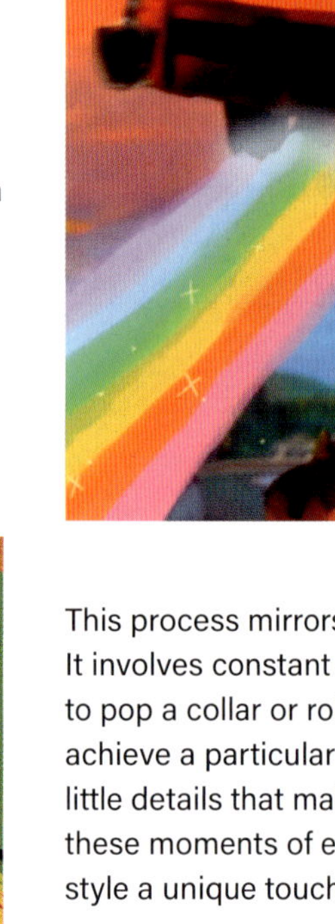

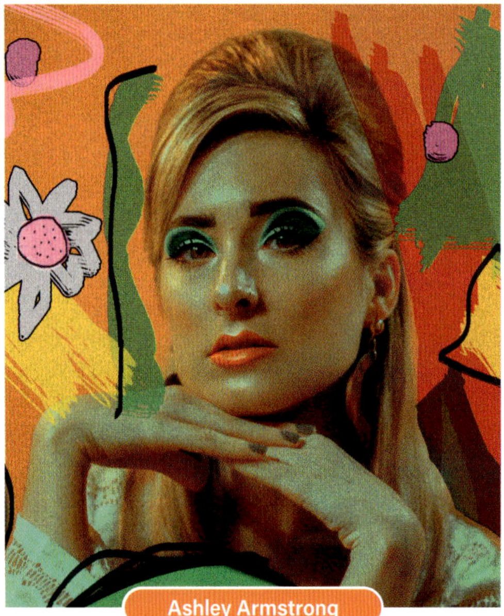

This process mirrors editing in every sense. It involves constant adjustments, like deciding to pop a collar or roll up the shirt sleeves to achieve a particular look or vibe. Often, it's the little details that make all the difference, and these moments of editing are what give your style a unique touch.

The same concept extends to various creative endeavors. When making music, you'll inevitably edit your song, adding, reducing, or rearranging elements to bring it all together. Editing is prevalent in almost everything we do, including makeup, where you continuously make choices about what to add or tone down for your finished look.

What's interesting is that we often believe we
need a fully formed, perfect plan from the start.
But the reality is different. All you need is a core
idea and a sense of what you want to convey or
feel. Editing comes in toward the end to make
the overall process more enjoyable and
free-flowing. Editing is the secret sauce that
allows you to shape and refine your work as
you go along.

Sometimes, we get stuck thinking that
everything must be perfect from the start, but
in reality, editing is the Holy Grail that lets you
say what you want to say. It's fluid and
adaptable. If you're not happy with your initial
work, you can edit it again, make additions or
subtractions, or step away and return to it later.
Editing equips you with the tools to be less
reliant on extensive planning.

I have a strong command of lighting and
technical skills, but if you were to see my

photos before I edit them, you might think
they're just "fine." While it's crucial to get the
lighting right and ensure correct exposure, the
real magic happens during editing. This
approach allows me to have fun and make
changes as needed, knowing it will turn out
okay in the end.

Since I often film by myself, I anticipate adding
extra elements during the editing process,
maybe even incorporating camera movements
because I'm a one-person crew. This means I
often shoot with a locked tripod, knowing that
can enhance and build upon what I've captured
later. I've developed a system that works for
me. It allows me to relax during the creative
process, even if my camera tilts slightly or
things fall off the set.

Your editing process can be tailored to your
unique style and needs, regardless of the
medium you work in.

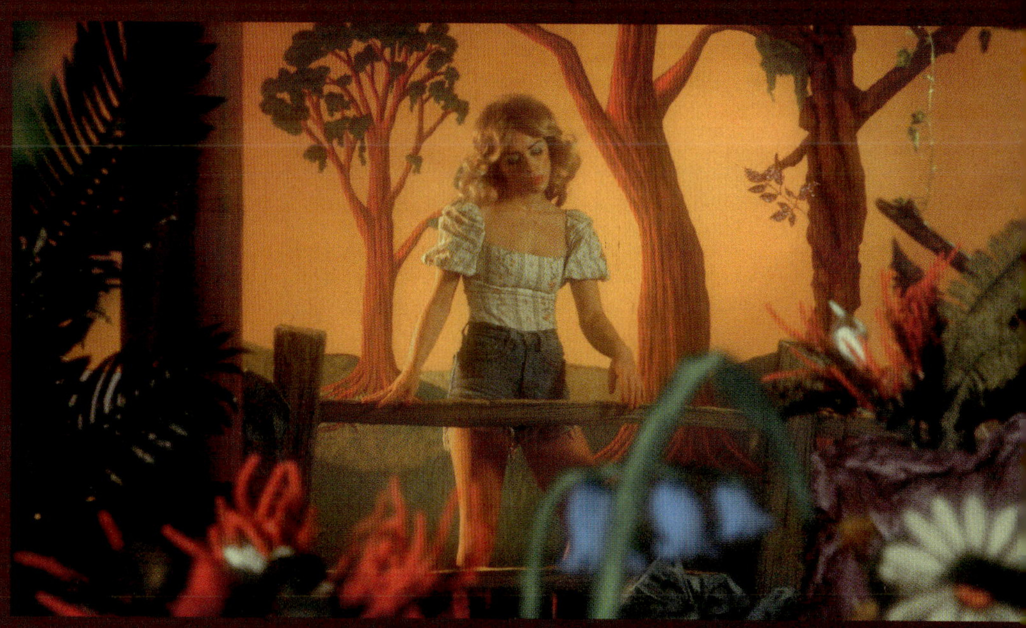

HAPPY ACCIDENTS

When you go into a project aiming for perfection right from the start, you limit yourself to never making those delightful "happy accidents." These are the moments of pure inspiration, the instances when you look at a piece of art, hear a song, or see an outfit or room design that makes you wonder, "How on earth did they come up with that?" Often, these remarkable creations happen entirely by accident. If you come in to a project too hot with a rigid, perfect plan, you might miss out on these spontaneous bursts of creativity.

That's why my creative process involves editing. I experiment with what I believe works best in the moment. I add elements, ideas, or details that feel right and then I refine and explore different angles afterward.

Editing essentially involves piecing together all the elements you've created to make them harmonious. I usually begin by creating a basic storyline or map without getting into the nitty-gritty of detailed editing. This initial step helps ensure that the overall story flows cohesively. Once I have the big picture laid out, I delve into the finer details, emphasizing particular aspects that enhance the narrative. It's a flexible approach that I believe works across various editing scenarios.

When I'm editing, I often revisit my initial story outline or shot list. These lists typically consist of a few bullet points, offering me a loose structure to work with. However, I don't rigidly adhere to them. This is especially advantageous when I'm working without dialogue. It allows me to remain open to the creative process, potentially stumbling upon precious happy accidents that can breathe new life into a project. For example, I might lay out all the clips I've captured and realize that reversing the order tells the story more effectively or that a moment I initially thought belonged at the end is more impactful at the beginning.

A crucial aspect of this process is learning to trust your instincts. Your brain has a natural rhythm that can signal when something is dragging on too long or needs more time to breathe. I often watch my work repeatedly until I feel that the timing is just right. Trusting your creative intuition is key to effective editing.

Furthermore, editing isn't just about technical adjustments; it's also about conveying emotions. Different styles of cutting, the timing of cuts, and the way they're executed can all influence the emotions the audience experiences. I've learned much about this by studying movies and observing how various filmmakers employ different editing techniques to convey emotions. It all boils down to timing and how you edit around those emotional moments you want your audience to feel.

In essence, everything can be edited in one way or another, and it's possible that these editing styles play a role in why you're attracted to certain things. Whether you appreciate slow-paced editing, disjunctive and wild cuts, or a bit of both, you might discover connections between editing styles and your personal preferences. Editing is a dynamic process, one that offers room for exploration and the occasional delightful surprise.

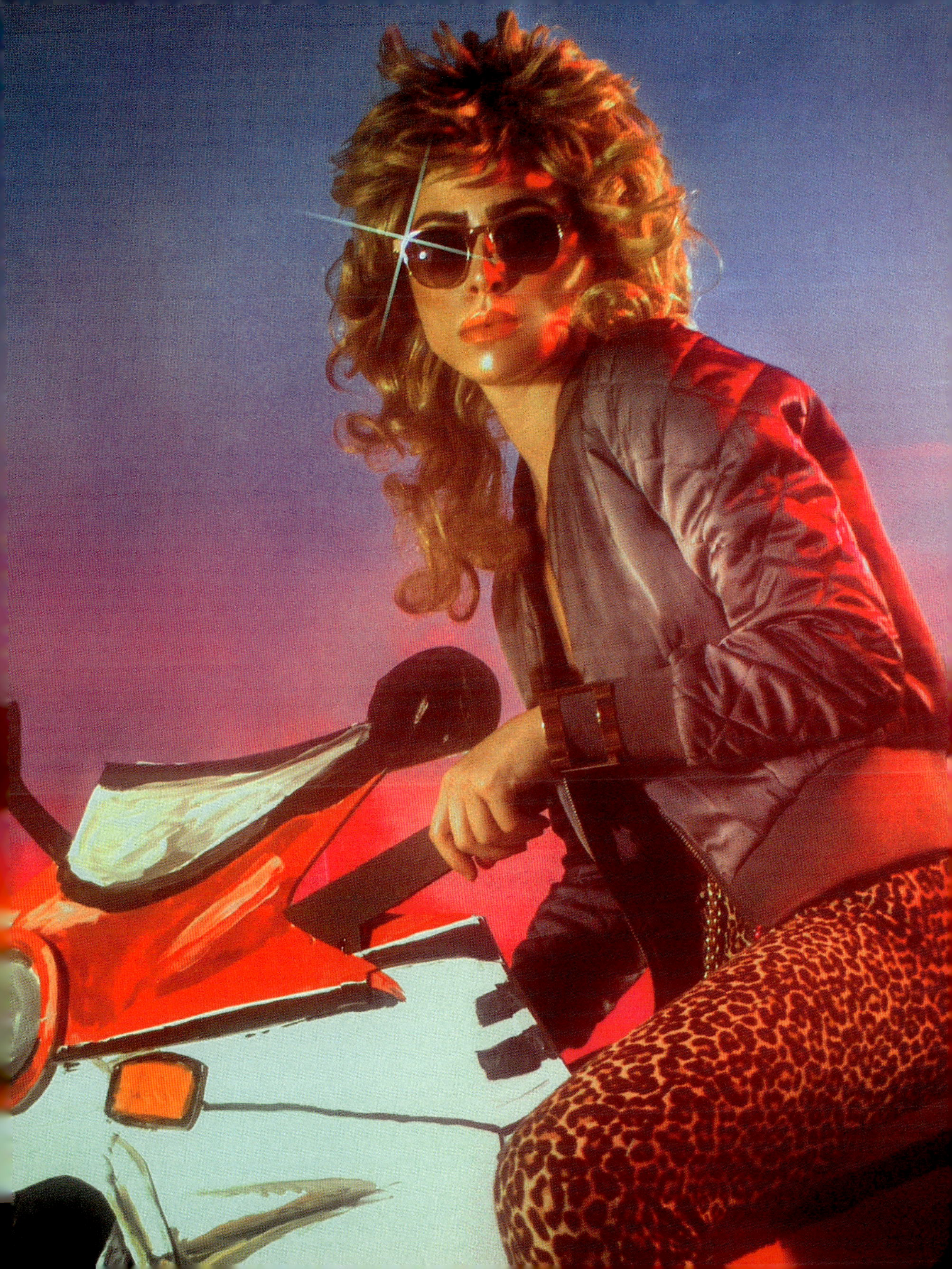

EDITING ACROSS DISCIPLINES

For interior design: If you're designing a room, you may not begin with a detailed floor plan. Instead, you might add various elements, possibly more than necessary, and then evaluate what works and what doesn't. It's a process of addition and subtraction—you start with a loose concept and refine it through editing.

For fashion: Similarly, when creating an outfit, you might start with a few core pieces in mind but remain open to adjusting along the way. You then add or remove items until the look feels just right. This too is a form of editing where you're fine-tuning to achieve the desired aesthetic. I might begin by putting on a pair of pants and a shirt but then realize I need to add something else. What about a pair of earrings? Once I put them on, I notice the materials or colors clash, so I try a different pair of earrings. Now I realize earrings don't work at all. What if I try a hat instead?

For music and visuals: If you're composing music or working with visual content, editing is an integral part of the process. You might lay down tracks or capture footage without a complete vision in mind. Then, during the editing phase, you add, remove, and rearrange elements to craft the final product. Editing allows you to shape the emotional impact and pacing of your work.

JUSTIN CRAIG
Music Producer

When producing music, I'm constantly editing, rearranging, building up, and breaking things back down. I find it valuable to explore. You can go down a path for hours or days searching for something and still completely fail to find anything. Other times, you crack things open into a new realm that you weren't expecting. It's all worthwhile exploration.

Editing is a process of rethinking, reimagining, and fine-tuning, an opportunity to change and elevate the initial concept. Often, I've gone to mix a song where I thought the production was totally finished, done, a masterpiece . . . and then I just start muting things, essentially, erasing ideas. Sometimes in that process, the song reveals itself again but in an exciting new way. Other times, it's additive. What's missing? It's important to maintain perspective and to know when (and when not to be) precious about what you're making.

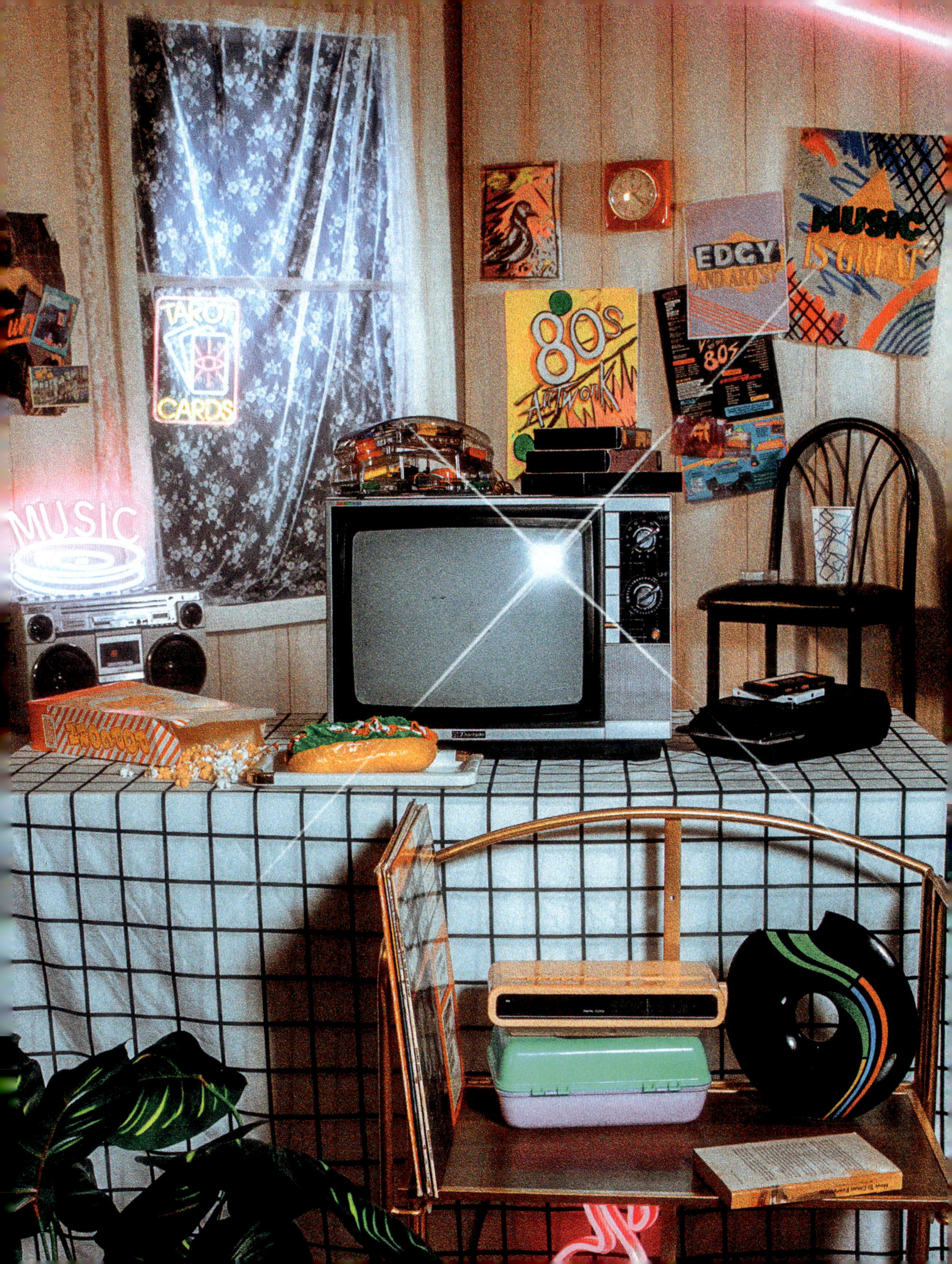
TAROT
CARDS
MUSIC
80's
Artwork
EDGY
AND AROSY
MUSIC
IS GREAT
80s
POPCORN

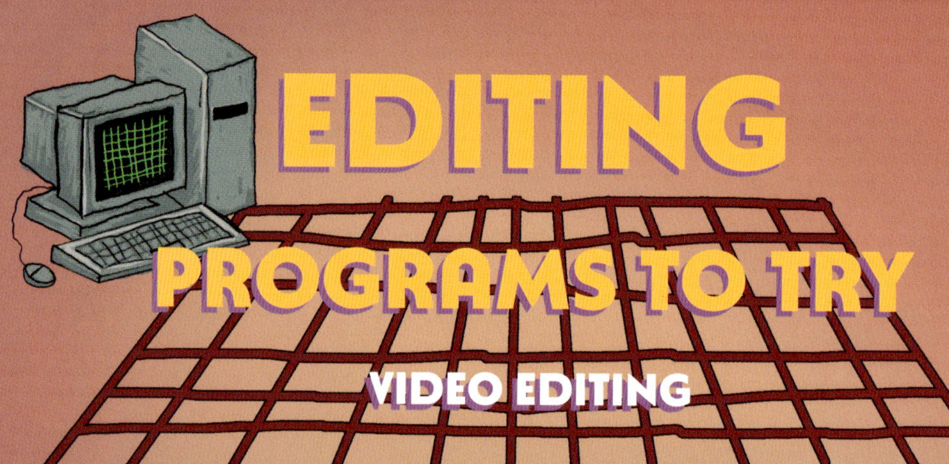

EDITING
PROGRAMS TO TRY

VIDEO EDITING

PRO FILM PRODUCTION

Adobe Premiere
Final Cut Pro
Avid Pro Tools
DaVinci Resolve

Adobe After Effects
Apple Motion
Blender
Nuke

VIDEO FX

CONSUMER FILM PROGRAMS

iMovie
Lumen5
Nero Video
Splice

CapCut
Videoleap
Canva

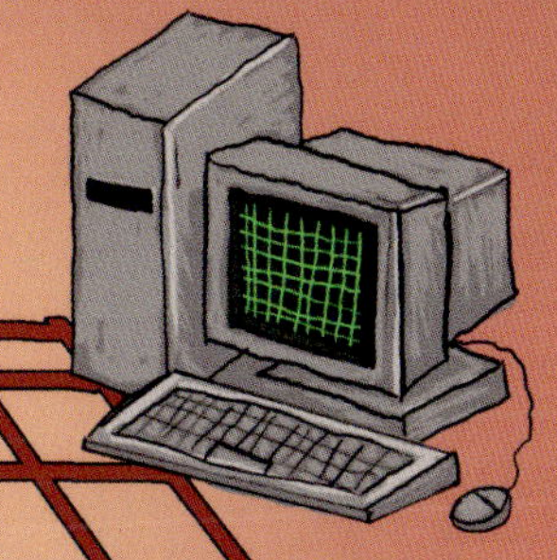

PHOTO, MUSIC, AND STORY EDITING

PHOTO EDITING

Adobe Photoshop
Adobe Lightroom
Canva

MUSIC EDITING

Pro Tools
Studio One
Ableton Live
Audacity
Logic Pro

DIGITAL ART AND DESIGN EDITING

Procreate
CAD
Adobe Illustrator
Adobe InDesign

SCRIPTWRITING

Final Draft
Arc Studio
Celtx
Scrivener

PRINT EDITING

Microsoft Word
Adobe InCopy
Grammarly

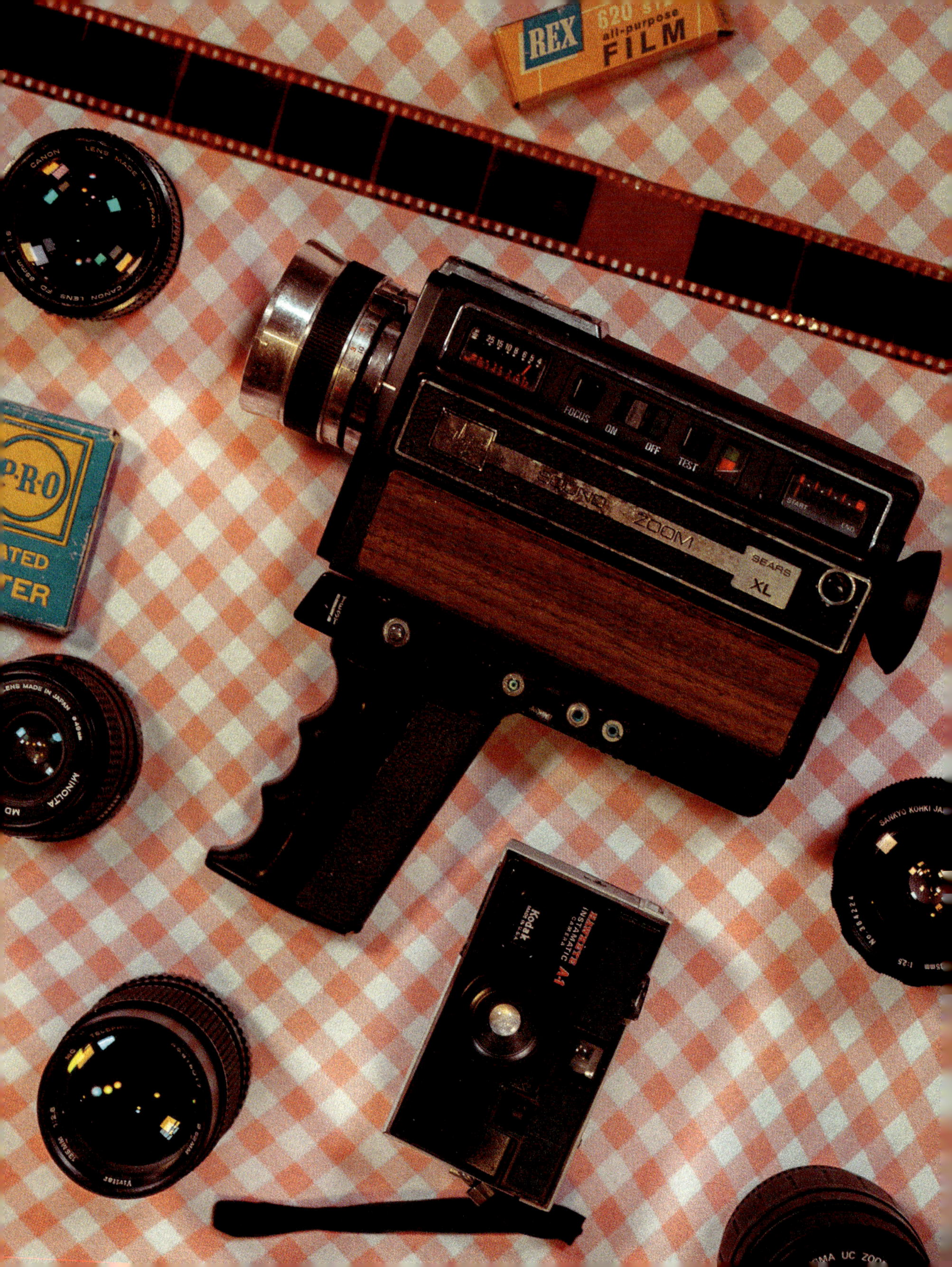
REX 620 SIZE
all-purpose
FILM
CANON LENS MADE IN JAPAN
CANON LENS FD 85mm 1:1.8
P·R·O
ATED
TER
LENS MADE IN JAPAN
MINOLTA
MD
ø49mm
FOCUS
ON
OFF
TEST
SOUND ZOOM
START
END
SEARS
XL
SANKYO KOHKI JA
No. 384224
35mm 1:2.5
Kodak
MADE IN U.S.A.
HAWKEYE
INSTAMATIC
CAMERA
A-1
MINOLTA
MD ROKKOR 135mm 1:2.8
SIGMA UC ZOOM

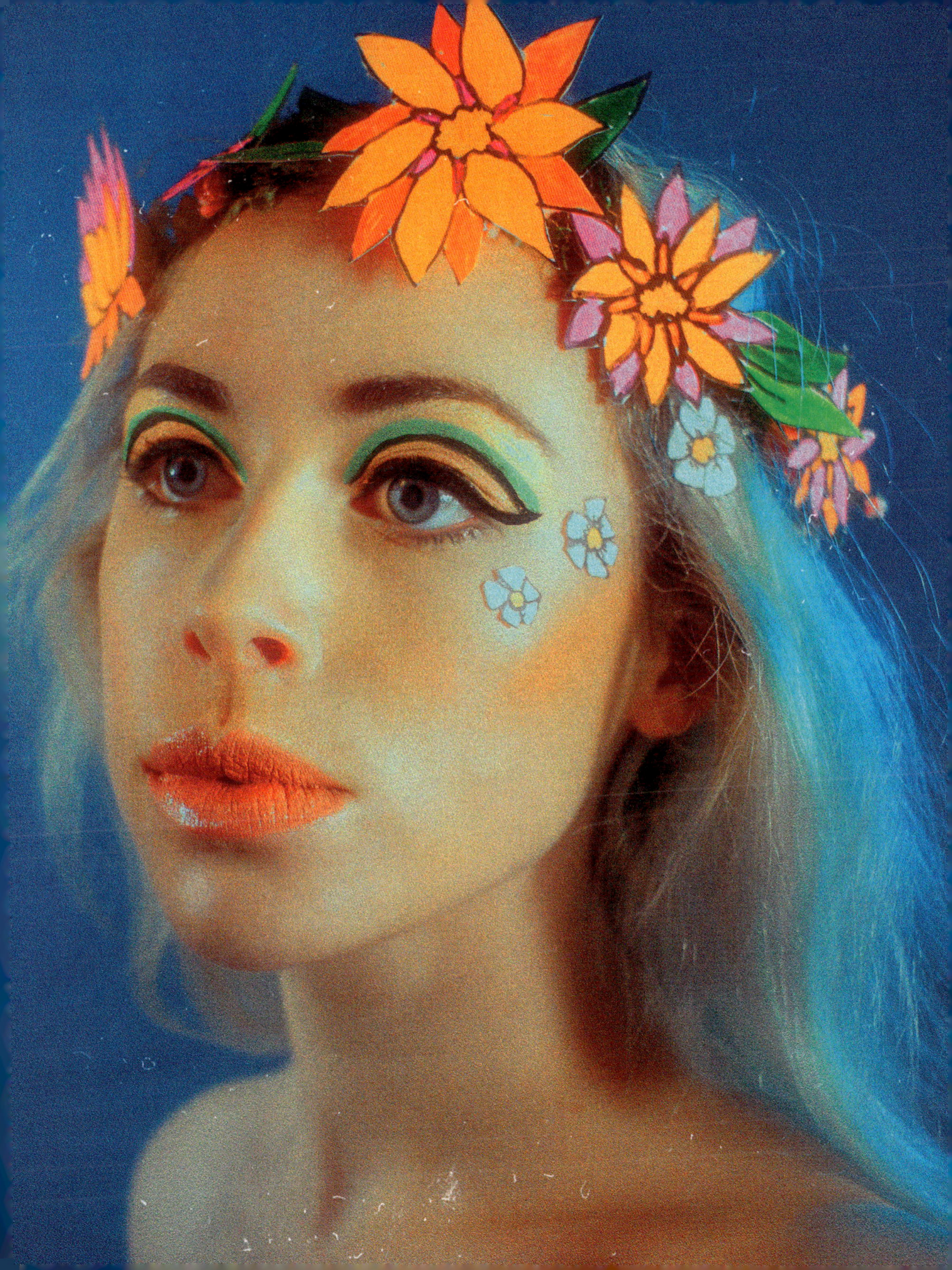

EDITING & POSTPRODUCTION EXERCISES

> Take the last 10 video clips in your camera roll and see if you can edit them together to create a montage or a narrative. Feel free to try adding text, color, music, and transitions to the clips to create something entirely new.

> Take a photo on your phone of something you like, such as an object, a color, a place, or a person. Use a photo-editing app and play around with all the different photo-editing settings (brightness, contrast, saturation, etc.). Try going through each setting and adjust the values until you end up with an image you really dig.

> Have someone select two random words for you to implement into a short narrative paragraph. One of the words must be the first word of your paragraph, the other has to be the last. What kind of narrative can you come up with to get from point A to point B?

> Record audio of yourself or someone else telling a story for a few minutes. Now, try and edit the dialogue down to just 1 minute. See if you can still include all the relevant details needed to tell a captivating and coherent story.

> Revisiting your list of influences from Chapter One can be a valuable exercise. If you've included any movies, artworks, photographers, or musicians, examine how these works were edited. The editing style might be one of the main reasons you're drawn to them. Do you notice any similarities in the editing of these pieces?

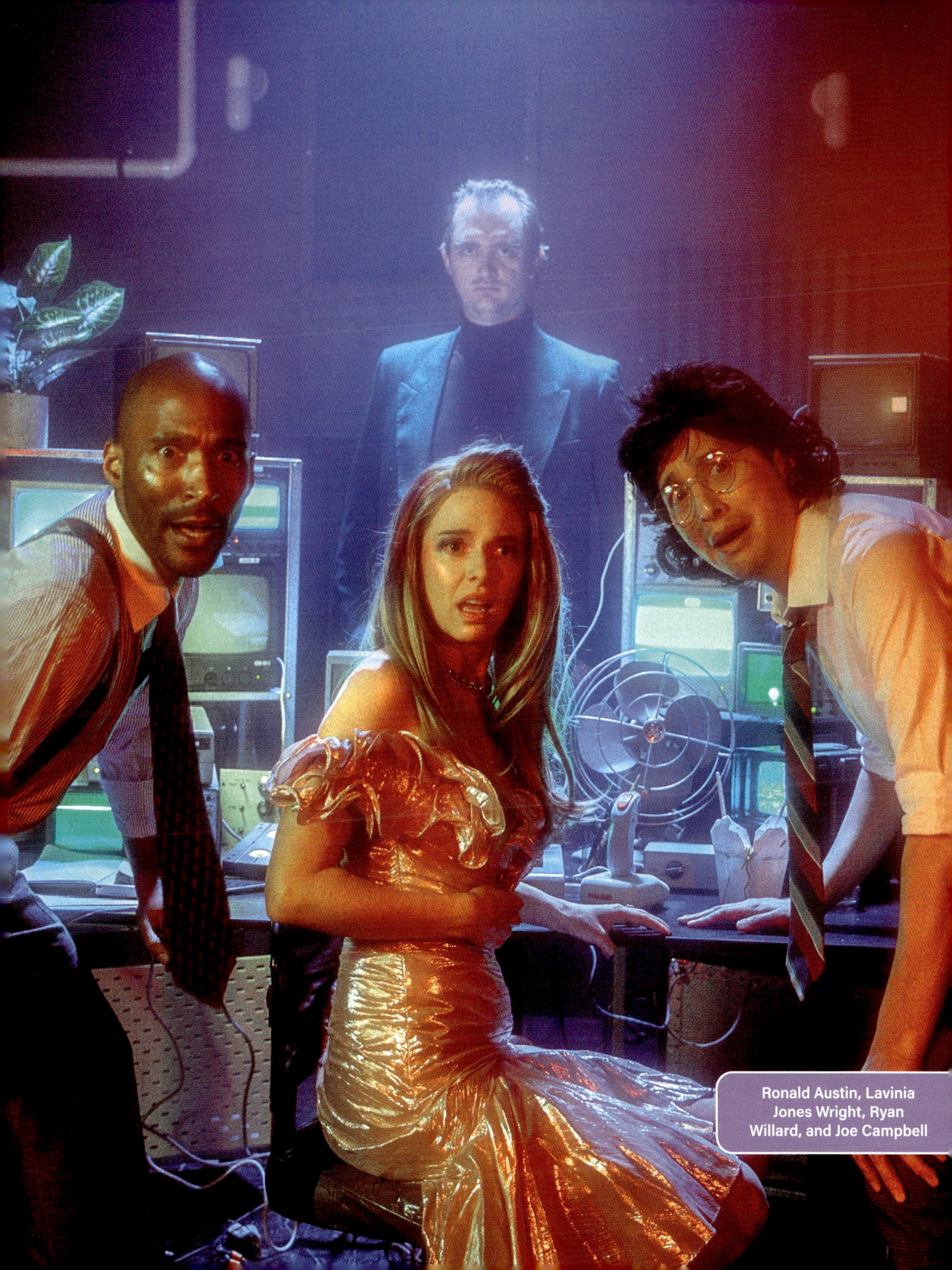

Ronald Austin, Lavinia Jones Wright, Ryan Willard, and Joe Campbell

QUESTIONS TO CONSIDER

- What type of editing or postproduction tools do you typically use? Can you use these same tools for the current project you're working on or could you try out some new tools or programs for a fresher result?

- What is the tone of your project? What emotion are you trying to convey through it? Is there anything you could change or remove to get closer to your desired intent?

- What is the pacing and flow of your project supposed to be like? Is it currently moving too fast or too slow? What can you change to speed it up or slow it down?

- Have you watched your project? Try to put yourself in the viewer's shoes. Are there any moments that feel uninspired? What could you add, remove, or alter to bring them to life?

- Who is the target audience for your piece? Do you feel your project will appeal to them? If not, what could you add, remove, or alter to reshape the final piece?

- Is there a specific outcome you want from this particular project? Do you feel that you are achieving it through its current state? If not, what alterations can you implement to ensure that your goal for the project is achieved?

- If you have already attempted editing and your project still isn't quite right, think about what specifically you want to improve. What is not working for you? Why do you think that is? What can you do to adapt it into something better?

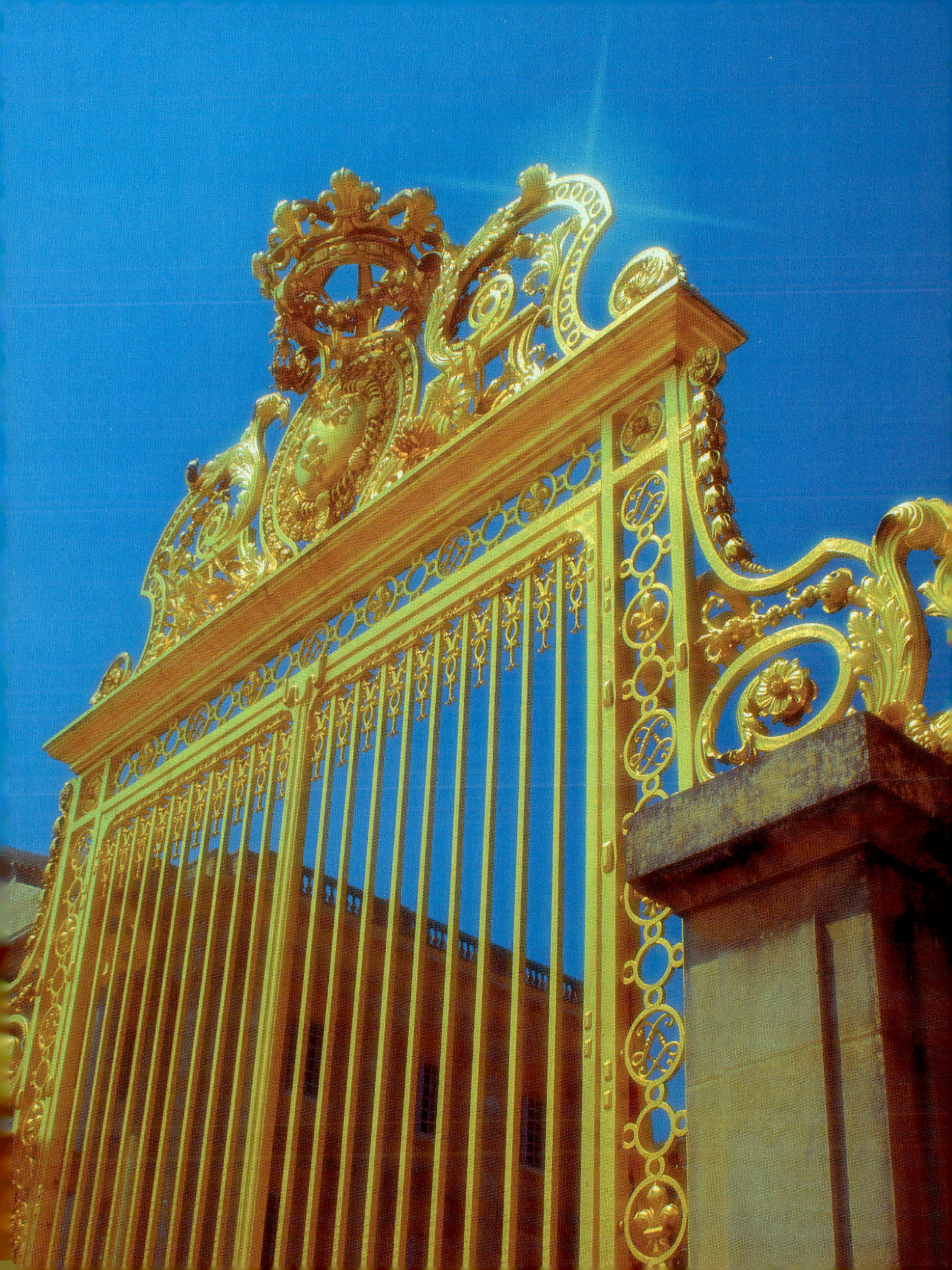

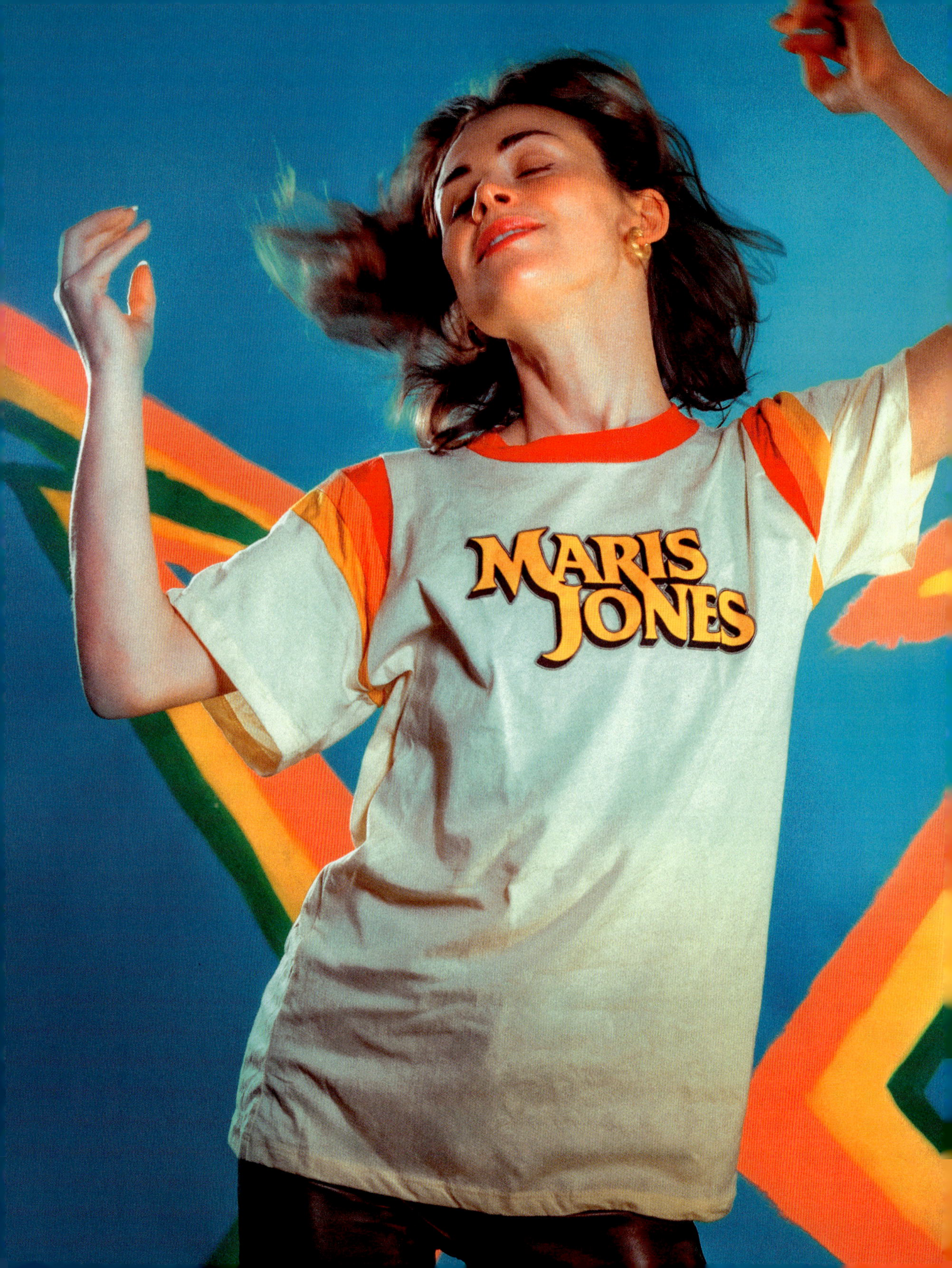
MARIS JONES

CHAPTER TWELVE

BECOMING YOURSELF

THE LONG & WINDING JOURNEY

If you've ever felt held back because you believed you had to be great from the start, let me reassure you—it's perfectly normal to be less than great when you begin any creative endeavor. Just as you can't pick up a musical instrument and play a masterpiece without practice, you can't master your artistic craft without making initial missteps. When you embark on your creative path, you're still discovering who you are.

Even after years of creative exploration, I still have so much more to uncover. It was only around the seventh year of my creative career that I began to truly understand my visual identity. Yet I'm still proud of all the things I created along the way. Each creative endeavor, regardless of its outcome, contributed to my growth and self-discovery. That sense of progress is something you should cherish and celebrate as you explore your own creativity.

So create. Create a lot. Share your work with the world. Don't concern yourself with acclaim, likes, or feedback. When you look back at everything you've created, you may spot flaws in every piece. But those flaws are the breadcrumbs that brought you forward. If you'd recognized them back then, you might not have made it to your current destination.

Your artistic journey is a tapestry woven from experiences, both great and flawed. I've crafted things that I'm immensely proud of, things I never knew I had within me. But they only became possible because of all the less-than-perfect creations that preceded them and taught me how to become a better artist through trial and error. Every piece I've made is dear to me since together they collectively define my artistic evolution. The magical part about this journey is that you don't wake up one day and exclaim, "Eureka, I've got it!"

Instead, you gradually realize that your creative pursuits have become an integral part of your life. You didn't need to sit down and strategize how to be "you." It's going to be something that happens naturally, over time. It's a beautiful moment when you do eventually truly grasp what kind of artist you are and what kind of work you want to make. One day, you may even think something along the lines of "This is who I am, and this is what I'm doing."

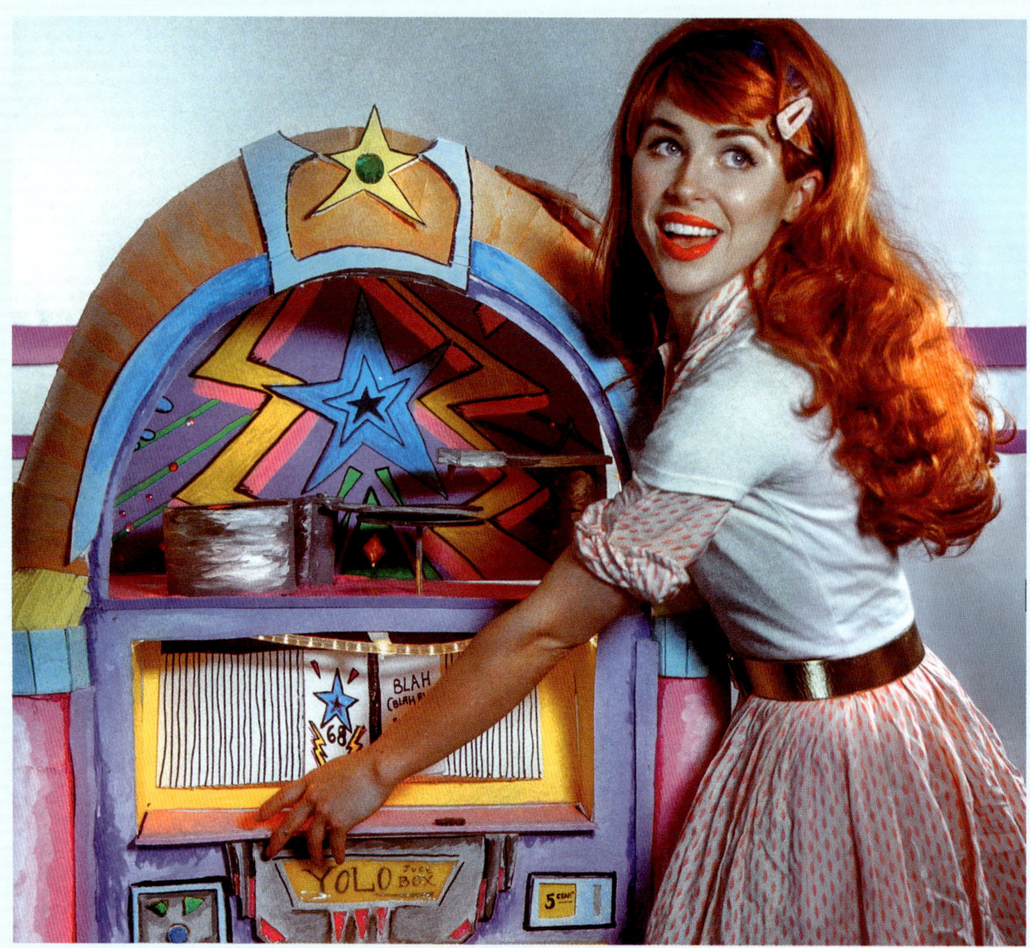

This journey allows you to look back and appreciate how far you've come—a luxury you'd miss if you aimed for perfection right from the start. Embrace the uncertainty of not knowing, and in time, you will uncover your unique voice. It takes time to truly understand who you are, what your hands can craft, and what your eyes can capture. You have to experiment, make mistakes, and experience the creative process in all its frustrating glory. However, within that frustration lies a profound sense of reward. I promise.

Your creative journey can be an adventure that never ends. Keep pushing boundaries, allow yourself to explore outside of your comfort zone, and always be open to trying new things. If you keep an open mind and are continuously willing to create, you'll uncover layers of creativity you didn't know existed within you. Embrace the imperfections for they are the stepping stones toward profound artistic fulfillment.

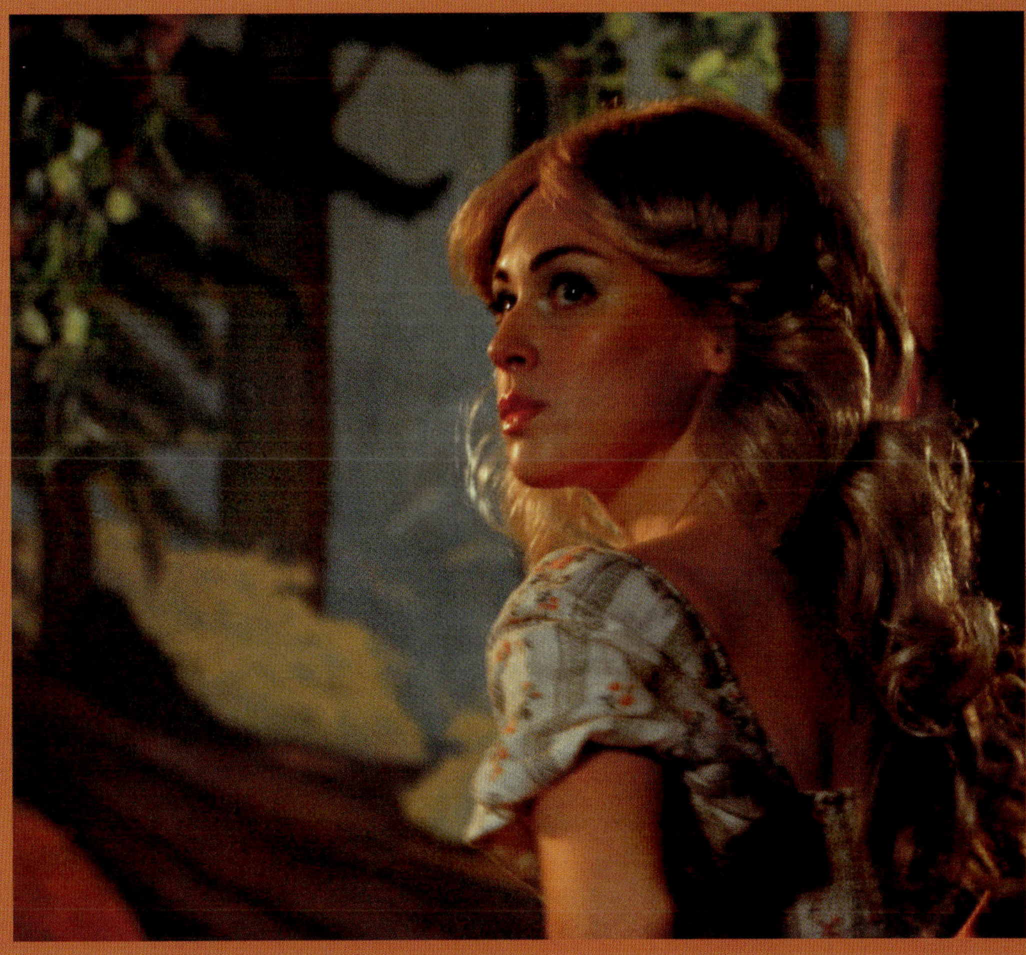

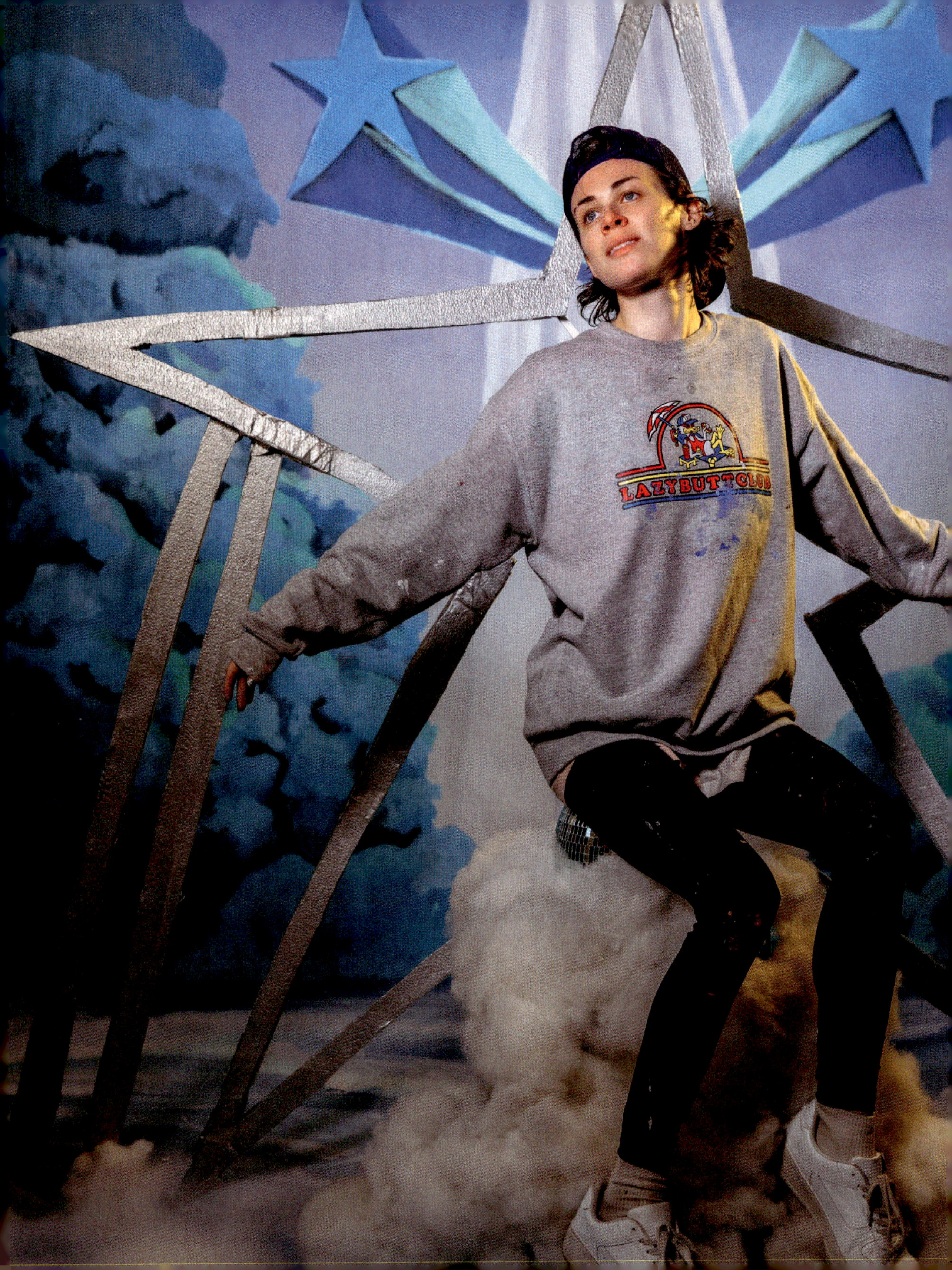
LAZY BUTT CLUB

YOU ARE ONE OF A KIND

We are vessels filled with memories and experiences, and how we express that wealth of information defines who we are. Your unique identity as an artist is built around how you translate your memories and experiences into tangible creations. Everything we create is added to a mosaic of collective memories. When people connect with what you make and the memories you share, they recognize a shared history, a common thread of feelings and emotions.

Your artistic aesthetic, style, and branding all draw from a multitude of different influences. It's impossible to create something entirely organic and unprecedented in today's world. We are sponges, absorbing a plethora of influences throughout our lives. How we process and combine these influences in our own unique ways is what shapes our creative identity. You are, in essence, the sum of your influences.

Think of creativity like cooking. You take various ingredients that already exist and combine them in a new way. You might think, "It's all been done before," but the magic happens when you infuse your own very specific perspective into the mix. Every fresh take on a familiar concept is a testament to our innate ability to reinterpret the world around us.

Art isn't about revolutionizing the universe or melting minds with groundbreaking ideas. It's about expressing what excites and inspires you. If your creations make you happy, that's what truly matters. Remember, if you don't enjoy what you're making, it's unlikely that anyone else will either. We bond over shared loves and dislikes, themes, and commonalities—this is why genres and subgenres exist in books, movies, music, and more.

Creativity is often portrayed as something that requires absolute originality, a departure from the norm. But, in reality, being disconnected from what others create would prevent you from connecting with them through your artistic creations. Being relatable is not a shortcoming—it's the essence of human connection. If something inspires you and it propels you off the couch, go for it. Pursue what excites you without the burden of feeling like your creations must be profound. Sometimes, making things that make you and others feel good is enough.

Creativity doesn't have to open a new portal in the universe or shatter people's minds to convey its point.

Revel in the joy of creation. If you ever find yourself stuck or doubting your artistic abilities, remember that it's all about being yourself. Reflect on all the things you've loved throughout your life; in many ways, what you love defines you. Consider how you can best interact and react to the world around you, and forge a new path that's tailored just for you.

As you move forward, be sure to hold onto the lessons and memories that got you here. Keep those precious early memories and vivid fragments of your childhood close to your heart. Be sure to mine your history, as it is an important key to unlocking your future.

Now is the time to set this book aside and start putting together a new outfit, painting a picture based on a recent dream, or utilizing objects to create a still life that conveys your emotions.

Be unapologetically yourself, and watch as your creativity blossoms like never before.

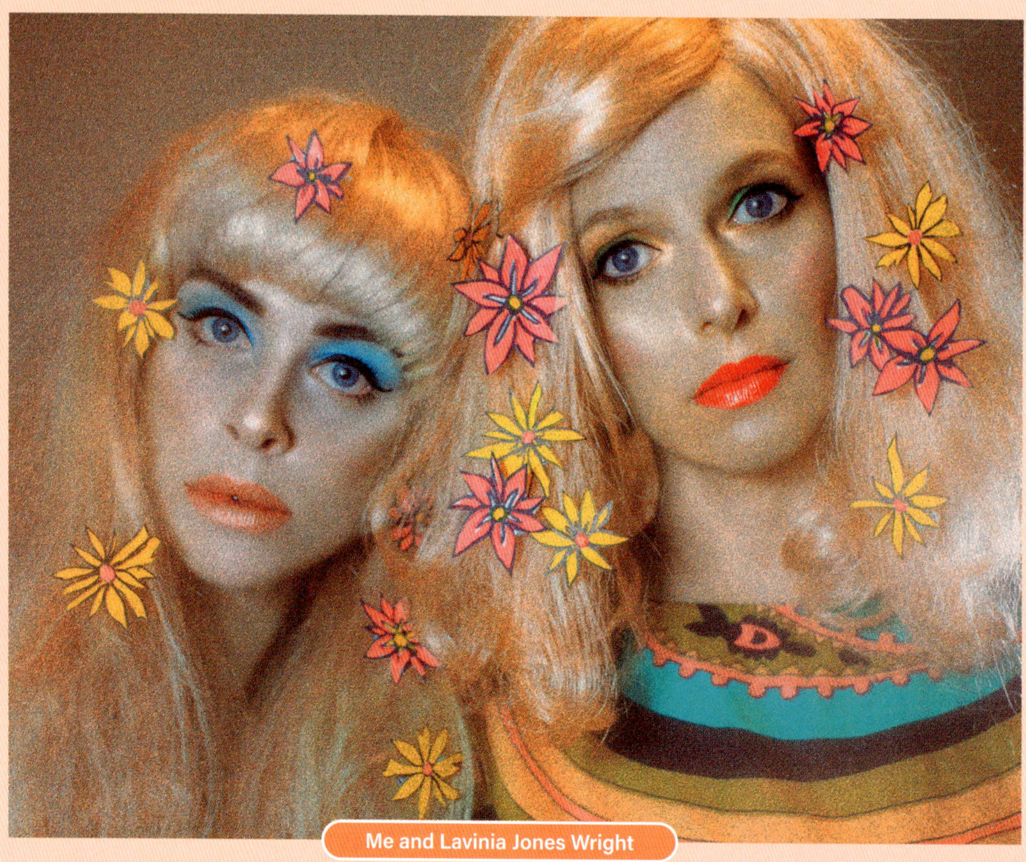

Me and Lavinia Jones Wright

Finishing Touches

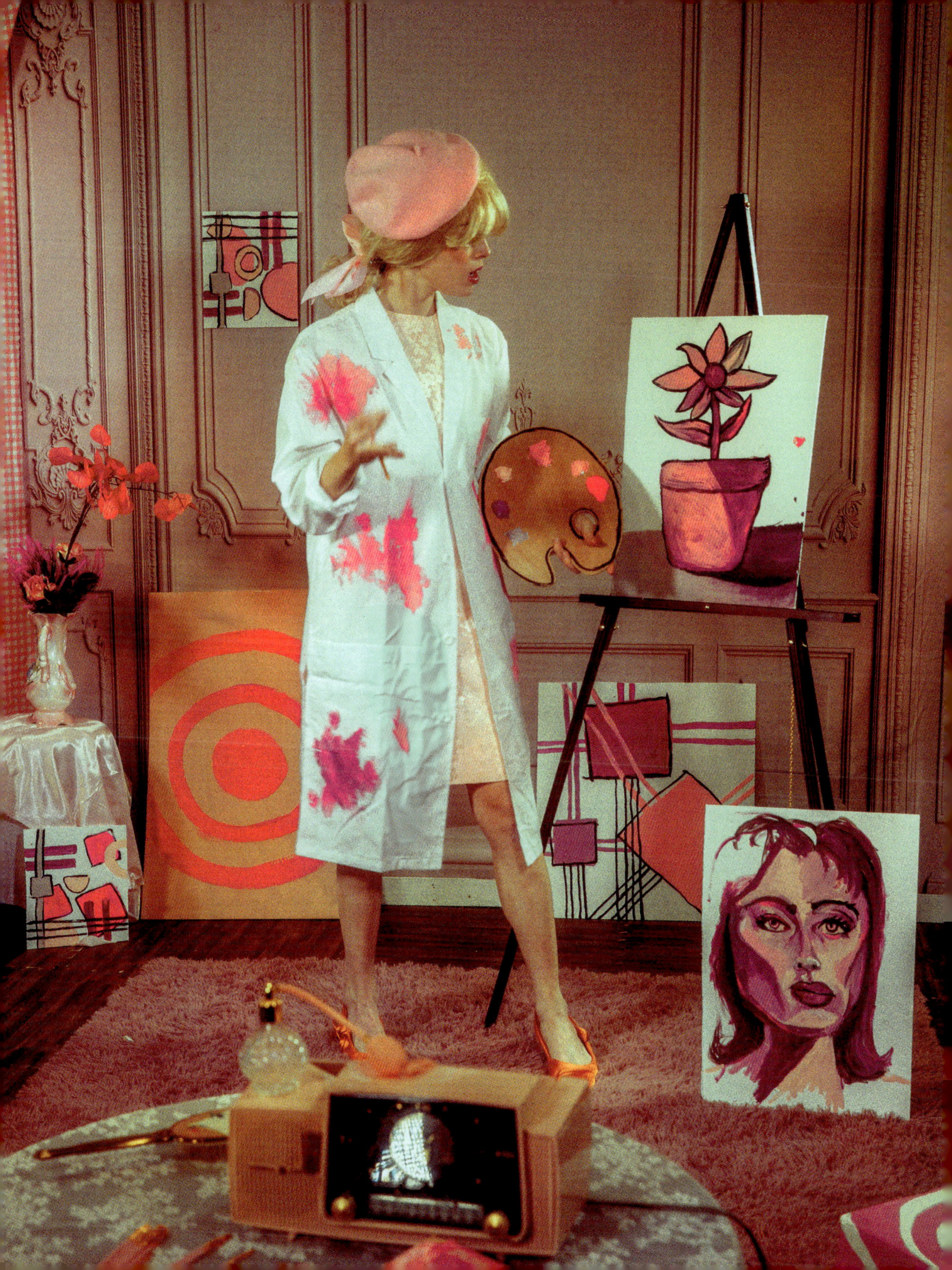

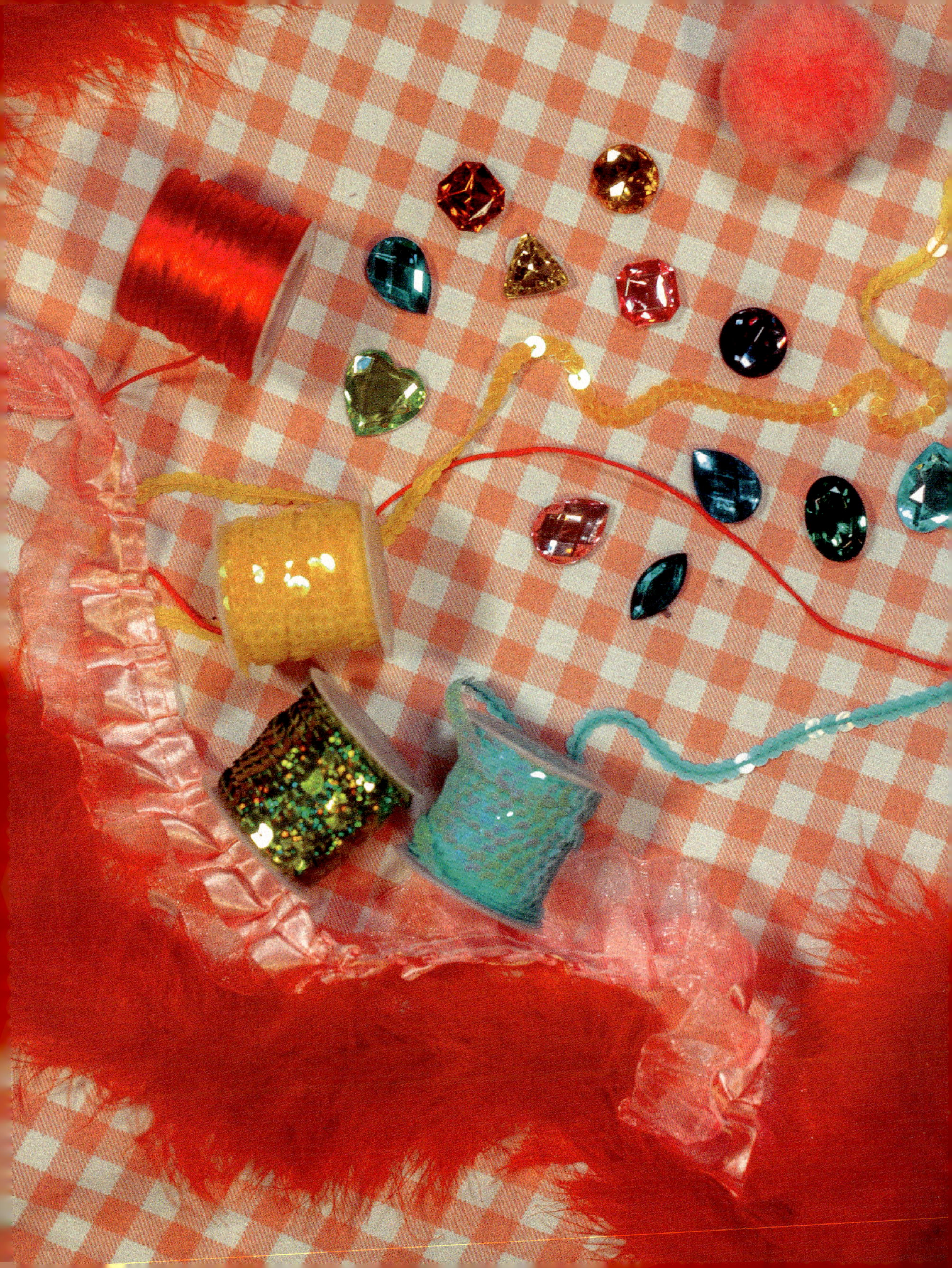

ACKNOWLEDGMENTS

To my wonderful best friend and partner, Talor Steinberg: Thank you for always putting up with me and my chaotic, creative mess. You have consistently been my biggest supporter, offering to help me in any way you can. I can't imagine my life without you. Your endless generosity has made every step of my journey that much more effortless and fun.

To my manager, Andrew Leib: I would be half of the creative I am today if it weren't for you. Thank you for continuously showing up and putting in the time to help me achieve my goals and dreams. I will never be able to find the words to describe how appreciative I am of all that you do for me on a daily basis. I am so glad we are on this wild ride together!

To my incredibly supportive family: Thanks for being just weird enough that I was able to grow into who I am as a creative. I don't know where I would be or what I would be doing if you didn't reinforce how it's a good thing to lean into your quirks and uniqueness throughout life. I love you all so much and am so thankful that you're my family. Special shout out to my sister, Lavinia, for all the fun, creative endeavors we do together and for also putting up with my chaos.

To my team at DK, Alexander Rigby, Bill Thomas, and Ryan Scheife: Alex, you amaze me beyond belief with your meticulous dedication to getting every part of this book assembled in time. Your job blows my mind, and through the hecticness of this project, you still managed to make every step of the process feel completely manageable and fun. Thank you for this opportunity. Bill and Ryan, thank you for helping this colorful and fun vision come to life. There were a lot of moving parts, but the book turned out perfectly, so thank you.

To the contributors: Thank you for taking the time to share your thoughts and wisdom on your areas of expertise. Not only are your contributions greatly appreciated, but it's also so cool to have multiple perspectives on these subjects. Thank you to everyone who was willing to have their photo featured in this book as well!

To all the people on the internet and in real life who have joined me along the way as I uncovered my creative self: It has been a long and unexpected journey, and I think it goes without saying, I wouldn't be the creative I am today if it weren't for all the generous support and kindness I've received on the way. I will be forever grateful. I truly feel like one of the luckiest people in the world to be able to create almost every single day. Thank you from the bottom of my heart.

To my friends for accepting I wouldn't be texting them back until I finished writing this book: Don't worry everyone, I will be texting you back more regularly now that the book is done. I am sorry texting always feels like such a big task for me. In all seriousness though, thank you for always being supportive of my antics. I love you all so much.

To my grandma: Thank you for loving clothes the way you did. My vintage collection would be nothing without your pieces. If I venture out into public in one of your coats, I always receive compliments, so thank you for making me look cooler than I actually am. (The orange coat on the cover of this book is hers.)

To my third- and fourth-grade teacher, Mr. McGee: Thank you for inspiring me. Because of your passion for technology and creating, you helped kickstart my love for video editing and helped reassure me that being creative was a special tool I could use throughout my adult life.

OTHER SOURCES FOR INSPIRATION:

BOOKS ABOUT ART AND CREATIVITY

Congdon, Lisa. *Find Your Artistic Voice: The Essential Guide to Working Your Creative Magic*. San Francisco: Chronicle Books, 2019.

Day, Felicia. *Embrace Your Weird: Face Your Fears and Unleash Creativity*. New York: Gallery Books, 2019.

Kleon, Austin. *Steal Like an Artist: 10 Things Nobody Told You About Being Creative*. New York: Workman Publishing, 2012.

Magsamen, Susan and Ivy Ross. *Your Brain on Art: How the Arts Transform Us*. New York: Random House, 2023.

Pivirotto, Nicole. *Color, Form, and Magic: Use the Power of Aesthetics for Creative and Magical Work*. San Francisco: Chronicle Books, 2021.

Rodsky, Eve. *Find Your Unicorn Space: Reclaim Your Creative Life in a Too-Busy World.* New York: G.P. Putnam's Sons, 2021.

Rubin, Rick. *The Creative Act: A Way of Being*. New York: Penguin Press, 2023.

Saltz, Jerry. *How to Be an Artist*. New York: Riverhead Books, 2020.

REFERENCE BOOKS

Adams, Sean. *The Designer's Dictionary of Color*. New York: Abrams Books, 2017.

Ang, Tom. *Photography: The Definitive Visual History*. New York: DK Publishing, 2022.

Dixon, Andrew Graham. *Art: The Definitive Visual Guide*. New York: DK Publishing, 2018.

DK Publishing. *Art That Changed the World: Transformative Art Movements and the Paintings That Inspired Them*. New York: DK Publishing, 2013.

DK Publishing. *Artists: Their Lives and Works*. New York: DK Publishing, 2017.

DK Publishing. *Design: The Definitive Visual Guide, Second Edition*. New York: DK Publishing, 2021.

DK Publishing. *Fashion: The Definitive Visual Guide*. New York: DK Publishing, 2019.

DK Publishing. *How Art Works*. New York: DK Publishing, 2022.

Ochs, Michael. *1000 Record Covers*. Cologne: Taschen, 2014.

Phaidon Press. *The Art Book, Revised and Expanded 2020 Edition*. New York: Phaidon Press, 2020.

St. Clair, Kassia. *The Secret Lives of Color*. New York: Penguin Books, 2017.

CREATIVE WORKBOOKS

Cameron, Julia. *The Artist's Way: A Spiritual Path to Higher Creativity, 30th Anniversary Edition*. New York: TarcherPerigee, 2016.

Scobie, Lorna. *365 Days of Art: A Creative Exercise for Every Day of the Year*. San Francisco: Hardie Grant, 2017.

Scobie, Lorna. *365 Days of Creativity: Inspire Your Imagination with Art Every Day*. San Francisco: Hardie Grant, 2019.

Smith, Keri. *Wreck This Journal: Now in Color*. New York: Penguin Books, 2017.

Wells, Megan. *Art Journaling: A Mixed-Media Guide to Unleashing Your Creativity*. Rye Brook: Peter Pauper Press, 2020.

DOCUMENTARIES ABOUT CREATIVITY

Abstract: The Art of Design (2017)
Art & Copy (2009)
Art and Craft (2014)
Bathtubs over Broadway (2018)
Beauty Is Embarrassing (2012)
The Creative Brain (2019)
Design & Thinking (2012)
Exit Through the Gift Shop (2010)
Objectified (2009)
Painters Painting (1972)
Why Man Creates (1968)

DOCUMENTARIES ABOUT SPECIFIC ARTISTS

The Andy Warhol Diaries (2022)
Between Me and My Mind (2019)
David Lynch: The Art of Life (2016)
Design Is One: The Vignellis (2012)
Drew: The Man Behind the Poster (2013)
Eames: The Architect & the Painter (2011)
Jean-Michel Basquiat: The Radiant Child (2010)
Kusama: Infinity (2018)
Marina Abramovic: The Artist Is Present (2012)
Moonage Daydream (2022)
Sky Ladder: The Art of Cai Guo-Qiang (2016)

MOVIES ABOUT ARTISTS

Artemisia (1997)
Basquiat (1996)
Big Eyes (2014)
Frida (2002)
Klimt (2006)
Lust for Life (1956)
Mr. Turner (2014)
Pollock (2000)
Seraphine (2008)
Showing Up (2022)
Surviving Picasso (1996)

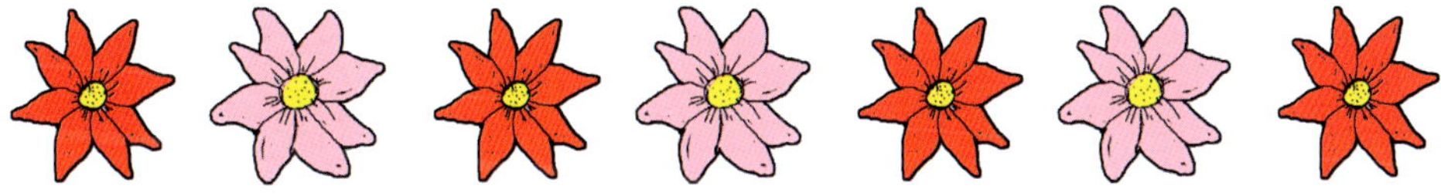

INDEX

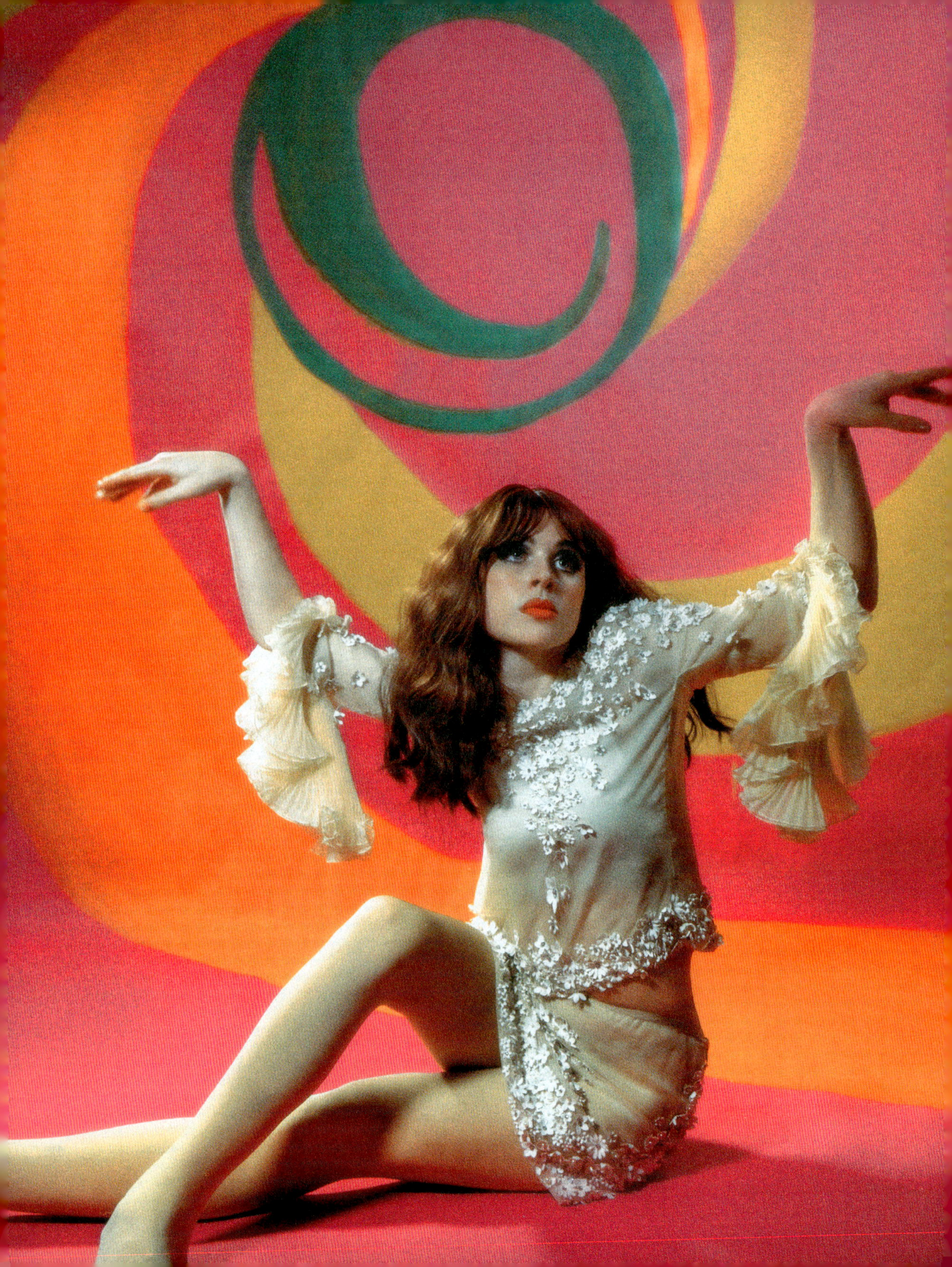

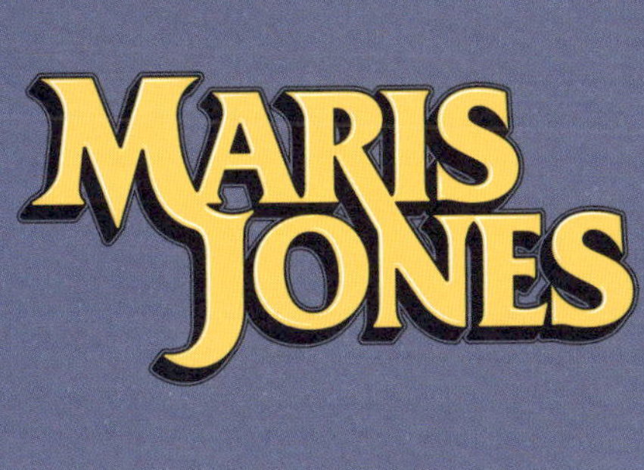

Maris Jones is the wildly popular content creator on Instagram and TikTok, with millions of followers who enjoy watching and listening to the creative and nostalgic videos and photos she shares online. Born in Philadelphia to artistic parents, Jones coped with the childhood isolation caused by her cerebral palsy by world-building and moviemaking alone in her bedroom at home. This artistic escapism led to an obsession with crafting sets and movies out of paper and cardboard.

Jones has been featured in publications like *Rolling Stone*, *Vogue*, *NYLON*, and *VICE*, and she has worked on major creative campaigns with brands like Valentino, Apple, YouTube, Universal Music Group, Hulu, Netflix, Gucci, and the John Lennon Estate. To her audience, she is a time traveler fueled by the thick sparkle of dreams. Jones is an adventurer without a road map who uses imagination as her only compass.

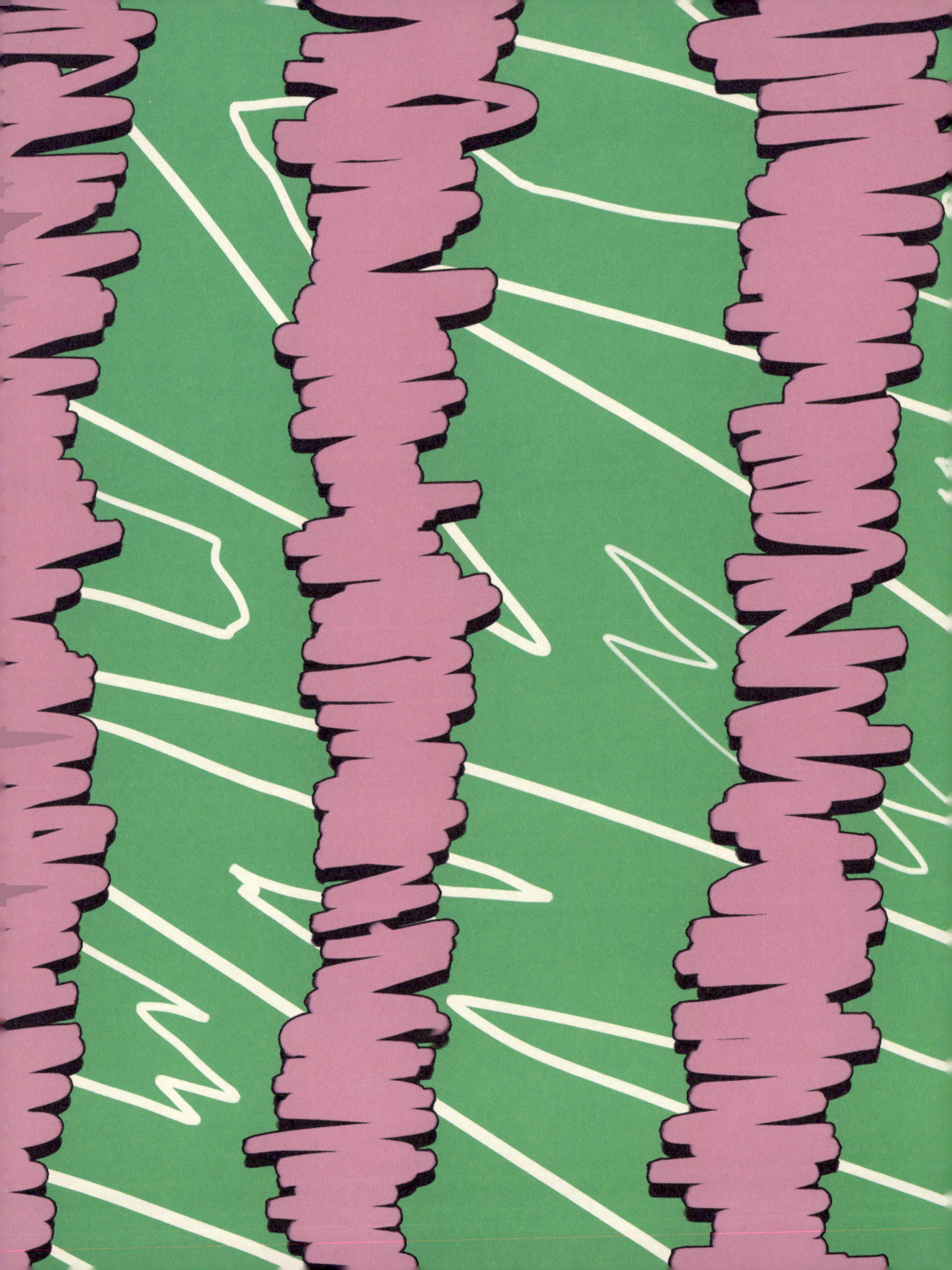